THE IMPACT OF CHRISTIANITY ON COLONIAL MAYA, ANCIENT MEXICO, CHINA, AND JAPAN

How a Monotheistic Religion Was Received
by Several Pagan Societies

THE IMPACT OF CHRISTIANITY ON COLONIAL MAYA, ANCIENT MEXICO, CHINA, AND JAPAN

How a Monotheistic Religion Was Received by Several Pagan Societies

Shinji Yamase

With a Foreword by
Robert M. Carmack

The Edwin Mellen Press
Lewiston•Queenston•Lampeter

Library of Congress Cataloging-in-Publication Data

Yamase, Shinji.
  The impact of Christianity on colonial Maya, ancient Mexico, China, and Japan : how a monotheistic religion was received by several pagan societies / Shinji Yamase ; with a foreword by Robert M. Carmack.
      p. cm.
  Includes bibliographical references and index.
  ISBN-13: 978-0-7734-5145-2 (hardcover : alk. paper)
  ISBN-10: 0-7734-5145-5 (hardcover : alk. paper)
  1. Christianity and other religions. 2. Christianity--Influence. I. Title.
  BR127.Y36 2008
  261.209--dc22

                                                                    2008013522
hors série.

A CIP catalog record for this book is available from the British Library.

Permission: Fotosearch, Waukesha, WI

The Edwin Mellen Press
Box 450
Lewiston, New York
USA 14092-0450

The Edwin Mellen Press
Box 67
Queenston, Ontario
CANADA L0S 1L0

The Edwin Mellen Press, Ltd.
Lampeter, Ceredigion, Wales
UNITED KINGDOM SA48 8LT

Printed in the United States of America

Table of Contents

List of Figures

Foreword

Robert M. Carmack
Professor Emeritus
State University of New York, Albany

This a thoroughly fascinating book on the impact of Western Christianity on the native peoples of Mexico and Central America, as well as of China and Japan. A unique point of view is expressed by the author in this very learned examination of how Christianity was received by so-called "Pagan" peoples. We are treated to a thorough description of the nature of Christianity brought to these New Worlds, and an even more thorough interpretation of the religious thinking of the native peoples subjected to Western political and religious domination.

Yamase argues with an abundance of documentary evidence that the encounter between Western Christian and native Mayas, Chinese, and Japanese can be fruitfully understood by examining their underlying cosmological points of view. In particular, the monistic view of Christianity is contrasted with the dualistic view of these so-called Pagan peoples. In Yamase's primary case of the Mayas, the Mayan dualistic view of the world made them able to incorporate Chistian ideas into their emerging colonial cosmology. Rather than a unilateral rejection of Christianity, and despite credible instances of resistance to it, the colonialized Mayas created reasonable reconstructions of their cosmologies that made it ii

possible for them to become Christian Mayas. Similar processes were at work in China and Japan, although christianization in those countries was not forced upon them through military conquest.

The author's discussion of original documentary sources, as well as scholarly studies, is most impressive. His selections, and translations of these selections, are always relevant and revealing. Western readers will be fascinated by texts from China and Japan, as well as from the Mayas themselves and early Spanish missionaries. Appropriately, the final chaper is devoted to a study of the Popol Wuj, the famous K'iche' Mayan epic. As with the previous chapters, Yamase attempts to show the dualism in that epic through its incorporation of Spanish Christian elements, and this provides a concrete summary of the overriding thesis of the book.

Yamase is not afraid to challenge many of the Western-based interpretations of the Mayas and their cultures, while also admitting that other ways of viewing the evidence should be considered. Overall, I find it difficult to conceive of any Western scholar of the Mayas or Christianity not being fascinated and stimulted by this unique book.

Acknowledgements

This research mainly discusses the relationships between Christianity and the Maya religion of the Spanish colonial period, whose phenomenon is often called Mayanized Christianity or religious syncretism. Although the main target of analysis is the colonial Maya texts, modern Maya's perspectives and ethnographic data will also be discussed.

The feature of this research is to revise and to analyze so-called 'Religious Syncretism or Fusion' mainly from a perspective of the world of paganism and dualism, though this manuscript is not very different from the popular style of traditional Maya studies. In order to consider the issue from a dualistic perspective, Christian history in other pagan cultures, including those of the Aztecs, the Incas, China, and Japan, will be considered as one chapter to constitute a comparative study.

Since the majority of academic contributions to this issue have been made by Western scholars belonging to the cultural sphere of Christianity, which is monotheism, it seems that their understanding of the idea of polytheism is still inadequate. In fact, while almost all researchers of Maya studies have noticed the importance of dualism within Maya culture, it is still rare to see a work generated from a perspective of dualism. This is especially true among researchers of the late twentieth century. Although my initial argument was published as a part of *History* iv

and Legend of the Colonial Maya of Guatemala, numerous points had to be removed due to limited space. Also, several points of my previous argument are still controversial. Therefore, it is suggested that presenting a more detailed view from the pagan world as a single volume will enhance current arguments about religious syncretism found among the Maya.

In my previous book, I presented somewhat controversial arguments based on a theory of dualism; 'the colonial Maya reconstructed their old cosmovision from Maya religions and Christianity'. This volume will further discuss this issue.

I thank Dr. Robert M. Carmack at the State University of New York at Albany, who reviewed the draft of this manuscript and wrote the Preface.

I also thank Dr. Brent Metz of the University of Kansas, and Mr. Vincent Stanzione in Guatemala, for reviewing this work. Another thanks goes to Dr. Mckenna Brown at Virginia Commonwealth University for introducing to me Mr. Stanzione, who is the author of a fascinating book, *Rituals of Sacrifice,* and has been engaged in preserving Maya traditions in Guatemala; and to Dr. Irene Blayer at Brock University, Canada, for spending her precious time.

A sincere apology must be given to Mrs. Patricia Schultz at Edwin Mellen Press for the delay of this publication.

As I am in Japan, it is not always easy to access to good reference sources of Latin American Studies. In addition, unlike in the Western world, the status of independent scholar is not always respectable in the Far East.

I thank Meta Brain, an unusual publishing house which calls itself 'a junkie publisher', for various arrangements for publishing my non-fiction style and general surveys on the Aztec, the Inca, and the Maya. Some discreet considerations arranged by Ms. Junko Ohta（太田順子）at that press are truly treasured and should be mentioned here.

Thanks to Mr. Takashi Kondo（近藤聖）for writing several advertising reviews of my Japanese books, which surely increased the sale of my books on various Pre-Columbian Civilizations in Japan.

The rapid development of electronic resources is becoming a great help for scholars who do not have a good access to research libraries. As one of them, J.B. Hare's *The Internet Sacred Text Archive CD-ROM* must especially be mentioned as one of most worthwhile contributions to this book, his CD was of great benefit as I completed this manuscript because it saved a vast amount time in searching for English translations of various Christian & Greek philosophers' texts and some classic academic works on religion. Among his scanned books, Manly P. Hall's controversial book (Hall 1928) was particularly interesting for me, although I do not make any reference to his book in this research. Other electronic libraries, such as the Christian Classics Ethereal Library and Biblioteca Virtual Miguel de Cervantes, a project maintained by Universidad de Alicante in Spain were also a great help.

Lastly, my thanks go to my late mother 山瀬英子, my late uncle 黒岡元, and my late father 山瀬邦良, who unexpectedly died on 21th December 2005. It must be emphasized that they have been indispensable in finishing this project.

Kanagawa, Japan. In a country of eight million gods.
Shinji Yamase 山瀬暢士

Note

Regarding names of the Japanese, the order surname – name is now conventionally used in Asian related journals and other media. However, this book follows Western convention (name-surname).

Proofreading of my English writing within this manuscript was largely done by **Scribendi.com**. Some small portion was proofread by **Accurate English Proofreading**. Although they provide these services commercially, I would like to acknowledge them here.

Introduction

Go into the whole world and preach the gospel to every creature. He who believes and is baptized will be saved; but he who does not believe will be condemned' (New Testament). [1]

...Of all these nations of [the Christian] *God our lord gave charge to one man, called St. Peter, that he should be Lord and Superior of all the men in the world, that all should obey him, and that he should be head of the whole race... he permitted him to have his seat in any other of the world... The man was called Pope, as if to say, Admirable Great Father and Governor of men...One of these Pontiffs, who succeeded that St. Peter as Lord of the world ... made donation of these isles and Tierra-Firma to the aforesaid* [Spanish] *King and Queen and their successors... Wherefore, as best we can, we ask and require you that you consider what we have said to you ...(Requerimiento of* 1509).[2]

Christianity is under control of the Emperor of the Southern barbaric people [南蛮帝王=Papal] *in Roma. Although Spain managed to conquer New Spain and the Philippines by sending her soldiers, the braveness of our* [Japanese] *Nation discouraged Spain and Portugal from making a military invasion of Japan. Thus, they decided to convert the Japanese to Christianity and later send an army to destroy Japan with the Christianized Japanese'* (Hapian 1970:441-442).

This book is an endeavor to present an ambitious study of the relationship between the Maya religions and Christianity, a perspective based on the ethnographical and historical context of the pagan and animistic worlds since the sixteenth century.

---

[1] Cited from *New Testament*: Mark:16, 15-16.
[2] Originally translated by Arthur Helps and published in Helps 1855:I:379-382. Reprinted in Yamase 2003b: Williams 1963:59-6.

The survey of colonial Maya religious texts will be a principal part of this research.[3] To date, numerous Maya documents written in the Spanish colonial period have been published. However, with the notable exception of the *Popol Vuh*, studies of those colonial Maya documents have been a relatively minor area of Maya studies. The reason for this trend can be explained in several ways, but the most important factor may be the fact that the majority of these Maya religious books are poorly understood by scholars. As the result of this, research of the colonial Maya had largely been based on sources written by the Spaniards, which often contain a strong bias. Although several important works utilizing colonial Maya sources have appeared since the late twentieth century which study the relationship between Maya religions and Christianity, it is often difficult to say that the colonial Maya texts are fully used to reconstruct the colonial Maya reaction to Christianity, because not only has no definitive comprehensive understanding of colonial Maya religious texts yet been made, but also private documents written by the Maya are few in number. A lack of adequate private texts, such as diaries or letters to friends, prevents us from understanding the colonial Maya interpretation of Christianity. In order to overcome those difficulties, the perspective of dualism and the view of the pagan world toward Christian civilization will be utilized in this research.

In the Muslim world, as in the past Christian world, dualism and pagan religions are often regarded as being inferior to or against Islamic teaching. It is known that Muslim fundamentalists of Afghanistan destroyed the world's biggest Buddhist idol. However, among the more moderate Muslims such strong hostilities towards pagan religions are no longer found. An interesting story, although I have forgotten the source, comes from a Japanese newspaper which cited an interview with a noted Japanese Buddhist. He has served the largest Buddhist temple, *Todaiji*, which has the largest Buddhist idol in Japan, and he is known as a scholar of

---

[3] For a summary of the colonial Maya texts of Guatemala, see Carmack 1973, Yamase 2002b:25-58, for that of the colonial Yucatec Maya manuscript, see *e.g.* Liljefors Persson 2000:51-78, Edmonson and Bricker 1985.

Islamic religious studies.[4] One day, a noted politician from Iran came to have a talk with him, and looking at the big idol in his temple, asked him: "*Why do you worship such an idol?*" As is known, worshipping idols is strictly forbidden in the *Koran*. The Buddhist monk replied: "*I know that the Koran frequently refers to the 'Face of Allah.' How do the Muslim people manage to understand this?*" Upon hearing this answer, the Iranian politician gave a hearty laugh, and stopped arguing about idolatry. However, this sort of religious conflict still turns up frequently today. The history of human beings reveals that we have killed one another for religious reasons. Religious struggles of the past often involved violation and massacre. In October 2004, in Iraq, Islamic fundamentalists blew up a memorial statue, constructed through Japanese funding, upon which a Japanese traditional style garden lantern and a Star as a symbol of Islam had been carved. The reason was, according to the fundamentalists, that the Japanese-style garden lantern represented a symbol of Buddhism.[5] On the other hand, the Japanese allowed the Muslims to construct their mosque in Japan, in spite of the old (but still current among some Islamic people) Islamic view towards traditional pagan and Buddhist religions. For the Japanese, all religions are equally important and thus giving honor to all of them at the same time is honorable.

After the Europeans ended the dark period of their medieval decline, they discovered the Americas and found them fully occupied by pagans. Since Christianiy had challenged old pagan religions, these newly discovered pagan religions were seen as enemies of the true faith. The *Bible* mentions that Jesus ordered the preaching of the Gospel all over the world.[6] Based on what Jesus commanded, the Spanish of the sixteenth century believed that preaching the Gospel and terminating pagan religions were the principal tasks of Christianity.

The sixteenth century can be said to be the period of the Iberian military and their spiritual conquest of the world. Within Mesoamerica, the first people who

---

[4] I remember reading this article in 2001.
[5] The Asahi Newspaper, Japan 9 October 2004. The fact is that the lantern is not a representation of Buddhism.

encountered the Spaniards were the Maya. The Maya inflicted a severe defeat on the Spanish force. In 1517, in spite of being equipped with guns and metal armaments, Francisco Hernández de Córdoba, the discoverer of the Yucatan Peninsula, was defeated by the Maya army and later died from numerous injures.[7]

Hernán Cortés, the conquistador of the Aztecs, also first landed on the soil of the Maya. He later defeated the Maya army of the Tabasco region. Nevertheless, he was not interested in conquering that area at that time, because little gold was expected to originate there. In the end he succeeded in the conquest of the great Aztec Empire.[8] After the fall of the Aztec Empire, although the Spaniards initiated the conquest of the Maya area, and Guatemala was soon subjugated by Pedro de Alvarado, the Europeans often had difficulties in maintaining an adequate military force on the Yucatan Peninsula. The Spaniards of that time were attracted more to Peru than to the Maya area, since the news of the discovery of another *El Dorado*, the Inca Empire, had reached Mexico. When the Inca lost their independence,[9] the Yucatec Maya still resisted the Spaniards strongly.[10]

As a result, after the fall of two powerful nations in the New World, the Aztec and the Inca, at the hands of the conquistadores, the Peten Itza, the last kingdom of the Maya, continued to exist even into the seventeenth century. Michael Coe comments that '...*the Maya are the toughest Indians of Mesoamerica, and struggle against European civilization never once halted*'.[11]

Although the Maya resisted Spanish invaders for many years, they were finally conquered. Since the Iberian States of that period justified their military conquest based on the bull of papal donation, religious extirpation of the conquered area was

---

[6] *New Testaments*: Mark:16, 15-16.

[7] A brief and efficient summary of the Spanish Conquest of each part of the Maya area, see Bricker 1981:13-52. For a detailed summary of the Spanish Conquest of the Yucatec Maya, see Chamberlain 1948, Cledinnen 1987.

[8] For the best account of the process of this war available now, see Thomas 1995. My briefer survey was published in Yamase 2003a, 2005.

[9] Hemming (1993) is still recognized as the best account of the fall of the Inca. My own account of this event (although in Japanese) was published as Yamase 2004.

[10] The most detailed account of the history of the Peten Itza is Jones 1989.

[11] Coe 1993:165.

conducted elsewhere in the Americas, followed by military suppression. Soon after the success of the military conquest, therefore, the Spaniards initiated their second conquest, often called the '*Spiritual Conquest*' of the Maya, partly due to the fact that the Spaniards needed a theoretical justification for the conquest. For the Spaniards, converting the Maya to Christianity was considered saving their souls from the devil.

Christianity of that era, which had battled with the Islamic religion for many years, was far more exclusive and intolerant of other religions than it is now. Within the Christian doctrine (as is also true for Islam), worship of idols is strictly forbidden, as idols are considered a representation of the Devil. Although the Europeans were once idolatrous in pre-Christian times, after their conversion, they began to identify their ancestral religions as a kind of 'black magic.' When the Spaniards discovered the Americas, they saw that the inhabitants of those lands practiced not more than black magic from the Spanish point of view. Since the majority of the Native Americans were idolatrous, they were treated as teaching about the Devil. The Spaniards thus initiated their plan to eradicate Native American religions.

From the beginning, Christianity had defined pagan religions as the teaching of devils. The Christian perception is that God became immanent and could only be seen in the person of Jesus, and represented in art. This tendency remained strong in the nineteenth century. A noted historian and writer of the nineteenth century, William H. Prescott, is known for his excellent works, the *Conquest of Mexico*, and the *Conquest of Peru*. He summarized the Native American religions as follows:

> It is a remarkable fact, that many, if not most, of the rude tribes inhabiting the vast American continent, however disfigured their creeds may have been in other respects by a childish superstition, had attained to the sublime conception of one Great Spirit, the Creator of the Universe, who, immaterial in his own nature, was not to be dishonored by an attempt at visible representation, and who, pervading all space, was not to be circumscribed within the walls of a temple. Yet these elevated ideas, so far beyond the ordinary range of the untutored intellect, do not seem to have led to the practical consequences that might have been expected; and few of the

American nations have shown much solicitude for the maintenance of a religious worship, or found in their faith a powerful spring of action. But, with progress in civilization, ideas more akin to those of civilized communities were gradually unfolded; a liberal provision was made, and a separate order instituted, for the services of religion, which were conducted with a minute and magnificent ceremonial, that challenged comparison, in some respects, with that of the most polished nations of Christendom. This was the case with the nations inhabiting the table-land of North America, and with the natives of Bogota, Quito, Peru, and the other elevated regions on the great Southern continent. It was, above all, the case with the Peruvians, who claimed a divine original for the founders of their empire, whose laws all rested on a divine sanction, and whose domestic institutions and foreign wars were alike directed to preserve and propagate their faith. Religion was the basis of their polity, the very condition, as it were, of their social existence. The government of the Incas, in its essential principles, was a theocracy.

Yet, though religion entered so largely into the fabric and conduct of the political institutions of the people, their mythology, that is, the traditionary legends by which they affected to unfold the mysteries of the universe, was exceedingly mean and puerile. Scarce one of their traditions - except the beautiful one respecting the founders of their royal dynasty – is worthy of note, or throws much light on their own antiquities, or the primitive history of man. Among the traditions of importance is one of the deluge, which they held in common with so many of the nations in all parts of the globe, and which they related with some particulars that bear resemblance to a Mexican legend.[12]

Prescott has said that it is surprising that many of these uncivilized American natives had a concept of a unique God close to that of Christianity. Thus, while he admonishes the prejudice toward the Inca civilization by the West, and accepts some superiorities of the Inca Empire over the West, it is also clear that his judgment of the superiority or inferiority of the civilization is still based on the view of Christian-civilization. In his time, the largest idolatrous state, China, which had officially recorded and treated the rest of the world as barbarous lands, began to show a rapid decline both in political and military power. The Ottoman Empire (Turkey), which had been a serious menace to the West for several centuries, also was in severe decline. Under such circumstances, it is not surprising that he left a notion of the achievement of the 'civilized' Christian people. According to Prescott's idea mentioned above, perhaps, the Maya religion can be categorized as a lesser one than that of the Inca, because the Maya did not have a clear concept of

---

[12] Prescott Chap.3.

a unique God who created the world and human beings. Although Prescott wrote an admirable work, therefore, the above quotation clearly suggests that the educated Westerners, as faithful Christians, still had some limited views of pagan religions, even in the late nineteenth century.

The Spanish of the sixteenth century used to to refer to the people who worshipped idols or images of Gods or the Buddha, such as American, Chinese and Japanese peoples, *gentil*, which means pagan. It is interesting that, in the sixteenth century, this word was not used to refer to Muslims, who forbid the worshiping of idols. Within Christianity, the *Bible* describes how those who worship idols are praying to evil spirits. Although as pagans, the ancient Roman people sometimes showed strong hostility to the emergence of and rapid development of Christianity, though the Roman Empire finally declared Christianity to be its national religion.[13] This historical process of the Christian spiritual conquest of Rome, which was somehow exaggerated in the European medieval period, became a fundamental concept of Western civilization. In some 'barbarous' areas of Europe of that time, such as Britain and the north eastern part of Europe, the propagation of Christianity was completed at a much later period. When the British were finally converted to Christianity, it was considered that they had become civilized because of their acceptance of the Gospel. For this reason, the European people, who originally worshiped idols in the time of the Roman Empire, came to have a view of history in which they abandoned worshiping idols and began to serve the Christian God, and equated this with the evolutionary process of civilization.[14] Therefore, the Christian people traditionally tend to consider those who worship idols to be somehow uncivilized. In the Western world, a dominant view had been that the pagan religions, the majority of which are animistic and dualistic, are still in the first, primitive stage of human history. In addition, a lack of the concept of a sole powerful deity among pagan peoples was argued as proof of their intellectual and

---

[13] As to the Spiritual Conquest of the Roman Empire, Fox (1986) is one of the good summaries.

cultural inferiority to Christians until the early twentieth century.[15]

Nowadays, the relationship between Christianity and Native American religions is more moderate, and the position of indigenous religions has somewhat been improved in the Americas. It is also true that both the Catholic and Protestants are now changing their past interpretation of pagan divinities. In 2004, for example, *Odin* and other ancient Germanic pagan divinities, who were once dismissed as Satan by the Christians, re-emerged as officially recognized 'gods' by the Church of Denmark. However, it is still true that apart from academic society, some ordinary people tend to consider pagan and animistic religions to be inferior to Christianity or to Islam. In many places, the Christian populations still tend to identify Native American religions as 'primitive', though less frequently than in the past. Moreover, as the Native Americans have been politically underrepresented in the Americas, in some places in which the social position of the Native American people is underrepresented (e.g., Latin America), indigenous religions are still blamed for sorcery, witchcraft and black magic. Indeed, violence against Native American religions has never ceased to date, and murders of Maya pagan shamans by Christian fanatics still frequently happen in Guatemala (see Appendix IV).

Because the Gospel does not allow belief in any God apart from the Christian Lord and the Maya of today are auto-identified as Christian under the influence of the strict Catholic teaching, they face an intellectual struggle as to how to accommodate their ancestral religious beliefs within the present Christianized culture. Because of this, they often fear that keeping and respecting their ancient beliefs might be a betrayal of the Christian teaching. In such social surroundings, it is not surprising that the Native Americans themselves often feel that their ancestral animistic and pagan religions are inferior to the Gospel, and in some cases, have tried to make their religions resemble Christianity (*e.g.*, by abolishing worship of idols). This trend tends to encourage the Native American people to undervalue

---

[14] This idea can easily be found in writings of the Spanish of the sixteenth century. For example, Acosta 1590, lib.5, chap.1.
[15] Yamase 2004:10-21.

their own traditional cultures. Unfortunately, the same phenomenon has been reported among the Japanese immigrants in the USA.

On the other hand, in the Far East, the religious and political climate is very different. Although monotheism, including Christianity and Islam, is accepted, their exclusive attitudes toward pagan and animistic religions have often been regarded as evidence of the 'immaturity' of their intolerance and thus paganism and animism have remained dominant from ancient times. In spite of the numerous efforts to develop Christianity in Japan since the sixteenth century, the Christian population in Japan is less than 2 percent of the whole population. The people celebrate festivals in numerous pagan temples. In East Asia, belief in various religions at the same time is a typical character of the Japanese and Chinese cultures. Although monotheism, such as Christianity, is respected as one of these religions (indeed, the Japanese do not hesitate to celebrate some of the Christian festivals), it is true that monotheism is often 'negatively' received as excessive and brutal fundamentalism, and the ideas of polytheism and animism are considered the better approach to peace and nature. Recently, while accepting some excellent notions existing in monotheism, pagan religious leaders and scholars in Japan expressed the view that the intolerance of monotheistic religions of other religions has caused most of the serious disputes of the world and that reviving the ideas of polytheism, and 'being tolerant of other gods,' is necessary for the realization of peace in the present world.

However, the Maya still have difficulty with such an opinion. The beginning of the suffering of Maya religions coincided with the arrival of the Christian people in the sixteenth century.[16] When the Spaniards conquered the Maya regions, it is well known that the Franciscans on the Yucatan Peninsula, led by Diego de Landa, practiced violent methods to expel the Mayas' old pagan religion during the 1560s. Several colonial documents state that numerous Maya people were injured and some were killed by the torture of the Franciscans. Although Landa was later removed from the Yucatan Peninsula due to his excessive brutality, the policy, suppression of the Maya religions, remained until the independence of Latin America from Spain. Even after independence, the political and cultural leadership of Latin American nations have been held by Spanish descendants, and Catholic monks have continued suppressing Native American religions. For the Christians, Maya religions are not a religion but are pejoratively labeled as cults. In addition to the Catholics, the Protestants also began to propagate Christianity and they were usually very hostile towards Native American religions. Consequently, in some parts of the Americas, Native American divinities are now considered a kind of evil spirit, even by the indigenous people.

However, in spite of the fact that colonial Catholic friars attempted to terminate pre-Hispanic Maya religions, often by using violence, continuous practice of the Maya pagan religion was frequently reported, even in the late colonial period, and of course, some practice of them can commonly be seen today. At the same time, most of the colonial Maya people also participated in Christian ceremonies. Similar phenomena can also be observed in a majority of Native American communities, and the Maya have sustained much of their traditional religion, even today. Have the Maya resisted Christianity? Thus, the relationship between Maya religions and Christianity from the Spanish Conquest to today remains an interesting academic issue, even today.

Colonial Catholic friars believed that Maya priests, called Chilam Balam, who were considered to hate Christianity, organized the continued practice of the Maya pagan religion. Moreover, the Spaniards considered that such pagan priests provoked the Maya people to revolt against the Spanish colonial rule. Nonetheless, the sacred texts of Chilam Balam, the *Books of Chilam Balam* contain a strong influence from Christianity. This religious phenomenon, found in the colonial Maya text, has often been called syncretism, and it was once considered a result of the confusion of both beliefs. Yet, scholars have also argued for many decades, that

---

[16] As to the spiritual conquest of the Yucatec Maya, see Clendinnen 1987:38-71, Chuchiak

11

religious syncretism, found in the *Books of Chilam Balam* and in the Guatemalan Maya texts, was generated to trick the Spaniards in order to hide their old religious beliefs. Indeed, researchers of colonial Latin American history have continuously provided evidence favorable to this view. Historical studies suggest that numerous colonial Maya religious practitioners refused to be converted to Christianity and sustained their ancient religions.

It is said, for example, that in order to continue their traditional rites, they only replaced the names of their old religious elements with those of Christianity in order to pretend that they had become good Christians. These kinds of colonial reports can be found in any part of the Americas. Consequently, the majority of researchers in this field consider that the religious syncretism found in the colonial Maya texts is a result of the colonial Maya's prudent way of hiding old Maya religious beliefs, or of a reluctant acceptance of Christianity. I do not deny that in most cases the Maya had to adapt Christian elements to hide their ancestral religion's customs and beliefs from their foreign ruler, the Spaniards, as this kind of religious phenomenon was frequently observed in Guatemala of the mid-twentieth century, well after the independence of Guatemala from Spain.

Another group of scholars studying the colonial Nahuatl people proposes that the colonial Nahuatl opted for both Christianity and their Nahuatl pagan religion at the same time.[17] Among them, Fernando Cervantes successfully argued a necessity for analyzing religious phenomena among Mesoamerican people from the perspective of dualism, though he does not use that term.[18] What was the case of the colonial Maya? For Maya who chose to ally with the Spaniards, it is likely true that they co-opted both the old and the new religions.

However, it is also true that the Maya were not always satisfied with the introduction of Christianity. For example, it is known that the Peten Itza, the last kingdom of the Maya, continued refusing to accept Christianity until the

---

2000. For the case of Guatemala, see Van Oss 1986, Yamase 2002b:182-190.

[17] Cervantes 1994:40-59, León-Portilla 1990:97-123.

[18] Cervantes 1994:40-46, Miller et al. 1993:81-82.

mid-seventeenth century. The remaining descendants of the Peten Itza are still refusing to be converted to Christianity. Nevertheless, although Christianity may have been considered very negatively by these anti-Spanish Maya, there is little evidence that the colonial Maya rejected Christianity as one of the various ways of preaching suitable for the Spaniards. Scholars like Matthew Restall point out that colonial Yucatec Maya religious texts, the *Books of Chilam Balam,* do not castigate the introduction of Christianity itself, although they express their lamentations for the sufferings introduced by Christianity.[19]

On the other hand, some scholars argue that the Christian influence found in the colonial Maya texts is evidence that those manuscripts were a product of Catholic missionaries. They have continuously argued that some of the colonial Maya texts, such as the *Popol Vuh,* are a fabricated product of the Dominican order.[20]

It must be noted that human belief is difficult to comprehend, and that the concept of religious hostility among the Maya is not the same as how Christian people have rejected pagan religions. The majority of the Native Americans generally considered both Christianity and their own religions to be homogeneous. The same reaction was observed in China and Japan. It is well known that while Christians have historically identified pagan religions as works of the devil, in other words, devil teachings, the Native Americans and Asians have regarded Christianity as one of the true religions, but meant for the Spaniards and other Europeans only. Such pagan people considered that the spiritual functions of Christianity are limited to the Europeans only and that Christianity is a necessary part of the world.

Although historical evidence is not always adequate, it can be suggested that the colonial Maya also recognized the homogeneous nature of Christianity with that of their own religions. It must be noted that although it is true that the Maya have refused to abandon their traditional religions and have often been hostile to

---

[19] Restall 1997:149.

Christianity, overemphasis of this point will result in excluding other important characteristics of Maya religions, their incorporative or cooperative nature, from our current analysis of the so-called religious 'fusion' found in the colonial Maya texts.

A survey of a colonial Maya rebellion in Highland Chiapas (1708-13) by Victoria R. Bricker revealed that the Maya rebellion against the Spanish was not intended to revive ancient Maya religions and customs, but to monopolize the control of the Catholic religion within the Highlands.[21] Although the Maya of that rebellion replaced their old idols with images of Catholic saints by the end of the eighteenth century, it is also true that old Maya religious beliefs still strongly survive there.[22] This suggests that those Maya did not abandon their old beliefs while incorporating Christianity. Why did they incorporate Christianity, the symbolic religion of the Spaniards? In the case of the Chiapas of the twentieth century, a Mexican scholar, Eugenio Maurer Avalos, argues that the syncretic religion of the Tzeltal Maya of Chiapas is neither Catholic nor Maya, but Maya Catholicism.[23] This may be the answer in the case of the colonial Maya. Yet, in the colonial Maya texts, such as the *Popol Vuh*, the Maya pagan deities evidently remain active, in spite of their acceptance of the rule of Christianity. Therefore, it is suggested that the idea of Maurer Avalos should not be applied to the case of colonial Maya.

In order to answer this 'mystery,' as I have argued in the previous work, in pagan cultures, Anti-Christianity does not always mean an 'exclusive attitude towards Christian ideas.'[24] It should also be understood that there is a fundamental difference between Christianity and the Maya religions. The major difference between them may be compared to the difference between 'history' and 'historical anthropology' (though there is now an emergence of an anthropological history

---

[20] Acuña 1975, 1983, 1998, Quiroa 2002.
[21] Bricker 1981:55-69.
[22] *Ibid.*:55.
[23] Maurer Avalos 1993.
[24] Yamase 2002b:234-55.

14

discipline). An argument based on 'history' tends to emphasize the evidence within a specific historical event. On the other hand, 'anthropology' tends to emphasize theoretical explanations. Although it is true that both the Maya and Christian people built a complex religious code, for example, the Maya have not generally been religious fundamentalists while Christians have been strictly theological for a long period. When new things are discovered, Christians of the past attempted to explain them within the context of the *Bible* only, because the Christian religion of the past placed absolute trust in the Christian *Bible*. This tendency can now be observed among some of the current Muslim fundamentalists. Such people tend to dismiss any phenomenon which their holy texts do not record.

On the other hand, although it is true that some texts, such as the *Popol Vuh,* are treated almost the same as the *Bible* among the Maya in general, the code of Maya religions is a Maya way of understanding and explanation of the universe.

A traditional explanation of the Maya concept, that is, the '*prophetic tradition of the Maya tends to blur the distinction between myth and history...The prophetic tradition ensures the conscious cyclical revival of selected aspects of Maya culture,*'[25] is certainly an important interpretation of the 'religious fusion' between Christianity and Maya religions. Nevertheless, it is also evident that prophetic tradition should not be regarded as the sole factor in such 'religious mixes.' For example, the colonial Maya often used Christian elements to hide their religion from violent Spanish evangelizations. Moreover, *nepantlism* (a neutral position between two religions) among the Mesoamerican people was also proposed in order to express the religious trauma of the Native American people in the sixteenth century.[26] More recently, others have proposed that the '*Maya and Native American religion blended into a set of a local variants on Catholicism.*' These three factors must have played an important role in religious mixing. However, are they enough? I will add another factor.

---

[25] Cited from Bricker 1981:180.
[26] León-Portilla 1990:71-2.

15

Because of the nature of the Maya religions, since the ancient times, when their old traditions and holy Maya scriptures failed to explain the emergence of newly and unexpectedly significant phenomena, the Maya historically reacted to this by modifying their code.[27] Moreover, Maya religions are essentially a way of communication between the people and nature. It can be said that in this type of religion, every individual has his/her own theology and religious code. In such a religious belief, incorporating Christian elements can take place as required to provide an explanation of new phenomena in the universe, even if the Maya actually disliked them.

This logic may be quite similar to the differences between ancient Roman and Greek pagan religions and Christianity on numerous points.[28] However, any study of the colonial Maya religious notion cannot be made at the same level as that of the ancient Roman by using old manuscripts, because the Maya left a far smaller amount of written text of their religious notions. The case of the colonial Maya should be studied from more various academic disciplines than that of the pagan Romans.

This book further develops the hypothesis that under the political, cultural, economical suppression of the Maya during the Spanish colonial period, the Maya traditional cultural tendency of reconstruction of their cosmovision became stronger. On this point, it must be noted that even though Catholic Christianity is far more fundamental than Maya religions, Catholic missionaries also made a serious attempt to incorporate pagan religions into Christian doctrine where European cultural, military, and economic force was a weak power. This case is found in Chinese history, and will also be discussed in this book.

In spite of the fact that the Maya were the most literate people within the New World in the pre-Columbian period, documentary evidence of the colonial Maya is not abundant. One of the major difficulties in considering the religious notions of the colonial Maya through the discipline of ordinary 'history' is a lack of a

---

[27] Yamase 2002b:

sufficient number of Maya private documents. Moreover, although colonial Maya half-religious chronicles survive, they are not easily understood and the authors of those texts are still unknown in most cases. It is often difficult to know the educational and religious background of the authors. Therefore, although some noted historians' works are undeniably indispensable references, it may be suggested that their focus on evidence within a specific period has a limitations for our understanding of the Maya. Under such circumstances, it may be said that the studies of the colonial Maya texts through ordinary historical surveys do not always produce a comprehensive understanding of the relationships between the Maya culture and Christian culture. Perhaps, an anthropological approach provides a better explanation of this phenomenon. Scholars have often tried to expand their research to ethnographical studies of the present day Maya in order to reconstruct the view of Christianity among the colonial Maya.

Apart from anthropological fieldwork, there are several other approaches. Archeological investigations bring us some useful understanding of the notions and beliefs of the ancient Maya, many of which still survive among the living Maya. Advancement in decryption of Maya hieroglyphics and studies of classic art have also unveiled the continuous existence of some fundamental concepts of the ancient Maya among the Maya of today. Although I have mentioned a negative view towards history as an academic subject in approaching the Maya, historical surveys cannot be ignored because they provide us with accurate information about the political and religious climate of certain periods of the past. Each of the disciplines has its own advantages and disadvantages.

Although analyses utilized by other 'traditional' Maya studies occupy a major part of this work, an ambitious attempt will also be included to 'understand Christianity from a perspective of dualistic cultures.'

The comparative study of different cultures in different parts of the world is an urgent task in any academic discipline. Some scholars have already mentioned that

---

[28] See Fox 1986:376-402.

a comparative study of missionary works in both New Worlds would result in a better understanding of the Catholic evangelization of colonial Latin America.[29] It seems that such an approach is more suitable for Western scholars who have a better capability of surveying Christian materials, than for me. What I will present in this volume is a comparative religious study, but also an attempt to understand Mayanized Christianity from the perspective of the pagan world. Comparing the reactions of each of the pagan cultures to Christianity and analyzing the conflicts among various religions in term of world history can also provide some essential keys to understanding the colonial Maya perception of Christianity.

The pagan's persecution of Christians in the early Roman Empire has been discussed in numerous works. What I will present is a comparative study of the 'Maya discovery of Christianity' as a part of the New World pagans' encounter with, or discovery of, Christianity of the sixteenth and seventeenth centuries. There is already an excellent collection of essays produced by noted researchers and edited by Gary H. Gossen, which discusses various aspects of conflicts between Christianity and Native American religions of Mesoamerica and South America since the Spanish conquest of the New World.[30] No doubt, that volume should be regarded as excellent one. Yet, at the same time, the almost inadequate consideration of 'Maya-Christian religions' from the perspective of dualism within that volume should also be pointed out. In spite of the fact that the importance of dualism (the term pluralism is more common today) among Mesoamerican culture is now recognized, I have often felt that this concept has virtually been ignored in some cases. Therefore, this work aims to revise the relationships between Christianity and Maya religions from a perspective of dualistic cultures.

In the sixteenth century, not only the Maya, but also the Aztec and the Inca, were confronted with a newly arrived religion, Christianity, and these other cultures are often used to present a comparative analysis of the colonial Maya's reaction to Christianity. Yet, this research does not confine itself to a focus on the

---

[29] Vogeley 1997.

18

'traditional' New World, the Americas. Nowadays, the term '*New World*' usually refers to the Americas only. In the sixteenth century, parts of Asia were also often considered another '*New World.*' It is well known that Christopher Columbus, the discoverer of the Americas, originally searched for China and Japan. Until his death, he believed that he had reached a part of China. Even in the late period, a sixteenth-century Spanish Franciscan, Fray Toribio de Motolinia, wrote that some *conquistadores* of Peru initially believed that they had come to the Americas to find *Cipango* [Japan].[31] Although the Westerners had already reached China and Japan through Marco Polo (c.1254-1324), the exact location of these lands remained obscure in the early sixteenth century. According to a Spanish historian of the sixteenth century, Juan González de Mendoza, the exact details of China remained a mystery to the Spaniards until 1575.[32] Therefore, it can be said that both Asia and the Americas were the New World for the Westerners of the sixteenth century. The first comparative analysis of pagan cults of these two New Worlds is the work of a sixteenth century Spanish friar, José de Acosta.[33] The present book is just the opposite of his work; while Acosta viewed pagan cults from his Christian perspective, the perspectives of paganism on Christianity is a main theme of this book.

As the result of the discovery of these two New Worlds, the Americas were conquered while the Asian civilization remained independent. As I have already mentioned, the justification of the conquest of the Americas was based upon the Papal Donation of 1492, by Pope Alexander VI, which granted the Spanish kings dominion over the newly discovered islands of the Americas on condition that the inhabitants were converted to Christianity. Since the Spaniards justified their military conquest of the Americas on the basis of the propagation of Christianity in those areas, the Iberian conquest of the Americas therefore involved not only military action but also forced religious conversion. From the sixteenth century,

---

[30] Gossen 1993.
[31] Motolinia 1985:lib 3, cap.11.
[32] González de Mendoza [1585] libro I, cap.I.

apart from the military and political struggles with the West, the Americas faced a confrontation with a newly arrived theological religion, Christianity.

It is said that the Christian religion was a part of the Spanish and Portuguese imperialism from the fifteenth to the early nineteenth century, and the Church within the New World often acted as a part of the institution of Spanish domination. In 1508, the Pope issued *Patronato Real*, which provided the Spanish and Portuguese crown with the coveted universal patronage over the church in the New World. This bull meant that the Spanish crown became the unique authority over the church within the New World. Under such a political and religious circumstance, it is not difficult to say that Christianity was considered the symbol of Spanish rule, and thus it often received strong resistance and hostility from the Native Americans. However in 1573, one year after the final collapse of the Inca state of Peru, the Spanish crown officially revised its past policy, and issued a new instruction.[34] In that, the crown states that new discoveries are not called conquests, that Christianity must be developed with peaceful methods only, and the right of domination over the people of newly discovered lands is justified only when there is spontaneous obedience from the indigenous residents. However, Christians in Asia had to pay compensation for their justification of the conquest of Latin America. In East Asia, the news of the Spanish conquest of the Americas and Philippines provoked a strong anti-Christian movement in Japan, large scale persecutions of the Christian population were frequently practiced and they were virtually expelled from Japan for nearly three hundred years. As a result, in contrast to Latin America, the small number of Christians in Japan survived on the margins of society, carefully hiding their Christian faith.

Later, in China, Christianity was introduced and was welcomed by a certain section of the ruling class. Yet the exclusive character of Christianity raised conflicts with Chinese traditional religions. After a long dispute, the Pope finally issued a bull in which he stated that the Roman Catholic Chinese were banned from

---

[33] Acosta 1590.

participation in Chinese rites. With its uncountable human resources, China at that time was a gigantic military and economic power. Since the sixteenth century, although the Europeans began to advance beyond China in some aspects, such military technology, such advantages had not become a serious concern for China because China still considered herself superior to Europe in numerous other ways. For China, Europe was a place of red-haired, barbaric people. For the Chinese Emperor of that time, therefore, the Pope was officially recorded as a vassal who paid tribute (the Pope was called the 'King of Propagation=教化王') and his messengers were never treated as diplomats, but as barbaric vassals before the Chinese Emperor until the late eighteenth century. All messengers from the Western and Islamic states acted thus, at least within the Emperor's place, because it was believed that the Chinese Emperor was granted his ruling power as the representative of the Lord of Sky (天子). A unique exception were diplomats from the Russian Tsar [Emperor], but they were only recognized as diplomats after the eighteenth century.

For Emperor Kang-Shi, therefore, the decision of Rome which forbade participation in Chinese rites among the Christians, was ridiculous, because it meant that he was ordered to do something by the Pope, who is, in theory, was his 'vassal' from a lesser civilization. As a matter of course, the bull of Roma provoked strong fury in the Chinese Emperor. The fact is that in spite of the hostility towards Christianity among a certain part of principal ruling class, the Emperor had made it possible to develop Christianity in China. The Chinese Emperor, who had once approved of Christianity, reversed the previous ordinance and initiated the policy of banning Christianity. This was the beginning of the history of the distress of Christians in China.[35]

Of course, because the pagan religion and political circumstances of each area were different, each area experienced a different type of religious confrontation

---

[34] The original text was published in CDIA: Vol. 16, pp.142-187.
[35] Yamase 2002b:250-5.

with Christianity. In Japan, although Shinto is the native Japanese religion and often shows striking similarities with numerous Native American religions, the main target of attack of the Catholic Church of the sixteenth century in Japan was Buddhism, since Buddhism was the most influential religion of that time. In China, although Taoism is a pantheistic religion and thus it can be said to be a comparative religion with those of Native America, the religious battle in China was raised between Christianity and Confucianism, the most respected philosophy within Chinese civilization. Therefore, it appears that each part of the two New Worlds had different historical anti-Christianity movements.

I do not insist that all pagan religions are the same, as the European scholars once argued in the Enlightenment period. There are some important fundamental differences between Native American and Asian religions. In Japan, it is generally accepted that there is no concept of a single creator of the world, while the Inca had *Viracocha* (yet, the Inca also worshipped the Sun God as an almost equivalent divinity; they also believed in a duality of *Viracocha*). While Japanese Shinto has traditionally regarded death as unclean, archaeological evidence suggests that the Maya, Aztec and Inca have not always considered it ominous. In the case of the Inca, although the Inca Emperor claimed that he was a son of the Sun, as the Japanese Emperor did, the concept of death was different. It is well known that in ancient Peru, dead persons were mummified and those mummies were treated as they would have been if alive. Fragmented parts of this belief remain in some local areas of the Andes. In addition, unlike the Inca and the Japanese, the religious concepts of the Maya are heavily influenced by their cycle-periodic notion, so that they often do not always have a clear distinction between the past and the present. These differences can be observed in the sexuality of their deities. For example, while Maya deities are often bisexual, Japanese deities are not.

Even if we confine our research to a single cultural area, such as Mesoamerica, there are numerous different types of religion, and thus each perception of Christianity could have been very different. Even among the Maya, each of Maya language groups had a different religious concept, although significant similarities among them can easily be pointed out. Furthermore, substantially different religious traditions and practices have been reported within the same Maya language group. Of course, every individual Maya would have a different religious mind. Therefore, because the Christianity of the sixteenth and seventeenth centuries encountered different types of religion in various places, some may argue that a generalizing historical process of idolaters' discovery of Christianity is difficult. In any academic discipline, it is generally believed that a comparative study often results in an overgeneralization and a fruitless oversimplification. As a comparative study of vast area of the two New Worlds, therefore, my analysis presented here will inevitably have some defects as a proper understanding of the Maya. Some may say that this volume is a vain effort.

Nevertheless, it must be pointed out that the essential concept of almost all pagan religions is dualism. Only when the significant similarities of religious concepts of those two New Worlds are considered, can a number of important common reactions towards Christianity be noticed. One of the aims of this research is to verify that the 'peculiar and confused Christianity' practiced among the Maya is commonly observed in other dualistic cultures, and that the so-called 'religious syncretism' found among the Maya is by no means a result of their confusion, but an intellectual reconstruction of two religions.

Although the Asian and Native American civilizations developed differently, a comparative study of the history of anti-Christianity during the sixteenth and seventeenth centuries is quite interesting. When we discuss religious issues, there are distinct similarities in those areas. Of course, I would agree that comparing the details of each religion is fruitless. As long as certain points, which will be mentioned below, are considered, I think that this research will yield some useful keys to understand the religious perceptions of the Maya people towards Christianity.

23

1: The majority of Native Americans and Far East Asians have a religious concept of dualism.
2: They are generally idolatrous.
3: They do not have a concept of religious sin.

From my point of view, the first point mentioned above, the 'concept of dualism,' although dualism in each culture is not the same, is extremely important when we consider religious hostility towards Christianity and the so-called religious syncretism between the Native American religions and Christianity. Thus, this work is better categorized as a comparative analysis of the perception of Christianity within dualistic cultures, and not as a comparative religious study. On this point, it may be said that this research also provides readers an opportunity to comprehend a difference between dualistic and monistic cultural perspectives.

What is dualism? Dualism is a concept attempting to discover a harmonious relationship between two opposing elements, such as day and night. Dualism is often referred to as negative and positive principles. The monism concept generated from Christianity and Islamic religion tends to regard eliminating evil as a true way of preaching the absolute good, the Lord (=*Allah*). Within dualism, on the other hand, any opposing element such as evil is treated as a necessary part of the universe. It is considered that true virtue is only generated from interaction between good and evil. An example may be that while the Hell in Christianity is defined as the land of the permanent enemy of the Lord governed by Satan, the *Popol Vuh* of the Maya treats their hell, *Xibalba*, as a necessary part of the universe, in spite of the fact that the punishment of the Hero Twins given to *Xibalba* is one of its core narratives and it is treated as a fearful place. This explains a fundamental difference between monism=Christianity and Maya dualism. While Christianity believes eliminating evil is the goal of human endeavor, the Maya consider that eliminating evil completely will result in a fatal destruction of the universe.

Previous studies on Maya concepts have often excluded this perspective. For example, it is often simply said that time is as a kind of life in the Maya conception. In that case, of what does time consist? The answer is the past and the present. In this respect, it may be suggested that the Maya concept of time is a representation of the dualistic notion generated by the past and the present. As will be argued in this research (e.g., the case of the *Book of Chilam Balam of Chumayel* of the Yucatec Maya), the Maya concept of time cannot properly be understood without grasping the dualistic understanding held by the Maya.

The importance of the inclusion of dualism in the current study of 'religious syncretism' among the Maya is to investigate the relationship between Christianity and Maya religion from this negative and positive principle. As will be discussed, although the colonial Maya and Nahuatl often found Christianity to be their opponent, it must be noted that the core ideological concept of the Maya is dualism. Therefore, it is suggested that in spite of frequent reference to their strong hostility toward Christianity found in colonial reports, the nature of their anti-Christianity should not be considered the same as anti-pagan views of the Christians. Although anti-pagan Christians usually opted for an eradication of pagan religions, pagan Maya did not respond in kind, due to their dualistic perceptions. By using various examples, this research will unveil that what the colonial Maya attempted to do was to seek a reasonable explanation of the emergence of Christianity rather than reject it. For example, here will be discussed that the *Book of Chilam Balam of Chumayel*, often called a book of hidden anti-Christianity or a merely confused one, did not oppose Christianity, but used it to reconstruct a new cosmovision of the universe.

The dualism concept found in colonial Native Americans has mistakenly been understood as a completely alien concept for the Western world. However, if we look at the Far East, a religious dualism which is quite close to that of the Native Americans, has remained a core concept since ancient times. Although Asian dualism considerably differs in some aspects, reading their ancient works can often assist us in comprehending the essential nature of dualism in general.

James Lockhart once argued that a realization of the true nature of colonial Nahuatl texts has called forth a *New Philosophy* with which to understand the sources and places them in their true context.[36] What is his proposed *New Philosophy*? From my point of view, the 'philosophy' must not be 'new,' but a variant of 'traditional' oriental dualism. In general, the Westerner or Western-educated Native American (including US-born Japanese Americans) have serious trouble in thinking and interpreting issues based on dualism. I have noticed through my communications with Westerners that the problems experienced by Western researchers in the field of Mesoamerican studies are substantially the same as the Western difficulties of comprehending Japanese and Chinese cultures. How many of them have actually read Chinese classical works, which are a treasure of the dualism concept?

After I finished my unsatisfying Ph.D. thesis (although some find 'vigor' in that text, it is really an annoying comment for me. The fact is that such passion did not exist. It was virtually written as a duty for late persons according to the Confucianism concept), I was looking for an alternative academic subject suitable to my status. At the time, I happened to know of a book which contained interviews with several living K'iche Maya shamans.[37] To be honest, I did not expect much from that book, as Maya studies are not a popular academic subject in Japan compared to the USA or Germany. However, although that book is not strictly an academic one, since the author carefully records the voice of the K'iche Maya shamans, numerous fresh ideas are provided. In that book, although arguments of the K'iche shamans merely represent one of various opinions among the Maya, I became interested in how those K'iche shamans speak of the importance of understanding dualism in order to comprehend some context of the *Popol Vuh* and the K'iche Maya understanding of Christianity.[38] Although the dualism concept of Mesoamerican cultures is often explained as 'dual thoughts,' when the Maya speak of dualism in Katuyasu Sanematu's book, it is quite similar to the positive and negative principle of the Chinese concept in many points. By reading 'confused'

---

[36] *Ibid.*
[37] Sanematu 2000.
[38] Also see Valencia Solanilla 1996, 2002, Alvarez 1999:47.

colonial Maya texts from the perspective of the positive and negative principle, I found that a more effective understanding of the colonial Maya texts is possible. Consequently, I became confident that the colonial Maya authors of the sacred text purposely made an ostensibly 'confused' Mayanized Christianity according to their concept of dualism. The aim of this research is to prove my hypothesis more clearly than in the previous book.

The relationships between Christianity and Native American 'primitive' pagan religions since 1492 have remained one of the controversial issues of Latin American studies. Are they a representation of religious syncretism, Native American confusions, or of hidden resistance to Christianity; the three interpretations mainly proposed. [39] Although the term of *nepantlism* (neutral position between two religions) has often been used to explain religious attitudes of the colonial Native Americans[40], a neutral position is not always adequate to clarify the concept of co-existence of two religious found in the colonial texts[41], because in such Maya texts, both religious beliefs have complex interactions with each other. From my point of view, the context of these texts should also be analyzed from the perspective of dualism, otherwise it is difficult to comprehend the Maya religious notion of Christianity. In the field of Maya studies, academic researchers have recognized dualism as an important element of the Maya culture.[42] Understanding Maya dualism is a vital key to understanding not only the context of the colonial Maya documents and beliefs, but also the relationship between Christianity and Maya religions. Dualism is now recognized to be an important part of the Maya culture by almost all researchers.

Nevertheless, when so-called Mayanized Christians are discussed (or Christianized Maya) with the cosmovision and religion found in the colonial Maya

---

[39] See Dussel 1981:66-7.
[40] *e.g.*, see León-Portilla 1990:97-122.
[41] See Cervantes 1994:56-57.
[42] Schultze-Jena (1954:62) mentions that this issue was first academically discussed around the 1880s. See Thompson 1954: 7-8. A recent discussion about Maya dualism can be seen in Edmonson (1993:67-8).

texts, the dualism concept has rarely been developed to a satisfactory level (at least in my view).[43] In such previous works, the relationship between Christianity and Maya religions is explained either as 'co-opting for either religious beliefs,' or as 'passive acceptance of Christianity' to define religious syncretism as a tactic to maintain the old pagan faith under Christian domination.

Although the use of 'co-opting' is quite acceptable, in my opinion, dualism is a more proper term to explain religious phenomena found in the Maya culture, because the Maya interchangeably worship Christianity and Maya religions at the same time, in most cases. As will be suggested in this book, the Maya systematically integrated Christianity into their dualistic beliefs.

At least until the early twentieth century, the Catholic and Maya religions practiced among the Maya after the Spanish conquest were often described as a religious confusion.[44] A US anthropologist, Oliver LaFarge, who appears to have noticed the importance of the duality of the Christian and Maya religions worshipped by the Guatemalan Maya, still called such religious phenomena 'confusion.'[45] Because most of his Maya informants did not have a good command of Spanish, he probably considered a religious fusion between Maya religions and Christianity to be a consequence of their syncretic confusion. Donaldo E. Thompson, another US scholar, also called Maya-Christian religious traditions among the Maya 'confusion.'[46] Yet, is the term 'confusion' a proper one to refer to religious practices among the Maya? Of course, I do not deny that since the sixteenth century, over time, both religions have been mixed by the ordinary and illiterate Maya in many cases, because the majority of colonial Maya were not well educated in Spanish so that they incorrectly received Christian doctrines. Perhaps, because of this, there was a long period during which the colonial Maya texts,

---

[43] A recent article of Victoria R. Bricker (2002) shows a significant progress in Western understanding of the Maya concept of dualism. She rightly points out that Christian and Maya religious elements are not confused, but are properly paired in the *Books of Chilam Balam of Chumayel*, a colonial Yucatec Maya text.
[44] For example, Wagley 1949:50.
[45] LaFarge 1947:103, 109.
[46] Thompson 1954: *passim*.

which contain 'distorted' Christianity, were considered to be evidence of the inferiority of the Maya intellect to the West in the nineteenth century.

Such a dismissive attitude toward the Maya has gradually changed, at least among academics. Eric Thompson, a great Mayaist of the twentieth century, proposed that Mayanized Christianity is a result of an unconscious eclecticism, a combination of ancient Maya religions and trivial features of Christianity.[47]

I am in favor of Thompson's opinion about Mayanized Christianity, to some extent. The majority of the Maya remained illiterate during the colonial period; they had to transmit their religious beliefs orally. This explains the hybrid religion found among the Maya, in that oral transmission tends to blur the original narratives unconsciously over the generations. The Maya of Chiapas have provided us numerous examples of this.[48] In the case of the Tolupan Indians of Honduras, who have traditionally relied on the oral tradition, this kind of unconscious blending (e.g., the native deities with Christian elements) is evident in some parts of their religious narrative.[49] Therefore, it can be suggested that among the Native Americans, unconscious blending of both religious beliefs into one belief system took place as a natural result.

Nevertheless, although there is some unconscious blending, it is also true that both religious systems are treated as substantially different concepts. This provides an argument against 'unconscious blending.' In addition, a doubt arises on this point: Can the idea of 'unconscious combination' be acceptable in the case of educated, literate Maya?

Thompson and other researchers tended to dismiss the important point that the authors of the colonial Maya texts must have been well educated. It has practically been ignored that they were reasoning people. Their intellectual ability should not be underestimated. For various reasons, such as very limited access to the Holy Scriptures, their comprehension of the Gospel may have been inadequate in some

---

[47] Thompson 1975:162.
[48] For example, see Gossen 1999.
[49] See Chapman 1992.

points. Can it be said that the Mayanized Christianity found in these texts was merely a product of Maya confusion or of their unconscious blending? Misunderstanding some theological issues of Christianity also took place in highly civilized areas such as Japan and China, because of their limited access to the Holy Scriptures. Therefore, it seems difficult to agree with these interpretations of 'unconscious mixing of two religious beliefs' in the case of colonial Maya documents. It is also almost certain that they never incorporated Christianity in a confused sense with their own religions, especially in the form of writing.

Internal evidence of these colonial Maya texts reveals that the authors of the colonial Maya appear to be different from colonial 'folk' Maya, who often spoke what they believed to be 'Spanish.' The context of the *Books of Chilam Balam* of the Yucatan suggests that the colonial Maya authors were capable of understanding not only Spanish, but also Latin! This fact proves that these authors were apparently educated. It is quite likely, therefore, that the authors of the colonial Maya texts must have consciously blended both religious elements.[50] Although Maya hieroglyphic materials were quickly disappearing after 1562, because the Maya elite had learnt Spanish from the friars, it is very probable that their old Maya traditions were already transcribed in the Spanish script. If so, knowledgeable colonial Maya must have used them as a unique source information on the Maya cosmovision. In this case, it is supposed that Christian elements found in the texts should purposely have been integrated with Maya traditional religious accounts by these educated Maya authors.

Two reasons for introducing Christian elements into the colonial Maya cosmovision can be proposed. The first one is to trick the Spaniards in order to protect written Maya religious scriptures. The second is that because of the difficulties of language, the concepts of Christianity were syncretized in a confused fashion with Maya elements in the colonial Maya religious texts.

---

[50] Bricker (2002) proves this point well.

On this very point, a question of the usage of the term 'syncretism,' has been was raised. Although the term 'syncretism' had a positive meaning of old, this was lost in the sixteenth century.[51] Any non-standard religious activity was considered evidence of the 'antichrist' by the Europeans of that period. It must be noted that even a Christian, Martin Luther, was called an 'antichrist.' It is not surprising therefore, that the colonial Spanish friars observed this Mayanized Christianity as evidence of antichrist sentiment among the Maya.

Although the Catholic Church changed its negative attitude towards other religions in the early twentieth century, the definition of syncretism remains somewhat 'an imperfection' and thus its presence is often regarded as an unenthusiastic one by the Christian population. Syncretism still generally refers to 'imperfect mixing = muddled circumstances' in Christian and Islamic cultures, and signifies a heretic concept. Therefore, syncretism between Maya religions and Christianity was considered 'inauthentic' Christianity by the Spanish friars. Because it is considered that Satan continuously made efforts to take people away from authentic Christianity, the colonial Catholic friars tended to conclude that the reason for this religious phenomenon was a result of deception by devils. In the later period, the intellectual ability of the Maya was often questioned. Because less educated Maya of the twentieth century do not always have a good command of Spanish (of course, Latin is out of question for them), some tended to consider syncretic Mayanized Christianity a result of their confused understanding of the Gospel.

However, although syncretic religions are still regarded as an improper version of Christianity by the Westerner, from a non-Western point of view, the localization of Christianity is often taken as positive. In Africa, for example, 'appropriation' is used instead of 'syncretism.'[52] This means that what the African practice is an authentic Christianity for them.

---

[51] Shaw and Stewart 1994:3-4.
[52] See Meyer 1994.

Therefore, in the first place, it must be asked 'What is authentic Christianity?' The fact is that Western Christianity is also a consequence of religious syncretism with old pagan religions. On this very point, the current 'authentic Christianity' may be said to be a product of a European-biased view. As found in the cases of Christian Platonism and Celtic Christianity in the Europe of the past, syncretism between ancient pagan religions and Christianity is not always a result of a confused mixture.

Therefore, 'reconstructing' instead of 'syncretism' may be properly used to refer to the issue of Mayanized Christianity found in the colonial Maya texts.[53] In this research, it will be discussed that the religious syncretisms found in the colonial Maya texts are not a result of confusion, but of intellectual efforts.

Although it was often said that the Maya after the Spanish conquest confusedly mixed Christianity with Maya religion, based on ethnographical works, not only the educated Maya, but also the folk Maya seem to have been religiously confused. Careful observations have revealed that the folk Maya, who do not have a good education, still separate Maya religions from Christianity. In the early twentieth century, Robert Redfield and Alfonso Villa Rojas reported that the Maya gods and the lord of Christianity were clearly distinguished by the Yucatec Maya in terms of two different ritual contexts, though their observation was often virtually ignored.[54] In the late twentieth century, Barbara Tedlock reports that she observed in the present-day Momostenango of Guatemala, a religious dualism of two very different religions, but neither was Catholic nor a part of a Christian-pagan syncretistic religion.[55] This suggests that they are not essentially confused with the doctrines of two very different religious traditions, and the Maya have historically and systematically interpreted Christianity within their own dualistic perception. In this case, both religions have a different role under a single Cosmos. Therefore, Christianity and Maya religions are essentially not syncretized. Nevertheless, the

[53] Yamase 2002b:259, Bricker 2002.
[54] Redfield et al.1962:124.

term of 'syncretism' remains popular, and the majority of researchers have been less concerned about Maya dualism in order to comprehend the meaning of colonial Maya texts with strong Christian influences.

As I am also a pagan, and a believer in Japanese Shinto, which shares similarities with Maya religions, comprehending their concept of dualism was not difficult for me at all. Nevertheless, I had never come to think of the importance of Maya dualism until I read Katuyoshi Sanematu's book published in Japan. I was ashamed of it. In fact, in my country, there are several quite interesting cases of religious 'fusion' between Christianity and Japanese traditional religions: one by folk-Christian Japanese people, another by a leading Japanese nationalist. They were used as comparative materials and the result of my research was included in my revised Ph.D. thesis, which has already been published.[56] In that book, I suggested the importance of understanding the so-called 'mixture' of Maya and Christian fundamentals from a perspective of dualism and of Christian scientific advantages, and that the Christian influence found in the colonial Maya texts could be considered the result of their reconstruction of a single cosmovision from two religions, rather than a religious fusion (or religious mixture). Although my arguments may be controversial in some aspects, I believe that at least a new standpoint has been added to the previous studies of religious 'fusion' between Christianity and the Maya religions. In fact, such cultural constructionism has been reported.

However, my research was obviously still imperfect. It is true that in the Guatemala of today, while some K'iche Maya opt for religious constructionism based on both Christianity and Maya religions, others are more fundamentalist in their ancient beliefs. It cannot be denied that the colonial K'iche may have belonged to the latter category. Therefore, soon after I published my work, I

---

[55] Tedlock 1991, see also Chiappari 1999:119-120. This kind of opinion was also presented in Dussel 1981:67, though he lacks substantial understanding of dualism.
[56] Yamase 2002b.

initiated preparation for presenting a more complete argument about Christianity from a perspective of dualistic cultures as a single volume.

It is commonly suggested that as the Spanish military success was considered evidence of the spiritual power of Christianity by the Maya, the acceptance of it was a logical choice for them.[57] Although this was also the case in the Japan of the sixteenth century, as a pagan, I am not satisfied with this kind of explanation. As will be discussed in this book, the people who have a concept of religious dualism have tended to identify Christianity as a religion homogeneous with their own, and thus, in theory, in most cases, although Christianity was basically considered to be harmful by such people, it was still considered to be one of various explanations of the universe. Moreover, although evidence is not always adequate, it must be pointed out that Christianity was initially welcomed at least by the ruling class, who could see the potential benefit of allying with the Spaniards, and by others in pagan countries. This is significant in that the Christians regarded pagan religions as works of the devil. Within the history of the world it is not rare to see that even if Christianity received strong hostility from pagan people, part of the Christian doctrine and knowledge were positively positively.

What I have insisted in the previous works is that current academic studies concerning so-called religious hybridization between Maya religions and Christianity during the colonial era give too much stress to Maya hostility to Spanish domination since the conquest, and that the Maya were treated as lesser citizens during the Spanish colonial period, resulting in an unbalanced understanding of the Maya reinterpretation of Christianity. The fact is that the Maya religions have been very incorporative since ancient times. However, since my previous research obviously covers a very limited part of the issue, my argument is evidently lacking some important issues that remain to be examined. Hence this work.

---

[57] Dussel 1981:67, Restall 1997:147.

Due to the catastrophic consequence of the Conquest, the Native Americans have often regarded Christianity as undesirable. In this case, it is obvious that analyzing the Native American concept of 'negative' must be done carefully, together with a consideration of their dualism. Nonetheless, in history of Latin American studies, while European and Native American traditional perspectives of deity have well been discussed, Native American concepts of 'evil' and 'negativity' have not always well been argued.[58] Fernando Cervantes pointed out the colonial Spanish excessive exaggeration of remaining pagan religious elements and practices among the colonial Nahuatl people as evidence of Anti-Christianity. His balanced argument should be mentioned here as a worthwhile contribution. However, as a result of this he is strongly reliant on European sources, no perspective from the dualism culture is substantially included in his argument. For that reason, I think that presenting an argument from the pagan and dualistic world is necessary. Differences in the concept of evil among the Maya from that of Christianity will be discussed in my analysis from my perspective of dualism.

Producing this book required a better understanding of the religious background of the Christian cultures of the sixteenth century, even though it is not my major focus. Therefore, it was necessary to summarize the history of the first encounter of the Spaniards and Native Americans from my own perspective.

In pagan animistic and Confucianist cultures, Christian cultures were a source of new discoveries. To be honest, after finishing this manuscript, my interest in the history of Christianity became stronger than in that of the Maya. In reality, my efforts to complete this manuscript were to explore Christian cultures more than the Maya and other dualistic peoples. On these grounds, the actual title of this book should be *A Pagan Exploration of Christian History.*

The early Christian ideas, such as Christian Platonism proposed by the early Christian Saints (such as Justin Martyr and Augustine), constituted the Christian view towards the pagan in the later period. In addition, several myths of the victory

---

[58] There are several works treating this issue, Cervantes 1994, Freidel 1993:176.

of Christianity over the pagan were invented in medieval Europe. These heavily influenced not only the ideas of the Spaniards of the sixteenth century, but also those of Westerners of today. Therefore, unless these issues are carefully considered, we can understand little of the various issues concerning the religious conflict between the Maya and the Spaniards (the Westerners of today). Therefore, the religious debate and ideas among the sixteenth-century Spaniards were investigated and will be discussed in this book to understand the fundamental conceptual difference of religion between paganism, animism and Christianity.

As a preparation for writing a comparative study of the Christian influence in the pagan world, not only is a good knowledge of the Maya and the Christian civilizations required, but also a good understanding of other pagan cultures. As a result, I have published three books on the Spanish conquest of the Aztec,[59] the Inca[60], and a reprint of several English translations of Inca material by Sir Clements Markham[61]. Preparing two books came about also because of my old interest in military history, which was one of the major factors in my going to the UK, though no one believed in my interest at that time. Another purpose of writing those books was to appeal and convey to the Japanese people an important fact, that the devastation of the 'barbaric' Native Americans caused by the 'civilized and self-conscious' Europeans resulted in the devastation of the 'barbaric and immature' Europeans (of course the Asians were also self-conscious at the same time) of the sixteenth and seventeenth centuries. This historical fact proves that although the Christians have often denied the dualism concept, their history has also always been subject to 因果応報 (retributive justice), one of the major concepts of dualism.

I must admit that both works were essentially written as non-refereed works for general readers, and never surpassed John Hemming's *The Conquest of the Inca*

---

[59] Yamase 2003a, 2005.
[60] Yamase 2004a.
[61] Yamase 2003b.

[62]and Thomas Huge's The *Fall of Mexico*[63] in terms of scale and academic value, except in some minor issues. Nevertheless, these experiences are a nice opportunity for me to collect numerous new materials and revise the history of the Spanish military and spiritual conquest. The process of writing has required me to read new materials more carefully, and has provided me a better understanding of the first confrontation between the Native Americans and the Spaniards, especially in Peru, than in the past, and it was quite useful to increase my knowledge of both in order to conduct this comparative research. Because a case study of the Inca was not included in the previous work, their history of resistance to the Spaniards provided me some new perspectives. As the result of these two works, I have noticed that there are some quite interesting keys to understanding pagan peoples' common interpretation of Christianity. All material read for those books subsequently became source materials for this volume. Chapter III 'Pagan Discovery of Christianity' is based on these books.

Chapter III of this volume, which is an unusual one as a part of Maya studies, was written to familiarize the non-pagan reader with the dualism concept. I believe that understanding pagan cultures from a perspective of dualism is quite useful, not only for the colonial Maya culture, but also for today's Maya, other Native Americans, and the Far East Asian cultures. Therefore, I hope that this book will be a useful reference for understanding somewhat complicated dualistic notions, not only for students of Maya studies, but also for those of pagan cultures in other areas of study.

This volume forms a peculiar comparative study. While comparative study is regarded as an interesting one, its argument often requires an oversimplification of complicated human notions, and thus there will come such critical comments on my research as that of Vincent Stanzione: "*the juxtaposition of thought almost always leads to a surrealistic perspective.*" Also, Asian pagans and Native

---

[62] Hemming 1993.
[63] Hugh 1995.

American pagans are geographically too remote from each other, and they have differently and independently developed since their beginnings.

The social and historical circumstances of Far East Asian and Native Latin American pagans is also so different. While the term *'religious peasant'* has been employed to refer to the Christian in the Far East, it has oppositely been used in Latin America. While Pope John Paul II made several speeches encouraging Japanese Christians to make a courtesy visit to pagan shrines (not for worship),[64] and while the monotheism found in Christianity is considered a peculiar thinking in Japan, such behavior has became a target of violent 'social cleansing' conducted by Christian fanatics in Guatemala. In the Far East, syncretism is often regarded as a sign of progress, but in Latin America, it is merely considered a sign of deceit or sin, and often is worthy of death. It can be said that the cultural and social view towards Christianity between the two regions has substantially differed. Therefore, there remains the fundamental question of the extent to which a comparison of two totally different cultural traditions' view of Christianity is meaningful and appropriate.

On this point, another critical view, also presented by Vincent Stanzione, may be valid: *"this is one of the stumbling blocks in this exhaustive comparative analysis: the two worlds in comparison, Japan and Southern Mesoamerica, differ so greatly that it seems inappropriate to compare the two. It would perhaps be of more importance to state the dissimilarities between Japanese and Mayan Christianity so as to understand their different stances towards Christianity."*

Given the above mentioned questions, although I believe a knowledge of Asian dualism will help in reconstructing the Native American dualism perspective, the lack of which in the previous views presented by Western academics, was

---

[64] When the US president George Herbert Walker Bush(1989-1993) visited the *Meiji Jingu,* a pagan temple honoring the Meiji Emperor (1852-1912) as a god, he actually worshipped in it in Shinto traditional style and some of the US fundamental Christian parties later strongly criticized "President Bush worshipping a demon".

criticized as vital by some K'iche Maya, it should be noted that this research has a certain limitation as a credible reconstruction of the colonial Maya.

Moreover, I remind the readers that this book is largely written from the standpoint of a pagan fusionism view, chiefly dualism, and the relationships between Maya religions and Christianity will predominantly be analyzed from that perspective, yet this view does not always represent that of the whole Maya and other pagan nations. The fact is that there are numerous beliefs and phenomena which cannot be explained from the perspective of dualism (*e.g.* political compromise is an example). As some Maya groups who refuse to be influenced from Spanish culture and Christianity indeed exist, it cannot be denied that the colonial Maya authors refused Christianity as an element of their dualism. What I argue in this book is solely one possible interpretation.

Although those who believe in monotheism may find my arguments here ironical, the purpose of this book is not to provoke any anti-Christian feeling, and I never intend to dismiss the ideas of Christianity and the Islamic religion. My late aunt was a Catholic nun and I have a close Muslim friend. As an ordinary Japanese, I do have respect for all kinds of religion, all over the world.

Chapter I: Maya Religion: As One of the Pagan Religions

...I have now argued sufficiently against those who believe that many false gods are to be worshipped for the sake of this mortal life and earthly things...Christian truth has shown these gods to be either useless images or unclean spirits and malignant demons: Created beings, at any rate, and not the Creator.(St. Augustine refuted the blame for Christianity raised by the remaining pagan population within the Roman Empire)[1]

But that Moses denominates angels gods, hear from his own words: 'The sons of God saw the daughters of men that they were fair; and they took them wives of all which they chose.' And a little after he adds, 'And also after that, when the sons of God came in unto the daughters of men, and they bare children to them, the same were giants...'(Gen. Vi. 2 and 4) That he means angels, therefore, by the son of God, is very evident:...For he appears to me to signify that the race of giants derived its subsistence from the mixture of the mortal and immortal nature. Would not, then, he who names many sons of God, and these not men, but angels, would not he have unfolded to men the begotten word, or son of God, or in whatever manner you may call him, if he had known him? But because he thought this a great thing, 'My first-born son, Israel' (Exod. Iv, 22))[sic]. *Why therefore, did not Moses say this of Jesus?* (From fragmentally surviving texts in which the Roman Emperor, Julian (361-363AD) accuses the Christians)[2]

I: Problems of Maya Sources

... Knowledge of the Gods is virtue, wisdom, and consummate felicity, and assimilates us to the Gods themselves. He [the reader] will find that the theology of Plato is the progeny of the most consummate science and wisdom, and that it is as much superior to all other theological systems which oppose it, as reality to fiction,

---

[1] Cited from Augustine 426:Book VI, Preface.
[2] Cited from Julian 361-3:79-80.

or intellect to irrational opinion. (The Roman Emperor Julian accusing the Christians)[3]

> *OUR knowledge of the mythology of the Maya is by no means so full and comprehensive as in the case of Mexican mythology. Traditions are few and obscure...*(cited from Spence 1913:Chap. V)

Numerous religious manuscripts written by the Maya people during the colonial period have been discovered in the past century, and almost all of them have been published. Nonetheless, the relationship between the colonial Maya and Christianity is far more problematical than that between the ancient Roman and Greek pagan religions and Christianity. In spite of the fact that the Maya were the most literate people in the pre-Hispanic period, investigating their surviving texts is often extremely difficult. The reasons for this situation may be explained as follows:

- **1:** Those surviving colonial Maya half-religious texts were most likely written for circulation among a certain group of highly educated Maya people, and thus it is not always easy for non-Maya readers to understand what the authors of these documents intended to record.
- **2:** Readers will find that within the *Books of Chilam Balam*, prophecy and history are inextricably entwined and often read like divine revelation.[4] This is also the same in part of the Yucatec Maya religion and the Christianity found in these books. In the *Books of Chilam Balam of Chumayel*, many readers may find that Jesus and other Christian saints are 'confusingly' merged with traditional Yucatec Maya religious figures, as if both are from a single religion. Although less so, the same problem for non-Maya readers exists in the case of the colonial Guatemalan Maya.
- **3:** The colonial Maya rarely left documents containing their personal religious beliefs. This makes it difficult to comprehend the colonial Maya notion of Christianity.
- **4:** Although the Spaniards of the colonial period wrote some important manuscripts describing the customs, rites, concepts and other various aspects of the Maya religions, the friars considered that understanding Maya religions was essential to evangelize the Maya. Nevertheless, it must be noted that with some exceptions, those texts were written by people who had little understanding of the Maya, who had a different

---

[3] Julian 361-3b:16-7
[4] As to the nine surviving Books of Chilam Balam, see e.g. Liljefors Persson 2000:65-71.

cultural logic from that of the Spaniards. For example, although almost all the colonial Spanish friars noticed that dualism was one of the important concepts among the Native Americans, it must be said that the understanding of it was generally impossible. For example, Francisco Ximénez, who made the first European translation of the *Popol Vuh*, translated two divinities of the K'iche Maya, *Tzacol* and *Bitol*, as *Creador* (= a single Creator). This clearly proves that this Franciscan did not understand the Maya concept of dualism, or intentionally mistranslated it as if the context of this K'iche mythological narrative was close to the *Bible*. The same problem has been pointed out in historical studies of other parts of the New World.

- ✔ **5:** Although considerable progress has been made, the details of colonial Maya religious ideas are not fully known, and thus it must be accepted that there are still difficulties of comparison of Maya religious doctrine with Christian ones.

- ✔ **6:** Some scholars believe that pointing out similarities between any two religions of the world is not difficult at all.[5] For example, '*The Jesus of the Gospels is said to have been tempted by the Devil in much the same way that Buddha* [of Buddhism] *was tempted by Mâra, the Evil One. Even the details of the two stories of temptation possess many features of resemblance.*'[6] In the case of Maya studies, both the Maya and the Christian Europeans have recognized a transcendent power over the human and nature. Were the Maya taught it by the Christian Europeans? The answer is likely 'no', because the fundamental conception of each religion is very different. The fact is that Christianity treats nature and the human as corrupted existences, but the Maya religions do not. Therefore, overemphasizing a small piece of similar conceptual frameworks of both religions must be avoided.

These points become strong obstacles for research, not only of the colonial Maya, but also of the majority of the colonial Native Americans.

There was a long period in which scholars tended to ignore Native American sources. It is now recognized that historians of colonial Latin America had virtually ignored the importance of the records produced by the Native Americans until the middle of the twentieth century. One of the fine examples is William Prescott's famous *The Conquest of Mexico* of the nineteenth century.[7] Since he heavily relied

---

[5] Yao 1997:5-12, Deloria 1994:81-2.
[6] Cited from Carus 1900:157.
[7] Prescott 1847.

on Spanish materials, he spread an exaggerated view of the Spanish conquest; claiming that the 'superiority of Western civilization vanquished the ancient American civilizations.'

Nevertheless, reading colonial Native American texts is said to be a difficult task. As I cited in my previous book, James Lockhart once pointed out that although most of the colonial Nahuatl sources ostensibly contain strong influences from the Spanish colonizers, they turn out to be more complex. They contain both indigenous and Spanish traditions, rather than simply one or the other.[8] Therefore, a realization of the true nature of Nahuatl texts has called forth a *New Philosophy* with which to understand the sources and to place them in their true context.[9]

The case of colonial Maya texts is more complex than that of colonial Nahua. The difficulties in understanding the colonial Maya religious texts, notably the *Books of Chilam Balam,* are perhaps well known among Latin Americanists. Although the difficulties of reading colonial Maya texts are often considered to be because of the intellectual inferiority of the Maya to the Europeans, their ignorance of a conceptual difference in the Maya way of thinking is the main difficulty. The majority of scholars of Maya studies are still non-Maya, and it appears that without a proper understanding of Maya religious thinking, those colonial Maya texts are poorly understood.

Because the Europeans of the sixteenth century considered religious syncretism negatively, it is not surprising that they often regarded Maya and Christian hybrid religions founded on the colonial Maya texts the result of the Maya's improper understanding of Christianity. Due to the difficulties in understanding the context of colonial Maya texts, therefore, especially the *Books of Chilam Balam,* it is true that there was a long period in which scholars tended to consider those texts as evidence of cultural inferiority of the Maya in comparison to the West. Some may consider that the uniqueness of the Maya religious conception created a very subtle religious fusion. However, as in the case of Japan, a

---

[8] Lockhart 1992:7.

stereotyped view, 'the specific uniqueness of the Japanese brain, which makes Japanese thought processes and linguistic expressions incomparable and therefore incomprehensible to and unlearnable by foreigners', which was once stated by the Japanese(!), cannot be applied to the study of colonial Maya texts.[10] As Klaus-Peter Koepping points out, such a fad concept essentially lacks a careful scientific analysis.[11]

On this point, however, there is a question. What is a scientific analysis? Although psychological approaches to human behavior, such as personal profiles in crime investigations, have proved effective, it must be noted that the notion of an ancient people is extremely difficult to reconstruct. Although any academic argument for religious syncretism of the past era remains subject to speculation to a certain degree, such difficulties can be overcome by utilizing several approaches.

First, the different cultural concepts between the Christian and the Maya must be comprehended. The principal religious preoccupation of the colonial Maya was the order of time. As will be argued, the cyclical periodic calendar system strongly influenced the Maya. Consequently, time was often considered a kind of God. In addition, as researchers are too obsessed with the Maya order of time, the importance of Maya dualism has often been ignored.[12] However, it is known that dualism occupies another fundamental part of Maya religious culture. These two fundamental concepts must be understood and used as a twosome when Maya religious concepts are considered.

The second point is to understand the substantial difference between Christianity and the Maya religions. Maya religions are not theological religions as Christianity is. Christianity tends to understand every kind of phenomenon within written religious materials that were believed to be given through Jesus and prophets like Moses from the one Lord, and they often dismiss anything

---

[9] *Ibid.*

[10] Cited from Koepping 1994:164, see *ibid*.165-6.

[11] *Ibid.*

[12] For example, Gutiérrez Estévez (1993:259) summarises that the conflict between the Catholic and colonial Maya traditional religions was between different conceptions and history.

contradicting the Christian idea found in the Holy Scriptures. On the other hand, Maya religions are an explanation of the universe, and they tend to incorporate any previously unknown phenomenon or idea within their existing theology.

Lastly, although any historical discipline primarily focuses on documentary evidence due to the inadequate number of documents, apart from documentary evidence, reconstructing the religious notion of the colonial Native Americans often requires evidence from related disciplines, such as anthropology, history, and archaeoastronomy. Due to the efforts of numerous scholars, considerable portions of those texts have now become more comprehensible than in the past. Nevertheless, although a careful analysis of colonial Maya texts is the most important, and several scholars have painstakingly investigated those Maya texts to find out the hidden meaning of their texts, it is never claimed that they are fully understood.

In the past century, Sir. Eric S. Thompson proposed that our understanding of Maya religions derives from six sources; (1) archeological evidence, such as murals, (2) hieroglyphic texts, (3) colonial documents written by the Maya, (4) Spanish records of the colonial period, (5) data collected by ethnological investigations from the living Maya since the twentieth century, and (6) Inquisitorial documents of practice of Maya pagan religions made by the Catholic church during the colonial period.[13]

Studies of Christianized Maya religions during the colonial period still follow almost the same methodology. Yet, I think that several further approaches must be added.

Liljeft Persson mentions that it is important to study both internal and external factors of the colonial Maya texts.[14]

She points out:

---

[13] Thompson 1970: 159-161.
[14] Liljeft Persson 2000:39.

45

Depending on which questions we ask of a text we get certain answers from the texts and its context; this in turn affects our understanding and interpretation of the text. For example, we might ask the following questions: Who is writing to whom, about what, when, where, and why? We might also be curious about the ideological frames of reference that affect both the production of and the reception of the text, and which also can differ from one historical period to another.[15]

This seems to be an essential key, because, no doubt, every colonial Maya individual had his own perspective on the Christian religion and Maya traditional religious belief. There is a noted example in Japan. Works of a Japanese Classical scholar, Atutane Hirata, are known for his 'peculiar' approaches to various religions of the world.[16] In spite of his strong hostility towards Christianity and the West, he did not hesitate to incorporate Christian religious elements into Japanese native religion. In this case, unless one looks at his educational career and personal letters, understanding his motive for the creation of such mysterious texts is impossible. A scholar who does not have a proper knowledge of Hirata's career, and the political and religious circumstances of Japan of his time, and his intentions, will certainly judge some of his books as little more than madness, theological texts written by a senseless and an eccentric person. The fact is that he analytically reconstructed a 'confused' description of Japanese gods from various religions, including the Gospel.

Unfortunately, due to a substantial lack of private writings of the colonial Maya authors, it must be said that a precise reconstruction of their notion of Christianity often remains a subject for speculation. In most case, a 'syncretic' study, which mixes colonial history and a notion of Christianity among the present day Maya, has only been used to hypothesize the intention of the colonial Maya authors.

This type of survey raises an important question: to what extent are data collected from the living Maya useful in understanding the colonial Maya texts? As Thompson pointed out long ago, because of the disappearance of the 'state' Maya

---

[15] Liljeft Persson 2000:39-40 also see Ivan Quiroa 2002:12.

religion, the folk Maya of today do not have knowledge of some of the leading ancient Maya gods which the ancient Maya priests recorded in their scripts.[17] Robert Redfield mentioned in 1941 that although the Yucatec Maya villagers still knew of old pagan gods such as *chaac* and *balam*, the Maya townsmen had virtually lost the knowledge of them.[18] In Guatemala, Leonhard Schultze-Jena, a noted German scholar of the early twentieth century, went to Guatemala in order to collect old mythological narratives and eventually got nothing.[19] Ruth Bunzel of the middle of the twentieth century wrote that she had an informant in the K'iche Maya of Chichicastenango who gave her complete Maya rituals for sorcery in spite of the potential danger. Yet, for this K'iche person, the context of the *Popol Vuh* was entirely strange.[20] In addition, either positively or negatively, Christian ideas have strongly influenced the Maya since the sixteenth century. Because of this, their religious beliefs have become very different from those of the ancient Maya in some aspects, and the Maya have often lost knowledge of their own myths.

Therefore, it may be said that the context of the colonial Maya texts was that of the colonial Maya elite, but not of the Maya peasants.

For example, some of the K'iche Maya now regard idols, which were worshipped by their ancestors, as great destructive powers.[21] Another example from the Tzotzíl Maya of Chiapas tells us that the lords of the earth, whom the ancient Tzotzíl must have regarded as gods, are now considered demons.[22] These examples suggest that some ethnographic data collected from the living Maya must be used with extreme caution when they are utilized as comparative data to analyze the ancient and colonial Maya religious beliefs.

On this point, it must be pointed out that the Maya of today are far more influenced by Western and Christian civilization. For example, in spite of the fact

---

[16] See Yamase 2002b:238-44.
[17] See Thompson 1970:161-5.
[18] Redfield 1941:2290269.
[19] Bunzel 1952:264.
[20] Bunzel 1952:264.
[21] Bunzel 1952:267-8.
[22] Gossen 1999:55-76.

that the colonial Maya did not have the concept of '*sin*,' several examples taken from Maya shamans of the early twentieth century and today clearly have it, although it is considerably Mayanized. Moreover, it must be noted that the idea of the folk people is not always that of the religious elite. In the case of Japan, for example, the ordinary folk Japanese tend to believe that the sacred objects of the Shinto religion are gods themselves. However, according to the official theology of Shinto, those sacred objects are not considered gods, but a temporal place in which gods come to rest or to communicate with the people.[23]

Yet, the information collected from the folk Maya is still useful. The Maya of today share a more closed cultural logic with their ancestors than do outsiders. Even though Maya gods virtually disappeared from public view after the conquest and were replaced by the Lord, Jesus and the Christian saints, other Maya divine elements (such as idols, the divine world, and the 260 days of the Maya sacred calendar) remain strong.[24] Therefore, from an anthropological perspective, interpretation of the colonial texts by the living Maya and their cultural perspectives are essential when we analyze colonial Maya half-mythological texts.

On this point, it must be noted that while knowledge obtained from the folk Maya people of today is commonly used in academic works, the current trend of dismissing works of the educated Maya of the twentieth century will result in an unbalanced understanding of Maya civilization.

It is true that the academic value of the modern educated Maya perspective applied to studies of the colonial Maya may be controversial, since they are living under a different cultural, political, and religious circumstance, and every individual of the Maya possesses a considerably different religious stance towards the Maya religions. Some have a fundamentalist view (though as will be discussed, even such people are not essentially exclusive), while others have a more relaxed vision.

---

[23] This type of misunderstanding of the nature of Japanese divinities has also been found in the well-educated class. For example, see Appendix II-B of this book.

[24] Bunzel 1952:266-7.

Some interpretations of the colonial Maya by the modern Maya have been published since the 1950s. While some are recognized in the scholarly world, others are not. Although the latter are often commented on as 'interesting,' they have often been dismissed by academics. In fact, to date, translations of the colonial Maya texts made by the Maya of the twentieth century have not always been appreciated within academic society, as will be considered, and because the modern Maya translator often subjectively translates the texts, their works are called 'peculiar' or 'off-the-mark.' Among them, a translation of the *Popol Vuh* by Adrían I. Chávez[25], is a good example. He is a K'iche Maya scholar of the twentieth century and invented a new orthography of the K'iche language. One of his major academic contributions is his new philosophical translation of the *Popol Vuh*. Although his translation has been regarded as an important work by some living Maya, the majority of non-Maya scholars call his translation 'off-the-mark,' because his linguistic analysis of the *Popol Vuh* is often considered peculiar. Because of this, his work has largely been ignored, especially by Western academics. Of course, I do not treat his translation of the *Popol Vuh* as a proper academic translation. Nevertheless, I do not favor those who have ignored Chávez's translation, because his view of the *Popol Vuh* represented in his Spanish translation, the *Pop Wuj*, must be seriously considered as a view of a Native K'iche Maya. On this point, the *Pop Wuj* published by Chávez can be important reference material for our understanding of the K'iche Maya perception of the *Popol Vuh*.[26]

If a researcher investigated folk Japanese religious rites and priests, but ignored everything written by them, would he understand the Japanese folk religions? The answer is absolutely '*no.*' All writings, including works lacking academic orientation, must be analyzed in order to comprehend the whole of the religious ideas among the Japanese.

---

[25] Chávez 1979, 1994.
[26] My early argument is Yamase (n.d.)

In this research, therefore, this kind of academically 'peculiar' work by the Maya of the twentieth century will be used as primary materials and examples of the Maya cultural logic and perspective.

It is true that interpretations found in these works by the Maya often contain strong personal bias, as those Maya authors often subjectively analyze the colonial texts. Therefore it can be said that such works of the Maya on the colonial Maya texts are not written in a scholarly fashion. Additionally, present-day Maya are not living under the same political and religious circumstances as the colonial Maya, and thus should not be considered good evidence of the perspective of historical study. However, it is known that the present-day Maya maintain many of the colonial Maya cultural traditions and those of the ancient Maya. For example, it is known that both ancient and modern Maya cosmologies are principally based on cyclical time. What is more important is that although the present-day Maya are more influenced by Western culture, they can still understand much of the cultural logic used by the ancient Maya not always understood by outsiders. Thus, it is suggested that their analysis of older Maya texts could be closer to that of their ancestors. Therefore, although data collected from the present-day Maya must be used with considerable caution, they must not be eliminated from our studies of colonial Maya texts. Nevertheless, those works are still a true example of real Maya people's religious views and can be considered an important primary source for understanding the Maya understanding of colonial texts, at least within the anthropological perspective.

In my previous works, I tried to blend all these approaches. However, although the development of Maya studies has been quite rapid during the last decade, we still have limited evidence in many cases. Therefore, I now propose the necessity to study Maya texts within the world of dualism.

First, we should add a 'Mesoamerican' context to the current study of Maya history. Colonial texts of the Mexican Highlands often provide some fundamental keys to understating the colonial Maya texts. It can be said that the context of the

Books of Chilam Balam of the Yucatec Maya represents the personal view of the colonial Maya. However, the nature of the writings found in these books, hardly understandable for outsiders, has prevented scholars from understanding their meaning. Art historians can often provide important pieces of evidence for our understanding of the colonial Mesoamerican people's religious views, which are often difficult to obtain in documents written in European script. Yet, art evidence is not always available. Consequently, reconstructing the history of the colonial Maya largely based on ordinary historical evidence can produce one-sided views. The particular problem is that the amount of surviving materials in the form of dialogues between the Native American and Catholic friars are quite few. Also, the majority of such surviving materials are of the Nahuatl, but not of the Maya. Therefore, scholars are often required to obtain comparative evidence from the other parts of the Native American civilization.

What I have mentioned above is not only the problem of Maya studies, but also of all Native American studies of the colonial period. Although the Nahua people left us a considerable amount of written materials, except for one noted document, the *Coloquio Doce* of the Aztec, only scattered information about dialogues between early Native Mesoamericans and Spaniards has survived.

Nevertheless, as the Spanish conquest of the Aztec was a memorable historical event for the Spaniards, and the central part of Mexico was an important political and economic base during the colonial period, there are numerous useful materials preserving early Nahuatl beliefs regarding Christianity. Conquistadors, such as Bernal Díaz del Castillo and Hernán Cortés, missionaries and some descendants of Nahuatl nobles left some important information with the Aztec lords about their religious beliefs and reaction to Christianity. Colonial reports of religious inquisitions provide quite useful material for our understanding of the attitude of Mesoamerican people towards Christianity. Though the majority provides only very scattered information, the inquisition against *cacique* of Tezcoco of the Mexican highlands, Don Carlos Ometochtzin, is known to be well documented, and thus it is a great help for us in understanding one of the colonial Nahuatl's views towards Christianity. Colonial records of confession also provide us scattered evidence, although these are not always available, to reconstruct systematically the religious beliefs of the colonial Native Americans. León-Portilla has summarized early colonial Nahuatl views towards Christianity well.[27] By combing the information collected from the early Nahuatl people, and sometimes from the Inca of Peru and Native North Americans, we can simultaneously conjecture the religious beliefs toward Catholic Christianity of the early colonial Maya. Because this information was written in the Spanish colonial period, Christianity was rarely attacked in plain form. However, it is not difficult to find some ironical views of the Native Americans regarding the introduction of Christianity. Although this research will not examine all of them, some will be analyzed.

Secondly, ethnographic works collected from modern Maya people can assist us in analyzing the colonial Maya texts. Although the current Maya people do not live under the same political and religious circumstance as the colonial Maya did, their religious life and view of Christianity is often a great help in reconstructing the religious mind of the colonial Maya. Of course, recent advancements in our understanding of Maya hieroglyphics must be added as a third approach. Understanding the religious beliefs of the ancient Maya people is now indispensable in order to decipher the colonial Maya texts.

Fourthly, while the number of scholastic works remains small, I believe that published studies of religious and mythological dialogues between Maya shamans and non-Maya interviewers will become indispensable references for all researchers in this field, because they are particularly useful in clarifying important conceptual differences between the Maya and the rest of the world.

---

[27] León-Portilla 1990.

II: Maya Religions, Dualism and the Universe: Their Differences from Christianity

> *The dualistic conception of nature has been a necessary phase in the evolution of human thought. We find the same views of good and evil spirits prevailing among all the peoples of the earth at the very beginning of that stage of their development...Nevertheless, it is not the final goal of human philosophy. As soon as the thinkers of mankind become aware of the dualism implied in this interpretation of the world, the tendency is again manifested towards a higher conception, which is a purely monistic view.*(Carus 1900:1-2)

> *When the Great Tao (Way or Method* [=dualism]) *become obsolete, benevolence and righteousness came into vogue. (Then) wisdom and shrewdness appeared, and there ensued great tricky hypocrisy.*(Lao-Tzu 580BC: Chap.18)

Since ancient times, Maya religions have heavily influenced the conceptual framework of the Maya. Understanding Maya religions is therefore an important task for Maya cultural studies. Maya cultures have not been fundamentalist. A noted US anthropologist, Gary H. Gossen, mentions his vision of the Maya of Chiapas: '*Mayas have always constructed ethnicity, cosmology, historical reckoning, and political legitimacy by drawing freely from symbolic and ideological forms of other ethnic and political entities-particularly those perceived to be stronger than themselves- in order to situate and center themselves in the present.*'[28] This kind of phenomenon can be observed in any language group of the Maya. This cultural tendency of the Maya seems to have been generated from their traditional religious perspective. Numerous scholars have pointed out that incorporating outside cultures is one of main features of Maya religions. However, there is a controversial point: whether the Maya have subordinated Christianity or have harmonized it with their religions. In addition, have they constructed their culture by 'freely' introducing alien cultural elements? The term 'freely' gives the impression that the Maya 'haphazardly' mixed various cultural elements. From my point of view, although it may be an unconscious and occasional confusion in some cases, the Maya should have had a certain established conscious pattern for

---

[28] Cited from Gossen 1999:259. I have also presented a similar argument in the case of the colonial Guatemalan Maya texts (Yamase 2002b),

adapting a foreign element in most cases. Based on this view, I believe that Maya cultural and religious assimilation would have been a product of their reasoned interpretation. As will be discussed, I believe that the established system of integrating alien elements into the Maya cosmos should be the logic of dualism. In this section, a brief discussion about Maya religions will be made.

The Spanish conquest of, and their colonial domination over, the Maya caused a massive decline in Maya religions. The religious system sustained by various small Maya nations disappeared, and the majority of the ruling class of the Maya became Christian in order to gain the favor of their new masters, the Spaniards. Nevertheless, at the folk level, Maya religions have never died out. In addition, the Maya elite often continue their traditional religious rites in secret places while outwardly accepting Christianity. This suggests that Mayanized Christianity has at times to be argued at two levels.

Historical evidence suggests that the colonial Maya understood Christianity within their own religious traditions, and thus their understanding of Christianity became different from what the Spaniards originally taught. The first Spanish friars simply used the *Tzacol Bitol* (K'iche deities, *Tzacol* and *Bitol*) in order to express the 'Christian God.' Later, as they noticed that use of *Tzacol Bitol* as the Lord resulted in confusion between K'iche deities and the Christian God, the friars replaced *tzacol bitol* with a Spanish word '*dios.*' Nevertheless, as will be mentioned, the colonial K'iche-Maya most likely understood the Spanish word '*dios*' via their dualism. When we talk about the relationships between Maya religions and Christianity, therefore, it is necessary to understand the Maya religious system, beliefs and other aspects. The Maya religious system is a very complex subject. Fortunately, since Eric S. Thompson's work, there have been good references on the Maya religions.[29] Based on such previous contributions, some important aspects of Maya religions will be summarized with my own analysis.

In this book, I prefer the use of the term 'Maya religions' to 'Maya religion.' The reason is simple. Not only the Maya, but also almost all the pagan civilizations, do not have a single, unified religious system, because there have always been local variations at any stage of their history. In Japan, for example, the fox is considered a divine animal, and temples to foxes can be observed in many places. However, in the Shikoku Island of Japan, the raccoon dog is worshipped as an alternative to the fox. The case of the Maya is more complicated. Because of the lack of a single, unified political organization across the Maya world, the Maya have also lacked a central religious authority like the Pope.

Before the Spanish conquest, each of the Maya states must have had a standard official religious code and unified doctrine of Maya religion. The Maya priest of every state must have held any religious ceremony in accordance with his country's instructions. Yet, after the conquest, the state system of the Maya gradually (or often quickly) disappeared. As the result of that, every religious leader in small local communities was allowed more room to create his own localized Maya religion.

In today's Guatemala, although there are some religious associations organized by the Maya, every K'iche Maya priest-shaman virtually has the freedom of his own religious practice. Such shamans practice religious rites derived from their way of understanding the Maya religions. As a result, the rites performed by each of them are often quite different,[30] though there have been attempts to unify their various ideas. In some Maya communities, such as the Lacandon Maya of today, whose societies have no specific priest or spiritual specialists, every head of the family unit performs his version of the Maya religion.

Of course, the Maya have several important religious scriptures, such as the lost hieroglyphic texts, the *Books of Chilam Balam*, and the *Popol Vuh*. Their use is not the same as the *Bible* of the Christians, however. While the *Bible* is defined as

---

[29] León-Portilla 1988, Thompson 1970, Edmonson 1993, Taube 1993, Holland 1963:68-154, Bunzel 1952, Milbrath 1999, Freidel et al. 1993, Gutiérrez Estévez 1993, Vogt 1969.

[30] As to this, see Chiappari 1999, Sanematu 2002.

the laws given by the one God, the pagan 'bibles' are essentially records of the past and prophecies made by ancient sages.

Although the *Popol Vuh* is often called the *Bible* of the Native Americans, it is a narrative of K'iche Maya deities and of the Utatlan dynasty. Unlike the Christian *Bible*, it provides no moral instruction. While the Christian *Bible* forbids worship of idols among its believers, the Maya holy scriptures have nothing about such matters. Although human sacrifice was practiced among the K'iche Maya up until the Spanish conquest, the *Popol Vuh* mentions it as a historical tradition. It never orders people to make a human sacrifice to Maya gods. The *Books of Chilam Balam* also only occasionally mentions moral duties. These books refer to the preciousness of stone, but they never order the people to worship idols. Some groups of the Maya have lost their ancestors' texts. The Lacandon Maya do not have a written sacred text. From my point of view, these situations have partly allowed the Maya to create a wide variety of individual religious practices and interpretations.

What is the standard Maya religion? This is a difficult question. Although the colonial period is obviously what we should treat as the standard Maya religion, reconstructing the Maya religion of the colonial period is not always easy, because sources available are not sufficient. Thus, information collected from various periods of the Maya has also been used.

When we discuss the system of Maya gods, that of the Yucatec Maya people of the late classic Maya and of the Maya lowlands of the classic Maya is usually mentioned as a standard example. Yet, as I have mentioned, each Maya language group has a slightly different local version.

For example, although *Chac* is known to be a classic Maya deity of rain and has been worshipped by the Yucatec Maya, this divinity was called *Tohil* among the late Postclassic K'iche Maya. Moreover, though *Tohil* is considered to be a deity similar to *Chac*, it is not the complete equivalent of *Chac*. *Tohil* has a slightly different character and seems to have had more roles than *Chac*. Nevertheless, each of the Maya language groups still shares some important fundamental elements. Therefore, a generalization of Maya religions can be made to a certain degree.

According to Yao, all religions may be divided into three categories: 1) theistic religions in which a single God acts as the ruler of humans and of nature (*e.g.*, Christianity and Islam), 2) humanistic religions (humans take the central position, such as in Confucianism), 3) naturalistic religion (nature occupies the central part of the Cosmos, such as in Taoism and in early Japanese Shinto).[31] However, the difference among these three is not always clear, as Yao mentions. It is commonly suggested that Maya religions are essentially a way of communication between people, nature and its gods or spirits. Although Maya gods have been recognized as an inspirational power, their basic role seems to have been as a mediator between humans and nature since the ancient period. Therefore, it may be suggested that Maya religions belong to the second category.

Yet, precise categorization of Maya religions is not an easy task. In fact, my argument based on the colonial Maya texts, which will be presented in the later chapters, is in favor of the opinion that the Maya religions should be categorized as naturalistic religions. At least, it can be summarized that the position of nature and humans in Maya religions is greater than in Christianity, so that the Maya religions can belong to humanist or a naturalistic religions (or both). There is no doubt that although the transcendent power of divinities has been recognized in Maya religions, their power is very limited as compared to the Lord of Christianity.

There is no doubt that Maya religions were originally created to explain natural and supernatural phenomena, such as astronomy and natural disasters, like many other ancient religions. It is not surprising that the Maya came to believe in the existence of transcendent powers behind natural and supernatural phenomena, including manufactured creatures. For example, the Lacandon Maya of the twentieth century lost the memory of their ancestors' great achievement, and believed the amazing ancient Maya ruins remaining in the tropical forest were a

---

[31] Yao 1997:12-7.

57

representation of supernatural power. They alleged these to be the houses of the
k'uh (Gods).[32]

Maya religions are known to have been idolatrous. No doubt, worship of idols
has been one of their major characteristics. It may be said that Maya idols are a
mere tool for communicating with their gods. Though uncertain in the very ancient
period, like other pagan people, the Maya seem to have considered that idols are not
gods themselves, but they are merely instruments to communicate with gods. Some
of the contemporary Maya longer regard a substitution as a living, divine thing.[33]

As Maya gods are by their very nature a heart or a spirit of nature, their
residence is in lakes, mountains, an old tree, caves and any other natural objects,
and each Maya god essentially exists within. Without idols, indeed, communication
with Maya gods could be made at any time, by offering incense, blood, and other
sacrifices directly to the lakes, rivers, mountains, or stars. Archaeological
investigations have revealed that the Ancient Maya made offerings directly in
caves and lakes. Therefore, idols are theologically a temporal residence of deities,
and thus they are not really necessary in theory. Yet, in numerous cases, there has
virtually been no clear separation between gods and idols. The reason for this may
be explained in that as the level of society advanced, the power of the ruling-class
also grew, and as a result, because the elite began to regard themselves as living
gods (often of the Sun, as seen in the Classic Maya cities), a confusion of the nature
of gods was created among the Maya. In some places, Maya idols are regarded as
actual gods to the present.

This confusion is quite common in pagan cultures. If someone reads the
Japanese sacred text of Shinto (the Japanese pagan religion), the *Kojiki*, s/he will
find activities of numerous human-shaped deities. The *Kojiki* illustrates them as if
they were human beings. Nevertheless, among the orthodox Shinto, it has been
considered since ancient times that no deity has a carnal body. The reason for this

---

[32] Boremanse 1993:326-8.
[33] Freidel et al. 1993:177. I do not discuss this issue in detail within this research. A more
detailed study may be published as a journal article or as a part of my forthcoming book.

58

may be the same as in the case of Maya. In the process of consolidating the power of the Japanese Emperor, it was necessary to define their ancestors as gods.

The same confusion was made by the ancient Romans. The fact is that the ancient Romans of the Empire period did not recognize idols themselves as gods, though some in the lower ranks misunderstood this concept. Roman idols were considered an instrument for imagining the faces of the gods and for communicating with them, and thus they were not alive.

In fact, with regard to the last pagan Roman Emperor, often called an apostate, Julian mentioned;

> *Statues and altars, and the preservation of the unextinguished fire, and, in short, all such particulars, have been established by our fathers as symbols of the presence of the gods; not that we should believe that these symbols are gods, but that through these we should worship the gods. For since we are connected with body, it is also necessary that our worship of the gods should be performed in a corporeal manner...*[34]

As Maya religions are strongly associated with agriculture, in spite of the Spanish policy of terminating Maya religions since the sixteenth century, they survive strongly in farming areas. While Christianity defines nature as a dishonored place, a strong tie between Maya religions and the agricultural environment (= nature) created an opposite view. In general, the Maya myth seldom strays far from the natural world. Therefore, contrary to the essential Christian concept, 'that humans and all other creatures in nature have sinned,' the Maya do not have this concept. While the Christians believe in Heaven as the sole residence of God, and the earth and Hell as that of Satan and evil sprits, the Maya have the gods of the sky, the earth, and the underground.

In Maya beliefs, all creatures of gods are good, as in other pagan cultures (*e.g.*, in Mesoamerica, North America, and Ancient Rome). In addition, all animals were considered equal to humans as a part of nature. For example, the Tzotzile Maya of

---

[34] Cited from Julian 361-3:106. see also *ibid*:107-111.

59

Chiapas believe that when a person is born, an animal is also born at the same time in the mountains. In their belief, both spirits are paired until they die.[35]

On the other hand, according to Christianity, it is said that the Christian God created all creatures within the natural world to serve humankind. Although the Maya religions received strong Christian influences after the Spanish Conquest, this concept, the Christian idea of nature and humans, has not always been accepted among the Maya.

In numerous pagan cults, Gods are often considered offspring of nature or of the universe (the difference between them is not always clear). Maya pagan religions are known for their animism. In general, animism gives a soul and a will to mountains, rivers, rocks, trees, stones, heavenly bodies, the earth, and sky, and in the case of the Maya, time is included. In general, pagan religions such as animism do not regard gods as rulers of nature, but as partners. Unlike the Christian religion, in Maya religions, there is no absolute deity who rules everything, and the number of Maya deities should be uncountable in theory. Maya religions have numerous gods. Each of these deities represents a supernatural and a natural phenomenon. That is, the number of Maya deities can be increased when a new supernatural or natural experience appears. In addition, Maya gods are an essence of nature and co-exist with nature. This point should also be taken into account when the Maya relationship with Christianity is considered.

For example, one of the Japanese Imperial Myths, the *Nihongi* (日本書紀) says:

> *Of old, Heaven and Earth were not yet separated, and the In* 〔陰〕 *and Yo* 〔陽〕 *not yet divided. They formed a chaotic mass like an egg which was of obscurely defined limits and contained germs. The purer and clearer part was thinly drawn out, and formed Heaven, while the heavier and grosser element settled down and became Earth. The finer element easily became a united*

---

[35] Holland 1963:100. This is also a typical idea of pagan cultures in general. Although Aristotle mentions that animals are inferior to the human due to a lack of reason, an ancient Platonist, Celsus', reply to Christianity suggest that the Roman and Greek pagan also regarded the animals as equivalent mortal things to the human (Celsus 178:84). Plato also argued that the souls of all animals, including the human, are good.(Plato 389?:153)

body, but the consolidation of the heavy and gross element was accomplished with difficulty. Heaven was therefore formed first, and Earth was established subsequently. Thereafter divine beings were produced between them.[36]

Or in some cases, Nature is considered to be the Gods themselves. The Creation Myth of the Navaho of North America tells us:

Here are the stories of the Four Worlds that had no sun, and of the Fifth, the world we live in, which some call the Changeable World. The First World, Ni'hodilqil, was black as black wool. It had four corners, and over these appeared four clouds. These four clouds contained within themselves the elements of the First World. They were in color, black, white, blue, and yellow. The Black Cloud represented the Female Being or Substance. For as a child sleeps when being nursed, so life slept in the darkness of the Female Being. The White Cloud represented the Male Being or Substance. He was the Dawn, the Light-Which-Awakens, of the First World. In the East, at the place where the Black Cloud and the White Cloud met, First Man, Atse'hastqin was formed; and with him was formed the white corn, perfect in shape, with kernels covering the whole ear. Dolionot i'ni is the name of this first seed corn, and it is also the name of the place where the Black Cloud and the White Cloud met.[37]

It is true that some pagan cults have better placed the position of the gods than the Navaho and the Japanese. The Inca and other ancient Peruvian peoples, for example, believed their supreme deity, Viracocha to be the creator and ruler of the world. Yet, because they did not consider the issue of conflict between the carnal body and the spirit (their treatment of mummies as human could be good evidence to support this point), it cannot be concluded that the Incan deities strayed from nature like the Christian Lord.

In the case of the Maya, although the influence from Christianity must be considered, the colonial Maya texts, such as the *Popol Vuh* and the *Books of Chilam Balam*, tell us that gods created the world. In those texts, Maya gods are not clearly (at least in our view) mentioned as offspring or a consubstantiality of Nature. Nevertheless, the creators in the Maya religions are by no means the same as those

---

[36] Cited from The *Nihongi* 1896:Book 1.
[37] Cited from O'Bryan 1956: The Creation.

in Christianity, because, as will be discussed, in Maya beliefs the world is merely a part of the universe.

While the Christian (and Islamic) God is the ruler of nature and the human, Maya gods, like ancient Greek, Roman, Chinese and Japanese gods, are essentially arbitrators between the two. So Maya gods should be regarded as a kind of a superior partner of the human, and although the humans were considered creatures (or often the descendants) of gods, the concept of the sinful human as a creature of God does not usually exist in pagan cultures.

In the case of the Maya, with the introduction of Christianity some of them now use the term 'sin (=*pecado*)', but the Maya religions did not originally have such a concept.[38] In addition, sin is differently received, compared to Christians, by the Maya of today.

Scholars like Dennis Tedlock have argued that like Greek mythology, the narrative found in the *Popol Vuh* originated from the Maya knowledge of astronomy. By watching the sky, the Maya must have understood that the ellipse of the Sun and the moon take place at regular intervals. In fact, ellipses are one of major concerns of surviving Maya hieroglyphic books. In addition, the ancient Maya were corn farmers, living in tropical surroundings. Because this environment has a dry and wet season, they became interested in the temporal cycle and created a complicated calendar system.

As a result, the Maya established a cyclic periodic notion, and it became one of the major features of the Maya civilization. In this concept, all is dominated by the cycle of constant time. Though the cyclical time concept is not particular to the Maya civilization but to the Mesoamerican civilization, the Maya version is known for its complexity. Because Maya cyclical time has been closely associated with the daily life of the Maya, its influence in the Maya ideology cannot be ignored.

---

[38] E.g. see Bunzel 1952:292-4.

62

The cyclical time concept of the Maya is clearly associated with their complicated calendar system.[39] Unlike the concept of linear time, this concept often makes our analyses of Maya belief difficult. The Maya once had a long-count calendar system, whose initial date started in 3,113BC, as a close equivalent of Western Christian and Islamic dates. In this, 13 *baktun* (1,872,000 days, about 5,128 years) is defined as one cycle of time. It is likely that the ancient Maya had a concept of time proceeding in a linear fashion. By using this calendar, the ancient Maya were able to have a fixed point in the past, and were made to thought of any historical and mythical event in terms of time. However, this long-count calendar system gradually became unpopular. The use of this calendar substantially ceased in the late post-classic period (1,200-1,500AD). When the Spaniards discovered the Maya, this calendar system, was not used anymore. With the disappearance of the long calendar system, the Maya of the Yucatan Peninsula began to use an abbreviated version of it, the so-called short-count calendar system which consists of 260 *Tun* = 13 *Katún* (1 *Tun* =360), about 256 years. It treats about 256 years as one unit, like our 'one century;' this calendar was used as standard in Mesoamerica. Yet, this calendar does not have any system of clearly distinguishing the previous 13 *Katún* and the present 13 *Katún*. Thus, the short calendar system can be said to have a difficulty in recording the past of more than 256 years ago. With the increasing popularity of this short-count calendar, in my opinion, an interesting concept of time among the Maya was gradually created, that is, to blur the past and the present. This concept is not found, as such, in the Christian, Islamic, Chinese, and Japanese cultures, which are based on a linear-time concept. Therefore, it can be suggested that for the Maya, the past *Katun* was not precisely the past, but 'another world.'

In Guatemala and other Maya lands, the disappearance of the long-count calendar system seems to have been much earlier, although we do not know the exact period. The Guatemalan Maya used only the 365-day *haab* calendar for

---

[39] The full explanation of various Maya Calendars can be seen in most of the good textbooks

63

cultivation and the 260-day almanac for religious rites. By meshing both calendars, a periodic cycle of 52 years (18,980 days), called a Calendar Round, can be made. Like the short-count calendar system, this system also lacks a system of dating the 52-year cycle so that no distinction between the previous 52 years and the present 52 years can be made. This is the same in the case of two previous cycles of 52 years. As on the Yucatan Peninsula, making the past and the present indistinct is one of main philosophical features of the Guatemalan Maya. The Maya considered that at the end of each *Katún* (or 52-years cycle), there is a significant event, such as the destruction of the world and the sun. Through this notion, everything, including any god, has its beginning and end. The Maya have traditionally considered that the power of gods can decline at the end of a certain time cycle. In colonial Maya religious texts, such as the *Books of the Chilam Balam of Chumayel* of the Yucaten Peninsula, each *Katún* cycle has one lord. Each of these Lords was considered a deity. It is interesting to note that while the destruction of Maya deities after the emergence of Christianity is mentioned in this text, the lords of *Katún* are referred to as active. In a sense, this fact suggests that the deities of this time are often superior to other types of gods in the Maya cosmos. Also, it may be proposed that the Maya divine world may have been based on a dualism between the Lords of time and the Gods of other supernaturals. This issue will be argued in the last part of this chapter.

Although the living Maya do not use the calendar system of their ancestors anymore, their vision of the world is still dominated by the belief in a periodic cycle. Therefore, it is often suggested that the Maya have been obsessed with the periodic-cycle. Occasionally, Maya calendaric time itself (a lord of *ahau*) functions as a kind of god in Maya belief. As will be discussed, the cyclic or periodic notion also constitutes one major aspect of Maya dualism.

The Maya religions are categorized as polytheism, yet each of the Maya language groups has a concept that all Maya deities are aspects of a unitary

on the Maya. For example, Sharer (1994:556-581).

perception of godhood (such as *Ka'koch* of the Lacandon Maya). Therefore, Munro S. Edmonson says that polytheism is a poor description of the Maya belief.[40]

The *Popol Vuh*, the holy sacred text of the K'iche Maya, and painted vessels of the classic Maya suggest that the Maya once developed a rich narrative of family relationships among various Maya deities, similar to ancient Greek myths. Yet, a full reconstruction of the ancient Maya myth seems to be impossible.

None of the supernatural powers is perfect. For example, no storm can last for a year. The sun, the most noticeable power in nature, loses his power during the night, and is sometimes 'eaten' by a weaker counterpart, the moon. The power of Maya gods, as a representation of the supernatural, also reflects the limited power of these supernatural phenomena. No Maya god is as perfect as the Christian Lord. Among the Maya Gods, *Itzamna* has been proposed as the most important God, although there may be some arguments whether *Itzamna* is *hunab Ku* (the principal god of the Maya pantheon). *Itzamna* (God D) and its local variants has generally been considered to be the supreme deity of the Maya gods as he carries the Maya hieroglyphic '*ahau* (=lord, principle)'. Contrary to the case of the Christian god, the function and power of *Itzamna* are limited compared to the Christian Lord and Islamic *Allah*. For example, when we read the beginning of the *Popol Vuh*, the existence of somehow anonymous, invisible superpowers may be noticed, though there is no evidence that it is a local equivalent of *Itzamna*, and it is not mentioned as the creator of the world like the Christian God. The *Popol Vuh* mentions that the world was created by a pair of gods, *Tzacol* and *Bitol*. No doubt, this concept represents the fact that any supernatural power in nature does not keep its power all the time (=non-eternal). For example, the sun was regarded as an important deity, but there have been frequent solar ellipses. Therefore, the ancient Maya considered solar ellipse evidence that something greater than the sun eats it.[41]

Every Maya deity has its own function within the Maya cosmos. Like pantheistic religions of other parts of the world, a Maya deity usually has multiple

---

[40] Edomonson 1993:67.

aspects and manifestations. A Maya deity, *Itzamna* was considered lord of the heavens, of day and night, and inventor of writing.

In some points, Maya religions may be said to be quite similar to the ancient Greek and Roman religions. Like *Zeus*, who capriciously troubles humankind, one Maya deity has a positive and negative character at the same time, but Maya gods are different from ancient Greek and Roman gods in other aspects. The Maya people have their own original notion of gods. Unlike Roman and Greek deities, few of the ancient Maya gods are in human form. In most cases, they are in animal form. Yet, human-like divinity can be observed in all periods of Maya history, and the majority of divinities found in the *Popol Vuh*, the Maya myth of the sixteenth century, are described as having a human-like existence. For example, although *Cipacna* is narrated as if he has a human form, *Cipacna* means crocodile, and thus it can be said that *Cipacna* may previously have been a deity in animal form. It may be that as time passed, the Maya gradually changed the animal form of their gods to a human form ('anthropomorphic form'). The *Popol Vuh* mentions that monkeys were the previous human beings. The *Popol Vuh* says that although the ancestors of monkeys once had their towns, due to their imperfection as creatures of god, their civilization was destroyed, and the remainder of them escaped into the forest and became monkeys. However, the monkey is often used as the image of the god of the sun. In addition, some animals, such as the jaguar and snake, appear to have been considered divine animals among the Maya. In general, animals are treated as members of the universe equal to humans. As I have mentioned before, this point is also a significant difference from Christianity, in which all animals were made as lesser creatures by God, and they are considered to serve human beings.

As in other pagan religions, another important concept of Maya religions is dualism. Although pluralism is now used instead of dualism, it will be argued that the essential logic of Maya, 'ostensible' pluralism, is substantially based on a complicated combination of several dualistic ideas. When we discuss the issues of

---

[41] The *Book of Chilam Balam of Chumayel*, Luxton 1995:46-7.

the Maya religions, animism is always discussed as one of their core concepts. Without a consideration of dualism, as will be argued, we could understand very little of the essence of animism. While the Islamic religion and Christianity believe in the existence of a sole powerful and eternal divinity as a creator and lord of all things, dualistic religions explain that any phenomenon is created and maintained by a pair of gods (sometimes more than two). As I have mentioned before, the Maya deities never stray from nature, unlike the Gods of Christianity and Islam, because nature is often considered a partner of the Maya gods or a godlike existence.

While Christian and Muslim doctrines insist that everything is under the control of a single holy power, in Maya religious belief, the emergence of every phenomenon is considered a result of the interaction of different types of multiple divine existences. For example, the *Popol Vuh* explains that the world was created by two divine existences, *Tzacol* and *Bitol*.

There has been a tendency in the Western and Islamic cultures to regard the dualism concept as one of a primitive culture. However, in China, another gigantic cultural area of dualism, this concept has been continuously developed as the most respectable concept. In the Far East, dualism is often considered useful in reducing conflicts among different cultures. As Fernando Cervantes pointed out in the case of the colonial Nahuatl,[42] it can be said that the core concept of Maya dualism is also quite similar to the traditional Chinese thought of the interacting principles of Yin and Yang [陰陽思想: male and female or the positive and negative principles] in some aspects. In general, the Maya dualism is often suggested to be *doble Mirada* (dual thought), Victoriano Alvarez argues that the Maya dualism is *La Visón de dos principios asociados* (the vision of two associated principles), and it is called '*K'abawil (Cabawil)*'.[43] I prefer the position of Alvarez, because rendering the cultural context of the Maya cultures becomes more comprehensive, as

---

[42] Cervantes 1994:40-46.
[43] Alvarez 1999:47.

presented in my previous work.[44] Unfortunately, as the ancient and colonial Maya did not leave us their philosophical argument on their dualism, there have been debates on the exact nature of Maya dualism. It is known that a dualism of Death and Life existed in Mesoamerica from the ancient period.[45]

Although that idea may well have been written in Maya hieroglyphic texts, such texts did not survive. Therefore, there is no evidence that the Maya once systematically developed their dualism like the ancient Greeks and the Chinese. Nevertheless, the surviving codexes clearly suggest the dualistic concept. On one page of the *Madrid Codex*, there are three gods receiving honey from bees. The god on the right-side is the Maya death god, *Cisin*, in the middle is *Chac*, the rain God, and *Itzamna* is sitting on the left. This scene proves that the ancient Maya treated both negative and positive deities equally. As Ruth Bunzel points out in the case of the K'iche Maya, the Maya gods are not friendly or hostile by nature. She notes that there is a ceremony for making a friend of the Lord of Sickness. Although they can be unpleasant in some situations, they become friendly in certain cases.[46] This concept is by no means a result of confusion, but of the harmonious nature of Maya religions. As will be argued, it is almost certain that various powers of Christianity were considered in this Maya dualistic concept.

---

[44] Yamase 2002b.
[45] See Miller *et al.* 1993:81.
[46] Bunzel 1952:267.

68

(Figure 1: the *Madrid Codex* cited from Brasseur de Bourbourg (1869-1870))

The texts of Taoism of China are particularly useful in order to understand the essential concept of the dualism proposed by Alvarez. In the *Tao Te Ching*, the ancient Chinese sage, Lao-tzu (580-500BC:2), says:

'天下皆知美之為美、斯惡已、皆知善之為善、斯不善已、故有無相生、難易相成、長短相形、高下相傾、音声相和、前後相随'
(All the people in the world recognize beauty as the beautiful one, from which [the idea of] ugliness is recognized [at the same time]. [In the same way, the idea of] the good is established, from which [the idea of] the evil is established [at the same time].

Therefore, existence and non-existence were born from each other. Difficulty and ease compensate mutually with each other. Length and shortness make the one clear figure of another. Height and lowness arise from the contrast with each other. The musical tone and voice harmonize through the relation of one with another. The being before and the one behind give [the idea of] following another mutually.)[47]

[47] The text cited from Lao-tzu 1997:8. Ogwa's interpretation and notes of the original Chinese text (*ibid.*:8-10) were useful. The English translation attached to the Chinese text is a corrected and

In this theory, everything is created by, and is maintained by two very different existences. Even if one of them has a negative value for the human being, it is still considered a necessary element of the world.

Also, the *Tao Te Ching* says;

> 道者、万物之奥、善人之宝、不善人之所保、美言可以市、尊行可以
> 加人、人之不善、何棄之有、
> (*Tao*[48] is the most honored place of all things. The good men make it a treasury; bad men are guarded by it, admirable words can purchase honor; (its) admirable deeds can raise their performer above others. Even those who are not good are not abandoned by it.)[49]

The idea of Taoism is that *Tao* = the true virtue (or reason) is generated by keeping the balance of the goodness and the evil. In other words, true virtue can embrace both good and evil at the same time. Although there are numerous local differences in dualism among pagan religions, the essence of Taoism is also the core concept of the majority of pagan religions. This is especially true in the case of Japan and other countries surrounding China, whose beliefs were strongly influenced by China.

Unless the dualism concept is well understood, understanding this ancient Chinese text, the *Tao te Ching,* is difficult.

Let us cite a part of the *Tao te Ching* as an example;

---

modified version of the English translation, which contains numerous misunderstanding of the original text, published in Lao-tzu (580-500BC:2).

[48] '*Pinyin DAO (Chinese:*道 *'road,' or 'way'), in Chinese philosophy, a fundamental concept signifying 'the correct way,' or 'Heaven's way.' In the Confucian tradition, tao signifies a morally correct path of human conduct and is thus limited to behaviour. In the rival school of Taoism (the name of which derives from tao), the concept takes on a metaphysical sense transcending the human realm. ...One aspect of the tao, however, can be perceived by man, namely, the visible process of nature by which all things change. From an observation of the visible manifestation of the Absolute Tao, it is possible to intuit the existence of an ultimate substratum that is the source of all things. Awareness of this process then leads toward an understanding of the Absolute Tao*'(cited from Britannica 1999:Tao).

[49] The text cited from Lao-tzu 1997:140. Ogwa's interpretation and notes of the original Chinese text (*ibid.*:140-1) was useful. The English translation attached to the Chinese text is a corrected and modified version of the English translation, which contains numerous misunderstandings of the original text, published in Lao-tzu (580-500BC:62).

大道廃　有仁義　智慧出　有大偽。

In an English translation published in the early twentieth century, the above text was translated as:

When the great Reason is obliterated, we have benevolence and justice.
Prudence and circumspection appear, and we have much hypocrisy.[50]

This translation, produced by a Japanese and a US scholar, is quite acceptable. Yet, there is a significant problem for Western people in their translation at the same time. 大道 = *Great Tao* is translated as *Great Reason*. Although this rendering is correct, the problem of this translation is that they fail to restore the dualistic concept behind the original Chinese text. In general, when this Chinese text is given as an isolated sentence, the Chinese, the Japanese, and some Western specialists in Asian studies can bear in mind that *Tao* is a representation of the Virtue and the Reason generated from the dualistic interactions, but ordinary readers cannot. From the perspective of the dualism, it can be suggested that the above sentence from the *Tao te Ching* also contains a kind of irony towards the popularity of the monotheistic concept. However, in Western societies, the readers would not find this 'hidden meaning' in the text, and they may conclude that the context of this text is also in the Holy Scriptures of Christianity. The case of the Maya is the same. Unless the readers pay attention to the dualistic concept, what they can understand from the Maya texts will be very little.

Of course, the concept of dualism found in the Taoism of China is not the same as that of the Maya. In addition, no ancient Maya writing gives us a clear philosophical argument about dualism as a Maya idea, and thus we cannot easily assume that ancient Maya philosophers developed their theoretical logic of dualism as did the Chinese. In the case of the Maya, for example, the concept of *Tao* does

---

[50] Lao-Tzu 1913:Chap.18.

not exist in Maya cultures, and, as will be argued, although the stones or the *ceiba* tree play something of a similar role, they are substantially different from the *Tao*.

The prime concerns of the Maya religions are generally 'time and its cycle.' Moreover, it is not certain that the ancient Maya possessed a notion that '*everything can be created out of nothing.*' Also, it is unlikely that the Maya possessed an equivalent of the Chinese concept that everything will be separated into two elements, *Ying* (陰 negative) and *Yang* (陽 positive). Furthermore, unlike in Taoism, the Maya gods are generally bi-sexual. *Chac*, a Maya deity of rain, is usually manifested as male, but it is occasionally shown as female.

Also, perhaps because of the notion of periodic cycles, the past (previous *Katún*) and the present (or the future *Katún*) also constitute a dualism. There is a good example. It is known that the King of the Peten Itza, the last kingdom of the Maya, predicted to the Spaniards their acceptance of Christianity and abolition of idols by 1697. Although this reaction is often considered to be evidence of their resistance to Christianity, another interpretation is possible. This is that the Peten Itza understood the relation between Christianity and Maya deities in dualism, the former as a future one, and the latter as a present one.[51] Because the Peten Itza often destroyed churches and killed Catholic monks, some may be suspicious of my view, yet in this case this issue must be considered on another point. The Maya had a view toward two religions, Christianity for the Spaniards and Maya gods for the Maya.[52] It should be noted that this view can constitute a dualism. Therefore, it is suggested that in this case, the Peten Itza's view of Christianity must be comprehended by using two dualism concepts (the past and the present and the Spaniard and the Maya).

The Maya often used a more complicated concept than dualism. It was the conception of four directions, that is, a four-in-one conception. This idea was, and still is, manifested in the four world directions and their coupled colors: East, red; North, white; west, black; and South, yellow. Maya gods were thought of in terms

---

[51] López de Cogolludo 1971:II:253-4.

of four dimensions, each occupying one of the four world directions. For example, there were four Chacs (rain gods) who could be worshipped singly, each in association with his world direction and color, or regarded collectively as one. It is well known among Mayaists that the *Annales of the Kaqchikel* records that Maya ancestors came from four *Tulan* in four directions.[53] Therefore, some may prefer the use of 'pluralism' to that of 'dualism.' Yet, it should be noted that such 'pluralism' is simply a complex combination of several dualism concepts in most cases. Therefore, I am not inclined to use the term 'pluralism.' When the colonial Maya texts are analyzed together with the logic of dualism, therefore, this concept (though a variant of dualism) should not be eliminated from our consideration.

Nevertheless, it must be noted that even though there are some serious differences between Taoism and Maya beliefs, the essences of the Taoism idea of dualism are easily found in Maya cultures.[54] Everything was essentially considered in dualism by the Maya. Even now, the Maya consider that any single Maya deity has a dualistic character. A Maya deity can have both negative and positive aspects at the same time.[55]

In spite of the importance of dualism among the Maya, some basic references on Maya thought written by respectable scholars have discussed little.[56] Although Ruth Bunzel noticed the important essence of dualism among the religious ideology of the K'iche Maya at Chchicastenango, she did not conceptually analyze the meaning of Maya dualism.[57] For example, as I have mentioned, while Eric S. Thompson clearly understood the system of Maya dualism, he did not include any perspective of dualism in his conceptual analysis. The importance of dualism among the Maya was proposed by a K'iche Maya scholar, Adrián I Chávez, in 1979,

[52] Yamase 2002b:227-8.
[53] Otzoy 1999:101,154.
[54] See Thompson 1970:199, Yamase 2002b:232-3.
[55] LaFarge 1947:103-4, Buznel 1952:268.
[56] For example, León-Portilla 1988, Restall, 1998.
[57] Buznel 1952:266-9, see also Holland 1963:94.

but his work was overlooked by formal academics due to his very subjective translation of the *Pop Wuj*.[58]

More recently, although Fernando Cervantes correctly identifies the nature of the positive and negative principles among the Mesoamerican people, though it seems that he is still struggling with this very alien concept.

The *Maya Cosmos*, written by David Freidel and Linda Schele,[59] and Victoria R. Bricker's recent article[60] prove that the recognition of the Maya duality concept has greatly improved among the academics over the decades. However, from my point of view, the authors still seem to have a difficulty in grasping the essence of this unfamiliar concept. Why have these researchers not presented their analysis of Maya thinking based on this concept? Perhaps, the reason for it may be due to the fact that the Maya have rarely spoken of the importance of dualism as one of key aspects of their philosophical and religious culture. In my opinion, another more important reason is that Western researchers, who are still the majority in the field of Mesoamerican studies, essentially have a difficulty in understanding the concept of dualism. Indeed, during conversations I have often found that many Westerners (including my former British supervisors) did not always make sense of my arguments so that I was often frustrated, though my Chinese friends did not have such a problem. The reason was plain, that the Japanese and Chinese sometimes (not always) consider an issue dualistically so that the problems were not raised. Although educated Westerners of today know the logic of dualism in their 'brain,' they have a serious difficulty of thinking about a matter dualistically in a real situation, due to their lack of practice of the dualistic philosophy.

In general, the Islamic and Christian people of today still tend to consider the Positive and the Negative Principles one of the chaotic, primitive, or mysterious occult characteristics of the Oriental and Native American cultures. However, this idea is commonly found in any pagan culture worldwide, including ancient

---

[58] Chávez 1979. see Yamase 2005b.
[59] Freidel et al. 1993.
[60] Bricker 2002.

European history. It is evident that ancient European pagan cultures once had this kind of dualism as one of their own cultural principles, because the concept of dualism is one of the main contexts within their mythology. Indeed, one of the noted critics of Christianity and a Neo-Platonist, Celsus, wrote the following text to oppose Christianity in 178AD:

> ...there can be no decrease or increase of evils in the world-neither in the past nor in the future. From the beginning of time, the beginning of the universe, there has been just so much evil, and in quantity it has remained the same... evils are not caused by God; rather, that they are a part of the nature of matter and of mankind; ...because things happen in cycles, what is happening now-evils that is-happened before and will happen again...What this means theologically is that neither good nor evil can possibly increase on earth...[61]

It must be noted that numerous ancient pagan religions within the Roman Empire agreed to treat gods and demons as a couple constituting a part of the cosmic system, even though each of them obviously is in conflict. This fact suggests that the ancestors of the Europeans once had a full understanding of the Chinese concept of dualism, the Positive and Negative Principles.[62] However, Greek pagan philosophers, who deeply influenced the later Christians, were not always in favor of ideas based on dualism. Although the denial of dualism did not gain popularity among the ancient Greek sages,[63] contrary to the Maya and the Chinese, they did not constantly consider it to be a demonstration of harmony, but they sometimes thought of it as a synthesis (=more chaotic than harmonious), especially when issues of the soul were involved. Their early attempt to reject the logic of dualism between the flesh and the Spirit can be found in Pythagoras' (580-500BC) ideas. Later, the Greek pagan philosophers, especially the Platonists, did not consider dualism as a harmony in the relationship between the Spirit and the flesh. In the *Phaedo*, while accepting dualism within the physical world,[64] by

---

[61] Cited from Celsus 178:V, p.81-2.
[62] Pagels 1995:130.
[63] Aristotle 1976b:300-322 (184a-192b)
[64] Plato 389?: 47-51, 70-71.

pointing out the invisibility and immortality of the soul, which proves the Soul has a non-physical existence, the existence of the human soul is treated as an exception to the natural balance within the material world (= Nature).[65] Thus, the Platonists rejected the idea of 'the Soul as one principle cooperating with the other principles within the natural [=human] world.' In this way, the Platonists separated the Soul from Nature sustained by the logic of dualism. Based on this idea, they argued the conflict between spirit and body, and they identified the latter as simply an instrument of the Soul but not as a collaborator with it. Also, Aristotle, a rival of Plato, accepted the Soul as the master of the flesh,[66] and argued that the Soul, which was confined by the flesh, is in a condition as if it had become sick, losing original liberty, as Plato says.[67] These were taken as evidence that in the relationship between Nature and the transcendent (Spiritual) world, Greek pagan people denied the logic of dualism.

It must be noted that neither Aristotle nor Plato denied divine character and the immortality of Nature.[68] After the Christian victory over the pagans, the majority of such ancient Greek pagan texts were condemned, or were forgotten by the Christianized Westerner. Plato's concept of the soul was later integrated into Christianity and became one of the core parts of it. As a result, only selected works of Greek philosophers continued to be read as pagan classics of a dead culture. Therefore, from my point of view, in spite of the fact that fragmental notions of harmonized dualism consisting of the Spirit and Nature have remained in European and Western cultures, Westerners often regard it as a chaotic contradiction or primitive concept. Consequently, they often have difficulty in comprehending some important basic concepts of the logic of dualism found among the pagan people of today.

---

[65] *Ibid.*:71-80, p.52-78., Aristotle 1976c:246.
[66] Aristotle 1961:40-3.(1254a-11-1255a). 1976c:241
[67] Aristotle 1976c:246.
[68] Aristotle 1976a:201. In his logic, although the flesh can be corrupted, elements of it will remain as immortal things, and thus the ancient Greeks concluded that Nature is immortal and divine.

On the other hand, as I have mentioned before, because the Maya religions are animistic, their central concept is that the entire universe is theoretically alive. Unlike Platonism, moreover, there is no positive evidence that the ancient Maya insisted on a separatism of the soul from the physical world.[69] Like other animistic religions, such as the Shinto of Japan, divine essence for the Maya possesses a tree and stone temporarily when he needs to communicate with the people and a divine physical object itself is not thought of as the god. However, in practice, Maya idols, as a substitution, are often living, divine things. The reason may be that in general, animistic and pagan cultures, including China and Japan, have been less concerned about the separation and conflict between the spirit and the flesh, and the definition of the spirit, than the Christians have. For example, the Tolupan of Honduras consider that the first Native Americans were immortal, and thus it can be said that the flesh and the spirit are a twosome for them. Therefore, I think the ancient Maya were not also interested in this kind of issue, though there is no solid evidence. Distinguishing the spirits from the physical world is technically impossible in their type of religion.

Today, in most cases, the K'iche Maya use the Spanish words, '*corazón* (heart)' and '*espíritu* (spirit)' in order to translate the terms of divine existence in their own language (e.g. *kuxtal, pixan* in the Yucatec and *gux* in the K'iche). The use of 'spirit' gives an impression that the Maya have traditionally regarded divine existence as transcendent powers as the Christians have done, and the use of '*corazón*' makes us imagine that the Maya did not have a clear concept of the separation of divine power from physical existence within nature. They have not concluded which Spanish word is more suitable. Because the colonial Spaniards translated these Maya terms as '*alma* (soul, spirit),' North Americans and Europeans often prefer the use of '*espíritu*,' and thus the term 'spiritualism' is frequently used in academic books without much consideration of the issue of 'what is the exact character of the Maya spirit?'. Certainly, the '*kuxtal*' or '*pixan*'

---

[69] See Freidel et als. 1993:181-182.

of the Maya should be quite similar to the '*spirit*' of Christianity, but there must be some crucial differences.

Apparent influences from the Christian ideology among the Maya of today sometimes make my analysis of the original Maya belief of spirit-like-beings difficult. Archaeological remains of tombs and offerings suggest that the Maya recognized the existence of the soul of the human, which continued living after death. Although the concept of the immortality of the Soul seems to have existed in Maya cultures from the ancient period, it is evident that the Maya have not treated the Soul as an exception to dualism within nature, unlike the Platonists and the Christians. At first, the Maya did not always consider the Spirit as an invisible thing, because blood was thought of as the Soul.[70] Second, they considered that gods have their own physical world in which mountains and rivers exist, like our own world. Third, none of the Maya religious texts, including those that received strong influence from Christianity, discuss the issue of the conflict between the flesh (or Nature) and the Soul. Fourth, in the Classic period, the kings of ancient Maya states claimed that they were divine humans as the sons of the Sun, like Jesus Christ of Christianity. The colonial Maya also had the term '*ku vinik,*' the divine human[71], and that of '*K'ul,*' the divine thing (=*e.g.* idols).[72] Next, '*kabavil (Kabawil)*' of the K'iche language signifies not only idol, but also god and the most precious *copal*.[73] Although the Maya deities do not have a carnal body in theory, this is evidence that the ancient Maya had a concept of carnal = spirit in some cases as the result of their confusion, which is also seen in the Japanese pagan religion, Shinto. The last reason is that the essence of Maya religions is a direct interaction between spiritual power and human beings. Both are a pair with the other. Therefore, it seems to be

---

[70] Holland 1963:99-105.

[71] *Diccionario de Motul* 1935:523.

[72] *Diccionario de Motul* 1935:527. Although '*K'ul*' is often translated as 'holy sprit' (e.g. in Freidel et als. 1993:176-7), I think this kind of rendering is improper, because it is evident that '*K'ul*' refer to both sacred physical object and spirit alike.

[73] The contemporary K'iche Maya often use *Kabawil* in order to express something like the dualism concept, or *Tao* of Taoism or the unitary notion of godhood, although the clear definition has not been made.(Yamase 2002b:232, 248-9)

true that the Maya notion of the Soul or Spirit is to believe the Soul as a corporative pair within the physical world.[74] Thus, it can be suggested that the Maya have traditionally considered that the Soul and the body are a twosome constituting one being, and the relationships between both are interdependent. Also, as I have mentioned before, although the concept of spirit had existed among the Maya before the Spanish conquest, the Maya concept of the separation of the soul from the material is not clear as in Christianity. That is, the colonial Maya were not interested in the distinction between the soul and flesh. Even the Maya of today do not completely accept the Christian belief that *'the soul is conflicting with the flesh.'* Based on what I have argued, therefore, it is suggested that the use of 'Heart' instead of 'Spirit' may be more appropriate to specify the character of Maya deities.

Natural phenomena, time, and the specific materials and plants occasionally become god-like living things or the god as in the Taoism of China (and Japanese and Chinese localized versions of Buddhism). This suggests that for the Maya, not only 'conventional' gods, but also other non-spiritual beings can act in almost the same way as gods (these living divine things should be distinguished from idols which are a temporal house of gods). By this logic, the Maya gods are not always paired with other gods only, they are sometimes coupled with other types of divinities. Unlike in Christianity, a Maya god can be paired with a physically divine existence, which has an equivalence to that Maya god, in order to do his work under some circumstances. This difference in interpretation of dualism between the Maya and Platonists may have resulted in a superficial understanding of Native American dualism among Westerners. In any case, when we analyze the colonial Maya texts, it must always be borne in mind that there are occasionally some god-like beings, which are sometimes superior to the 'real' gods.

Contrary to the Maya's belief, the denial of dualism within Christian ideas is collectively observed in their arguments about the conflict between evil and good. Christianity (and Islam) defines Satan, a former angel, who revolted against the

---

[74] I have used Boremanse (1993:343-7), Edmonson (1993:70-72), Shultze-Jena (1954:50-2),

Christian God, as a ruler of the underworld, or Hell. In Hell, Satan has a complete, independent world. In spite of being a merely product of God, Satan has almost an equal power, is a master of this world, and causes negative effects on human beings. According to Christian doctrine, the current world remains under the rule of Satan until the prophecy of the second arrival of Christ is fulfilled. God and Satan are always contrary to each other, and thus the elimination of Satan is an important task of God. Destruction of Satan does not mean a collapse of the world in Christian theory, therefore.

In the case of the Maya, they also had deities of death, such as God A, a death deity: known as *Yum Cimil* (often *Ah Puch*) in Yucatan. In Guatemala, the lord of *Xibalba* is considered equivalent to him. He closely resembles *Mictlan* of the Nahuatl). Today, the Yucatec Maya still believe in the existence of this god as a negative one.

This god is not an equivalent to Satan in Christianity. While Satan is considered an opponent to the God of Christianity, Maya God A is merely a deity of death-related events. Since only God A and *Itzamna* have two Maya glyphs, the importance of God A seems to be equal to *Itzamna* within the Maya cosmos. He ruled *Mitnal*, the lowest of the nine Maya underworlds, and was god of the day *Cimi* (the day of death). In some aspects, this Maya god is similar to Satan (Lucifer). Like Satan, God A causes disorder in the world. He uproots or destroys trees planted by *Chac*, the rain god. As a god of death, moreover, the Maya have feared him from ancient times. Nevertheless, God A has been considered a positive deity in some situations. This point is a definitive difference of God A from the Satan of Christianity (and Islam).

It must be noted that God A was associated with the god of war and of human sacrifice (God F). His close association with the god of war suggests that, in some specific events, the Maya believed it was necessary to gain his power for victory. In other words, this example suggests that when a negative deity becomes a partner of

---

Wagley (1949 :60-64) in order to consider this issue.

another one, the Maya considered that the pair of gods had a positive function in certain situations.

These examples clearly suggest that, like in other pagan religions, from the ancient period, the Maya have thought that any phenomenon within their cosmovision is a result of interactions between two different divine things. In the classic period, although God A had been considered a god bringing to the world a negative influence, this god was an important element of the world. God A was merely a god of death-related events, and was not an enemy of other gods.

In the Christian doctrine, unlike in Maya religions, the Christian God, his angels and saints, never pair with Satan and his subordinates; rather, it is considered that the destruction of Satan is necessary to restore proper order in the world. On the other hand, in Maya theology, since every natural and supernatural element is a part of the cosmos, any god who represents such phenomena is a necessity in the world. Therefore, because termination of negative deities would mean a total destruction of the world, none of them can be eliminated. That is, 'if light is killed, shadow will also die.'

The Maya have apparently understood Christian concepts through this logic since the Spanish conquest. The concept of the Christian Satan was not introduced in the Maya cosmos. For example, the battle between Satan and the Lord is not mentioned in the colonial Maya texts, in spite of the fact that it was a principal Christian concept among the Spaniards of that period. This suggests that for the Maya, all supernatural powers were '*dios* (=gods).' Maurer Avalos pointed out that in spite of the fact that the friars frequently attempted to appropriate a Maya negative deity in order to speak of the devil since the sixteenth century, the concept of Satan was not fully understood by the Tzeltal Maya. Their long efforts resulted in the fact that *Chopol Pukuh*, a Tzeltal Maya deity, is not yet regarded as Satan or demon but as a merely minor evil '*dios*=god' by the Maya. [75]

---

[75] Maurer Avalos 1993:232. *Pukuh* is regarded as a black demon among the Tzotzil Maya, see Gossen 1999:55-76.

In addition, the concept of Hell in the European Christian idea did not exist among the pre-Columbian Maya. As I have mentioned, the Maya have a concept of the underworld, and the *Mitnal* of the Yucatan and *Xibalba* of Guatemala are known.

The colonial Yucatec Maya feared *Mitnal*, because it was considered a place of torment. Diego de Landa, a Franciscan bishop of Yucatan of the late sixteenth century, recorded what his Maya informants told him:

> *The people have always believed in the immortality of the soul, in greater degree than many other nations, even though they were not so civilized; they believed that after death there was another life better than this, which the soul enjoyed after leaving the body. This future life they said was divided into good and evil, into pains and delights. The evil life of suffering they said was for the vicious, and the good delectable for those whose mode of life had been good. The delights they said they would come into if they had been of good conduct, were by entering a place where nothing would give pain, where there would be abundance of food and delicious drinks, and a refreshing and shady tree they called **Yaxché**, the Ceiba tree, beneath whose branches and shade they might rest and be in peace for ever.*
> *The torments of the evil life, which they said awaited the wicked, lay in going to an evil place below the other, and which they called **Mitnal**, meaning hell, where they were tormented by demons, by great pains of cold and hunger and weariness and sadness. They said there was in this place a chief demon whom all the rest obeyed and whom in their language they called **Hunhau** [or **Cumhau**]; also they said that these good and evil after-lives had no end, because the soul itself had none.[76]*

One may argue that the above-quoted Maya notion of *Mitnal* is considerably closer to that of the Hell of Christianity, though the reliability of information provided by Landa remains questionable. Alfred M. Tozzer suspects that what Landa wrote about the Maya doctrine of retribution with a heaven and a hell seems to have been a reflection of Christian teaching.[77] In fact, the concept of retribution with a heaven and a hell cannot be seen in the colonial Maya half-religious texts,

---

[76] Cited from Landa 1566: sec.XXXIII, p.57-8. **Hunhau** is considered one of the variants of *Yum Cimil, Kisin* or *Ah Puch*.

The concept of immortality of the soul is still observed in K'iche Maya. They consider that spirits of the dead are superior to those of the living people (Shultze-Jena 1954:96).

[77] Landa 1941:131, note 615, 132 note 617. The K'iche-Maya at Chichicastenango of the middle twentieth century, reject Christian ideas of the afterlife (Bunzel 1952:269-70).

such as the *Books of Chilam Balam*. Yet, since there could have been various Maya notions of *Mitnal* in the pre-Columbian period, we cannot completely dismiss what Landa says, unless other solid evidence opposing his information is discovered.

Research on the Maya of the twentieth century has revealed existence of a quite similar notion among the Maya.[78] The Maya often feared the Gods of the Underground = *Mitnal* or *Xibalba*. The Tzotzil Maya of the twentieth century believed that during the daytime, the Gods of the Sky and the Sun were confining the gods of death underground. In the night, however, the gods of death could come out from underground to attack humans. They called the underground '*el mundo inferior* (the inferior world),' and were afraid of going out at night.[79] It may be said that the Tzotzil Maya's idea of the underground is somehow similar to the Hell of Christianity.

Even if Landa is correct, and *Xibalba* and *Mitnal* may be similar to Hell in some aspects, it is almost certain that they are not an equivalent of the Hell of Christianity, as is the case for God A.

The Maya considered the underworld = *Xibalba* to be a holy place while fearing it. It is known that in the Classic period (250-900AD), Maya kings communicated with their ancestors and gods in caves or labyrinths, which were considered entrances to *Xibalba*.[80] This fact suggests that the Classic Maya did not believe that spirits of the dead would go to Heaven, and that the Maya concept that 'Heaven = Paradise for good people' from the sixteenth century was possibly introduced by the Spaniards. Therefore, the Maya concept of an underworld is not an equivalent of the Hell of Christianity. Nevertheless, since the colonial Spaniards translated, *Xibalba* of K'iche and Kaqchikel Maya, and *Mitnal*, a Yucatec Maya

---

[78] See Holland 1963:69, Redfield 1941:125-6.
[79] Holland 1963:97.
[80] Rivera Dorado 2000:158.

word, simply as '*el infierno* (the Hell),'[81] resulting in numerous misunderstandings of the Maya concept of the underworld.

It should be noted that because the Maya considered the underworld an indispensable part of Nature, *Mental* or *Xibalba* are often cooperative with the celestial realm of the sky in order to sustain the universe. J. Eric. S. Thompson summarized this logic well:

> *The sun god, for instance, was primarily a sky god, but because he passed at night through underworld on his eastward journey from point of sunset to point of sunrise he became one of the nine lords of the night and underworld.*[82]

I have previously pointed out that in the *Annals of the Kaqchikel* of the Kaqchikel Maya, *Xibalba* is mentioned as a positive being (a creator of 'Precious Obsidian) in the creation myth, in spite of the fact that they generally considered *Xibalba* negative. This phenomenon can be observed in the *Popol Vuh* of the K'iche Maya[83] and among other Maya.[84] The Chichimec people of Mexico claimed that they came from seven cases, for example. At Teotihuacan, a gigantic city in the Mexican highlands of the Classic Period, it was revealed that the temple of the Sun, the largest construction in that city, was built above a cave. This suggests that the Mesoamerican people tried to associate their origin with the underground world as a holy place. These facts also suggest that although the underworld has been regarded as a world of Satan in Europe, the Mesoamerican people considered it differently.

I have previously argued that when we consider the phenomenon of so-called Mayanized Christianity, this fundamental difference of religious concept must be considered carefully, because the Maya traditionally re-interpreted emerging

---

[81] E.g. Ximénez 1985:615, Coto 1983:295, *Diccionario de Motul* 1935:629, 920, *Diccionario de San Francisco* 1976:239(in this dictionary, a word '*Metnal*' is given). *Xibalba* is mentioned as '*diablo*' (Satan) as a Yucatec Maya word in *Diccionario de Motul* (1935: 920).

[82] Cited from Thompson 1970:199.

[83] Yamase 2002b:214, 232.

[84] See Thompson 1970:199.

religious and cultural elements within their dualism. Dualism still dominates the Maya concept of religious issues and daily life.[85]

For example, when the K'iche-Maya adopted a Spanish word in their language, apart from its original Spanish meaning, they added another neutral meaning to that word as in their own language. Schultze-Jena provides us an example. '*niño*' in the Spanish language signifies 'a boy.' However, when the K'iche-Maya use this word, '*niño*' means not only 'a boy,' but also 'a neutral sex child.'[86] Ruth Bunzel recorded that the K'iche Maya of Chichicastenango often use the words 'the divine world (*mundo*)' to invoke the sacred power.[87] Although Buznel considered that it refers to the heart of the sky mentioned in the *Popol Vuh*, as in the case of other Maya divine things, *el mundo* among the K'iche Maya has various meanings, and '*mundo*' is often used to signify things which have no relation to the earth.[88] In my view, the divine '*mundo*=world' may refer to the virtue of the universe, something like the *Tao* of Taoism in China, although this point cannot be made clear at this moment. In addition, as I have mentioned before, 'idol' also has several meanings, including 'god.'

By pointing out the existence of the notion of bisexualism and the duality of the deities among the Maya, the importance of the Maya dualism has been recognized by some European researchers from the late nineteenth century.[89] Yet, it is true that it has not always been fully considered in analyses of the colonial Maya texts. Although Schultze-Jena considers dualism of the K'iche-Maya to be bisexual, as I have argued, the Negative and the Positive Principle is also an important concept within their dualism. As has been argued and will be discussed, the Maya dualism is a necessary part of understanding their religious belief and cosmovision as well as other cultural elements.

---

[85] Yamase 2002b:212-4.
[86] Schultze-Jena 1954:62.
[87] Bunzel 1952:264-5.
[88] *Ibid.*:264-9.
[89] Schultze-Jena 1954:62-3.

No doubt, as a religion of the Spaniards, Christianity was negatively received by the majority of the colonial Maya. Nevertheless, the theory of Maya dualism had room for Christianity to be integrated within the Maya cosmos. Indeed, even though the colonial Maya made several brutal attacks on the Christian Church and often refused to accept Christianity as their own sole religion, there is no evidence that they rejected it as a religion. Although it was treated negatively, it is almost certain that Christianity was recognized as a negative partner of Maya ancient divinities within the Maya universe.[90] Since the Maya dualistically comprehended the role of deities, the Christian god and his subordinated ones were no exception to that psychological belief. The Maya began to look for the positive aspect at the same time.

As will be discussed in the latter part of this book, this kind of reaction towards Christianity is found universally in the dualistic world. For example, the colonial Nahuatl of the Mexican highlands considered that *Maria,* who is originally a mere human in the Gospel, is coupled with the Christian Lord as queen of the heaven to rule the world.[91] This case proves that the Mesoamerican people tended to reject the monotheism found in the 'European' Christianity.

As another example, the myth of the Tolupan in Honduras provides us an interesting view.[92] Although by the late twentieth century, many of their traditional religious customs had disappeared, they were not Christianized yet.[93] The Tolupan received Christianity unconstructively, perhaps because of their conflicts with the Spanish and Ladino after the Spanish conquest. They used the elements of Christianity in order to stress the difference between the Ladino and themselves. Two gods, '*Tata Dios*' and '*Our Lord*' were generated from Christianity. Both are subordinated to the *God Toman, the Elder and the Younger*, the supreme gods of the Tolupan. *Tata Dios* belongs to Toman the Elder who rules the East Sky, and *Our Lord* to Toman the Younger who rules the West Sky.

---

[90] Yamase 2002b:Chap.6.
[91] Damrosch 1993:148-9.
[92] I have used Chapman 1992.

Although *Tata God* is assigned to look after the Ladino, he often fights and holds them in contempt. Another god, 'Our Lord,' is portrayed as the instigator of death on the Earth and is regarded as an enemy of the Tolupan, yet the savior of the First Native American.[94] In their myth, one of the Tolupan supreme gods, Toman the Younger, ordered Our Lord [likely originated from Christ] to go to the Native American nation:

> *We Mortals, ourselves, asked for death because we are troublemakers.*
> *Our Lord gave us fetid vapor to spread sickness, to plague Indians forever*
> *after...In the times of old, people didn't die. During the time of the First*
> *Nation, there was no fetid vapor; people lived peacefully with Our Lord...But*
> *later, they all got angry with us....*
> > **Toman***: Now go to the Indian Nation.*
> > **Our Lord:** *No, I won't go.*
> > **Toman:** *You must go. You alone. Didn't they kill you? Didn't they bury*
> *you?*
> > **Our Lord:** *No, it was the Jews. Oh! Oh! What a headache I have!*
> > **Toman:** *...The Indians are not your enemy.*
> > *....Three days later, Our Lord returned. He had forgiven his enemy...*
> > **Our Lord:** *...It's true, you are my friend...I've forgiven you and now, Old*
> *Indian, you'll become my father in law.*
> > **The First Indian:** *I agree....*[95]

Anne Chapman believes that these Gods (Our Lord and Tata Dios) found in the Tolupan myth originated from Christianity, and are parodies of the Christian faith.[96] Our Lord in their myth should be regarded as a demonstration of Tolupan's contemptuous view of the Ladino's behavior since the Spanish conquest. In the following myth of the Tolupan, Our Lord is described as a snob.

Chapman also recorded:

> **Our Lord:** *No thank you, Señor, I like the Indian women better. Now I'm*
> *going to the Earth to heckle the men and to embrace the women...'*
> *Our Lord came here to make love to our women. He didn't respect*
> *anyone. He got on top of them, embracing them, caressing them and making*

---

[93] Chapman 1992:11-2.
[94] Chapman 1992:105-119.
[95] Cited from Chapman 1992:108.
[96] *Ibid.*:274-5.

love to them. He did everything of that sort....Then Our Lord fled, trying to
hide from the men. He shouted to Mother Earth, 'Open up for me!'
    Mother Earth: *No. I won't open. Only the Mortals have the right to*
open me.[97]

Another part of her record of the Tolupan myth says:

    Our Lord didn't want to pay for food. He didn't like food that was bought.
He wanted it to be given to him.... I won't buy love, either. If it's free, yes.[98]

Although Christian elements are ostensibly confusingly mixed, if we analyze the above texts from a perspective of dualism, they accommodate Christian elements into Tolupan cosmology perfectly. It must be suggested that some internal conflicts within each god can be explained perfectly by positive and negative principles, which are an important element of dualism. The above-cited narratives tell us that the Tolupan often negatively received the Christian Gods as if he is a 'devil' god. Nonetheless, unlike Satan of Christianity, these 'originally Christian' gods never oppose *Toman* (the Elder and the Younger), though they do complain about *Tomans'* orders. Moreover, despite the fact that Christianity is considered negatively and is made fun of by the Tolupan, it is evident that its divine nature is not dismissed.[99] He sometimes acts as one of various positive gods. This fact suggests that *Tata Dios* and *Our Lord* in Tolupan myths are recognition of Christianity as a part of the cosmovision, according to Tolupan's dualism. The Tolupan incorporated Christianity within their cosmovision in order to explain the arrival of the Ladino and their long abuse of the Native American. In other words, many of negative aspects of their life are ascribed to the Christian God and spirits. I propose calling this type of religious mixing 'dualistic religious reconstruction.'

In the early eighteenth century, there were several Maya revolts against the Spaniards.[100] What they did not expel Christianity, but created their own Christianity. Therefore, in such a case, it may be said that the Maya divided the

---

[97] Cited from *ibid*:111-2.
[98] Cited from *ibid*:112-3.
[99] See Chapman 1992:105.

88

cosmos by using two different Christianities, one for the Spaniards and another for the Maya, though their old belief was not completely ignored, as pagan elements have often been reported in Chiapas.

The authors of the *Book of Chilam Balam* of the Yucatan Peninsula used a different type of dualism.[101] As will be discussed later, they used the past and the present in order to constitute a dualism consisting of Christianity and Maya pagan religions. The *Books of Chilam Balam* of the Yucatec Maya are famous for the difficulty of their context. This is especially true in the narratives containing strong Christian influence. Some readers may find that Christian and Maya elements are mixed confusingly, and would say that the Christian doctrine found in these books looks like a 'chaotic' or 'primitive' understanding of the Gospel by the colonial Maya. Others argue that the strong persistence found in Christianized Maya myths is evidence of the colonial Yucatec Maya's prudent hiding of their old religious beliefs from the Spanish extirpations of Maya pagan religions.

However, I am not in favor of either position. Firstly, I believe that the Christian doctrine found in these texts is by no means a result of Maya confusion.[102] Although some of the 'confused' Christianity found in these documents may be a 'hidden resistance to Christianity,' this judgment seems not always to be correct. The fact is that there is no solid evidence that the authours of these Maya texts hid Maya religious elements through trickery. I have previously argued that because the colonial Maya understanding of Christianity must have been formed within the Maya dualistic culture, the ostensible difficulty of a 'fusion' between Maya and Christian elements found in the *Book of Chilam Balam of Chumayel* should be interpreted from the perspective of dualism. In other words, the *Chumayel* represents a Maya cosmovision: one cosmos and two religions. In fact, as will be discussed in the next section, it is evident that the ostensibly 'confused' Mayanized

---

[100] For these incidents, see Bricker 1981:55-69, Gosner 1992.
[101] For example, see Redfield et al.1962:124.
[102] Bricker (2002) also proves that the context of the *Chumayel* is not a product of confusion.

Christianity found in the *Chumayel* was created analytically through dualism by the colonial Maya authors.

Before going into an analysis of the *Chumayel*, it is useful to understand to what extent the creation myth has been significant among the Native Americans in general. A North American Native American, Vine Deloria, Jr. discussed the difference between Christianity and Native North American religions. He says:

> *Indian tribal religions and Christianity differ considerably on numerous theological points, but a very major distinction that can be made between the two types of thinking concerns the idea of creation. Christianity has traditionally appeared to place its major emphasis on creation as a specific event while the Indian tribal religions could be said to consider creation as an ecosystem present in a definable place. In this distinction we have again the fundamental problem of whether we consider the reality of our experience as capable of being described in terms of space or time-as 'what happened here' or 'what happened then.' ... Christians see creation as the beginning event of a linear time sequence in which a divine plan is worked out, the conclusion of the sequence being an act of destruction bringing the world to an end. The beginning and end of time are of no apparent concern for many tribal religions.*[103]

This could be applied to the case of the creation myth found in the colonial Maya texts. For the Maya, a creation myth is not a memorial of the achievement of the Lord, but merely one of ordinary historical events. Unlike Christians, the Maya have had several (two or four) creations since the beginning of their history. For the Maya, although the creation myth is still an important event, its degree of importance is far less than it is for the Christian. In theory, even if the Christian Lord is incorporated with such a belief, he would merely be the creator of 'only one' of the various worlds in the Maya universe. This point will be considered later, with the Maya dualism. This is the same in other pagan cultures. The Aztec also considered that the world was created several times, for example. In Japan it is suggested that the Creator became a subordinated god to the ruling god who was

---

[103] Cited from Deloria 1993:78.

born after the creation.[104] In the case of the Inca, there were several Creators of the world, in spite of the fact that *Viracochan* was regarded as the supreme Creator.

In Maya cultures, the importance of the Creator in religion also seems different to the Lord of Christianity. For example, *Itzamna*, the Lord of Maya gods, carries the title of *Ahaw*, but no evidence of his identity as the Creator of the World has been found. In pagan religions, the Creator of the world is not always necessarily the supreme deity. For example, although *Tzacol* and *Bitol* are mentioned as the Creators in the *Popol Vuh*, the same manuscript tells us of the existence of four divinities in the cosmos prior to the Creation. Nevertheless, these deities are practically ignored after the Creation in the *Popol Vuh*, where it refers to *Tohil* (or possibly *Naxit* as a living god) as the ruling god of the world. On this point, it may be suggested that Creators in Maya religions were not considered a supreme deity.

When we study the dualism of the pagan cults, including the Maya cultures, moreover, an important fact is that the majority of them are animistic. As found in numerous other animistic and dualistic cultures, the dualism concept of the Maya is found not only in the interactive relationship among Maya deities, but also among certain physical elements of nature and the Maya gods. This concept should not be considered through the rather ambiguous term of 'pluralism,' but in terms of 'multiple sets of dualism,' although there are some exceptions. Therefore, Christian divine elements found in colonial Maya texts should be considered in this way. Maya dualism does not always consist of Maya gods and Christian divine elements, but it often does consist of Maya divine time, divine materials, and Christian holy elements. This point will be argued in the next section. Although a similar attempt has already been presented by Victoria R. Bricker[105], I chose to examine different parts of the *Chumayel*.

---

[104] See Appendix I of this volume.
[105] Bricker 2002.

III: Religion as a Part of the Universe: The Case Study of the 'Religious Fusion' between the Yucatec Maya Religion and Christianity

> *It is, indeed, my opinion, that the sun (if we may credit the wise) is the common father of all mankind; for as it is very properly said, man and the sun generate man. But this deity disseminates souls into the earth not from himself alone, but from other divinities; and these evince by their lives the end of their propagation.* (The Roman emperor, Julian. Cited from Julian (361-3b:41))

The existence of Christian elements within the Native American cosmovision has sometimes been regarded as the result of the primitiveness of that cosmovision.[106] However, modern scholars do not hold this view.[107]

My analysis of the colonial Maya texts will suggest that, at least, the colonial, educated Maya logically placed Christian elements into the traditional Maya cosmovision. In my opinion, the issue of the influence from Christianity found in a colonial Yucatec Maya text is useful to verify the issues mentioned up to this point. The *Book of Chilam Balam of Chumayel*, one of the important colonial Yucatec Maya religious texts, will be examined as an example. Although the religious phenomena found in this text are still regarded as a religious mixing, this text suggests that the colonial Maya comprehended Christianity via dualism consisting of Christianity and the Yucatec Maya religion. I do not disagree that the authors of the *Chumayel* occasionally mixed Maya concepts with Christian ones.[108] However, overemphasizing this point is not acceptable. Although they are ostensibly mixed, as will be argued, a careful analysis suggests that each of them is still essentially treated as an independent religious system.

Let us examine the actual text. Richard Luxton, a British scholar, produced a more readable translation of the *Chumayel* than those from the past.[109] Nevertheless, the text of *Chumayel* may still be difficult for the majority of readers.

Let us look at two parts of the *Chumayel*:

---

[106] Dussel 1981:67.

[107] e.g. Bricker 2002, Yamase 2002b.

[108] As to colonial Maya reconstruction of their myth based on the Christian concept, Bricker (2002) is a successful result.

'*16. THE MORTALITY OF THE NATIVE GODS*

[This] is very necessary [for] the health introduced into one's spirit. These are the precious stones proclaimed by Our Father Spirit; This is the first meal, this balche [sic] wine, With which we respect him here, We, the ruling people. Great is the exhortation separating the worshippers From the uncertainties of their gods. These precious stones are the recognized image of the true god, Our Father God, The Father of heaven and earth, True God. However, the first gods were mortal gods. The power of their worship [is] ended, Their judgment broken by the benediction of Our Heavenly Father. It is perfected, The redemption of the multitude. It is perfected, the resurrected life. True god, True Dios. When He blessed heaven and earth, Then the judgment of the [old] god was broken for Maya people, Your heart despairing of your god, truly. This is the account of the world in those times. This is because it has been written, truly. Because it did not happen, In the time of working these books, truly, Many volumes of discussions, truly, That might be inquired in the face of Maya people, If they comprehend how they were born and settled the world Here in the forest, truly.'[110]

Some may say that the above quotation from the *Chumayel* is an example of the colonial Maya's superficial acceptance of Christianity. The above quoted text tells us that the colonial Yucatec Maya recognized the power of the Christian God as a ruler of the New Period.[111] Since this kind of logic is seen in another *Book of Chilam Balam*, the *Tizimin*, it appears that the colonial Maya clearly considered that the power of their old gods had ended.[112]

On this very point, some may consider that contrary to the case of the Tolupan, the colonial Maya accepted the superiority of the Christian Lord to the Maya gods. Yet, the fact is different. The *Chumayel* says; '*However, the first* [Maya] *gods were mortal gods*' (in the original Maya text; *Bacacix* (however) *yax* (first) *kuobe* ([*sic*] gods), [were] *hauay* (mortal or perishable) *kuob* (gods)). On this point, it must be

---

[109] My own review of his translation, see Yamase 2002c.

[110] Cited from Luxton 1995:75. Also see Roys 1967:98 (The Creation of the World).

[111] The Supreme deity mentioned in the *Chumayel* does not have to be considered a sole god. Our Father God (*Cayumil ti Dios*) may be a different deity from the True God (*Hahal ku*). It may be two gods, or a pair of two gods. In fact, they use two names, True God (*Hahal ku*) and True Dios (*Hahal Dios*) to mention the Christian God in a single sentence (Luxton 1995:75). *Ku* is a Maya term to refer to God and *Dios* is of the Spanish. Therefore, the supreme deity mentioned in the *Chumayel* may have dualistic character, one as of the Maya, another as of the Christian Lord (Yamase 2002b:262-3). If this view is correct, the mortal gods mentioned in the *Chumayel* may be the lesser Maya deities.

[112] See Yamase 2002b:229-231.

noted that the author(s) of the *Chumayel* still considered their old gods 'gods.' In the *Chumayel*, unlike the Christian texts, the Christian God is not treated as the sole Lord of the Universe. Their acceptance of the Christian Lord was not a dismissal of their old gods. They are neither treated as devil sprits, nor mentioned as 'dead.' It is important to notice that, as will be discussed, their own gods are treated as the lords of the past *Katún* cycle. In other words, the Maya did not recognize the Christian god as the sole almighty and eternal God as mentioned in the Christian Holy Scriptures. Because, the Maya evidently considered that the gods of Maya, too, had power as the gods in the past. This part of the *Chumayel* should be understood on the basis that the gods of the Maya lost their divine power and the era of the God of Christianity was newly arrived. As I have mentioned, the Maya have been influenced strongly by the periodic-cycle notion. In the Maya belief, no gods, worlds, or suns have immortal, divine power. Their power can decline in a particular cycle of time. So, it may be said that the Maya recognized Maya gods of the past and the Christian Lord and other holy existences (e.g. angels) of the present as a pair. This logic of dualism allowed the colonial Yucatec Maya to replace old Maya gods with the Lords and the saints.

The Christian God was perhaps understood as a mortal divine power in this Maya concept, as the immorality of the Christian Lord is not (at least directly) mentioned in the *Chumayel*. Alternatively, it is suggested that the colonial Maya may have concluded that there are two types of gods, '*mortal*' Maya gods, and the '*immortal*' Christian Lord. If the latter view is correct, the immortality of God, which is one of the key elements of the Gospel, was not a serious concern for the colonial Yucatec Maya.

As for the praise of the Christian God found in the *Chumayel*, it is possible to suggest that administration of the 'present' world was transferred to the Christian God from the old gods of the Maya for a period of one *Katún*. Therefore, the acceptance of the Christian God among the Maya was not as the absolute Lord of the universe as in Christianity, but as a new master of a certain period within the Maya universe.

It must be noted that the *Chumayel* says, '*These are the precious stones proclaimed* [Instead of 'proclaimed,' I prefer 'foreseen' as the meaning of *patah*] *by Our Father Spirit ... These precious stones are the recognized image of the true god, Our Father God, The Father of heaven and earth, True God*'. As the precious stones (*tunil*) are said to be the image of the Christian Lord in the *Chumayel*, precious stones are evidently treated as the key element of Maya religions in the *Chumayel*.[113] It is also obvious that the Maya evidently rejected the Christian fundamental idea of 'idol (precious stones) = house of devil spirit.' It is also apparent that the colonial Maya tried to relate Maya traditions to the Christian God.

Looking at another part of this text will provide another view. Let us look at another part of the *Chumayel*:

19. THE BIRTH OF GOD AND A NEW SOCIAL ORDER

The Lord be with you.' The completion of the words of their sermon When there was no sky and earth. There it was reborn while the world was submerged When there was no sky or earth. Then three-cornered stone of grace came into being, The forming of the god [and] the rulership, For no heaven had been made. Then was the birth of the seventh stone In the seventh katun, Hanging in the spirit of his breath, The seven predestinies. Then, they say, was the stirring Of the seven graces also. Seven are the saints also. When they were still virgin Was when the birth of the first stone of grace came about. One infinite grace When there was an infinity of darkness Without God existing then He had yet to receive His Godhead, Then He remained inside the grace All alone by Himself inside the darkness When there was no sky or earth. Divided in two parts [was] the ending of the katun, But the birth was not to occur In the first katun. He was there and heard-. 'A god at this place for me,' God came into being [And] in two parts He departed. Then He became man In the second infinite stone of grace. Then He emerged in the second katun, 'Alpicon' the name of the born angel. Departing He endowed the second grace The second infinite darkness Because there was no one to be there. Then He received his sacredness all by Himself, alone When He came and departed. 'Affirm.'

---

[113] The *Chumayel* says that ordinal stones were created after the birth of Adam and Eve (Luxton 1995:107).

Sweet was His discourse When He received His divinity all by Himself,
alone. Then He departed, He went to the third infinite stone of grace, 'Dawn
of the Yearbearer,' the name of the angel. This was the third grace.[114]

Past researchers often called the above part of the *Chumayel* '*the most mystical*
and hermetic in the Book of Chumayel'[115] or '*some outstanding examples of*
admixture...a strange confusion of references to angels, directions and colors, the
Trinity, and ritual stones and number of paganism.'[116] However, in my view, this
part of the *Chumayel* is systematically organized according to Maya dualism. By
applying the theory of dualism, this part of the *Chumayel* is relatively easy for the
readers to comprehend.

'Saints,' 'virgins,' 'angels,' and possibly 'three'[117] were apparently introduced
from Christianity. Because, in this text, the Spanish term '*Dios (Ds in the text)*' is
not always used to refer to the God but often *ku* or *kuil*, it is not completely certain
that the above-cited narrative of the *Chumayel* is always talking about the Christian
God. The creation and fall of the Maya gods is mentioned in the previous part of the
Chumayel[118], and it can be suggested that the God found in this part of *Chumayel*
refers to the god of Christianity.

It must be noted that the above-cited text from the *Chumayel* says: '*There it*
was reborn while the world was submerged when there was no sky or earth. Then
three-cornered stone of grace came into being, the forming of the god [and] the

---

[114] Cited from Luxton 1995:91. Also see Roys 1967:107-8 (*The Ritual of the Angels*).

[115] Luxton 1995:270.

[116] Thompson 1954:14.

[117] '*The three cornered*' mentioned in the *Chumayel* may have been an influence from a
Christian source, because the traditional Maya considered the world to have four corners. In general,
stone is often regarded as the earth in animistic cultures. Therefore, 'stones' mentioned in the
Chumayel, might refer to something like the heart of *Mitnal*, the sky, and the other holy place, or the
hearts of the universe, which mentioned in the beginning of the *Popol Vuh*. If this view is correct,
the stones mentioned in the *Chumayel* are the superb deities of the Maya. However, as the *Chumayel*
clearly distinguishes these stones from Gods, it is evident that the colonial Maya's concept of the
stones was different from their concept of Gods, and thus there is no evidence supporting my view.
Another possible view can be considered. A Maya hieroglyphic, '*tun* (=stone)' ⬚ has a phonetic
value of '*ku*'. A Maya term, *Ku* also signifies 'God'. In general, when ⬚ refers to 'a stone', it is
spelled as ⬚ '*tun ni*'. However, it may be suggested that the use of ⬚ among the ancient Maya
resulted in a confusion between stone and God.

[118] See Luxton 1995:76-89, Roys 1967:99-107.

rulership, for no heaven had been made.' The author of the *Chumayel* placed *'three-cornered stones (ox amay tun g[raci]a)'* above the god. As long as we read this sentence straightforwardly, it is evident that this text refers to the Christian Lord as an offspring of the three precious stones. Because stone was frequently used to express a cycle of time among the Maya, and the Maya deities were subject to a cycle of time, it may be that they considered the Christian Lord as an offspring of time as a result, like the Maya deities. Yet, in this moment, there is no solid supporting evidence that *'three-cornered stones (ox amay tun g[raci]a)'* were considered the Lord of time by the authors of the *Chumayel*.

The Christian often regards the world as a solid part of the universe. On the other hand, the Maya, like the other Native Americans, believed the world to be a temporal creature within the universe, and thus that the world would be destroyed at a certain point of time, as the previous ones were. Therefore, as I have argued before, the importance of the Creation myth of the world is less than that in the *Bible*. Although the Christian Lord was recognized as the ruler of the New World, for the Maya, that world simply is a part of the universe. Therefore, I suggest that for the colonial Maya, the true ruler of the Universe is 'the precious stones.' This suggests that the Maya authors did not accept the Christian Lord of the whole universe, but a lord of one of the worlds (= the present world). Moreover, the colonial Yucatec Maya often regarded time as a better one than spiritual things = gods.

From what I have argued up to now, it seems to be plausible that the concept of god for the Maya is very different from that of Christianity. For the colonial Yucatec Maya, those who have the supreme divine power are 'the precious stones' which control the gods.[119]

Unlike in Christianity where the saints are not treated as gods or angels, the Maya saints mentioned in the *Chumayel* are almost the same as human gods (*ku*

---

[119] See note 117.

vinik [*winik*]).[120] This suggests that although there are strong influences from Christian materials, the *Chumayel* was based on the traditional Maya concept of deities. On this point, the second citation from the *Chumayel* was once commented on by Ralph L. Roys as '*The following ritual is an example of the manner in which the Maya superimposed Christian doctrines on their own religious conceptions.*' [121] He also commented, '*Even in their Christian worship we find among the Maya an unconscious tendency to adapt the new religion to their own psychology.*' [122] Although I do not prefer his use of the terms 'superimpose' and 'psychology,' his opinion is acceptable to me. However, as I have argued before, were they unconscious efforts? Although it may be controversial, as will be discussed, there is no evidence that the colonial Yucatec Maya combined Maya and Christian elements confusingly.

One of the current popular ideas of this religious 'mixing' among the present-day Maya is that the Maya created a new religion from both traditional Maya religions and Christianity. However, as will be argued, the case of the colonial Yucatec Maya texts seems to be different.

This is an interesting issue. Although the *Chumayel* accepts the end of the Maya gods, another important element of the Maya cosmos, the stones, were continuously mentioned as an associate of Christianity.

In the first citation of the *Chumayel*, it is said, '*These are the precious stones proclaimed by Our Father Spirit.*' The text seems to state that the Christian Lord is the lord of the precious stones. This statement contradicts that of the second citation from the *Chumayel*: '*Then three-cornered stone of grace came into being, the forming of the god [and] the rulership, For no heaven had been made. Then was the birth of the seventh stone in the seventh katun, hanging in the spirit of his breath,*

---

[120] At the initial stage of Spanish evangelization in the sixteenth century, the Maya replaced the names of Maya gods with those of Catholic saints in order to keep their old pagan faith. For the Maya, there was no distinction between God and saint. The Maya still keep this notion. Vogt (1969:367) reports the Tzotzil Maya and the Tzeltal Maya of the twentieth century regarded saints as Gods. Also see Maurer Avalos 1993:236-238.

[121] Roys 1967:107 note 2.

[122] Roys 1967:201.

the seven predestines. Then, they say, was the stirring of the seven graces also. Seven are the saints also. When they were still virgin was when the birth of the first stone of grace came about.' This passage apparently tells us that the three-cornered stone is a better existence than is the Christian God. The same statement can be found in another part of the *Chumayel*. The *Chumayel* mentions that although the Christian Lord was created by himself, he was born in the stone.[123]

'*Three cornered Stone*' (*ox amay tun* g[raci]*a*) and '*these Precious Stones*' (*Lay u tunil*) which are mentioned in the *Chumayel*, seem to be different in nature. Therefore, if we think that they are different stones, there might be no problem. However, if these two types of stone are the same, how can we analyze this 'paradox?' I think that the 'contradiction' found in the *Chumayel* may have been a result of the Colonial Yucatec Maya's struggle to combine dualistically the concept of two different religious traditions.

The idea of god-like (or superior) stones must have existed among the various ancient and colonial Maya groups.[124] Although it is not information from the Yucatec Maya, the *Annals of the the Kaqchiquel* of the Guatemalan Highlands recorded that *Xibalba*, one of the four elements of the Maya universe, created the precious stone.[125] It is suggested that they considered the precious stone to be an offspring of the universe. Although in the *Popol Vuh* the precious obsidian is not directly associated with the K'iche Maya gods,[126] it must be noted that these kinds of special stone(s) are often treated as an authority independent from Maya gods within the Maya universe. This Kaqchikel text does not tell us that the gods were created either by this stone or by the universe. In addition, the ethnographical data from the living Maya does not provide information on it.[127] Therefore, although it can be said that the precious stone may refer to the altar on which the ancient Maya offered human victims, the exact function of that stone in the Kaqchikel Maya

---

[123] Luxton 1995:108-9, Roys 1967:114.

[124] Yamase 2002b:204-9, Freidel 1993:178.

[125] Otzoy 1999:101,154.

[126] Tedlock 1996:163. My early argument on this stone is made in Yamase 2002b:209.

[127] My previous hypothesis on this type of stone is in Yamase (2002b).

cosmos is not clear. Yet, it is clear that the divine stone is treated as a divine thing, which is always (or sometimes) superior to the gods. It is possible to consider that like the lord of *Katún*, these 'precious' stones may refer to something like a supreme concept of time, and may have been the lord of time. Yet, as I have discussed in the case of the *'three-cornered stone,'* there is no solid evidence supporting this idea. Therefore, at this moment, I will define these special stones as 'a supreme existence, like a superior god.'

From this fact, it may be proposed that the ancient Maya believed certain stones to have a god-like existence but to have a different position from an ordinary god in the Maya cosmos. Two possible orders of various elements within the Maya universe may be summarized, as in Table 1 or Table 2.

If the colonial Yucatec Maya had a notion of 'the precious or divine stone > the Gods,' a tie between the stones and the Christian God mentioned in the

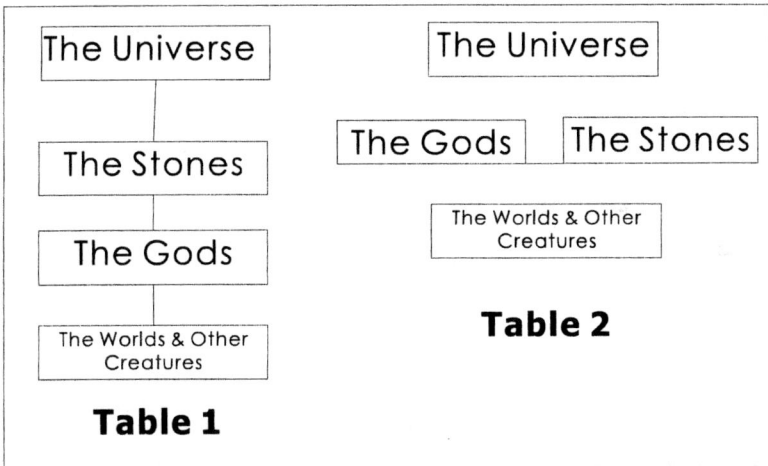

Table 1

Table 2

Chumayel can be explained by the logic of dualism. My hypothesis is that for the Maya, although the old Maya gods were lesser divine elements than the stones and thus the Maya did not have difficulty in dismissing them, they did not accept the superior position of the Christian Lord over the stones. In Christianity, the Lord is of the whole universe. On the other hand, stones are often superior (or equivalent) to gods in the ancient Maya belief. When they tried to combine these concepts as one, there was a serious contradiction. For the colonial Yucatec Maya author(s) of the *Chumayel*, dismissing the belief of the other was impossible. The Christian God and Maya stones must have been understood as an equivalent pair of the present world within the Maya cosmos. Therefore, the Maya author(s) could not have accepted either the inferiority of the stones, the supreme divine element of the Maya, to the Lord of Christianity, or the reverse. The conclusion invented by the colonial Yucatec Maya to overcome this problem seems to be accepting the superiority of one of them to the other in some aspects. By doing this, both the Christian Lord and the Maya precious stones became an equivalent pair working under the Maya cosmos. The *Chumayel* says that the Christian Lord was born by himself only as one element of the cosmos, but his birth was associated with the stone, which is an equivalent existence of the Lord. It is noted that their solution is perfectly explained by dualism. By this logic, I consider that the author(s) of the *Chumayel* explained that the Christian God was born within the Maya universe as one element of it (see Table 3).

Apart from those discussed before, there is another possible representation of dualism in the *Chumayel*. The story of the creation of the humans and others was virtually taken over by that of the Christianity, and it says that the first human beings are Adam and Eve who were created by the Christian Lord.[128] This change was necessary because the author(s) of the *Chumayel* accepted that they were living in the era of Christianity. The Maya's own version of the creation story of the humans must have been eliminated.[129] However, the author(s) of the *Chumayel* insisted that the birthplace of the Maya people was inside the stone.[130] By placing a precious stone as a (somehow superior god-like) partner of the Christian Lord, they successfully (at least in their view) managed to insist that the Maya people were

---

[128] Luxton 1995:107.

[129] We do not have information on the descriptive creation myth of the human of the Yucatec Maya. That in the *Popol Vuh* has been used as the standard of the Maya.

[130] Luxton 1995:94. It says '*Sihon* (birth)-*tun* (then, finally) *u tunil* (in the stone)' (Then, we were born in the stone). Roys (1967:109) reads *Sihontun* as the name of a stone.

created by the Christian God, a (perhaps 'negative') partner of the Maya precious stone, as a historical incident of the Maya universe.[131] Therefore, I suggest that the Christianized Maya religious beliefs found in this text could be a result of the colonial Yucatec Maya effort to reconstruct their cosmovision.

Based on what I have mentioned up to this point, it can be suggested that the author(s) of the *Chumayel* defined 'religion' to be a part of 'the universe = the cosmos.' What the *Chumayel* shows us, is not a religious mixing, but a reconstruction of a cosmovision. As will be mentioned in the next chapter, this

Table 3: New Cosmic Order

concept (one universe and two religions) is now proposed by the Guatemalan Maya people.[132]

There is another issue. The fact is that while the author(s) of the *Chumayel* accepted that the era of the Maya gods had ended, the Yucatec Maya in villages continued worshipping them together with the Christian God and other holy

---

[131] Luxton 1995:109.
[132] Chiappari 1999:124 note 9.

persons.[133] Among the folk Maya, each religion has had its own religious function and space in 'this present' world. In other words, Christianity and the Maya religions have co-existed. Therefore, this difference may suggest that the view of two religious systems presented in the *Book of Chilam Balam of Chumayel* only represents that of an urban area in which the Maya were more Hispanized. The descendants of the Peten Itza, the last kingdom of the Maya, still refuse to accept Christianity. Also, the concept of the precious stones is not preserved among the contemporary Maya. These examples also suggest that the opinion and belief of the colonial Maya priests do not always represent those of all Maya.

Based on these arguments, the case of the Guatemalan Maya texts of the colonial period will be discussed. Yet, in the next chapter, the Christian view towards pagan religions will be made prior to my analysis of the Guatemalan Maya.

---

[133] For example, see Redfield et al. 1962:124-6. It is possible to consider that the dead Maya gods were considered a partner of the present Christian God and saints, though there is no solid and good historical evidence.

In the Christian mind, the death of the Lord means the gravest catastrophe such as a total destruction of the Universe. On the other hand, the death or defeat of the gods does not always have an equivalent significance among the Maya and other Native Americans. For example, *Quetzalcoatl* was said to be defeated and to be expelled by *Tezcatlipoca* at the end of the Toltec Empire, but worship of it was continued as one of principal ceremonies among the Aztec. Another example can be taken from the *Popol Vuh*, in which although the lord of *Xibalba* killed *Hunapu* and *Hunahau*, later they were reborn in order to take revenge. These examples show that the death and the defeat of a God of the Mesoamerican people does not always mean their permanent disappearance.

Chapter II: Christian Discovery of Pagan Religions[1]

Leopold - But in that War against the barbarians [the Native Americans], great damage and slaughters of people are committed, as usually happen, which constitute a reason to avoid the wars. The danger of that war is as serious as that of the civil wars among us.

Democrates - On the contrary, there is a difference between a right and pious war and an abominable civil war. In many cases, innocent people are involved in unjust war. On the contrary, [in war of justice,] those who [committing religious sin, such as worshiping pagan idols] are defeated and surrendered are [essentially] well deserved to receive punishment; so, when this difference becomes greater, the reason of dissuading to fight for constant principles, valiant, and right, will be less important.[2]

I: The Birth of Christianity and its Difference from the Pagan Religions

Julian also adds to these things, that Christ himself says that the law ought to be preserved; for his words are: 'Think not that I am come to destroy the law or the prophets: I am not come to destroy, but to fulfil [sic].' (Matt. V, 17.) And again, 'Whosoever, therefore, shall break one of these least commandments, and shall teach men so, he shall be called the least in the kingdom of heaven. (Matt. V, 19.) Since Christ has indubitably commanded punishments for those who break even one of those mandates, but you in sort break all of them, what mode of apology can you invent? For either Jesus speaks falsely, or you are not perfectly observers of the law. (The last Pagan Roman Emperor, Julian's accusation of the Christians)[3]

李路問事鬼神。子曰、未能事人、焉能事鬼。敢問死。曰、未知生、焉知死。 *Chi Lu asked about serving the spirits of the dead. The Master [Confucius] said, 'While you are not able to serve men, how can you serve their spirits?' Chi Lu added,*

---

[1] Dussel (1981) was quite useful to finalise this chapter.
[2] Cited from Sepúlveda 1984:27.
[3] Cited from Julian 361-3:94.

*'I venture to ask about death?' He was answered, 'While you do not know life, how
can you know about death?' (Confucian Analects* 500BC: Book 6, Chap.11-12)

*...while we are in the body, and while the soul is mingled with this mass of evil,
our desire will not be satisfied, and our desire is of the truth. For the body is a source
of endless trouble to us by reason of the mere requirement of food... when we have
the least possible concern or interest in the body, and are not saturated with the
bodily nature, but remain pure until the hour when God himself is pleased to release
us. And then the foolishness of the body will be cleared away and we shall be pure
and hold converse with other pure souls...*(Plato in the *Phaedo* [1871])

Although I am specialized neither in Christian studies[4] nor in ancient Roman
history, not only the history of confrontation between pagan religions and
Christianity, but also the typical character of Catholic Christianity since its
beginning must be summarized for comparative purposes. The 'Christianity'
chiefly discussed in this book is, of course, the Catholic Christianity of the
sixteenth century. The reason is clear. Although various sects of Christianity such
as Mormons and Protestants are now in Guatemala and other parts of the lands of
the Maya, Catholic remains the dominant sect and it has influenced almost all
aspects of the living Maya since the colonial era. Although issues related to Japan
discussed in the next chapter have to involve the views of the Gospel expressed by
Unitarians and Protestants, since these will be discussed in that chapter, they will
not be considered in this chapter.

The Spaniards of the colonial period were generally hostile towards
indigenous American religions. They considered them enemies of the Christian
God to be terminated as soon as possible, because the majority of the Spanish of the
sixteenth century had a fanatic Catholic Christian mind. Not only the brutal
conquistadors and nationalists, but also those who (such as José de Acosta, Fray
Toribio de Motolinia and Cieza de León) were sympathetic to the Native
Americans, often regarded the devastations given to the latter during the Spanish
conquest God's impartial punishment for the Native Americans' evil religious
practices (idolatry, human sacrifice etc.). After the military conquest of the New

---

[4] As a non-Christian writer, I have found MaGrath (2001) a particularly useful introduction to
numerous essential matters of Christianity.

World, therefore, the spiritual conquest to exterminate the remaining pagan cults became the main concern of Spain. However, it must be said that their strategy of the evangelization of the New World was much too careless. Before arguing this matter, the early history of Christianity will be discussed.

Christianity was initiated as a faction within Judaism, in order to complete the law given by his previous prophets, as Jesus said. Like Judaism, Christianity is often categorized as a theistic or theo-centric religion. Although rapidly changing today, Christianity was one of the most exclusive religions in the world for many centuries. It is true that the stance of Christians towards other religions, especially pagan religions, was denial from its beginning. As time passed, this hostility of Christianity toward paganism increased.

Christianity, as well as Islam and Judaism, are generally called monotheisms. It is true that Christianity also accepts the existence of holy divine spirits apart from their one God. Contrary to pagan religions having numerous gods apart from the supreme deity, all lesser divine powers are called angels by Christians. Also, although they are considered to be merely messengers of the Lord, they are sometimes mentioned as if each of them has a specific function, similar to a pagan god.[5] These Christian angels form a kind of pantheon of gods in the Christian doctrine. Therefore, it is not always correct to define these three religions as monotheistic. So how are they different from the majority of pagan religions?

While almost all pagan religions, including Maya ones, consider that there are numerous divine gods, who are an essence of nature, the Christians accept only one deity, who is invisible and does not have any physical representation. Therefore, according to Christian theology, God does not exist in nature.

Thus, Christianity can be called a religion of separatism from nature. As Christianity was created as a challenge to ancient pagan religions, all forms of paganism, including the ancient cults of classical Greece and Rome, were regarded as cults of evil spirits.

Therefore, it can be said that the history of Christianity is a history of a battle with pagan gods. While ancient Greek and Roman pagan religions tolerated people believing in another religion at the same time, Christianity required baptized people to have exclusive devotion to it. The Christians dismissed Roman deities as Satan. Because the Roman Emperor was at the same time the supreme priest of the Roman pagan religion, the birth of Jesus Christ and of Christianity meant the beginning of a challenge to the Emperor. Therefore, although the Roman pagan people may have initially welcomed this new religion as the birth of a 'new deity,' without much understanding of it, subsequent violent persecutions of Christianity by the Empire was a natural course.[6] Nevertheless, Christianity rapidly attracted the people. This is generally explained as follows: it admitted all ranks and both sexes equally, contrary to existing pagan religions.

In 1920, Edward Carpenter summarized the difference between the ancient pagan religions, including the Aztec example, and the Christian religion, as follows:

> ... a certain ascetic attitude towards sex was one of the most salient marks of the Christian Church; and that whereas most of the pagan cults (though occasionally favoring frightful austerities and cruel sacrifices) did on the whole rejoice in pleasure and the world of the senses, Christianity--following largely on Judaism--displayed a tendency towards renunciation of the world and the flesh, and a withdrawal into the inner and more spiritual regions of the mind. The same tendency may be traced in the Egyptian and Phrygian cults of that period.... Another characteristic of Christianity which is also very fine in its way but has its limits of utility, has been its insistence on 'morality.' Some modern writers indeed have gone so far--forgetting, I suppose, the Stoics--as to claim that Christianity's chief mark is its high morality, and that the pagans generally were quite wanting in the moral sense! This, of course, is a profound mistake. I should say that, in the true sense of the word, the early and tribal peoples have been much more 'moral' as a rule--that is, ready as individuals to pay respect to the needs of the community--than the later and more civilized societies. But the mistake

---

[5] For example, see The *New Testament*: Revelation 7:1. In that, four angels are mentioned as if they are controlling the wind as independent gods.

[6] Fox (1986) well summarizes the history of the Christian victory over the pagan in the Roman Empire. It is interesting that Porphyry, who is a Neo-Platonist and was known as a noted enemy of Christianity in the second and third centuries, referred to Jesus Christ as an exceedingly pious man.(Augustine 426: Book XIX, Chap.23, p.955)

> *arises from the different interpretations of the word; for whereas all the pagan religions insisted very strongly on the just-mentioned kind of morality, which we should call civic duty to one's neighbor, the Christian made morality to consist more especially in a mans duty to God. It became with them a private affair between a mans self and-God, rather than a public affair; and thus led in the end to a very obnoxious and quite pharisaic kind of morality, whose chief inspiration was not the helping of one's fellow-man but the saving of one's own soul.*[7]

Although the Maya religions were not included in his analysis, I believe that his summary can largely be applied to the difference between the Maya religions and Christianity.

The Christian religion talks about the existence of the human as sin.[8] The first human beings, Adam and Eve, were the first sinners (they ate apples against the order of the Lord), because of Eve's carnal desire caused by the flesh. According to this belief, as Adam and Eve were banished from Eden, it is clear that Christianity defined the earth as a place of exile. In addition, it can be said that Christianity defined the physical world as a representation of sin. While the Christian makes life a sin and makes death a release from sin, the Chinese Confucianists argue that both should be treated homogeneously. This is one of the important differences between Christianity and pagan religions. Thus, the main purpose of worshipping the Christian God within Christianity theory is to ask him for forgiveness for the original sin committed by Adam and Eve. Only the Christian God can make human salvation possible. Although this kind of interpretation of the Gospel was strongly opposed by Pelagius (c354-418?), who stressed the essential goodness of human nature and the freedom of the human will, his party did not last for long, and was eventually condemned. Since then, this view has been proposed repeatedly with no substantial success.[9]

In Maya religions, on the other hand, the *Popol Vuh* tells us of the destruction of the previous three humans, because of their imperfections. It may be suggested that the human in Maya belief is a trial product of the gods. This Maya concept is

---

[7] Carpenter 1920:198-199.
[8] The *New Testament*: Roma 3:10, 23.

obviously different from the 'sinning human' of Christianity. For that reason, although human beings are treated as creatures of gods, due to a lack of the notion of sin, the position of the human is far better than in Christianity. That is, the relationship between gods and humans in Maya religions is to show a piety to gods with offerings, the so-called 'give and take.' Although it is not a precise description of the nature of Maya religions, it may be suggested that Maya divinities are closer to 'transcendent partners of the human being, an irregular form of harmonized dualism,' with the Christian God being a stern ruler of the human being and of nature.

In various pagan religions, in general, it is rare to see a concept of sin and salvation. The people worship their pagan gods to ask for certain benefits and express their thankfulness. Although the Tolupan of Honduras define themselves as 'Children of Death,'[10] this 'death' only signifies a natural phenomenon of their mortal status and their fear of epidemics and disasters within nature.[11] The term 'Children of Death' of the Tolupan does not equate with the Christian concept of 'the sinning human.'

Christianity divides the human being into body and spirit much more clearly than Maya religions do. Contrary to Maya religions, the Gospel says that the human body is considered to be opposing God.[12] In the theory of dualistic religions, such as those of the Maya, a life is created by an interaction between the flesh and the spirit. On the other hand, the *New Testament* says; '*The Spirit is the life-giver; the flesh does not benefit at all.*'[13] This idea in Christianity is not based on the Greek philosophers. The Platonist's idea of the superiority of Spirit over carnal materials is merely a discussion of the physical issue that although the flesh disappears after death, the soul does not do so. On the other hand, in the Gospels, it is considered that the Soul is morally corrupted by the flesh.

---

[9] Also see Deloria 1994:80-81.
[10] Chapman 1992:275-6.
[11] See Chapman 1992:111-2.
[12] The *New Testament*: John 6:63, Roma 8.
[13] Cited from the *New Testament*: John 6:63.

109

According to the *New Testament*, humans are easily corrupted, in spite of existence of the Law of Moses. The reason explained is that although the Law is holy, just and right, so that it is agreed within the human innermost mind, it is spiritual so that the flesh of the human always opposes spiritually good Law.[14] There are numerous examples that the souls of the human were easily spoiled by worldly and carnal desires and materialized cultures, in spite of an excellent Law given by God through prophets like Moses. Therefore, Jesus may have considered that because any physical thing can easily corrupt a good soul, stressing a separation of the soul from any other material thing within nature is necessary for the salvation of human beings. Additionally, in this logic, He may also have concluded that any spirit existing within a physical thing, such as an idol, which had often been over-decorated by the mentally corrupted priests and rulers in order to deceive the people, cannot avoid being corrupted, and a better soul cannot co-exist in such a material. It is also evident that the Supreme God, who must be perfect in every aspect, cannot live in nature. Therefore, it was suggested that the Christian God does not have any substance.

The Saint Martyr Justin (c.100-165) later argued about the vagueness of the idols:

> And neither do we honour with many sacrifices and garlands of flowers such deities as men have formed and set in shrines and called gods; since we see that these are soulless and dead, and have not the form of God (for we do not consider that God has such a form as some say that they imitate to His honour), but have the names and forms of those wicked demons which have appeared. For why need we tell you who already know, into what forms the craftsmen, carving and cutting, casting and hammering, fashion the materials? And often out of vessels of dishonour, by merely changing the form, and making an image of the requisite shape, they make what they call a god; which we consider not only senseless, but to be even insulting to God, who, having ineffable glory and form, thus gets His name attached to things that are corruptible, and require constant service.[15]

---

[14] Roman 7:12-25.
[15] Cited from Justin, First Confession Chap.XVI., p.166.

A noted influential Christian theologian, St. Augustine (c.354-430), mentions in his attack against Roman pagan religion, the following:

> *But all these things, our adversaries say, have certain physical interpretations; that is, interpretations in term of natural phenomena – as if in this discussion we were seeking physics rather than theology, which is an account not of nature, but of God. For although the true God is God not by opinion but by nature, nonetheless all nature is not God. For although the true God is God not by opinion but by nature, nonetheless all nature is not God.*[16]

Consequently, in Christian philosophy, the human being and the nature in which they live is also treated as a corrupted world, inferior to the world of spirits. By this logic, the Christian God is considered the Lord = Ruler of his creatures. Apart from the one Lord, the existence of other divine spirits is accepted to be angels. Yet, it is considered that they are servants and messengers of the Christ, but not gods.

On the other hand, although the supreme pagan deity is generally believed to be the Creator of nature = the world (or an offspring of it) among pagan people, the function of such a supreme deity is usually to act as a mediator, adviser, administrator or partner with his creatures, rather than to be an absolute ruler. On the other hand, for the Maya, nature has not always been considered inferior to the spiritual world, because nature is not a sinful place. Rather, it is sometimes treated as a kind of residence of the gods, and thus the position of nature in Maya belief is far better.

In fact, as I have mentioned in the previous chapter, the invisible and non-physical Christian Lord is coupled with the visible and physical precious stone(s) in the colonial Maya religious text, the *Chilam Balam of Chumayel*. This suggests that contrary to Christian doctrine, the colonial Maya religious leaders regarded the Christian God, the leader of the spiritual world, as a harmonious partner of the physical substitutions. Thus, the Christian concept of denial of the physical world did not exist for the Maya. Although the term 'spirituality' has

---

[16] Augustine 426:Book VI, Chap.8, see *ibid.*:Book IV Chap.12, p.159-160.

widely been used to refer to Native American religions, divine things were not confined to spiritual power among the Maya.

The Christian doctrines emphasize the conflict within the spiritual world. They stress more the confrontation between Satan=Lucifer (evil) and the Christian God (good) than previous religions did. For example, although in the *Old Testament*, Satan is not regarded an adversary of God, Satan gradually became the main adversary in Christian thought.[17] Interestingly, in the Christian history, as the goodness of the Christian Lord became more emphasized, along with the rapid increase in the Christian population, the power of Satan increased at the same time. This example suggests a curious fact that although the Christians always tried to persuade belief in the one God of the universe, they have not managed to deny the validity of dualism.

> *Accordingly, while the belief in good spirits tended towards the formation of the doctrine of Monotheism, the belief in evil spirits led naturally to the acceptance of a single supreme evil deity, conceived as embodying all that is bad, destructive, and immoral.*[18]

This evil Satan is called the prince of this world, the great dragon, the old serpent, the prince of the devils, the prince of the energy of the air, the Antichrist.

Within the Christian world, Satan is theologically a single evil spirit, a former angel. According to Christian doctrine, Satan was originally created as one of the superior angels by the Christian God, and was named Lucifer. However, because he and other angels challenged the Christian God, He ordered the remaining faithful angels to expel the rebellious angels. This battle ended with a victory for God, and the rebellious angels fell into Hell, the underworld in which they continued intervening in the Christian God's affairs.

---

[17] For example, see Pagels 1995:39-62. Her book is one of the most readable summaries of the evolution of concept of Satan in the early Christian history.

[18] Carus 1900:1-2.

Yet, as I have mentioned before, the conflict between the Lord and Satan is not a main concern of the *New Testament* and the *Old Testament*.[19] Indeed, early Christians did not emphasize the horrible power of Satan. Among first-century Christian materials, reconciliation with Christianity's opponents is an important practice of the Christian.

The *Bible* says:

> You have heard that it was said, 'Love your neighbour and hate your enemy' But I say to you, Love your enemy and pray for your persecutors[20]

In theory, as an angel, Satan is inferior to the Lord, and thus the power of Satan in this present world should be negligible. Also, because the power of an angel as a creature of the Lord is so limited, Satan should not have a significant power over the human being. Based on these facts, it is suggested that with regard to almost all negative phenomena in the physical world, it can essentially be said that they were given as a punishment from the Lord due to man's original and everyday sin. The *New Testament* says that all creatures work together for good.[21] This suggests that Satan is also a good part of the universe, although he may be a troublemaker on some occasions. Nevertheless, after the Gospel was widely spread within the Roman Empire and it gained a position as a dominant religion, not only the chief of evil sprits, but also the Jews and all pagan deities began to be called Satan. A little later, the definition of the devil was argued through a broad interpretation. A theologian of the third century, for example, Origenis (Origen, c.185 - 254), wrote that the term Satan sometimes refers to anything opposing the Christian God and his flock.[22] Therefore, it can be suggested that as Christianity became a dominant philosophy of the Empire, the Christians became more intolerant of their opponents as vassals of Satan.[23]

---

[19] E.g. Pagels 1995:xvi.

[20] Mattew 5:43-44.

[21] Roman 8:28.

[22] Origenis 246~9?:Part II, Book 10, p.700-1, also see Pagels 1995: 135-141.

[23] See Pagels 1995:179-184.

Unlike God A of the Maya, the Satan of Christianity (for the later Christians) is never coupled with the Christian God or his angels to create a positive phenomenon. The *Bible* says, '*And the God of peace will shortly crush Satan under your feet.*'[24] It was repeatly argued that although Satan (or Lucifer) is a powerful immortal spiritual power, his ability is inferior to that of the Christian God.[25] Thus, because he is a mere prince of evil spirits (spirit is considered inferior to god in Christian theology), Satan is not regarded as an equivalent existence of the Christian God. He is always opposing the Christian God and his sole purpose is the negative influence on human beings.

Therefore, one of the important essences of Christian culture may be summarized as a denial of dualism, especially the positive and the negative principles. Although it is not greatly discussed in the *Bible*, St. Augustine's attack on Platonism clearly proves that dualism, one of the fundamentals of Greek and Roman philosophies, was considered merely a confused understanding of divine matters by the Roman Christians.[26]

St. Augustine wrote in his *City of God*, "*If anyone should employ two nurses for an infant, one to give nothing but food to him and the other nothing but drink, as the Roman employed two goddesses for this purpose, Educa and Potina, he would certainly seem to be foolish, and to be behaving like a comic actor in his own home.*"[27]

The above quotation proves that the early Christian did not consider dualism as a harmony, but a chaotic situation.

There is an exception. That is Jesus Christ. Because Christianity defines existence of the flesh as sin, the body of Jesus as human flesh became a serious problem. In the case of Jesus Christ, the coexistence of his spirit as God (positive) and his human body as sin (negative) is contradictory. In addition, that Jesus Christ

---

[24] Cited from *The New Testament* Roman 16, 20.
[25] Augustine 426: Book XII Chap.3, p.501-2.
[26] Augustine 426: Book VI Chap.9, p.257, Book IX, pp.359-389, see especially *ibid.*: Chap.23, pp.387-9.
[27] Cited from Augustine 426: Book VI Chap.257.

existed, as a physical existence, is inconsistent with the invisibility of God mentioned in the *Bible*. Furthermore, the insistence of the Christian on Christ as the son of God, suggests that Christianity denied its principle of monotheism and was taken as evidence of the fraud of Jesus. Pagan people, such as Celsus, attacked these points effectively.[28] Hence, a theory called the Trinity (regarding God, Jesus Christ, and the Holy Spirit as a single divinity) was invented in order to overcome these controversial issues. Consequently, while pagan idols were dismissed, the worship of the figure of the crucified Jesus Christ, who is paradoxically a part of the invisible Christian God, has been accepted to date. This 'contradictory' theory was poorly understood by the pagans, including the Chinese Christian converts of the sixteenth century.[29] In my country, apart from the Christians, the majority of the Japanese of today regard the figure of Jesus as an idol.

Like the Trinity, fragmented conceptual legacies of the dualism of the European pagan period still survive in the Western cultural concepts of today. However, a strong tendency to regard monotheism as best was generated in the Western mind. Because of that, intolerance of other religious beliefs, especially of paganism, became a core of Christian civilization. As the result, they have usually considered syncretism the equivalent of 'confusion'.

When we investigate any religious issues of Latin America and Asia during the sixteenth and seventeenth centuries, it must be noted that almost all contemporary Spanish and Portuguese commentators held a fanatical Christian view of the pagan. It is natural that those people whose mind was dominated by Christian philosophy were never able to understand any social and religious phenomena generated from the conceptual framework within the dualism of the Native Americans (or the Asians). Rather, they concluded that any concept based on dualism found in the New Worlds was evidence of lesser intellects among the Asians and the Native Americans.

---

[28] Celsus 178:VIII, p.103-5, Julian 361-3:47.
[29] Young 1983:67.

Contrary to Christianity, as I have repeatedly argued, Maya religions are based on dualism. In a sense, there are numerous 'contradictions' similar to the Trinity of Christianity within Maya doctrines. Even if one of the Maya deities is demonic, he must not be destroyed. Although it is true that the K'iche-Maya '*Bible,*' the *Popol Vuh,* also narrates a 'punishment' of positive Twin Gods given to the negative deities of *Xibalba,* this conflict should not be considered the same as the relationship between the Christian God and Satan. As I have argued, what the *Popol Vuh* tells us is merely chastisement given to *Xibalba* but not a total destruction of *Xibalba.* There is little evidence that the colonial Spaniards fully understood this concept. In the case of the relationship between Christianity and Maya, therefore, a consideration of this kind of harmonious dualism must be included.

Also, although a religion often signifies the whole universe in monotheistic cultures, this concept cannot always be applied to pagan cultures. Quite often, a pagan religion is a part of a cosmovision.

There is an interesting report by a US anthropologist, Christopher L. Chiappari. Although in orthodox religious studies, a religion is normally considered to consist of transcendence [often simply a god or goddess] of the human and nature,[30] the present-day Guatemalan Maya prefer the use of the term 'cosmovision' to 'religion'. According to the educated Maya, however, a religion, which is merely a part of the Maya cosmovision, involves the gods and the humans only.[31] By using this logic, the Maya justify having both Maya religions and Christianity at the same time.[32]

Although this idea may sound peculiar, this logic seems not to be a new concept created by the K'iche Maya of the twentieth century. Indeed, as I have discussed in the previous chapter, this logic was used in the *Books of Chilam Balam* by the colonial Yucatec Maya. As I argued there, the *Books of Chilam Balam of*

---

[30] Yao 1997:12-17.
[31] Chiappari 1999:124 note 9.
[32] Sanematu 2000: 241-8, Yamase 2002b:248-9.

Chumayel almost certainly tells us that Christian and Maya deities are a partner (or a subordinated part) of the precious stones, presumably the symbol of the Yucatec Maya universe.

Therefore, it is possible to conclude that this type of logic has universally existed in various Maya groups from antiquity. It may be suggested that the Maya manage to accommodate Christianity and traditional K'iche Maya religion into a single Maya cosmovision, which is sometimes called *K'abawil*. Although *K'abawil* was often considered to be referring to a god or idol, it is now regarded as something like the *Tao* of Taoism among certain parts of the K'iche Maya. In dualistic cultures, each of these religions interacts with another in certain situations. This concept is sometimes named *K'abawil*, and it may be called a K'iche Maya way of the Trinity (cosmos, Christianity, K'iche Maya religion). Thus, it can be said that *K'abawil* is a unitary notion of godhood. In this interpretation, a unitary notion of godhood consists of both the K'iche Maya religion and Christianity. Each of those two religions has its own unitary notion of godhood (in the latter, a unitary perception of the God and spirits). It may be argued that this conceptual framework was generated to avoid the conflicts between two entirely different religions. The case of the Maya is not a typical one within the dualistic world.

In the case of Asia, it can be said that an Asian version of 'the Trinity' is a co-existence of Confucianism, Buddhism, and a local native religion. For example, the Chinese have traditionally compromised three religions, Confucianism, Buddhism, and Taoism, as if each of them is equally important. That is, although there are three different types of religions, all of them are explaining one truth (in Chinese 三教一道 or 三教一帰). This concept seems to have been generated under the strong influence of the dualism concept of Taoism, although no solid evidence exists. When Buddhism was introduced in China, although the traditional Chinese gods must have been subordinated as supporting gods of the Buddha in the original Buddhist idea, this concept was rejected by Chinese dualism (likely of Taoism). Gods of any religion had to be equally treated. Consequently, the superiority of the

117

Buddha was not accepted, and Buddhism was integrated into a Chinese Trinity which comprised their cosmos. Almost the same ideology was proposed in Japan and Korea.[33] Almost the entire Western world of the sixteenth and seventeenth centuries (and today) observed this belief as chaotic. For example; a Portuguese Jesuit monk, Matteo Ricci (c.1552-1610), commented that this Chinese practice simply resulted in increasing the number of faithless people.[34] Another Portuguese Jesuit, Alvarado Semedo (c.1585-1658), wrote that the Chinese were attempting to fuse all three into one, without breaking any of the religious precepts of these three religions. He observed the Chinese religious mind and described it a mysterious behavior.[35] In the case of Japan, Alejandoro Valigano described the Japanese co-opting various religions as 'chaotic'.[36] In a sense, they were correct. The contemporary European did not notice that Buddhism in China was heavily Chinesed, as if it were a totally different religion from the original Buddhism, in some aspects. As a monotheistic religion, Christianity could not allow this practice.

On the other hand, as I have written before, the ironical fact is that the Trinity of Christianity is just as 'chaotic' for pagan people. As will be mentioned in the next chapter, Christianity was also included as a part of this Asian 'chaotic' Trinity. The Catholic Church of the sixteenth century never accepted this 'barbaric' version of the Trinity. However, when a new religion is received from another place, a certain localization of the original concept cannot be avoided. Christianity is no exception. It is noted that in the Roman era, a certain localization of the original Christianity was made to compromise with and to attract pagan converts. The increasing number of angels and over-decorated ornaments, paintings and Church buildings instead of idols are examples. Moreover, accusing the Jews, who have the Law of God, but not the Romans who were pagans, in Matthew, and a mysterious

---

[33] In Japan and China, the relationships among these three religions have not always been harmonious, nor have relationships among religious leaders of each religion. For example, Confucianism's hostility towards Buddhism was seen in both countries, although it was not aimed at abolishing Buddhism completely.
[34] Ricci 1982:lib.1, cap.10.
[35] Semedo 1562:cap.17.
[36] Valigano 1583:Cap.9, p.60.

118

exclusion of some Gospels, such as the *Gospel of Mary* and the *Gospel of Thomas* found on papyrus fragments in Egypt, from the *New Testament* might represent a Christian history of localizing the Gospel.[37]

Today, there is an interesting example of the Japanese version of 'the Trinity'. The majority of Japanese conventionally give a certain function to each of three religions, Shintoism, Buddhism, and Christianity.[38] They generally choose traditional rites of Shinto for annual celebrations, Buddhism for funerals and other rites associated with death, and Christianity for weddings and some 'fashionable' celebrations. According to the Buddhist calendar, many choose to marry at a 'Catholic or Protestant' church. It appears that these three different religions constitute a unified single godhood (or cosmovision) for the Japanese. The Christian Lord and angels have been integrated as members of the group of 800 million Japanese gods who maintain the Japanese cosmovision. Not surprisingly, the Japanese clearly understand each of these three teachings is different, and this Japanese 'chaotic' religious practice is poorly understood by the Westerner and the Muslim. The fact is that although the majority of the Japanese do not exactly know the meaning of Christian doctrines, such as the ban on worship of idols, they unconsciously believe that interactions among different religions will bring good fortune for them. For them, an important virtue, which each of these religions provides, is that the differences and contradictions found in their religious philosophy do not have significant implications. If I may mention my relatives at this point, my late aunt was a Catholic nun, and she maintained a respect for traditional Japanese religions at the same time. In general, the Japanese do not

---

[37] Pagels 1995:63-88. The *New Testament* was canonized about 200AD, almost two hundred years after the death of Jesus, and thus during that period, a possible movement to eliminate some Gospels containing unfavorable concepts for the leaders of early Christianity.

[38] Although Confucianism has traditionally been counted as one of the religious beliefs in Japan, it is now regarded as a classic philosophical moral teaching for the Samurai rather than as a religion by the majority of the Japanese. Although the influence from Confucianism is still very strong in the Japanese culture, an almost total lack of worship of Confucius within Japan culture may well support this view.

approve of a religion dismissing other religions or Japanese who devote their faith to only one type of religion.

In the feeling of the Chinese and Japanese, because every religion tries hard to improve the believer and seeks true virtue, then all rightly deserve honor. It is true that the Westerner, including Japanese Christians, have contemptuously called this Asian religious custom 'atheism' since the sixteenth century. However, in Western countries, this principle also functions as an important one. For example, the antimonopoly and free competition principle in business, which Westerners love, are theoretically the same as the religious thought of the Chinese. Do the Westerners believe that monopoly in the religious world is the best situation for improving human morality? What we are practicing is the theory of the dispersion investment in various religions. As a result, the total number of the registered population of each religion is more than 60 percent of the actual population in Japan.[39]

What the Japanese of today are practicing is essentially the same as the majority of the Maya of today. Nevertheless, the fact is that the former are virtually overlooked and the latter are accused. This differentiation has been, of course, generated by the difference in social status between the Japanese and the Maya.

The Christian rejection of the harmony between nature and the spirit resulted in stronger denial of idols as a physical representations of divine things than that of Judaism. What was the origin of the denial of idols in Christianity? Let us look at the *Old Testament*. The fourth of the Ten Commandments of Moses tells us;

> *You shall not make for yourself an idol, whether in the form of anything that is in heaven above, or that is on the earth beneath, or that is in the water under the earth. You shall not bow down to them or worship them; for I the LORD your God am a jealous God...*[40]

The initial purpose of denying idols by the prophet Moses may have been to eliminate the corruption of the pagan priests who cunningly used idols in order to

---

[39] Obara 1998:213.
[40] *Exodus* 20:4. cited from Metzger et al., 1995.

120

deceive the people. The *Old Testament* says that although the Ancient Babylonians believed that idols were living gods,[41] when Daniel revealed that the priests and their families used the idol of Bel to deceive the king, the king noticed the foolishness of idols.

The *Old Testament* certainly prohibits worshipping idols, and in Wisdom Chapter 14, idols are mentioned as the cause of evil, yet it does not refer to idols as Satan. The reasons for the banning of idols given in this source are: 1) God became jealous, 2) idols are merely soulless objects, so that worship of them is no more than ridiculous.

In the Christian religion, idols became more closely associated with Satan than in Judaism. As I have mentioned, although Jesus Christ said that he was also living bread, the Christians defined anything of the physical world (=flesh) as inferior and opposite in existence to the Spirit. Therefore, within Christianity, idols as physical things had to be more strongly dismissed than in Judaism.

The *New Testament* says;

> *Live by the Spirit, I say, and do not gratify the desires of the flesh. For what the flesh desires is opposed to the Spirit, and what the Spirit desires is opposed to the flesh; for these are opposed to each other, to prevent you from doing what you want. But if you are led by the Spirit, you are not subject to the law. Now the works of the flesh are obvious: fornication, impurity, licentiousness, idolatry, sorcery, enmities, strife, jealousy, anger, quarrels, dissensions, factions, envy, † drunkenness, carousing, and things like these. I am warning you, as I warned you before: those who do such things will not inherit the kingdom of God.[42]*

Also,

> *The rest of humankind, who were not killed by these plagues, did not repent of the works of their hands or give up worshiping demons and idols of gold and silver and bronze and stone and wood, which cannot see or hear or walk. And they did not repent of their murders or their sorceries or their fornication or their thefts.[43]*

---

[41] *The Bel and the Dragon* 3:1-21. in *ibid.*
[42] *Galatians* 5:16. cited from Metzger et al., 1995.
[43] *Revelation* 9:20. cited from Metzger et al., 1995.

From the above text cited from the *New Testament*, it appears that idols are rejected as non-spiritual objects, as in the *Old Testament*. It has been believed that the Lord is formless so that any figure of Him should not be made to avoid a misunderstanding of Him.

In the Christian belief, the one God lives as a spiritual being in Heaven only, but not in idols or any other substitution. Therefore, although the Christians often manifestly accepted spiritual powers existing in idols, they considered it a consequence of the fact that evil spirits used idols to deceive the people.

As a result, since any idol of pagan gods was considered a representation of Satan and his fellows within Christian doctrine, all pagan religions theoretically were enemies of Christianity.

Nevertheless, in the early period of Christianity, because the early Christians were a small religious party within the Roman Empire, the empire of pagan religions, it was obviously impossible for them to deny the whole of pagan religiousness.

As I have discussed, the early Christians integrated Platonism and Aristotle's work with the Christian theology. It is known that Platonism had a significant impact among the educated people in the Roman Empire. During the second century, Justin Martyr (c.100-165) and Clement of Alexandria (c.150-211~215?) were known as the defenders of Christianity against attacks from pagan religions. On this, it should be noted that they valued classical philosophy and the literature of pagan cultures.[44] For example, Plato often publicized his view against idols, which were coincident with Christian teaching.[45] Therefore, the early Christian Saints selected certain parts of Platonism in order to justify the Gospel theologically, and persuaded the pagans to be converted. This is called Christian Platonism, in which similarities of Platonist ideas to Christianity, such as the theory of the immortality

---

[44] *e.g.*, see Justin's the *Second Apology*.
[45] Justin (*The Hortatory Address to the Greeks*, Chap.XX, p.282) argues that Plato was hinted by the doctrine of Moses and other prophets while in Egypt.

122

of spirits, were often used to prove the rightness of the Gospel. By pointing out the fact that Platonists (and Neo-Platonists) recognized the supreme deity over all pagan gods, Justin argued that Platonists already supposed the existence of the Christian God. He used this to praise the classic Greek philosophers' efforts and intellect in approaching the Christian God. Justin and Clement only rejected polytheistic myths, cults, and ethical doctrines incompatible with Christian principles. Thus, although the idea presented by Platonists represented a quite close one to Christianity, they failed to recognize the true context of the Gospel, because the philosophers tried understanding the truth of godhood with imperfect human intellect and reason only. In short, the Roman pagan religion was treated as a false understanding of Christianity. Therefore, this suggests that the early Christians were much more tolerant of pagan cults than those of the later period were. This kind of idea can also be seen in the works of St. Augustine of the fifth century and other important Christians. In the case of Augustine, he even praised some ideas presented by a prominent anti-Christian philosopher, Porphyry, in order to prove the accuracy of Christian teachings.[46] He mentions in his *City of God*, '*He is the God whom Porphyry, the most learned of philosophers – though the bitterest enemy of the Christians – acknowledges to be a great god, even according to the oracles of those whom he supposes to be gods.*' [47]

St. Augustine did not regard the whole of ancient Roman and Greek religions as false. Rather, he incorporated them into Christianity. *Jupiter*, whose name etymologically corresponds to the Greek *Zeus*, was the supreme deity of the Roman religion. His purpose was to define ancient pagan religions as a necessary step in the human approach to Christianity. He argued that the Roman god, Jupiter, is the same deity as the Christian God, and all other Roman gods are merely parts of Jupiter.[48] This idea presented by the early Christian saints was inherited by the

---

[46] Augustine 426:Book XIX, chap.23, p.953-960.
[47] Cited from Augustine 426:Book XIX, chap.22, p.953.
[48] Augustine 426:Book IV, p.143-186.

Catholic friars of the sixteenth century, though Plato and Porphyry were replaced by Aristotle, the popular Greek philosopher of that time.

Under pagan religions' dominant climate, early Christians were forced to provide counter-attractions in order to gain popularity over polytheistic religions. This was done by incorporating pagan religious elements within Christianity.

One noted example might be the date of Christmas, commemorating the birth of Jesus Christ. In spite of the fact that in the eastern part of the Roman Empire, January 6, was originally celebrated as Christmas Day, December 25 was gradually accepted as the day of Christmas during the fourth century. Although the reason for this change remains uncertain, it is generally thought that early Christians wanted the date of Christmas to correspond with that of the pagan Roman festival celebrating the 'birthday of the unconquered sun' (the day of the winter solstice). In this way, early Christians were often forced to make a compromise with old Roman and Greek pagan religious cults. As will be mentioned in this book, the colonial Maya and Nahuatl people later reversed what the ancient Christians practiced in the Roman era; they tried to make the date of their traditional festivals correspond with those of Christianity.

Moreover, in spite of the insistence of a single Christian God, the Christian religion increased the number of angels and saints as did pagan pantheons. Unlike old pagan religions, the early Christian did not give the female any religious role. Therefore, as one of the counter-attractions, the cult of the Virgin Mary was soon produced by the Church to provide a divine female within Christianity. Additionally, by establishing an organization of convents for females, Christianity offered a place for women who became nuns in clerical society. Although pagan idols were removed, numerous images of saints were painted. Although those images were not considered physical alternatives to pagan idols, it is true that creating those images was a kind of compensation for lost idols. In addition, numerous figures of the crucified Jesus Christ have been used. Therefore, it is suggested that the early evolution of Christianity is a history of the Christian adaptation of selected pagan elements. In spite of the fact that Jesus probably defined the flesh as sin in order to make people understand, 'A simple life which is not blinded by love of gain caused by carnal desire, is the unique path to happy life,' the paradox is that the Christians began to build shrines for the corpses of the Christian saints, and their shrines were becoming packed with works of art, as in the pagan temples of the past.

There is no doubt that the sixteenth century's Catholic friars kept the past mythic success of converting the Roman Empire in their mind. However, as I have mentioned, the spiritual conquest of the Romans required of Christianity many adaptations to the old pagan religious elements.

After the collapse of the Western Roman Empire, the triumph of the past spiritual conquest of the Roman Empire was greatly embroidered with later invented myths during the medieval period in Europe. During the medieval period, it was often fanatically imagined that after the Roman Emperor, Constantine I (also known as Constantine, the Great: ruled c.312-337) chose Christianity as the state religion, except for a short period of setback, Christianity was quickly spread within the empire and pagan religions promptly disappeared.

In the sixteenth century, an Englishman, John Fox (or Foxe c.1517-1587), wrote his famous book, the *Book of Martyrs* (the original title is the *Actes and Monuments of these Latter and Perillous Dayes*), in which he says;

> *Thus Constantine, sufficiently appointed with strength of men but especially with strength of God, entered his journey coming towards Italy, which was about the last year of the persecution, A.D. 313. Maxentius, understanding of the coming of Constantine, and trusting more to his devilish art of magic than to the good will of his subjects, which he little deserved, durst not show himself out of the city, nor encounter him in the open field, but with privy garrisons laid wait for him by the way in sundry straits, as he should come; with whom Constantine had divers skirmishes, and by the power of the Lord did ever vanquish them and put them to flight.*
>
> *Notwithstanding, Constantine yet was in no great comfort, but in great care and dread in his mind (approaching now near unto Rome) for the magical charms and sorceries of Maxentius, wherewith he had vanquished before Severus, sent by Galerius against him.... Constantine, in his journey drawing toward the city, and casting up his eyes many times to heaven, in the*

> *south part, about the going down of the sun, saw a great brightness in heaven, appearing in the similitude of a cross, giving this inscription, In hoc vince, that is, 'In this overcome.'*
>
> *...Constantine himself often times reports, and also to swear this to be true and certain, which he did see with his own eyes in heaven, and also his soldiers about him. At the sight whereof when he was greatly astonished, and consulting with his men upon the meaning thereof, behold, in the night season in his sleep, Christ appeared to him with the sign of the same cross which he had seen before, bidding him to make the figuration thereof, and to carry it in his wars before him, and so should we have the victory.*
>
> *Constantine so established the peace of the Church that for the space of a thousand years we read of no set persecution against the Christians, unto the time of John Wickliffe.*[49]

However, the real fact is different. One apparent error of Fox is, for example, that the persecution of Christianity was continued even after 313AD. It is true that Constantine I had stressed himself to be the servant of the God.[50] Yet, although there is no doubt of Constantine I's devotion to Christianity, it must be noted that until just before his death, he remained *Maximinus Pontifice* (the supreme pagan priest), according to the empire's tradition. In fact, he continued to participate in some important pagan practices, especially of the sun god. Some argue that because the Christian population was still small in number at this time, it was also necessary for the emperor to compromise with the pagan people who remained the majority of his people.[51] Even if such opinions are fully taken into account, as Ostrogorsky points out, it would have seemed strange to call Constantine I the first Christian Emperor of the Roman Empire.[52] For example, the *Against the Christian* of Porphyry (a Neo-Platonist, a fierce critic of Christianity in the Roman Empire, c.234-305), was condemned to be burned in 448AD. It was more than one hundred years later than the death of Constantine I. This may well prove the continuous tolerance of traditional pagan religions in the Roman Empire. It is true that later writers mythically overstated Constantine's religious zeal toward Christianity.

---

[49] Fox ca.1560 Chap. I.
[50] For the relationships between Constantine I and Christianity, see Fox 1986:609-662.
[51] Fox 1986:657-8, Marrou 1980:34-8.
[52] Ostrogorsky 1957:43.

Since the ninth century, the Roman Catholics have claimed that Constantine I donated half his empire to the Catholic Pope. The *DONATIO CONSTANTINI* (*Donation of Constantine*) is a Latin document that discusses the theoretical donation by the Emperor Constantine I to Pope Sylvester I (c.314-335) and his successors of spiritual domination over the other great bishops and over all matters of faith and worship, as well as temporal dominion over the entire Western Roman Empire. It was claimed that the gift was motivated by Constantine I's supposed appreciation to Sylvester for converting him to Christianity.

It seems true that this document was forged in order to legally claim the independent power of the Pope from the strong control of the remaining proper Roman authority, the Byzantine emperor, who had lost virtually all capability of supplying military aid to Rome by that time. This faked text also helped create a victorious feeling, 'the great success of the spiritual conquest of the Roman' among the West Europeans. In any case, it was considered genuine by many, including enemies of the papal claims to power throughout the European Middle Ages.

However, the fact is different. Such a myth was invented well after the seventh century. Later historians exaggerated Constantine I's devotion to Christianity. It must be noted that Constantine I merely stated that Christianity was one of the state's favorite religions, and he tolerated all other religions at the same time. In addition, the majority of the members of the Roman senate continued to be pagan believers, and the Pope continued to be treated as a vassal by the Roman Emperor, and later by the Byzantine Emperor. The successor of Constantine I, Julian (c.361-3) was known as an apostate, and practiced persecution of the Christians in his efforts to restore Hellenistic pagan cults within the empire. This also suggests that the power of the pagan elite was considerable in the Europe of the late fourth century.

Although the official view of Catholics has tended to minimize the effects of this emperor, it should not be overlooked that the Roman Empire was still largely dominated by pagan people. Even in the later period, there was a strong belief that the Roman emperor was still the unique lord of the world, and that he was directly chosen by gods (later by the Christian God) or the Roman citizens, but not by the Pope. Justinian (Byzantine emperor: reigned c.527-565) is a good example. He was certainly a devotee of Christianity and he is the first Roman emperor to completely root out paganism. For him, the victory of Christianity was a sacred mission of the Roman Empire. Yet, this emperor who re-conquered Italy and numerous lands belonging to the former Western Roman Empire in order to revive the Ancient Roman Empire, did not recognize the Pope as the lord of the Spiritual World at all. The fact is that Justinian intervened in every aspect of ecclesiastical matters of Rome as a person entrusted by the Christian God. The final judgment on any Christian rites also rested with him. These facts clearly contradict the existence of *DONATIO CONSTANTINI*, which claims the independent power of the Pope from the Roman Emperor.

Now, *DONATIO CONSTANTINI* is considered a fake, and presumably written in Germany of the late eighth century. This document was first proved a counterfeit by an Italian humanist, Lorenzo Valla (c.1407-1457), in 1440, and his book was published in Germany in 1517, though a controversy lasted until the eighteenth century.[53] Although Valla's attack on the myth of Constantine I was used by the Protestants in Germany to oppose the Pope, therefore, the sixteenth century's Catholic people were still mentally dominated by the myth of the 'miraculous and dramatically immediate conversion of the Roman Empire into Christianity.'

Although a noted professor of Salamanca University, Francisco de Vitoria, referred to *Donation Constantini*, as '*if there was such a thing*'[54] in his lectures, he does not absolutely deny its authenticity. The great Spanish humanist Bartolomé de Las Casa's book provides us evidence that Constantine the Great's exaggerated zeal to Christianity was still dominant in the sixteenth-century Spanish mind.

Let us look at a part of Las Casas's '*Apologia:*'

---

[53] See Britannica 1999: Valla, Lorenzo.
[54] Vitoria 1989:85.

> *...Constantine the great* [Constantine I] *waged wars on unbeliever in*
> *order that, once they had been subjected his rule, he might remove idolatry*
> *and faith might be introduced more freely...The Church History says that*
> *Constantine was happier about the conversion of this nation than he would*
> *have been had the great Roman Empire been enlarged by the addition of new*
> *kingdoms and empire.*[55]

It is obvious that the historical fact, Constantine I's tolerance of all religions during his time, seems to have been completely ignored by Las Casas.

Also, the myth of Constantine I can be observed in the work of Las Casas' enemy.

> ...in short, provided that it is possible, all of the impediments and the
> worship of the idols will disappear, and the pious and justifiable law of the
> Emperor Constantine [I] against the pagan and the idolaters will be
> renewed.[56]

It is true that the spiritual conquest of the Roman Empire succeeded steadily, with minor setbacks, after Constantine I, and it became a core part of the Roman Empire. Yet, it must be pointed out that its progress was very slow.

Within the Christian doctrine, pagan religions are defined as works of the Devil, and thus worshipping idols is considered a sin. Therefore, pressure against paganism within the empire was gradually increasing in the fourth century. The Roman Emperor, Theodosius I (reigned c.379-395), abolished the title of *Pontifex Maximus* as a Roman emperor, and made orthodox Christianity an ingredient of good citizenship in the empire. Under the rule of Theodosius I, many pagan temples were closed or even destroyed. However, in general, even during the reign of Theodosius I, pagan religions were tolerated in many Roman imperial provinces. For example, the school of the Neo-Platonists continued their teaching in Athens, because of Theodosius I's hesitation in destroying such an admirable classical academy. Moreover, the Roman Senate was still a place of pagan people. Although the political power of the Senate of the Roman Empire had decreased considerably

---

[55] Cited from Las Casas 1992:Cap.34, p,279-81.
[56] Sepúlveda 1984:84-5. My translation.

129

by the late fourth century, the members still openly opposed the Christianization of the empire in 382, 384, 389, 392, 402, and 403AD.[57] The pagans only gradually became Christians.

Even in 410, pagan people still had certain influence within the empire. It is known that in 413, St. Augustine began to write his *City of God against the Pagans*[58] in order to answer the allegation raised by the pagans that the introduction of Christianity was responsible for the sack of Rome in 410AD. The end of Greek paganism took place by order of the Byzantine Emperor, Justinian, in 529, almost two centuries after Constantine I's approval of the Gospel.

Another example can be taken from Egypt. The ancient Roman Republic subjugated ancient Egypt. As the Romans considered ancient Egyptian pagan deities to be an obstacle to their domination, shrines of Egyptian gods were placed under direct control of the Roman Empire and the Romans paid for their maintenance. Even after Christianity became the favorite state religion of the Roman Empire in 313AD, the empire's support to ancient Egyptian pagan religions continued and Theodosius I continued supporting them.

Consequently, until a Byzantine Emperor, Justinian, decided to end imperial financial support for pagan temples, Egyptian pagans were largely unmolested and the imperial government paid their sustenance. Even after this period, the persistence of pagan religions in Egypt was frequently reported. By now, it is clear that the Roman Empire took great care in abolishing ancient indigenous religious beliefs in its subordinated lands.

Yet, as I have discussed, this story was somehow forgotten by the church-related people of the sixteenth century, due to later exaggerations of the success of the spiritual conquest of the Romans. It is not difficult to suppose that by reading the mythically-fabricated history of early Christianity, the Spanish friars expected too much from their evangelic activities in the New World. However, it must be noted that this myth still survives in the minds of today's Christians. In

---

[57] Marrou 1980:140-5.

130

1981, for example, Enrique Dussel, an Argentine and noted historian (later he became a Mexican), wrote: '*A few centuries after the beginning of Christianity, the whole of the Roman Empire had been Christianized.*'[59] The fact is that even this admirable historian retained a biased view generated long ago.

II: The Spanish Spiritual Conquest of the New World[60]

The Chinese Scholar says: The things in this world are many and dissimilar, and, in my humble view, they cannot emerge from a single source any more than can the rivers and streams, the sources of which are located in a variety of different place. Now, however, you assert that there is only one Lord of Heaven. Will you kindly give me reason for this' (Matteo Ricci)[61]

You [the Christians] *say, 'The immortal angels stand before God, those who are not subject to human passion, and these we speak of as gods because they are near the godhead.' Why do we argue about names? ... Whether one addresses these divine being as gods or angels matters very little, since their nature remains the same.* (Porphyry, the prominent pagan critic of Christianity in the Roman Empire)[62]

As the Spanish Crown justified the conquest of the Americas in the sixteenth century because of the Papal donation, the conversion of the indigenous inhabitants of newly discovered lands was a duty. Numerous pagan religions found in the Americas proved that the Native Americans had been under the domination of Satan. By converting them to Christianity and saving them from Satan, therefore, Spanish rule was theoretically justified. Tomas Lopez Medel, a Spaniard of the sixteenth century who acted as an *Oidor* in Guatemala, wrote about the religions of the Maya and the Aztec, as follows:

Where neither God is, nor dwells, all good luck and every reason and justice, and the ultimate and the end of all the evils that can come to a nation, and people is without the news of, and is taken away from the true God. The

---

[58] Augustine 426.
[59] Cited from Dussel 1981:296.
[60] Based on Yamase (2005:38-62, 248-270), this part is written as an expanded version. On this issue, numerous publications have appeared. While León-Portilla (1990), Ricard (1966) and Hanke (1965) remain essential readings, I have found following as useful for this volume; Doverger (1993), Frost (1993) and Marzal (1993), Greenblatt (1993), Gutiérrez (1993).
[61] Cited from Ricci 1985:86-87.
[62] Cited from Porphyry 1994:84.

emulator of the works of God and the father of the lie and the principle and entrance of all ills, the devil, just as he put all his study and care in taking man away from the road of God and deceiving and blinding the peoples with all false religions...They, without excepting any nation, in thousand of kinds of abominable idolatries...

The island Indian worshipped the devil and were well subjected...In the New Kingdom was flower of all the superstition and idolatry, and I pray God that it may not be today, ... In Mexico and Yucatan and Guatemala and in all those provinces in that region, idolatry was utmost and the devil was well serviced at the expense of these peoples. ... They were in all parts of Mexico and in those neighboring provinces, the sacrifices of gold and silver and of the fruits which they collected... also they killed even men alive in large numbers, and very usually blood was taken from the men of their own members.[63]

The Spaniards (and the other Europeans) of that period generally considered the existence of the pagan deities a challenge to the Christian Lord. Those pagan deities were called Satan and were considered to destroy the good order established by the Lord.

It was often very difficult for the Maya to forget their old deities, even after they were converted. It was a natural reaction when a person was forced to be a Christian. Since Christianity is monotheistic, however, it was assumed that surviving pagan traditions among the Native Americans after their conversion were a result of the deception of Satan. An example from Peru: Las Casas argued that because pagan gods [of course, he called them 'devils'] initially refused to speak to the people who were converted to Christianity, though they found such tactics meaningless, they ordered the people to worship both Christianity and them.[64]

Since the Catholic Church regarded pagan religions as the teachings of Satan, their termination was an important task. However, perhaps, experience from conversion of the remaining Muslim population after the *Reconquista* of the Iberian Peninsula, led the Spanish Crown evidently to undestand that completing evangelization in Spanish America would take a long time.

It is known that the Spanish Crown never permitted the publication of a famous work of Juan Ginés de Sepúlveda, a noted Spanish scholar of the sixteenth

---

[63] Translated from Lopez Medel 1990:326-7.
[64] Las Casas 1992:libro2, part2, chap2.

century, the *Demócrates Segundo*. This was in spite of the fact that he justified the Spanish conquest on the basis of the continuous practice of several sins, such as worshipping idols and human sacrifices in the Americas.[65] This was because abuse of the Native Americans by the Spanish colonists who followed the views of Sepúlveda reached its climax in that time. It was known that the Inca Emperor, Manco Inca, raised his '*reconquista* of Peru.' His rebellion caused serious disorder in Peru.

Some colonial documents of the Spanish crown suggest that the Spanish crown understood that harsh conversion and punishment of the indigenous people of the Americas would not bring an effective result.[66] It is clear that practice of unnecessary violations against the native population had caused social instability in the new colonies and that their rebellion, which would lead to destruction of the native population, had to be avoided. Since the Spanish crown never intended to make the new colonies a source of supply for Spain, the Native Americans were necessary as labor.

However, the majority of missionaries engaged in the conversion project did not understand the intention of the Spanish crown, though it was partly because the crown did not issue a law banning the inquisition of the Native Americans until 1571.[67] The early Spaniards did not remember the historical process of the spiritual conquest of the Roman Empire. Christians of the sixteenth century had numerous advantages over pagan states, such as military and technological power. In fact, two powerful states of the Americas, the Aztec and the Inca, were conquered within a short period, though it is now believed that the Spanish military advantage was not the main factor in the conquest.

Since the friars observed a certain semantic purity, moreover, they thought that pagan religions practiced in the Americas were evidence of sin, and people's souls could not be saved from evil spirits if they did not spread Christianity. Unlike the

---

[65] Sepúlveda 1984.
[66] See *Proceso inquisitorial del cacique...*(1980:XII-XIII). Kobayashi 1995:134-5, García Icazbalceta 1947:3, 172-3.

early Christians in the Roman Empire, therefore, the Spaniards did not see any necessity to adjust Christianity to indigenous American pagan religious traditions. For them, no compromise with pagan religion should be made, because it meant a defeat of the Christian God by Satan, and thus the aim of evangelization of the Americas was to introduce an exact copy of European Catholic Christianity.

However, forced conversion is not allowed in Christianity. The *Bible* never orders the Christians to punish pagan people. It says:

> *So I write you now that if a pretended brother is immoral or greedy or idolatrous or abusive or drinker or a robber, you must not associate with him, nor even eat with one of that type. What business of mine is it to judge outsiders? Do you not have those within the church to judge? But outsiders God will judge. Expel that wicked person from your own company.*[68]

The *Bible* apparently mentions that only the Christian God can punish those who have committed sins. In spite of this, the missionaries tended to use forced conversions. In Spanish America of the sixteenth century, the Franciscans had almost a monopoly. The Franciscans of that period had a solid notion that the day of Last Judgment was approaching, and that if the Native Americans were not quickly converted to Christianity before that day, Satan would take many souls. Therefore, while insisting on the necessity of defending the Native American, the Franciscan evangelization tended to be *en masse* without proper instruction, and in some cases, they even justified the mistreatment and slaughter of indigenous peoples.

During the Spanish conquest of the Aztecs, it is well known that Hernán Cortés massacred the citizens of Cholula before he went to the Aztec capital. It is recorded that one of the first twelve Franciscans in Mexico, Fray Toribio de Motolinia (Benavente) (c.1500?-1569), later told Bernal Díaz del Castillo, a former foot soldier of Hernán Cortés, that the slaughter of Cholula was a great event, because the Mexican people were entrapped by fear and the subsequent conquest was made easy. This Franciscan priest appears to have considered that, however atrocious

---

[67] Greenleaf 1988: 92-3.
[68] *New Testaments* Corinthians 6, 11-13.

events may have been, so long as Christianity was developed and accepted among the Mexicans, everything was justified.

> *...que fueron los primeros frailes que Su Majestad envió esta Nueva España, después de ganado México, según adelante diré, fueron a Cholula para saber e inquirir cómo y de qué manera paso aquel castigo, y por qué causa, y la pesquisa que hicieron fué con los mismos papas y viejos de aquella ciudad, y después de bien informados de ellos mismos, hallaron ser ni más ni menos que en esta relación escribo, y no como lo dice el obispo. Y si por ventura no se hiciera aquel castigo, nuestras vidas estaban en mucho peligro, según los escuadrones y capitanías que tenían de guerreros mexicanos y de Cholula, y albarradas y pertrechos, Y que si allí por nuestra desdicha nos mataran, esta Nueva España no se ganara tan presto ni se atreviera [a] venir otra armada, y ya que viniese estuvieran siempre en sus idolatrías. Yo he oído decir a un fraile francisco de buena vida, que se decía fray Toribio Motolinía, que si se pudiera excusar aquel castigo y ellos dieran causa a que se hiciese, que mejor fuera; mas ya que se hizo, que fué bueno para que todos los indios de las provincias de la Nueva España viesen y conociesen que aquellos ídolos y todos los demás son malos y mentirosos; y que viendo lo que les había prometido salió al revés, y que perdieron la devoción que antes tenían con ellos, y que desde allí en adelante no les sacrificaban ni venían como en romería de otras partes como solían y desde entonces no curaron de él y le quitaron del alto cu donde estaba, o le escondieron o quebraron, que no pareció más, y en su lugar habían puesto otro ídolo. Dejémoslo ya, y diré lo que mis adelante hicimos.* (they were the first [twelve] friars whom His Majesty sent to this New Spain, after Mexico was gained, as I will mention later, they went to Cholula to know and to inquire how and of which way that punishment was done, and for that reason, and the search made, was with the same Papa [=pagan priest of Cholula] and old men of that city. After they were well informed, they found the about the same in this relation which I write, and not as in what the bishop [Bartolomé de Las Casas] says[69], and if that punishment was not unexpectedly made, our lives would have been in much danger, as the swarms and captains had Mexican and Cholula warriors, and earthworks and equipment. If there we are misfortunately killed, neither this New Spain would not have been gained so quickly nor dared another Navy to come. They would always be idolatrous as they were.
> I have heard that a good Franciscan friar, Fray Toribio Motolinia, said, if that punishment [that slaughter] could be avoided and they [=the inhabitants of Cholula] [would not] have given the cause of what was done, there is nothing like this. But it was already done. It was good, because all the Indians of the provinces of New Spain saw and knew that those idols and all the others are bad and deceitful. They saw what the idols promised, led them to misfortune. They lost the devotion that they had with them before, and since then neither did they offer sacrifice to them nor they came to make a pilgrimage from other parts [of Mexico] as they used to do. Since then they

---

[69] See Las Casas 1981.

did not care for that idol and they cleared of it from the high *cu* [=temple] where it was. Whether they hid it or broke it, it is not seen. In its place, they have put another idol. We now leave this story, and I will mention what we did before.)[70]

It must be noted that one of the Franciscan friar's logical arguments used to justify such harsh evangelization in the Americas was amazingly similar to a work written by Juan Ginés Sepúlveda, an extreme Spanish nationalist of the sixteenth century. He is known for his work, the *Demócrates Segundo*.[71] Although this work was banned and not published, it was widely circulated in the form of handwritten manuscripts among the Spanish nationalists, and greatly influenced their ideology:

> (**Leopold.** – According to this, do you think that the pagans must be forced to receive the faith, in spite of the protest [against any forced conversion of pagan people] of Saint Augustine, whose testimony is mentioned before? **Democrates.** – If I believed so, I may confirm my opinion with great authorities. In truth, if it could be made so, I would think and support myself that this was the greater obligation of the charity, because 'What is greater benefit which we can do to an unfaithful man, than the faith of Christ? Yet, I think it is not acceptable that as I have said before, without the will [to be a Christian], there is no place for the faith, thus conversion cannot be forced. According to the testimony of Saint Augustine and great theologians, baptizing persons against their will, or their children who have not reached the age to understand the reason, and usually follows the will of their parents in most part, is vain and sometimes a pernicious work. By this, I do not insist that those who are unwilling [to accept Christianity], must be baptized, but, inasmuch as possible, we take them aside from the precipice, even against their will, we have to teach the truth to those who walk an a nomadic path, by means of pious warnings and evangelical predication.[72]

In spite of the fact that all theologians had been in denial of the use of violence against those who committed religious sins in Christianity, Sepúlveda encouraged

[70] The Spanish text in Díaz del Castillo 1977:Cap LXXXIII, 249. My English translation. As the reliability of Díaz del Castillo has often been criticized, the above quote may not be true. In fact, Toribio Motolinia always criticized the cruelties of the Spaniards in Peru (Motolinia 1987: Lib.III, Cap.XI). However, as this Franciscan priest was personally impressed with Hernán Cortés and was critical of the activities of Las Casas who had also severely attacked Hernán Cortés, it is likely that he tried to minimize the negative consequence of the Conquest of Mexico caused by Cortés. See Motolinia 1555.
[71] Sepúlveda 1984.
[72] My translation of the Spanish text (translated from the original Latin text by Angel Losada) cited from Sepúlveda 1984:65.

certain uses of violence, including military action on the grounds of justice in the evangelization of Christianity.

However, the *New Testament* and other writings of the saints never order the punishment of the pagan. Use of violence against the pagan or forced conversion was not practiced by the early Christians but was by the early Muslims.[73] Therefore, although torture of the remaining pagans was still openly practiced in Europe at this time, it may be suggested that this argument was about early Islam.

In order to validate his theory more effectively, therefore, Sepúlveda stated the Native Americans' incapability of understanding the true teaching of Christianity (such as a lack of literacy), and attempted to use the concept of the natural slave.[74] By defining the Native Americans as lesser human-beings=natural slaves, defined by Aristotle[75], he insisted that such inferior human beings must be dominated and educated by the best Christians, the Spaniards, in order to receive the Catholic teachings. Although Sepúlveda was criticized for his extreme nationalistic views by numerous Spanish humanists of his time, from what Díaz del Castillo tells us, it seems clear that such opinions had already become popular among the sixteenth century's Spanish friars before Sepúlveda established his theory to justify the Spanish conquest of the Americas. Let us look at another part of his book:

> Leopoldo. ---- Demócrates, You seem to teach that evil should be done so that good happens, in spite of the disapproval of Saint Paulo in the *Espitola to the Roman*. Then, this war without committing sins cannot be done, or less badly, is very difficult, and it causes many wrongs, as the reality of this war is demonstrated, since war has never been done without offense against, damage to, large disadvantages of and loss of the barbarians.[76]
> Demócratas ---Leopoldo, Even if that reason has some strong points, it does not have so many other strong points and does not oppose this war

---

[73] '*Jews and Christians were assigned a special status as communities possessing scriptures and called the 'people of the Book' (ahl al-kitab) and, therefore, were allowed religious autonomy. They were, however, required to pay a per capita tax called jizyah, as opposed to pagans, who were required to either accept Islam or die.*' cited from Britannica 1999: Muhammad and the Religion of Islam.

[74] Sepúlveda 1984:35-6. See

[75] Aristotle 1961:29-47.(1254a-1255b-40)

[76] My translation of the Spanish text (translated from the original Latin text by Angel Losada) cited from Sepúlveda 1984:76.

[although I do not know] concerning the remaining other wars, whichever chief cause may be made. Therefore, a war never has been carried on and finished without large damages and loss, some offense and damage. Moreover, it is difficult for those who make a righteous war to avoid harm and insult. Yet it is not inferred that making a war seems completely impossible. Neither a principal should be responsible for a war of justice that is made for right reason, nor for an unjust one, nor the crimes committed by the soldiers without his consent. At the same time, for that crime, neither it converts the just reason nor the unjust, nor it becomes worthy of condemnation. The Christian laws order us to avoid dangers and occasions to commit sin. Nevertheless, the laws do not order us to do so when a need exhorts us to avoid another much worse one [e.g., idolatries, human sacrifice], or if it invokes the public and great goodness [such as Christianity, Spanish education, technology].[77]

It is evident that Sepúlveda justified the conquest of the Americas by using a variation of 'the Positive and the Negative Principles,' because his logic apparently follows the line that 'a negative is necessary to create a positive.' Apart from this, the number of victims killed by the Spaniards during the conquest of Mexico was far smaller than those annually killed in the ceremony of human-sacrifice at Tenochititlan, the Aztec capital.[78] By overemphasizing the benefits of the introduction of Christianity and its civilization, he considered the damage given to the Native American to be a serious issue.

For those like Sepúlveda, the living as human beings was to follow solely the Christian doctrine, and pagan idols had to be destroyed as soon as possible.

The Franciscans of this period, including Motolinia, opposed the cruelties inflicted by the Spaniards. Nevertheless, in Europe, since the madness of witch hunting from the medieval period had not ceased, torturing heretics was still widely practiced, and the Maya could not be an exception. They also became subject to this act of sheer madness. Like Diego de Landa, the bishop of Yucatan, the Spanish did not often hesitate to use excessive violence towards the Maya. It is almost certain that there was another motive for such practices, the creditable avarice among the Franciscans. In order to leave their name as the victor of evangelization in the New

[77] My translation of the Spanish text (translated from the original Latin text by Angel Losada) cited from Sepúlveda 1984:76-7.
[78] Sepúlveda 1984:61. He stated that about twenty thousands were sacrificed every year (ibid).

World, some dared to use violence to force the indigenous people into Christianity. Such missionaries pursued the immediate result and often pressed the natives for conversion to Christianity by using violence.

Consequently, the majority of the Native Americans became Christians with little understanding of Christian ideas and doctrines. For such people, accepting Christianity did not mean a total abandonment of their own deities. It is rather natural that those newly converted people continued worshipping their old pagan deities, because some of them must have become Christians only due to fear of the Spaniards.

Yet even among the people who became faithful Christians, abandoning their old pagan religions was often difficult. For them, accepting their old deities as Satan was not possible. Consequently, they often continued their old pagan rites secretly, or renamed their old deity the equivalent of the Christian saints. This phenomenon is often called '*nepantlism* (reluctant acceptance of Christianity).'

For those who received violence from the Spaniards, it is not surprising that their Christian faith was not a real one. By secretly worshipping old pagan idols, they continued resisting Christianity. Of course, for those who sustained independent states and indulged in resistance to the Spanish colonial domination, Christianity was not acceptable. The Peten Itza of the Maya and the Neo-Inca state led by Manco Inca are known examples. They refused Christianity. Nevertheless, even though they identified Christianity as a 'symbol of the enemy' or regarded it as a target for assault, I think that due to the dualistic nature of pagan religions, the Christian god was likely regarded as something like a 'negative' god, but not as a 'devil or Satan.'

On the other hand, the Catholic friars observed the continuous practice of ancient religious rites among the Native Americans as evidence of their still being deceived by Satan. Therefore, the majority of the friars believed that any remaining pagan cults must be exterminated at once. Even today, although the Roman Catholics have already accepted the existence of some divine concepts of other religions, many Catholic friars in Guatemala (and in other parts of America) are not very satisfied with the Catholic Maya who still worship the old Maya deities.

There was one exception in the sixteenth century, which was a certain part of the Dominican order led by Bartolomé de Las Casas. Bartolomé de Las Casas criticized the brutal treatment of the Native Americans by the Spaniards, and became an influential person with the Spanish crown. He is known for his counter-argument against Sepúlveda in the Valladolid debate in Spain.[79]

He is also known for his insistence on 'tolerance of Native pagan religious cults.' He considered that evangelization of Native Americans must be made by their spontaneous conversion.

During his lifetime, writing several books and conflicting with others, Las Casas insisted that harsh conversion into Christianity must not be practiced and ancient American pagan religions must be tolerated until the Native Americans became fully capable of understanding the Christian doctrine.

If we read the *Bible* carefully, an interesting fact can be pointed out. It was said that offerings to idols were made not to God but to the Devil, but it never mentions that the Christians must punish believers of idols. It is true that the *Bible* mentions that the pagans will receive the last judgment of God after their death, and will go to Hell as the result of their devotion to devils, but it mentions also that whether they should be punished or not is solely dependent on God's will. In other words, the *Bible* says that exterminating or punishing the practices of pagan religions is not included in the scope of human justice. Yet, Sepúlveda argued that although those pagan people cannot be punished by any Christian, there is no doubt that such practices (e.g. human sacrifice) were against the natural law[80] as a legal state system, and such pagans were humiliating the Christian God. For him, because the definition of 'just war' was a 'fight for retaliation,' he insisted that the wars against the Native Americans were justified as righteous wars of retaliation for the

---

[79] For the background of this debate, see Pagden 1987:109-145, Brading 1992:79-101, Hanke 1965, 1974, Yamase 2002b:81-6.

humiliation given to the Christian God.[81]

This logic was not justified. The *Bible* says:

> *Bless your persecutors; yes, bless and do not curse them…Do not avenge*
> *yourselves, dear friends, but leave room for divine retribution; for it is written,*
> *'It is Mine to punish; I will pay back, says the Lord..*[82]

On the other hand, from the early times, Las Casas argued that any use of violence should not be made, except for protecting Christians from attack by the pagan. Furthermore, he declared that if the Spanish crown found it impossible to convert the Native Americans without destruction of their society and life, the crown must abandon its conquest of the New World.

Under such political circumstances, the religious aspiration of that period was dominated by a fanatical Christian view of pagan religions, i.e., 'all these religions were works of Satan.' One of the major intentions of Las Casas was to counter that opinion among the fanatical Christians and nationalistic Spaniards.

To oppose Sepúlveda, furthermore, Las Casas wrote two important works, the *Apologia* (1548-1550?)[83], and the *Apologética Historia Sumaria.*[84]

Las Casas aggressively opposed Sepúlveda in every aspect by introducing a historical example that the great Roman Emperor Constantine I, who was supposed to have been a great adorer of Christianity, never waged a war against the pagan people in order to remove paganism. Las Casas thus rejected Sepúlveda's justification of war against the Native American on the grounds of their devotion to pagan religions.[85] His argument was essentially based on Aristotle's assertion that spiritual activities depend on the natural environment and on physiological conditions, which justified the various religious practices of the Native Americans, and assumed their intellect. When considering the strong influence of Augustine

---

[80] Philosophy, understanding of right or fair dealing held to be common to all humankind and derived from nature rather than from the rules of society, or positive law.
[81] Sepúlveda 1984:58-60.
[82] The *New Testament*: Roman Chap.12:14, 19
[83] Las Casas 1992.
[84] Las Casas 1967, 1995.

141

found in Las Casas' works, it seems to be true that he tried to identify Native American religions as a kind of Platonism.

It is now known among historians that Las Casas relied on the logic found in St. Augustine's classic Latin works, such as the *Confession*[86] and especially the *City of God.*[87] That is, all men by virtue of the natural light predictably seek for and serve [the Christian] God. While attacking the 'errors' of Platonism, Augustine praised the wisdom of Plato, whose philosophy was partly considered to be quite close to the Gospel.[88]

Augustine says:

> *If Plato and Porphyry had been able to communicate to one another certain statements which each of them made singly, they might well have become Christianity.*[89]

Augustine's assertion in the above text is interesting. He concluded that not only a wise pagan philosopher, Plato, but also Porphyry, a bitter Roman pagan enemy of Christianity, unconsciously understood some fundamental concepts of the Gospel. Las Casas' attitude towards Native American religions seems to be quite close to that of Augustine towards pagan philosophers. It is true that although Las Casas did not openly refer to Platonists and Neo-Platonists in his works, unlike Augustine, without any doubt he was aware of the ancient Platonist ideas cited in Augustine's *City of God*. It may be suggested, therefore, that he tried to prove all Native American pagan religious practices to be a progressive process toward perception of the Christian Gospel.

In the *Apologética Historia Sumaria*, he considered all pagan religions to be a representation of the Native Americans' diffuse way of understanding the one true [Christian] God.

---

[85] Las Casas 1992:Cap.34, p.279-284.
[86] Augustine 401.
[87] See Brading 1992:99-100.
[88] Augustine 426:Book VIII, Chap.4-9, p.316-325.
[89] Augustine 426:Book XXII, Chap.27, p.1169.

Las Casas further argued that;

1: Cannibalism practiced among the Native American is not essentially evil, unless they kill a person for that purpose.[90]

2: Human sacrifice is not always evil.[91]

In the process of opposing Sepúlveda, Las Casas argued, for example, that the *Bible* clearly mentions that his Father, the Christian God, sacrificed Jesus Christ. He cited this narrative as evidence that human sacrifice is not always against the natural law. By quoting the works of Saint Thomas, Las Casas further tried to prove that offering sacrifice is accepted in natural law.[92]

On this point, Las Casas pointed out that before knowing the Lord of Christianity, the ancient Romans, who created a magnificent civilization, and the Spanish, also practiced human sacrifice, as the Native Americans were doing in the sixteenth century. By introducing examples of human sacrifices practiced by the ancient Romans, Greeks, and other peoples found in the Holy Scripture, Las Casas says:

> human victims, as we have proved elsewhere from Augustine, Cherysostom, and Valerius, it is not surprising that, when afflicted and pleasing to God, that is, men... there is some probable natural reason by which men can be led to sacrifice human beings to God and, as a result, that is not easy to persuade the Indians, within a short period or by a few words, to refrain from their traditional practice of human sacrifice.[93]

He applied the theory to the human sacrifice practiced in the Americas. First, he insisted that because punishing those who were committing the crime of sacrificing guiltless persons could not be done without harming other innocent people, no castigation must be made to them through war. He insisted that the Native Americans were offering human sacrifices to 'false gods (the sun, idols, and animals, etc.)' whom they erroneously considered 'true gods,' and their religious beliefs clearly suggested that, like the ancient Greek and Roman philosophers, the

---

[90] Las Casas 1992:Cap.33, p.212-220.

[91] Las Casas 1992:Cap.34-7, p.221-242..

[92] Las Casas 1967:Lib.III, cap.LXXII, 375.

[93] cited from Las Casas 1992: Chap.36, p.238-9. Also see *ibid.*: Chap.37.

Native Americans tried to understand the meaning of the Gospel within their best possible intellectual capability. Therefore, even if their awareness of the Christian God and his words was far from perfect or they worshipped devils, such mistakes should be regarded as their innocent ignorance of the true Christian God or a result of a deception made by Satan, and thus the Native Americans were not directly sinful.[94]

In short, Las Casas found the pagan religion to be evidence that the Native Americans had intellect. By identifying the Native American religious and cultural system as better than those of the ancient Greek, Roman and all other cultures,[95] he unofficially argued that the Native American religions were better organized than those of the ancient Western civilization. If religious ideas and philosophies of the Native Americans were proved equivalent to those of Moses and the Greek philosophers or better, no destruction of Native American beliefs could be made in theory. I think this was Las Casas' aim.

As Tzvetan Todorov has already discussed, this kind of logic was generated by the Spanish *Conquistadors*' justification of their excessively brutal mistreatment of the Native Americans because of their practice of paganism and human sacrifice.[96] These practices were exaggerated by Spanish chroniclers and the *Conquistadors*, and were considered against natural law. On the other hand, as MacCormack points out, the aim of Las Casas was to understand the origin of human perception of God.[97] Las Casas believed that all humans are by nature religious. In this process, Las Casas tried to prove that although essentially an error, idolatry and human sacrifice are a natural step on the path to understanding the existence of the Christian Lord, so such natural mistakes should not always be regarded as sin.

Las Casas explained human sacrifice as follows: the Native Americans paid their maximum respect to what they believed to be gods, by offering their most precious possession, the human body. Human sacrifice found in New Spain was

[94] Las Casas 1992: Chap.31, p.204-5, Chap.32, Chap.35, p.230.
[95] Las Casas 1967: tomo I, lib.III, Cap.CLXXXIII, also *passim*.
[96] Todorov 1999:186-190.

144

evidence that the Native Americans had greater devotion to their gods than those who offered mere animal sacrifices (easier to practice than offering a human). Therefore, he concluded that those who were practicing human sacrifice in the New World had the most pious attitude to their deities.[98]

From his point of view, this religious zealousness among the Native Americans could be seen as superior to that of the Christians.

Furthermore, he pointed out that while the Native Americans believed in the existence of numerous gods, they also supposed the existence of a single, supreme, transcendent god among them. According to him, this 'supreme God,' worshipped by the Native American, was actually the Christian God. He argued this to be evidence of their inspirational perception of the Christian God.[99]

What I have mentioned up to this point can be found in any good work on Las Casas. Because the purpose of this section is to understand the background of the religious beliefs of the Spaniards of the sixteenth century, it is necessary to examine the background of Las Casas' attitude towards the pagan by reading his texts in chronological order.

It seems that Las Casas got his idea from his opponent. The early Christian saints, such as Justin Martyr and Augustine, already practiced the kind of logic known as Christian Platonism used by Las Casas. They regarded Plato and Aristotle as wise pagan philosophers who understood some important aspects of the Gospel. However, the later Christians did not treat Plato, Aristotle and other pagan Greek philosophers as 'semi'-Christian. It was thought that these ancient Greek sages had fallen into Hell.

Las Casas' enemy and a prominent Spanish nationalist of the sixteenth century, Dr. Juan Ginés de Sepúlveda, was considered the best authority of his time on Aristotle, the ancient Greek pagan philosopher. As one of the fanatic Christians of that time, Sepúlveda justified the Spanish conquest of the Americas on the grounds

---

[97] MacCormack 1993:119.
[98] Las Casas 1967:Cap.183.
[99] Las Casas 1967:Cap.120, 122, 126.

of the practice of idolatry and human sacrifice among the Native Americans. However it is also known that he was not always in favor of Christian rigorism,[100] and it must be noted that he did not define all paganism as evil:

(**Democrates.** -...so, by divine instinct and teaching of nature, Socrates, Plato, Aristotle and other philosophers admitted the existence of a unique God...

Leopoldo. -Perhaps, you believe that Plato and Aristotle admitted the existence of one God, when, at every step, they speak to us of many gods...

Democrates.- To use the word 'God' as a metaphor is neither impious, nor contrary to the sacred Holy Scriptures:... In this way, therefore, the children of God call him God, although exactly by nature, there was only one Son of God. Saint Paul says, *all are children of God by the faith*; and Saint Juan [says; they are so] in the Gospel: *the Lord gave them authority of being made as children of the God to those who believe in his* name. In conclusion, the wise philosophers remembered and they named many Gods, but expressed in popular style and metaphor. In this way, we call the incorporeal substances angels, and they sometimes called them intelligences and gods in other times. Already as if admitting the existence of innumerable angels, they imitate the simplicity of God. We believe in the existence of a unique God, in the same way that they believed that there were many substances of these in Heaven. Nevertheless, they certainly considered the existence of the single greatest God...Aristotle testifies to it by expressing it as... God, even being one, nevertheless is called with many names which we give them for their works. In this way, call Jupiter as to the author giving it the life... According to Saint Augustine...he has the same opinion, not only of Aristotle, but also of almost all the sages of paganism, calling God in the air, Jupiter, and the same one in the air, Juno; in the sea, Neptune; ... As Saint Augustine said, he was assured that Jupiter was adored, even though by those who worshipped the unique [Christian] God without simulacrum [=the idols], but HE is named with another name.[101]

In addition, he says:

Leopoldo.– How could they reach salvation with the natural law only, those philosophers, and honest males of paganism?

Democrates.- ... Dogma is admitted by all the theologians in that there can be no salvation; but you know that the same theologians interpret this doctrine with indulgence and amplitude. When they handle the salvation of the previous Holy Fathers before the coming of Christ, neither have they assured, nor do they require that all of them [Greek pagans] have an explicit faith in Christ, but they [the Greek sages] were not pleased with certain occult

---

[100] Several scholars have already discussed this issue, for example, see Gutiérrez 2003:248-50.
[101] Sepúlveda 1984:47-8.

and enigmatic beliefs. By this reason, there are reasons to believe that those philosophers and as many as believed in the existence of one God and in his providence for human things, also had a certain faith in Christ. ...For this reason, we can believe that the ancient [Greek pagan] philosophers, [pagan] followers of justice, and the other pagan virtuous ones educated by them, had a faith in Christ, and they could be saved by the natural law before his [=Jesus] arrival.'[102]

It is evident that Sepúlveda, who justified the brutal conquest of pagan states, praised the ancient Greek 'pagan' philosophers at the same time. The saints of early Christianity used the ideas of Aristotle and Plato to theologically prove the Christian idea. However, they also stated that even though the Greek sages were great, it was impossible to know and comprehend the content of the Christian Gospel through human intellect alone.[103]

The amazing fact is that he treated the Greek pagans almost as Christians. Surprisingly, Sepúlveda argued that even believers of other religions could receive relief of the Christian God after death, as long as they believed in the Christian Lord and lived according to the natural law.

Since a possible salvation of non-Christians had already been argued by the early saints, such as Paul and Thomas Aquinas, Sepúlveda simply recalled the opinions of the past.[104] It was generally said that before the arrival of Jesus Christ, only those who followed the Mosaic law (= Judaism) were able to receive salvation after death. How did Sepulveda manage to categorize Greek pagan sages as Christians?

Although Plato and Aristotle were beloved philosophers of the early saints, those saints never mentioned any possibility of their salvation. It is almost certain that Sepúlveda, as the best authority on Aristotle of his time, was impressed with Aristotle's scholarship and respected this ancient pagan philosopher so much that he could not send him to Hell. Therefore, he apparently wanted to save Aristotle and other respectable pagan philosophers from Hell.

---

[102] My translation of Sepúlveda 1984:52-3. Also see *ibid*.:51.
[103] e.g., Justin *The Hortatory Address to the Greeks*, p.277.
[104] Sepúlveda 1984:52-3.

Although early saints did not speak of the possible salvation of Plato and Aristotle, it is also true that they often declined to mention their fall into Hell. On this point, some saints argued that the ancient Greeks and Romans had a faith in the Christian God, called *Jupiter* or *Zeus* by them, so that those ancient pagans may be called semi-Christian, in spite of the fact that they did not follow the Mosaic law. So the Roman and Greek pagans were not totally rejected by the early Christian saints. As Sepúlveda says, this idea was found in Augustine's *City of God*.[105] Saint Augustine neither considered the possibility of the salvation of the ancient Greek sages, nor the possibility of their fall into Hell. But Augustine argued that the *Jupiter* of the Roman Empire (and *Zeus* of the Greeks) was the Christian God. Also, the *Bible* says that whoever confesses before the Christian Lord will be saved.[106] Based on this, Augustine seems to argue that an unbaptized person had the possibility of salvation after his death.[107]

Since the possibility of the salvation of non-Christians had already been discussed,[108] the idea of Sepúlveda was nothing new. There was room for Sepúlveda to rescue his beloved ancient masters. But since faith in the Christian God was not a sufficient to defend the Greek philosophers, identifying the natural law as an alternative to the Mosaic law was necessary for Sepúlveda.

Thus, what Sepúlveda called the natural law, is the law which was produced by human natural perception and intellect only, and it had to provide almost the same mandates as did the Mosaic law. As a result, he concluded that as long as the pagan people had faith in the Christian God, and managed their social and religious life according to the natural law, their souls would be treated as Christian.

In short, it is evident that he tried to reason and prove the following: in spite of the fact that any reasoning pagan people, such as the Greeks and Romans, were naturally able to comprehend idolatry as a sin against God, lesser 'barbaric' people such as the Native Americans committed idolatry and human sacrifice as a result of

---

[105] Sepúlveda 1984:47, Augustine 426:Book IV, Chap.12.
[106] John 3-5, Matthew 10-32.
[107] Augustine 410:Book XIII, Chap. 7, p.547-8.

148

the inferiority of their natural law. Therefore, it can be said that although Sepúlveda accepted his favorite paganists as Christian, his acceptance of pagan religion inherently selective.

Nevertheless, almost all Catholic friars of his period did not rescue even the Greeks and the Romans. In general, the Catholics of the sixteenth century did not emphasize any possibility of the salvation of pagans.

Matteo Ricci, who is known for his unusual respect and affection for the great and prominent Chinese philosopher, Confucius, never mentioned that this philosopher must have received salvation from the Christian Lord, though he made several attempts to rescue him by inventing a 'new, better' Hell. On this point, it must be said that Sepúlveda was ironically much more tolerant of polytheistic pagan religions than was Las Casas and other Catholic friars, at least in the early stages.

Sepúlveda concluded that those who, like the Native Americans, were a lesser human and acted against the natural law, because of their sins, must be punished by the Spaniards as the representatives of the Lord. However, there was a notion in the Christian culture that sins of the ignorant should not be punished.[109] According to Sepúlveda, even ignorant sin must be punished.

Sepúlveda argued:

> In this way, therefore, the same as the ignorance of each of the things, the ignorance of the right or the law does not remove the sin. Therefore, one has a carnal affair with a woman, who was secretly replaced [with his wife], as we have said. This person does not see the affair [which was] voluntarily [made by him], because he does not know the material which he treats, or the object from where he takes his reason for the moral act. In addition, he was ignorant that that law ordered him to know [who is that woman, before a carnal affair]... the natural laws, at the same time, are divine, as we have previously said. They have a universal application and all the mortals follow them ... and all can know them. Another very distinct case is he of that case who was observed justly ignorant and invincible, which cannot be exceeded with study, therefore this removes the will at the same time and erases completely the sin. It would be found in such cases of ignorance, according to the judgment of

[108] For example, see Gutiérrez 2003:241-8.
[109] For example, Saint Thomas's *Summa Theologica, 1a-2ae.xix,6* (Thomas 1960:292).

149

Saint Agustin, that they find nobody to learn [the Gospel].[110]

The conclusion of Sepúlveda was not obviously to accept idolatry and human sacrifice as exceptions.[111] He argued that although sin resulted from some ignorance, it should not be excused, and any such excuse must be applied to only the case caused by deception of others, such as a person who has a carnal relationship with a woman. Because, as a duty, the Native Americans must have known of the prohibition of idols in natural law, Sepúlveda argues that their idolatry could not be excused. If he excused this, his defense of the Spanish conquest would not have been justified. Why were idolatry and human sacrifice considered sins? It is true that the *New Testament* prohibited the Christians from worshipping idols, but it did not order Christians to punish non-Christian idolaters. Long before the time of Las Casas and Sepúlveda, there was endless dispute as to whether idolatry and human sacrifice were sins or not. Offering animal sacrifices to the Lord is not necessarily a sin in Christianity. The *Old Testament* records that Moses killed oxen as a sacrifice to his [Christian] God and he sprinkled their blood onto the altar and the people of the Israel in order to make the covenant with the Lord.[112]

In the *New Testament*, on the other hand, Jesus said that his body was bread and his blood, wine, and that people who ate and drank them would make a covenant [with the Father].[113] This suggests that he stated that a part of the God = Jesus was sacrificed for the people as their daily meal. Therefore, in Christianity, the flock has to eat its Lord. However, although Jesus discouraged the people from killing animals for sacrifice, he never defined animal sacrifice as a serious sin. Therefore, although the human bloodletting practiced among the ancient Maya and other Mesoamerican people was considered horrifying and ghastly by the Spaniards of the sixteenth century, the fact is that offering the blood of animals was

---

[110] My translation of Sepúlveda 1994:103-4.
[111] *Ibid.*:104.
[112] *Exodus* 24:4-8.
[113] *Luke* 22:14-23.

acceptable, according to the *Bible*, although it was not recommended according to the *New Testament*. However, as human sacrifice was strictly forbidden by Moses' Ten Commandments, 'Thou shalt not kill', it is considered a serious sin against the Lord.

There was a strong belief that the human being, by nature, never sacrificed a person and worshipped idols. By this logic, unless they were idolaters, no nations ever practiced human sacrifice. On this basis, it was often claimed that human sacrifice and idolatry were against the natural law. So human sacrifice and idolatry were considered a result of Satan's deception of people. Yet, there has been some disagreement as well. For example, Francisco de Vitoria also discussed this issue, and he concluded that human sacrifice is not always lawful.[114] If the Native Americans were simply deceived by Satan, then Satan must face the punishment of God. According to Sepúlveda, however, any intelligent human beings have by nature the ability to understand human sacrifice and idolatry as serious sins against the Christian Lord. Therefore, Sepulveda thought that even if it is supposed that the Native Americans did not learn these prohibitions from a Christian before the arrival of the Spaniards, it was not an excuse for them to avoid the punishment of God; rather, by his argument, they were merely human-like animals.

His theory is self-contradicting. Sepúlveda discussed in another part of his text that the intellect of the Native American is low as compared with the humans of other countries. Based on this, it can be said that the Christian God will forgive the sin of human sacrifice and other sins, because those sins are a result of the low intellectual level of the Native Americans. If they were human-like animals, they could not be sinning, because the salvation of animals is not considered in the Gospel.

Sepúlveda made a further distinction between the ancient Greek pagan and the sinner. In order to make certain Greek pagan sages the exception to sinful people, He distinguished a sin committed in a state system from a sin made by a private

---

[114] Vitoria 1485?-1546: 212-217.

151

individual. He wrote:

> ...those same theologians offer [the case] of the habitants of Seir, Moabitas, and Ammonitas, whom God protected and prohibited the children of Israel to attack. With this case, they try to show that idolatry is not a sufficient reason to wage war against the pagans... although the common people were idolaters, it is probable that there were many people who kept the natural law, they worshipped the single true God and they maintained the religion and institutions of their ancestors by that time.[115]

Sepúlveda clearly thought that even if the people in a society were idolaters, as long as the upper class people in the society were suspicious of idolatry (and obviously human sacrifice), knew the existence of the Christian Lord (even though unconsciously), and that the social order was maintained by natural law, then that pagan society would be excused from punishment by the Christian Lord.

This logic was also used to save the Greek philosophers from Hell, as the ancient Greeks were known for their idolatry. On this point, it must be said that although Sepúlveda did not make a clear citation, the ancient Greek sages were not always in favor of idolatry. For example, the *Phaedo* of Plato says:

> ...*the body is a source of endless trouble to us by reason of the mere requirement of food; and also is liable to diseases which overtake and impede us in the search after truth: and by filling us so full of loves, and lusts, and fears, and fancies, and **idols**, and every sort of folly, prevents our ever having, as people say, so much as a thought.*[116]

The same author says in the *Sophist*:

> 'Str. *And if there is deceit, then all things must be full of idols and images and fancies.*'[117]

On the other hand, the fact is that the Native American did not fall into this category so Sepúlveda justified the destruction of the Native American states based on the following three facts: (1) idolatry was openly practiced by the ruling people

---

[115] My translation of Sepúlveda 1984:104-5.
[116] Cited from Plato 1871. Bold by the author.
[117] Plato 360BC.

at state festivals, (2) human sacrifice was also systematically celebrated at state events, (3) cannibalism was also legally approved. That is, the sin in the New World was not the sin of individual people but of public states. Thus, together with his assumption that the Native Americans were natural slaves, he concluded that the Spanish should have the right of waging war against their sins.

On the other hand, although it is sometimes ignored among scholars,[118] it is surprising that Las Casas, who has generally been considered 'tolerant' of the pagans, had initially a far more fanatical Christian view than Sepúlveda. It is well known that Las Casas stated in 1519 that, *'Aristotle was a Gentile, and is now burning in Hell, and we are only to make use of his doctrine as far as it consistent with our Holy Faith and Christian customs.'* [119] It is known that the *Apologia* was written in order to contest Sepúlveda's *Domócrates Segundo*. In the *Apologia*, he again criticized Aristotle: *'Good-bye, Aristotle! ...This chase was different from the one Aristotle taught. Although he was a profound philosopher, he was not worthy to be captured in the chase so that he could come to God through knowledge of the true faith.'* [120] Based on this opinion, all pagan believers in the New Worlds would also be condemned by the Christian God. In order to oppose Sepúlveda, therefore, Las Casas needed to find a new perspective to save the Native Americans from the devastation caused by the Spaniards.

There was no doubt that idolatry and human sacrifice were publicly approved in numerous Native American states and communities. These religious customs were not approved by the Church and were against Mosaic law. Therefore, by emphasizing a limitation of human intellectual ability to understand the Gospel without the help of those who taught it, Las Casas attempted to conclude that 'those sins' were 'inevitable natural error in the early stage of history of any humankind of high intelligence,' in order to excuse pagan religious practices. Also, he pointed out that the Native Americans had never heard the context of the Gospel before the

---

[118] Because I am not a specialist of Las Casas, I may have overlooked the works discussing this issue.

[119] Cited from Hanke 1965:124. He does not mention the source material.

153

arrival of the Spaniards. By that time, although Las Casas had already argued in the *Apologia* that '*the worshipers of idols, at least in the case of the Indians, about whom this dispusion has been undertaken, have never heard the teaching of Christian truth even through hearsay; so they sin less than the Jews or Saracens, for ignorance excuses to some small extent,*'[121] and he tried to prove this more efficiently in the *Apologética Historia Sumaria*. In order to stand up for the Native Americans, it is obvious that Aristotle, also a pagan, had to be in Heaven. Las Casas was forced to change his mind on Aristotle in order to defend the lives of the Native Americans. In addition, he had to present a view that all pagan people actually worshipped the Christian Lord. In order to insist upon this, all the supreme deities of various pagan religions had to be the Christian Lord. This required him to accept *Zeus* of the Greeks and *Jupiter* of the Romans as the Christian Lord. Although he does no clearly mention it, Las Casas transformed Aristotle from a gentile into a semi-Christian.

In the *Apologética Historia Sumaria*, Las Casas wrote:

> By the recited reasons, all nations of [pagan] barbarians and the wild [pagan] people in the world were able and can induce, to know and to understand that there is some Lord, Maker, Mover and keeper of all things, who is more excellent than man... to whom all the men call God....the men profess God without faith. Aristotle also said in book I, Chap 30 of the *coelo et mundo*, that all men agreed with this, that glorious first body that is the heaven, is the real palace and place of the most supreme one Lord who is God. All the Greeks and the other first peoples had knowledge of the [Christian] God.[122]

In another part of the *Apologética Historia Sumaria*, he also wrote; '...it is not said that many of these who follow idolatry are inexcusable. Because they have an ignorance, because if they were helped in what they should do, they are arranged so that God lit them...Some of these [pagans] feel invincible their ignorance, and by

---

[120] Cited from Las Casas 1992: Cap.4, p.40-1.
[121] Cited from Las Casas 1992:Chap.9, p.78.
[122] Las Casas 1967:tomo I, Lib.III, cap.LXXII, p.374. My translation.

154

this means they are excused.'[123] In the *Apologética Historia Sumaria*, although indirectly, Las Casas implied the potential salvation of Aristotle as an idolater (otherwise his logic cannot be justified).

Lewis Hanke argued the *Apologia* to be a prototype of the *Apologética Historia Sumaria*.[124] In my view, Hanke's hypothesis can be supported by the different attitude towards Aristotle found in two works of Las Casas. It is clear, therefore, that Las Casas suddenly changed his view of the Greek pagan sage in a period of several years. He seems to have concluded that all pagan religions were essentially a worship of the Christian God. The reason for this might be considered a result of what Sepúlveda hinted to Las Casas, and also that Las Casas had not carefully read the works of the old Christian saints.

Both Las Casas and Sepúlveda agreed that innocent errors should not be punished as sins. However, Sepulveda argued that as human sacrifice and idolatry must naturally be noticed as sins even without knowledge of the Gospel, any human committing those errors could not be excused. On this point, therefore, it was necessary for Las Casas to prove that idolatry was not against the natural law. Although he previously denied any possibility of killing idolaters and to depriving them of their property, it must be pointed out that in the *Apologia*, he never accepted idols as divine things. He wrote, '*Even though the Indians cannot be excused in the sight of God for worshipping idols...they can be completely excused...they are following a 'probable error'...*'.[125]

As I have mentioned before, the thinking of Las Casas is based on Saint Augustine. Augustine wrote:

> But among all these vices and crimes and manifold iniquities, there are
> also the sins that are committed by men who are, on the whole, making
> progress toward the good. When these are judged rightly and after the rule of
> perfection, the sins are censored but the men are to be commended because

---

[123] Las Casas 1967:II, Épílogo, Cap.CCLXVI, p.647.
[124] Hanke 1974:74. Edmund O'Gorman (in Las Casas 1967: Tomo I, XXXIV-XXXV) mentions that there is no internal evidence that the *Apologética Historia Sumaria* was written prior to 1552.
[125] Cited from Las Casas 1992:Chap.34, p.221. See *ibid.*: 221-4, Chap.37, p.342-3.

they show the hope of bearing fruit, like the green shoot of the growing corn. And there are some deeds that resemble vice and crime and yet are not sin because they offend neither thee, our Lord God, nor social custom. For example, when suitable reserves for hard times are provided, we cannot judge that this is done merely from a hoarding impulse. Or, again, when acts are punished by constituted authority for the sake of correction, we cannot judge that they are done merely out of a desire to inflict pain. Thus, many a deed which is disapproved in man's sight may be approved by thy testimony. And many a man who is praised by men is condemned.[126]

He thought that in the process of human cultural progress, committing some sins could not be avoided. Although Sepúlveda used this type of logic in order to justify the Spanish sin of the brutal conquest of the Americas, Las Casas used it to excuse the Native American sins of human sacrifice and idolatry. Therefore, Las Casas concluded that worshipping pagan idols (devils) was not only not a religion, but was evidence of the intelligence of the Native American.

He later wrote in the *Apologética Historia Sumaria*:

Hay otra razón o señal ser natural la idolatría, ... porque cuán presto pudo aparecer alguna señal o vestigio de la alteza, sabiduría, divinidad de Dios en los ídolos o en las estrellas o en los hombres o en otras cualquiera cosa, conviene a saber, o porque se le decían las cosas por venire o por la hermosura della, o por el bien que dellas les venía o beneficio que recebían dellas, según dice Aristóteles, III, Politicorum, caitulo....sin mucha consideración se inclinaban a adorar y hacer reverencia a aquellas cosas en que veían aquellas señales de excelencia de Dios...y podían les comenzaron a ofrecer sacrificio que, como es ya dicho, se debe a sólo Dios.[127]

(There is another reason or sign that the idolatry is natural, ...how prompt some signs or vestiges of the highness, wisdom, divinity of God could appear in the idols or in the stars or in the men or in any other thing, ... as Aristotle says in Book III of the *Politicorum* (*Politics*) chapter.... without a great deal of consideration [=by nature], they are inclined to worship and to bow to those things in which they saw those signals of excellence of God...and as it has already been said, they could offer sacrifice which should be made to the God only.)

If the ancient Greek sages could receive the salvation of the Christian Lord, as Sepúlveda insisted, there is no reason why the Native Americans, whom Las Casas believed to be better than those sages, could not also. By examining aspects of

---

[126] Augustine 401:Chap.IX.

156

Native American religions similar to monotheism, such as the common existence of the Supreme Deity over the pagan pantheons, Las Casas tried to suggest that all men naturally sought to find and serve the one true God of Christianity. Therefore, it is not surprising that modern scholars often refer to Las Casas as a unique sixteenth century European who discussed the Native American religions from the native point of view.[128] Gustavo Gutiérrez wrote in his magnificent book about Las Casas: *'His contribution has been decisive in the arenas of human right, religious freedom, democratic institutions, and the effort to understand the 'other' of Western civilization.'*[129] Las Casas certainly contributed to the human rights of the Native American. However, it is questionable whether he contributed to their religious freedom.

One may think that Las Casas tolerated and justified Native American pagan religions and accepted their existence. It has been suggested that, in 'Christianized' Europe, his argument was probably the first attempt to question a Christian path to God as a unique one, which was also perhaps the first unconscious attempt to present a hypothesis that 'the origin of all religions came from a single True God' in the sixteenth century.[130] On this point, Hidefuji Someda suggests that Las Casas' insistence is not based on a Christian viewpoint of 'history=progress,' regarding instead the history of human beings as a progressive transformation.[131]

Nevertheless, a careful consideration of Las Casas' idea brings us to an opposite idea. As I have previously discussed, in the early stages, Dr. Sepúlveda first rescued the Greek pagan philosophers from Hell, while Las Casas damned Aristotle for his 'wicked' religious beliefs and expected that he was being tortured forever in [Christian] Hell.

Las Casas glorified the magnificent cultural standards and social order established by the Native American elsewhere in New Spain in order to make the

[127] Las Casas 1967:tomo I, lib.III, cap.LXXIV, p.382.
[128] Hanke 1974:142-3.
[129] Gutiérrez 2003:XV.
[130] See Todorov 1999:189-193, also see Brading 1992:90-3.
[131] Someda 1995:340-1.

157

Spanish understand the intellectual capability of the Native American. Moreover, he enthusiastically attempted to remove negative views of the Native Americans from the discussions held in Spain.

Las Casas' idea clearly suggests his refusal to categorize cultural standards according to the Christian perspective, as Someda argues. Nevertheless, because Las Casas simply adopted the ideology of the early Christian saints in the case of the Americas, as David A. Brading points out, Las Casas' idea was not particularly innovative or sensational within the history of the Christianity.[132] The basic concept of Las Casas is not so different from the Christian Platonism proposed by the early Christians. Las Casas somehow tried to prove all pagan religions were 'an incorrect path to the Christian Lord as a result of a lack of proper evangelization,' in the same way that Platonism was judged by the early Christian saints in the era of the Roman Empire.

Only selected ideas of the Greek philosophers, such as the immortality of the Spirit, were appreciated by Christian ideology. Platonism has been used as evidence that the ancient sages proved the rightness of the fundamental concepts of Christianity before the arrival of Jesus Christ. There is another example. In ancient Britain, Christianity was initially developed as 'Celtic Christianity,' which is a mixture of selected parts of both Christianity and the old Celtic, pagan religions. This so-called 'Celtic Christianity' tolerated both religions. Celtic pagan traditions were brought into the Church. Over time, with some important exceptions, the Celtic religious elements gradually disappeared. The remaining Celtic religious deities became part of Christianity, and thus Celtic Christianity became orthodox Catholic Christianity.[133] What Las Casas dreamed of in the New World was repeating this spiritual conquest of the Celts and Platonism. His view towards other non-Christian teachings should not be treated as the Unitarianism of today, which seeks closer ties with other religions. His stance towards pagan religions was therefore a 'tolerance,' but not an 'acceptance of their permanent existence.' Las

---

[132] Brading 1992:93.

Casas developed a discussion, seeing the human sacrifice and the idolatry of the Maya (and the other Native Americans), as 'the universal erroneous act' from a view of the preceding history of the human race.

Unlike pagan people, including the Maya, Las Casas never identified any pagan religion as homogeneous with Christianity. He concluded that no pagan people could understand the truly unique existence of the invisible True God in spite of the fact they originally had an old memory of a single true God, and as a result of this Satan deceived the Native Americans and their minds degenerated.[134] What he also insisted was that because the Christian God is invisible and unnoticeable, it is not surprising that the Native Americans had not managed to comprehend the fact that the Christian God had sole dominion over the world.[135] Therefore, he added that the pantheistic religions found among the Native Americans should be considered a result of their innocent failure of recognition of a single and unique [Christian] god, and thus their ignorance of the Christian God should not be punished.

A careful analysis of Las Casas' works also reveals that his insistence was designed to prove the sophisticated cultural level of the Native Americans' religious rites according to Aristotle's definition, devotion, and systems, but not to praise religious concepts and practices. The core of his theory was to assert the Native Americans as the same (or better) human as the ancient pagan Romans, Greeks, and Egyptians in terms of cultural standards and religious purity. At the same time, he wanted to categorize all pagan religions as the early stage of development of any human race before they attained Christianity. In fact, he mentioned the sophisticated religious and state system which the Native Americans possessed as proof that converting them to the Gospel would be far easier than converting ancient Romans and Germans.[136]

What Las Casas justified in the pagan religions is better and more efficiently

[133] see Hutton 1991:287-9.
[134] Las Casas 1967:Cap.121.
[135] Las Casas 1967: Cap.71.

159

summarized by Herbert Spencer of the nineteenth century:

> *Mr. Herbert Spencer bases religion on the Unknown, declaring that the savage worships those powers which he does not understand. In order to give to religion a foundation which even the scientist does not dare to touch, he asserts the existence of an absolute Unknowable, and recommends it as the basis of the religion of the future. But facts do not agree with Mr. Spencer's proposition. A German proverb says:*
>   *'Was ich nicht weiss*
>   *Macht mich nicht heiss.'*
>   *Or, as is sometimes said in English:*
>   *'What the eyes don't see*
>   *The heart doesn't grieve for.'*
> *What is absolutely unknowable does not concern us, and the savage does not worship the thunder because he does not know what it is, but because he knows enough about the lightning that may strike his hut to be in awe of it. He worships the thunder because he dreads it; he is afraid of it on account of its known and obvious dangers which he is unable to control.*[137]

Consuming much more space, Las Casas said essentially the same thing.

This means that Las Casas was about to appeal to the universalism which is common to all human beings, but not to the universal relation between the non-Christian religions and Christianity.

Let us look at his *Apologética Historia Sumaria*:

> *...conviene a saber, que aún no son regenerados por el santo baptismo, como al principio, antes del advenimiento de Cristo, todas las naciones (sacando los judíos) eran dejadas caer en la idolatría y en vicios que a ellas e siguen, por el oculto divino juicio ... La infidelidad destos tales no tiene razón de pecado en cuanto es no tener fe de Jesucristo ... No se dice aquí de la idolatría, la cual, en muchos, no será excusable porque hayan tenido ignorancia, porque si se ayudaran haciendo lo que debían, disponiéndose para que Dios los alumbrara, vencieran la ignorancia y esto paresce sonar la doctrina de los sanctos, por cuanto a algunos y a munchos de los mismos gentiles, algunos déstos sienten ser invencible su ignorancia, y así excusarse.*[138]
> (It is important to know that even though they are not regenerated by the holy baptism, as at the beginning, before the arrival of Christ, all the nations (except for the Jews) were untidy to fall into the idolatry and into vices which they followed, by the hidden divine judgment...The unfaithfulness of these

---

[136] Las Casas 1967:Cap.127.
[137] Cited from Carus 1900:7-8.
[138] Cited from Las Casas 1967:II, Epílogo, Cap.CCLXVI, p.647.

people was not a cause of sin inasmuch as not having faith in Jesus Christ... Here, it is not said that many of these idolaters are inexcusable. Because they are ignorant, because if they were helped to know what they should do, they could be arranged so that God lights them. They overcome their ignorance. And this seems to reprise the doctrine of the saints, inasmuch as [do this] to some and to many of the same pagans. Some of these [pagans] feel invincible in their ignorance, and by this mean they are excused.)

It is clear that Las Casas did not define pagan religions as proper teaching. By praising the Native American's devotion to their gods, he did not accept those gods as 'God,' but as a kind of Christian angel.

Let us cite the *Apologética Historia Sumaria* again. He talks about the situation of the Guatemalan Maya of the sixteenth century:

> *Tenían humilladeros antes de llegar a los pueblos, donde había unos oratorios como ermitas de ídolos, que llamaban mumuz, y déstos había de trecho a trecho en los caminos, donde hacían sus oraciones y ofrecían sus sacrificios, y aunque todo supersticioso, pero en todas sus obras buscaban y pretendían en confuse hallar a Dios.*[139] (They had places of worship in front of the towns, there were some orators at hermitages of idols, whom they called *mumuz*, and these were in places on the roads, where their prayers were prayed and they offered their sacrifices, and although all were superstitious, but in all their works sought and pretended in confusion to find [the Christian] God.)

After all, even for him, it was impossible to deny the core concept of monotheism. Therefore, for Las Casas, pagan religions and worship of idols are a 'natural error,' which all humankind had made before they were converted into Christianity.[140] What Las Casas proposed during his lifetime was to terminate pagan religions with peaceful methods, which would take considerable time.[141]

By defining the Natural Law as another divine code, Sepúlveda emphasized its function as if it were a good alternative to the Gospel, but Las Casas did not do this to the same degree. Although the reason is not clear, a hypothesis can be presented. Orthodox Christian parties criticize Unitarians of the twentieth century, who sometimes became paganized Christians, because their ideology of tolerating

---

[139] Las Casas 1967:tomo II, Lib.III, Cap.CLXXIX, p.224.
[140] Las Casas 1967:tomo I, Lib.III, Cap.LXXIV, p.381-7.

certain parts of pagan religions threatened to make Christianity a mere moral code. For the Catholic and the Protestant, Christianity must be unique divine law. This kind of view may have been in Las Casas' mind. In my opinion, because accepting the natural law and other religions as a kind of alternative has a potential danger of downgrading Christianity from a divine teaching to a mere moral code, Las Casas used 'innocent error' to refer to other religions.

Undoubtedy he is one of great humanists of world history, and his insistence that the Spaniards must give up the evangelization of the Native American due to the catastrophic damage caused by the Conquest is respectable. Nevertheless, he never came to understand the concept of the dualistic culture, and he gave pagan religion a lower status. As a faithful Christian of the sixteenth century, he must not be condoned for it, because even if Las Casas had reached a conclusion that a religion had the same or superior value to Christianity, it is certain he could not have presented such an idea in public. In order to defend the Native Americans from the very religious-minded Europeans, he did have to compromise on some issues. Yet, even for him, gods of pagan religions were essentially 'erroneous, defective, and lesser' deities, and their worship must eventually be terminated in the long run, with the exception of local, conventional religious events acceptable within Christian doctrine.

Let us cite a part of the *Apologética Historia Sumaria*. Las Casas talks about the people of Middle America:

> *no dudosa de aquí* [en] *adelante al mundo todo, la ventaja incomparable que estas naciones, en especial las de tantas y tan grandes provincias como eran las que dijimos comprenderse dentro de la que se nombraba la Nueva España, a todas las más del mundo, señaladamente a las griegas, y mucho más a las romanas y no menos a las hebreas, cuando idolatraban, en la modestia y religiosa honestidad, templanza, orden, reposo, gravedad, silencio, lágrimas, ... concluido en los seis precedentes capítulos haber hecho ventaja las naciones de la Nueva España a todas o a las más gentes del mundo idólatras, mayormente a los griegos y más a los romanos, y a todas, en lo tocante a sus sacrificios,... conviene a saber... La tercera, en la preciosidad*

---

[141] Las Casas 1992: Chap.34, p.225.

y valor de los sacrificios...[142]

(...it is not doubtful, from now on, in the whole world, that these states, especially so many and so large provinces named the New Spain, which we comprehended the inside of, have an incomparable advantage over all of the world, especially the Greeks, and a great deal the Romans and not less than the Hebrews. When they were idolized, in the modest religious honorableness, moderation, order, rest, gravity, silence, tears, ... I have concluded in the previous six chapters that the nations of New Spain have done advantage to all or to the peoples of the idolatrous world, greater to the Greeks and more to the Romans, and to all, in it concerning their sacrifices, ... It is important to know; ...The third, in the preciousness and value of the sacrifices..)

In the same work, although Las Casas praised the people of New Spain (the Middle America) as better than the Peruvian people in terms of the number of religious ceremonies and the quality of offerings to the gods[143], he apparently preferred the Peruvian people to the former in term of religious character. Let us look at Las Casas' conclusions about the Peruvian people:

Por consiguiente, queda manifesto y muy manifesto cuánta ventaja hicieron éstas a todas las otras o a las más del mundo, ... más dignos y más nobles y más limpio o menos lleno de haces de errores de idolatría, concepto y estimación y conocimiento de la excelencia y perfecciones de Dios o de los dioses que tenían por verdadero Dios...[144]

(Consequently, it remains clear and very evident as much as advantage which they did these, to all the others or to the majority of the world, ... much worthy, much noble and much clean or less full of making errors of idolatry, concept and estimation and knowledge of the excellence and perfections of God or of gods which they possessed for the true God.)

It is certain that Las Casas concluded that both the Peruvian and Central American religions were better than the ancient Roman and Greek pagan ones. However, it is also evident that Las Casas never accepted pagan religions as essential teaching for human beings. By comparing the above two citations, it can also be noted that his idea clearly suggests that the Peruvian people were better than the Central Americans, because the former were less idolatrous and knew the excellency of the true God as the lord of other gods. He cited Peruvian religion as

---

[142] Las Casas 1967:TomoII, lib.III, Cap.CXCIII, p.292-3.
[143] Las Casas 1967:Tomo II, Lib.III, Cap.CXCIV, p.294
[144] Las Casas 1967:Tomo II, Lib.III, Cap.CXCIV, p.296.

the least corrupted pagan religion according to his Christian standards.

As he mentioned that the Guatemalan Maya believed in the existence of good and evil angels or spirits,[145] it is certain that Las Casas considered some of the Maya deities to be good angels. Nevertheless, Las Casas never changed his stance into 'idols = demons.' Because the Maya worshiped their gods through idols, almost all the Maya deities were devils for Las Casas. In fact, in another part of the text, he called all their pagan gods '*sus pecados Dios* (their sinning Gods)'[146] with the exception of their supreme deity.

Contrary to such Christian reactions towards pagan religions, as will be discussed, although the pagan people of the sixteenth and seventeenth centuries often showed a strong resistance to Christian domination and Christianity, there is little evidence that they rejected Christianity as a religion. For example, the famous anti-Christian Asian political leaders, such as Hideyoshi Toyotomi （豊臣秀吉）of Japan and Chen-Lung （乾隆帝）of China, regarded Christianity as a homogeneous religion of their own.[147] While suppressing Christianity as a barbaric and mean teaching, they did not initially treat Christianity as a false creed as the Christians did pagan religions. Although Toyotomi Hideyoshi stated that Christianity is a conceited, 'saucy' religion, Christianity was still considered acceptable. Indeed, he later explained the reason to the envoy of Portugal as follows: principally, a human being should be able to choose any religion freely, whichever meets that person's need. And because each religion instructed the people in an appropriate way to worship the Godhood within a specific region, in general, it is usual for one to believe that a traditional religion of one's native place is more suitable. Although Las Casas was of course far more humanistic than the Japanese military dictator, who had twice made brutal invasions of Korea, it is also evident that on the point of religious matters, Toyotomi Hideyoshi was much more tolerant and open-minded than Las Casas. The reason for this different view can be

---

[145] e.g. Las Casas 1967:tomo II, Lib.III, Cap.CCXXXV, p.507.
[146] Las Casas 1967:Tomo I, Lib.III, Cap.LXXXV, p.441.

explained as the consequence of different perspectives towards the universe. While Hideyoshi regarded religion as a part of the universe, as I have argued in my discussion of the *Chumayel* in the previous chapter, for Las Casas, a religion (= Christianity only) must embrace the whole universe.

Las Casas' view towards pagan religions was far from the concept of religious 'freedom.' This point of view may be proved in a comparison between he and a Japanese anti-Christian philosopher of the nineteenth century. Works of a Japanese Classical scholar, Atutane Hirata (平 田 篤 胤　c.1776-1843), are the best documented and known example of anti-Christian revisionism (let us call him a Japanese Sepúlveda because of his extremely nationalistic view). Like Las Casas, he also collected ancient religious narratives of various countries. As Las Casas' was, one of the purposes of Hirata's analysis of Christianity was partly to understand the origin of the human perceptions of 'gods' in various parts of the world. During this process, he incorporated some Christian ideas into the Japanese religion, Shinto. As the ancient Christian saints attacked Roman pagan philosophers, Hirata defined Confucianism, (let us call this the Asian Platonism here) which constituted a vigorous intellectual faction in the Japan of his time, as an imperfect understanding of the nature of gods. The true gods could not be understood by the intellect of shrewd humans like the ancient Chinese sages. He also categorized Christianity as a diffused and primitive understanding of Japanese Shinto. On this point, it may be said that Hirata's view was quite similar to that of Las Casas. However, the stance of Hirata is essentially different from Las Casas. While being an excessive nationalist and anti-Christian, he did not dismiss the Christian *Bible*, but referred to it as one of the true narratives of the 'GODS,' although he defined it as a corrupted book written by the Southern barbaric peoples [=the European]. Hitara treated both the Japanese sacred texts and the Christian holy scriptures as almost equivalent old records of the GODS.[148]

Some may say that Sepúlveda and Las Casas also accepted certain parts of

---

[147] See Yamase 2002b:234-8, 253-4.

165

pagan religion as corrupted Gospel. Yet, it must be noted that while being an excessive racist, in order to incorporate Christian elements into the Japanese religion, Hirata even accepted the existence of holy spirits within Christianity, personages found in some parts of the Holy Scriptures, and several 'errors' in ancient Japanese sacred texts. This was impossible for Las Casas. In this process, some scholars argue that Hirata adopted the Christian concept of the sole Creator of the world from the Christian sources (as I have mentioned in the previous chapter, the *Kojiki*, the sacred text of the Japanese narrate the gods as if they are offspring of nature), because the concept of the sole Creator at the beginning of the universe had already been argued among some of the Japanese classical scholars well before him.[149] Therefore, it is still controversial whether Hirata's idea of the supreme deity as the Creator and Master of the universe was directly influenced by Christian sources or not. However, what is evident is that he used the *Bible* as important supporting evidence of his interpretation of Japanese classic works, and also he often mentioned that the truth should be supported by various sources in the world. Hirata treated the Christian *Bible* as one of true ancient records through which he could find a unique path to the 'GODS' and to the reconstruction of the true context of the cosmos.[150]

This point is a significant difference between Hirata and Las Casas. For the pagan, their scriptures are generally 'ancient Records of a particular region,' but not the 'Word of God' provided by the past 'selected divine' prophets. In such a culture, prophets were not always taken seriously, but the 'antiquity of the scriptures' was. Moreover, the pagans made the ethnicity of a religion an issue and attacked Christianity as a religion of the foreigner.

The Tolupan of Honduras also integrated Christianity into their cosmovision in

[148] See Yamase 2002b: 234-7, 252-3.
[149] Tahara 1963:119-122. Tahara is critical of those who overemphasized the impact of Christianity within Hirata's works, because for Hirata, the Christian materials were merely one of his source materials. As the main target of Hirata's criticism was Confucianism and Buddhism, he favored the ideas of Christianity and found Taoism useful to discredit Confucianism.
[150] My early arguments on Hirata's reconstruction of the true way of the gods can be seen in Yamase 2002b:234-246. For more details of his life and career, see *e.g.* Tahara 1963.

spite of their dislike of it. They chose to reconstruct their traditional cosmovision, which is able to explain the existence of Christianity as an exterior religion, like Hirata, and, although lesser deities, the Christian God and Jesus are almost homogeneously treated.

On the other hand, Las Casas found Native American pagan religions to be proof of their limited understanding of the Christian God due to a lack of instruction. He (and Sepúlveda) tried to understand pagan religions within Christian theology only. No doubt, his aim was to 'repair' the imperfection of pagan religions, which is a 'correction,' but not a 'reconstruction.' The works of Hirata are somewhat different from Hideyoshi Toyotomi and Chen-lung, as Hirata tried to make Shinto not a part of the universe, but as its unique religion, like Las Casas. Nevertheless, in spite of the fact that Hirata proposed Shinto as the unique truth of the universe, the conclusion reached by Hirata was virtually a 'reconstruction' of the cosmos from the sources of various religions, whereas Las Casas maintained the superior position of Christianity over other religions. Why was there such a serious difference between the Christian and the pagan people? I think the phenomenon found in the ideas of Hirata is representative of a dualistic culture.

Like the Japanese, other Asians and Native Americans, the Maya have also traditionally interpreted incoming culture within their dualism. In other words, Christianity was regarded as a religion homogenous with their own. This difference of attitude toward an alien religion must be taken into account when issues of Mayanized Christianity are discussed. Therefore, it may be said that Las Casas and other Christians tended to comprehend pagan religions in their monistic minds; on the contrary, Asians and Native Americans understood the existence of the Christian Lord with their dualistic minds.

The conflict between Sepúlveda and Las Casas continued. Some followed the former and others, the latter. It is known that Las Casas was well received by numerous Spanish intellectuals, including the members of the Royal Council of the sixteenth century. A sixteenth-century friar, Francisco Falcón, for example, wrote a letter to the Spanish king with apparent influence from Las Casas, in which he denied the crown's right of domination over the New World.[151] Perhaps, as a result of such humanists' efforts, the peace treaty of Acobamba, which considerably favored the Inca, was eventually agreed between the Neo-Inca and the Spanish crown in 1569.[152] In that treaty, forced conversion to Christianity is not mentioned as a duty of the Inca.

Contrary to Las Casas' opposition to the conversion of people without a full understanding of Christian doctrines and their own will, the Franciscans still tended to opt for mass conversion. The policy of the Franciscans resulted in an increase in the so-called dual believers. It was not an inevitable situation. Nevertheless, the Franciscans regarded any remaining pagan elements among converted Native Americans as a serious crime against Christianity. On the Yucatan peninsula, from 1562, the bishop of Yucatan, Diego de Landa, tortured the Maya during his campaign against the remaining Maya religions. However, his campaign was short-lived. The crown ordered him to leave due to his excessive brutality.

On the other hand, the Spanish king did not always regard humanitarians' activities as positive for the stability of colonial administration.[153] In fact, he advised Francisco de Toledo, the fifth viceroy of Peru, to be cautious in his activities in Peru. While removing works of Las Casa from the public on approval of the crown[154], therefore, Francisco de Toledo and his advisers revived the logic of Sepúlveda in order to terminate the remaining Inca influence over the Andes. Yet, in 1573, one year after the complete fall of the Inca, the crown officially stated that '*future discoveries are not called conquests and only peaceful methods must be employed.*'[155] So, the result of the great debate between Las Casas and Sepúlveda

---

[151] Falcón 1567.
[152] The full text of the treaty of Acobamba and its accompanied documents were published in Guillén 1978.
[153] Levillier 1935: tomo I, p.126-7, Hanke 1965:162-3, Hemming 1993:396.
[154] Hanke 1965:163, Zimmerman 1938:105 note 14.
[155] CDIA, vol.16., p.142.

seems to have ended with the victory of Las Casas, at least in the state's ideology. The Spanish crown never allowed the works of Sepúlveda and of Pedro Sarmiento de Gamboa to be published, despite the fact that both were written to justify the military conquest and Spanish domination of the New World.[156]

However, as historians have mentioned, the victory of Las Casas did not produce overall positive result. The theory of Sepúlveda was widely used by the colonial Spaniards. Even in 1595, a Franciscan, Fray Gerónimo de Mendieta (c.1524-1604), praised Hernán Cortés, the conqueror of Mexico, as a new Moses,[157] although at the same time, he also accused the Spaniards of brutal treatment of the Native Americans as an undeniable fact, and praised Las Casas for his unusual efforts to defend the Native Americans from the destruction caused by his nation.[158] Moreover, the number of Dominicans sent to Spain decreased markedly after the sixteenth century.[159]

Outside New Spain, for example, the Dominicans of the seventeenth century in China were known for their intolerance of Chinese religions, contrary to Las Casas' defense of the 'Native American practice' of pagan religions. The majority of Las Casas' policy was inherited by the Jesuits rather than by his fellow Dominicans.

A noted Jesuit of the sixteenth century, José de Acosta (c.1540-1600), further developed Las Casas' theory. By pointing out several cultural distinctions achieved by the Native Americans, Acosta admonished exaggeration of the superiority of the Spaniards over them.[160] In addition, he criticized excessive Spanish nationalist arguments about the justice of the Spanish conquest of the New World.[161]

However, on several important points, Acosta's attitude towards the Native Americans (and the Asians) was fundamentally different from that of Las Casas. Firstly, certainly due to his fear of the Spanish royal authority, his stance was more

---

[156] Sarmiento de Gamboa 1572.
[157] Mendieta 1595: Book III, Chap.1, p.53-58.
[158] Mendieta 1595: Book IV, Chap. 1, p.77-8.
[159] Borges 1977:481-535.
[160] Acosta 1590:Lib.6, Cap.1, Lib.7, Cap.28.
[161] Acosta 1588:Parte II, Cap.2-7. See Hanke 1974:133-4.

169

neutral, like the *nepantlism* of the colonial Nahuatl. Acosta referred to Las Casas as one of the anonymous, excessive critics of the *Conquistadors*.[162] Acosta also categorized all pagan people as 'uncivilized people.' In his view, the cultural standard of the Native American was of the lowest type.[163] Like Las Casas, Acosta referred to the traditional perception of the supreme invisible deity among the Native Americans as the Christian Lord, yet he considered it to be evidence that the Native Americans possessed no intellectual capability of understanding the true Christian God.[164] He even called the intellectual level of the Native Americans 'that of children.'[165] Moreover, although passively, he regarded the consequence of the destruction of the Native American states as a positive effect, because Christianity had became known among the Native Americans and it had ended the sins against the Christian God committed by them before Spanish domination.[166] In a sense, Acosta's view might be called hypocritical eclecticism derived from both Las Casas and Sepúlveda.

One of his books, *De Procuranda Indorum Salute Pacificación y Colonización* (1588), is interesting.[167] In this book, a gradual transformation from pagan religions to Christianity is discussed. He argued that some pagan traditions, which were not opposing Christian doctrines, must be preserved. For example, he insisted on the necessity of maintaining pagan temples, and that only idols must be removed from those temples. Moreover, by introducing a case from the early England of the pagan period. A rite of animal (=cow) sacrifice for pagan deities practiced among the English, was transformed into a religious celebration for the Christian God in which cows were killed as a meal for the people, but not as an animal sacrifice for Satan, and thus avoiding he sin of sacrifice.[168] His idea, however, does not provide

---

[162] Acosta 1590:lib.7, Cap.27.
[163] Acosta 1588:Prologo. The fact is that even Las Casas did not stop calling the pagan 'the barbarians' to the end. e.g. see Las Casas 1967: Lib.III, cap.LXXII, p.374..
[164] Acosta 1590:lib.5, Cap.3.
[165] Acosta 1588:Parte 1, Cap.8.
[166] Acosta 1590:Lib.7, Cap.27.
[167] Acosta 1588.
[168] Acosta 1588: Part III, Cap.24., p.295-9.

any innovative view of pagan religions.

Although Las Casas tried to prove all other religions probable errors before the Gospel, the European friars continuously treated pagan religions as devil worship. In Japan, a Jesuit, Alessandro Valignano (1539-1606), was known for his new approach of adaptation of national customs. Unlike other European friars, he accepted the intellectual ability of the Japanese, where before all Japanese traditional religions had been called childish superstitions or works of Satan.[169] In a report, he argued that when Latin was taught to the Japanese, none of the ancient Roman and Greek works (such as of Aristotle), containing the ideas of the pagan gentiles, must be used as textbooks.[170]

In the case of China, the Dominicans ignored Las Casas. Due to the Dominican insistence on intolerance of Chinese religious rites, Dominican friars were more cruelly persecuted than the Jesuits by the Chinese officials of the seventeenth and eighteenth centuries. A famous Jesuit, Matteo Ricci (1552-1610), was well received in some circles by educated Chinese, in spite of the fact that though he was strongly impressed with Confucianism, he never accepted the possible salvation of Confucius.

In addition, it is known that in Spain, Las Casas had been treated as a quisling.

The prejudged concept that monotheism is better than animism and dualism, and that Christianity is the final goal which all humans must eventually reach, remained among the Western cultures. At the end of twentieth century, Paul Carus wrote:

THIS WORLD OF OURS is a world of opposites. There is light and shade, there is heat and cold, there is good and evil, there is God and the Devil.
The dualistic conception of nature has been a necessary phase in the evolution of human thought. We find the same views of good and evil spirits prevailing among all the peoples of the earth at the very beginning of that stage of their development which, in the phraseology of Tylor, is commonly called Animism. But the principle of unity dominates the development of thought. Man tries to unify his conceptions in a consistent and harmonious

---

[169] Valignano 1583: Chap.3, p.27-31.
[170] Valignano 1583: Chap.12, p.78-80.

Monism....Monotheism and Monodiabolism, both originating simultaneously in the monistic tendencies of man's mental evolution, together constitute a Dualism which to many is still the most acceptable world-conception. Nevertheless, it is not the final goal of human philosophy. A soon as the thinkers of mankind become aware of the Dualism implied in this interpretation of the world, the tendency is again manifested towards a higher conception, which is a purely monistic view.[171]

And part of a work by the noted US writer of the nineteenth century, William Prescott:

It is a remarkable fact, that many, if not most, of the rude tribes inhabiting the vast American continent, however disfigured their creeds may have been in other respects by a childish superstition, had attained to the sublime conception of one Great Spirit, the Creator of the Universe, who, immaterial in his own nature, was not to be dishonored by an attempt at visible representation, and who, pervading all space, was not to be circumscribed within the walls of a temple. Yet these elevated ideas, so far beyond the ordinary range of the untutored intellect, do not seem to have led to the practical consequences that might have been expected; and few of the American nations have shown much solicitude for the maintenance of a religious worship, or found in their faith a powerful spring of action. But, with progress in civilization, ideas more akin to those of civilized communities were gradually unfolded.[172]

As Las Casas proposed three centuries ago, Prescott evidently considered the supreme God of the Inca to be the Christian God. Nevertheless, unlike Las Casas, this noted US historian did not accept the religious devotion of the Native American at the same level as the Christians did. Until the twentieth century, the emergence of the concept that each religion has a unique universal value had not appeared in the Occidental societies.[173]

In the twentieth century, people gradually began to be released from the fetters of the Christian thinking. Edward Carpenter summarized the historical Christian view towards pagan religions as follows:

---

[171] Carus 1900:1-2.
[172] Prescott Chap.3.
[173] In Japan, the Christians of the late nineteenth century often used 'natural error' to refer to traditional Japanese religions. e.g., Ozaki 1892:45-6.

To-day [1918] *we are witnessing in the Great European War a carnival of human slaughter which in magnitude and barbarity eclipses in one stroke all the accumulated ceremonial sacrifices of historical ages;...The mental attitudes, for instance, of Abraham sacrificing the ram, or of the Siberian angakout slaughtering a totem-bear, or of a modern and pious Christian contemplating the Saviour on the Cross are really almost exactly the same...For after all we see now that sacrifice is of the very essence of social life. 'It is expedient that one man should die for the people'; and not only that one man should actually die, but (what is far more important) that each man should be ready and willing to die in that cause, when the occasion and the need arises. Taken in its larger meanings and implications Sacrifice, as conceived in the ancient world, was a perfectly reasonable thing.*

Among those who appreciated pagan cultures more than Prescott, there has been a strong trend in the Western civilization placing pagan cults in apposition of 'primitive error' of the humankind.[174]

Consequently, in Western and Islamic cultures, a notion remains, even in these days, that monotheism is the last stage of a civilized people. This trend results in a biased view of 'the superiority of the people of European origin over the 'poor, less civilized, and barbaric' Orientals and Native Americans.'.

On the other hand, in Asia, the opposite view is seen:

When the Great Tao (Way or Method [=dualism]) *becomes obsolete, benevolence and righteousness came into vogue. (Then) wisdom and shrewdness appear, and great tricky hypocrisy ensue there.*[175]

By this logic, the region in which monotheism is dominant, is evidence that there have been numerous corruptions among the inhabitants of that land. Although Hirata did not speak directly of his view of monotheism, by reading his writings, it is almost certain that he would say: unlike other parts of the world where barbarous people became corrupted and disordered, the Japanese have by nature been excellent and perfect until today, therefore, God did not feel any necessity to send prophets to teach monotheism in Japan. In the case of China, the Chinese naturally questioned the reason why China, which was a much larger and more important place than other regions, is not mentioned in the Holy Scriptures. This initial question later formed an opinion that Christianity and other monotheistic religions

---

[174] Carpenter 1920:109-115.

are for the people in the West.

III: Spanish Version of Christianity in the New Worlds[176]

> We hold up our hands in horror at the thought of Huitzilopochtli dropping children
> from his fingers into the flames, but we have to remember that our own most
> Christian Saint Augustine was content to describe unbaptized infants as crawling for
> ever about the floor of Hell! What sort of god, we may ask, did Augustine worship?
> The Being who could condemn children to such a fate was certainly no better than
> the Mexican Idol (cited from Carpenter 1920:108-9).

William Prescott once wrote; *"But the doctrines* [of Christianity] *were too abstruse
in themselves to be comprehended at a glance by the rude intellect of a* [Aztec]
barbarian."[177] In the past, in works such as Prescott's, the Native American's
incapability of understanding the Gospel was often pointed out in studies of
religious 'syncretism,' but it is true that the context of Christianity is often
self-contradicting, even to its scholars. For example, the *Old Testament* says that
the Christian God as Spirit is, in essence, invisible and immense, and thus he cannot
really be expressed by any art or image. Nevertheless, the Christians also believe
that the first man was made according to the image of God.

As I have discussed, evangelizations in the two New Worlds were not
equivalent to the previous 'spiritual conquest of the Roman Empire.' In the time of
the Roman Empire, the Christians as a minority had to adopt several important
pagan elements to reduce hostility from the pagans. Consequently, a considerable
amount of pagan literature has survived today. However, the friars of the sixteenth
century often regarded the lingering influence of the Hellenistic pagan era as a
negative. In the New Worlds, therefore, it is not surprising that some friars
expected to create a much better Christian Kingdom. In the case of sixteenth
century Japan, Alejandro Valigano argued the necessity of burning all Japanese

---

[175] Lao-Tzu 580BC: Chap.18.
[176] For an useful introduction of the evangelization of the early colonial Guatemala, see
Stanzione, 2000:82-87.
[177] Prescott, 1843:book 3, chap.IX.

classic pagan literature.[178] On the Yucatan Peninsula, it is widely known that a Franciscan, Diego de Landa burnt precious Maya hieroglyphic codices, as he thought them to be a great obstacle to evangelization. As the result of their excessive passion for the purity of Christianity, the Christian evangelization of that era consequently resulted in the total destruction of cultural traditions in many cases.

In addition, although the early Christian people generally possessed a quite good awareness of Roman or Germanic pagan religions, the Spanish friars in New Spain did not always posses a full understanding of Native American religious concepts. It is true that some great friars, such as Francisco Ximénez, Bartolomé de Las Casas and Bernardino de Sahagún, who noticed the significance of the knowledge of Native American traditions for an effective evangelization, collected quite important ethnographical data and composed informative books. Nevertheless, the great majority of friars made this a limited field of study. Also, only a few of the friars managed to read the works of Sahagún or Las Casas. The works of Sahagún, for example, received persistent opposition to publication, and were not printed until the nineteenth century.

Therefore, in spite of numerous efforts of collecting ethnological information made by the Spanish friars, understanding Native cultures generally remained at the level of mystery.

Moreover, the friars often prevented the indigenous people from reading the whole Holy Scripture. Since the *Old Testament* contains some tales of pagan religions, the friars in the New World (and in Japan) were afraid that the indigenous people, who read the whole *Bible*, would misunderstand proper Christian teaching. Therefore, only selected portions of Christianity were introduced. What the colonial Spanish missionaries of the sixteenth century taught was not the exact context of the *Bible*. They made a concise account of the *Bible* and Christian doctrine as a textbook of Christianity for the Native Americans. In the case of

---

[178] Valigano, 1573.

175

Guatemala, the *Theología Indrum,* written by Domingo de Vico of the sixteenth century, is known. In Mexico, Pedro de Córdoba's work published in 1544 is one of the famous ones.[179] It is also known that the Portuguese friars in Japan (1590) and China later published almost the same textbook.[180]

Until 1555, there were numerous efforts to create Native American priests. In Mexico, for example, full Christian doctrine and Latin were taught for that purpose at *El Colegio de Santa Cruz,* which is also called the *Tolatelco* seminar. Spanish professors and Aztec noblemen collaborated well. One of the surviving works of this college is the *Libellus de Medicinalibus Indorum Herbis* of 1552.[181] This book is evidence that some colonial Nahuatl became competent in Latin.

However, negative opinions about the Native American's ability to comprehend the Christian faith were raised in New Spain, opinions which eventually reached the Spanish Crown. Ridiculously, those who expressed a negative view of the Native Americans insisted that Holy Scriptures should not be shown to them. They considered that not only did the Native Americans not efficiently understand the context of the *Bible,* but also that they would distort it. In my view, the latter rationale was the main cause of the ban.

Although it is not proper evidence, the case of Japan might explain the true reason for banning education of the Native Americans. In Japan, in spite of the fact that the Portuguese Jesuits of the sixteenth century accepted that the Japanese were the most reasonable among various 'barbaric' peoples in the world, certain Europeans were against granting education to the Japanese. For example, an Italian, Alejandro Valigano, who acted as the supervisor of the Jesuits, wrote a letter to Roma in 1580.[182] In his letter it is written that Francisco Gabriel, the head of the society in Japan, insisted that educating Japanese in Latin and Portuguese was not necessary, because if they acquired the full knowledge of the Holy Scriptures, the

---

[179] Cordóba, 1544.
[180] Dotirina-Kirisitan [1590]
[181] Cruz, 1552.
[182] Cited in Shûtte 1951:321-5. A Japanese translation of this letter is found in Matuda et al. 1973:301-3.

Japanese would not respect European friars and thus the religious order would not function well. According to Valigano, moreover, not only Gabriel but other Europeans had a notion that because the Japanese were an inferior race to the Europeans, Japanese monks must simply act as a mouthpiece for what European friars ordered. Valigano noticed that unless there were Japanese monks who knew Japanese traditions, the Church would attract nobody in Japan. In fact, some Japanese converts had already left Christianity due to a racist climate among the Europeans. Valigano later reformed the discriminative attitude towards the Japanese, and his reform resulted in increasing the Christian population in Japan.

However, although the Europeans were an ethnic minority in Japan, they became the ruling class in Latin America. Subsequently, as a result of several negativity regarding creating Native clergies, the ecclesiastical council finally decided in 1555 to forbid the creation of a Native American priesthood, and the majority of the Native Americans were prohibited from learning the entire Christian doctrine.[183] This discrimination may have played an important role in increasing the hostility towards Christianity among the Maya.

The ecclesiastical council's decision was clearly opposite to the sentiment of the early Christians. Like pagan religions in the era of the Roman Empire, Christianity in Latin America became a discriminative religion, which admitted its members according to their social rank.

This seems to be one of the major reasons for the failure of the Catholic spiritual conquest of the Maya. As Arimichi Ebizawa points out in his study of the Japanese Christians of the nineteenth century, the hierarchical structure of the Catholic Church was one of the major causes of the poor performance of the Catholic evangelization of Japan.[184] Within the hierarchical structure of the Catholic Church, for example, pastors are distinguished from ordinary Christians, and they are regarded as agents of the Lord. In this structure, the devotees of Catholicism cannot directly communicate with the Lord, and religiously had to rely

---

[183] See Hanke, 1974:24-7.

on their priests (though this concept is now being changed). On the other hand, every Protestant Christian theologically has a right to act as a priest. Although the Catholic policy was quite effective in avoiding syncretism or creation of new localized Christianity, this method has a certain defect.

Ebizawa argues that due to the different structural character of the Catholic and Protestant churches, the Catholics have generally been more passive. He points out that Japanese followers of Catholicism actively engaged in missionary work, were rare, whereas those of Protestantism popularized their belief and thought freely.[185] It must be noted that the same phenomenon can be observed in the Latin America today.

Therefore, in the case of the Catholics, it was clear that unless they created a Native American priesthood, a large number of friars had to be invited from Europe for efficient evangelization. Nevertheless, it is a well-known fact that during the colonial era, the numbers of friars were never adequate throughout Spanish America. Local communities always suffered from lack of a priest. In some cases, the existing priests' quality was also questionable. Consequently, because of a fear of decreasing income, the Spaniards in remote areas often discouraged their Native American laborers from going to churches a long way from their homes. As time passed, the number of secular churches became greater than the mendicant orders. The former were generally concerned with the Spaniards only.

The decision of hiding Christian writings from indigenous American people was also applied to various versions of the *Theología Indrum*. All of these were collected and locked away. When we consider the reason for the temporal success of the evangelization of China, the lack of an instruction book in their own language prevented the Maya from understanding Christianity.

There seem to have been some exceptions. Some of the *Books of Chilam Balam* of the Yucatec Maya prove that they had quite a good knowledge of Christian sources; probably the authors of these texts managed to read full

---

[184] Ebizawa, 1968:473-4.

178

Christian materials in church, even after 1555 (of course, they may have stolen these materials from churches). This suggests that under some specific circumstances, some of the educated Maya were able to consult Christian materials during the colonial period. Yet, this should be regarded as an exceptional case. In most cases, the Native Americans' knowledge of Christianity during the colonial period was limited to the context found in the concise versions of Christian doctrines. In fact, all the colonial Guatemalan Maya texts of the sixteenth and seventeenth centuries clearly prove that the Christian influence came from the *Theología Indrum* only. Therefore, when we consider the Christian influence found in colonial indigenous texts, the concise version of the *Bible* edited by the colonial friars is more important than the 'real' *Bible*.

For this research, I have used a colonial document called *Un manuscripto K'ekchí del siglo XVI*,[186] one variant of the *Theología Indrum*, and the work of Pedro de Córdoba. The former is a unique published version of the *Theología Indrum*. It was aimed at a more effective evangelization of the Guatemalan Maya. The latter was written to evangelize the Central Mexican people. However, the context is so much concise that the Native Americans only acquired a rude knowledge of the nature of Christianity. Indeed, although I read *Un manuscripto K'ekchí del siglo XVI*, and Pedro Cordoba's work,[187] I was never able to grasp the full nature of the Gospels from them.

The main purpose of these concise versions of Christian doctrines was, of course, to dismiss pagan religions as a teaching of Satan by emphasizing the existence of the one powerful God. However, it must be said that these materials were an extremely poor and problematic source. Although it is true that the texts narrate the power of the Christian Lord, the Trinity and the origin of Christian religion, *Un manuscripto K'ekchí del siglo XVI* essentially narrates the concise history of Christianity, without much explanation of its fundamental conceptual

[185] Ebizawa, 1968:473-4.
[186] María Bossú Z., 1990.
[187] Córdoba, 1540.

issues. Cordóba's work is considerably better than *Un manuscripto K'ekchi del siglo XVI* on this point. It provides a more comprehensive instruction of Christianity to the readers, though often much abbreviated. Nevertheless, I found that this work has several fundamental defects as a textbook of the Gospel for pagan people.

Let us cite a part of Cordóba's work:

> ... *God does not ask you to sacrifice your children, or kill your slaves, or any other living person, or cut your own flesh, or spill your own blood. He only wants you to love Him and honor Him as the true God, and not to consider any other as God, for there is no other God except Him. And those things that you worship as gods have no power. They cannot give you anything, because there is only one God. He is the one we preach to you, and He is very good. The gods you worship and honor as gods are only devils and evil enemies of the true God. The God whom we preach to you threw your gods from His house, as later we shall tell you, because they were evil, and they wished you ill. They ordered you to kill your children and your slaves and other persons, and they further ordered you to spill your own blood. But the real God of whom we preach, since He is good, loves Christians well, and will love you if you wish to be His friends. He does not want you to kill your children or your slaves, or any other person, nor does He want you to shed your blood unnecessarily.*
>
> *Our God is also very large, because He is in Heaven and on earth and in the air, and here and in Castile and in all the world, although you do not see Him, because God does not have a body. Since He does not have a body, we cannot see Him with the eyes we have of the body; but the soul, which has no body, very easily can see Him after it leaves the body. Even though we do not see Him here, He is among us and gives us life. If He did not sustain our lives, we would die at once. He is in all things and supports them in their being, and gives them power to increase and multiply in Heaven. He displays himself to His friends, very clear and beautiful, where you and we shall see Him if you become His friends, and if you become Christians.*
>
> *You should love this God who is so great and so powerful, so beautiful, so rich, and so good, and who loves mankind so much. And you should serve Him and take Him to be your God because there is no other God but Him.*
>
> *And you will recognize the deception in which you have lived by believing that Huitzilopochtli or Tezcatlipoca, and others whom you regarded as gods, were gods. They were not gods, but evil demons who deceived you, as we shall explain later, since there is not in all the world or in Heaven or on earth or in the sea any God except the one and only God who rules and governs and sustains everything.*

And this is the first Article that you must believe, so that you may go to Heaven to share and enjoy the pleasures that God has provided there for His friends.[188]

By emphasizing the deception of the Aztec gods, the text persuades the Aztec people to abandon these gods and to adore the Christian Lord. Although the context of this text matters little, there is an important point. One of the essential concepts of Christianity, as I have mentioned, is a denial of the harmonized relationship between the spirit and nature, including humankind. However, because orthodox Christianity accepts the theory of the Trinity, this concept is not always clear to non-Christian people. Indeed, these concise versions of the *Bible* do not provide a comprehensive explanation of the Trinity. Let us examine the text of Cordóba cited above.

In the above-cited text he says, "*Our God is also very large, because He is in Heaven and on earth and in the air, and here and in Castile and in all the world, although you do not see Him, because God does not have a body.*"

Yet, the text also says in another place: "*...God decided to become man and to take on human flesh from the Virgin Mary, He sent a very beautiful angel from Heaven ... who spoke to her on behalf of God, and told her... the Son of God joined in Himself a soul and body in the unity of one person.*"[189]

Cordoba's book also says "*...please understand well that the person of the Father, and the person of the Holy Spirit did not become man and take on human flesh, but it was only the person of the Son that took on human flesh and became man... *".[190] Although Cordóba tried to persuade the people that the existence of Jesus, a visual God, is the sole exception, he substantially failed to explain the Trinity. Moreover, the readers of his text may well consider that 'the Lord may consider the necessity of another Son in the future,' as frequently discussed by anti-Christian ancient Roman people.

Because of these defects, I was never able to comprehend the proper reason for

---

[188] Cited from Córdoba, 1970:60-1.
[189] Cited from Córdoba, 1970:87.

banning idols within Christianity. The text simply says, '*Do not worship idols!*,' and no explanation is provided as to why figures of Jesus Christ are an exception.[191] The issue of the Trinity is the same.[192] If some think that my lack of understanding was caused by my lack of intelligence, it may be. Yet, the fact is, that I eventually had to read not only a full version of *Bible*, but also the early and medieval saints' works, like those of St. Augustine, and numerous academic introductory works in order to understand these questions.

The situation was the same in China, although the Chinese were given much more information through communications with the West than were the Native Americans. Christianity was propagated chiefly by the Portuguese and French Jesuits in the China of the seventeenth century. The Catholic friars provided a concise version of the *Bible* to the Chinese, as they did in Latin America. Consequently, much confusion concerning Christianity wwas questioned by anti-Christian Chinese people.

I will cite a useful paragraph from John D. Young's book. He summarizes the ideas and knowledge concerning the Gospel presented by Yang Kuang-hsien (楊光先), a Chinese critique of Christianity in the seventeenth century.

> *Yang's broad knowledge of the stories in the Old Testament was derived from Li's pamphlet, but his understanding of the New Testament was very limited. His only source of information was Matteo Ricci's T'ien-chu shih-i, which never explained in any detail the Christian doctrine of the Trinity. Not knowing the relationship between the Father and the Son, Yang asked that if T'ien-chu, or Yeh-su (Jesus Christ), had come to earth for thirty-three years, who was taking care of his business in heaven during those years? ... if Jesus did come to earth during the Han dynasty, before Han times the world would not have had a God. Yang was perhaps illogical and confusing, but his ignorance of the doctrine of Trinity was excusable. Confucian literati of*

---

[190] Cited from Córdoba, 1970:86.

[191] The reason for banning the idols is mentioned in *Un manuscripto K'ekchi del siglo XVI* (María Bossú Z. ,1990: Cap.XII 80-1). According to this source, Satan (a Spanish term, *Diablo*, is used in the original text) ordered the people to make idols and to worship him in front of the idols, in spite of the fact that except for the Lord, none of the other deities must be worshipped. Yet, it does not explain why the figure of Jesus can be an exception.

[192] Of course, there is an explanation about the Trinity in *Un manuscripto K'ekchi del siglo XVI*. See María Bossú Z., 1990: Ca.XIX 111, Cap.28, 142-3..

nineteenth-century China were also puzzled by the same problem, Wei Yuan argued that Jesus never claimed himself to be God but only the son of God. Yang also found the doctrine of sin to be highly unsatisfactory. He was particularly concerned about why Jesus did not come to earth to save all souls. If God really was solicitous for Adam's welfare, Yang asked, why did God come down so late and not soon after Adam was created? Yang, like many Confucian literati of his time, believed that a perfect society was possible on earth if the teachings of the sages were followed. With such a this-worldly mentality, Yang was prompted to ask practical questions. If there were really an all-powerful supreme being named T'ien-chu, why then did he not bring happiness to all people on earth? Why was there no paradise on earth? Indeed, Yang's arguments had such a secular bent that the missionaries would be hard put to present a theological rebuttal in terms of Chinese thought...[193]

This type of question was continuously raised by the Chinese of the eighteenth century. A similar story can be observed in the case of anti-Christian Japanese scholars of the nineteenth century. Limited access to the Holy Scripture often resulted in the discrediting of Christianity and a confusion of its doctrines.

In the case of the Maya, it is now known that except for urban areas, due to a lack of a sufficient number of friars and often their poor knowledge of Maya tongues, the evangelization of the Maya was not always efficiently practiced. Almost certainly, the level of colonial Spanish evangelization was not more than the context of *Un manuscripto K'ekchi del siglo XVI* in most rural towns and villages. With such poor instructional materials, how many Maya managed to understand Christianity completely?

When distribution of the concise version of the *Bible* was forbidden in the late sixteenth century, it is not difficult to imagine what happened. In Guatemala, no surviving colonial Maya religious texts mentioned any Christian material apart from the *Theologia Indrum*. The fact is, that except for some elite Maya who practically became 'Spaniards,' the Spanish language remained a very alien language for the majority of the Maya during the colonial era. Even for those who could read Spanish well, access to the Holy Scripture was often impossible. In addition, the level of Maya language spoken by the Spanish friars was poor, even in

---

[193] Cited from Young, 1983:87. As to a published edition of Matteo Ricci's *T'ien-chu shih-i*, Ricci (1985) is a bilingual (Chinese and English) edition..

183

the late colonial period. I can imagine that the Spanish version of Christianity sounded like, 'Please confusingly comprehend the Gospel through your imagination!' to the Maya.

How did the colonial Native Americans manage to understand this paradox through poor interpreters? It is obvious that the imperfect understanding of the Gospel among the colonial Maya was not always caused by their 'inferior' intellectual ability. Although it is ostensibly confusing, I argue that Christian elements were analytically integrated into the Maya Cosmo in the *Book of Chilam Balam of Chumayel* of the colonial Yucatec Maya. It must be said that limited knowledge of the Holy Scriptures was another, and possibly more serious, reason for improper understanding of the Gospel among the Maya. However, it should not be overemphasized as the most important reason. The *Books of Chilam Balam* of the Yucatec Maya suggest that the authors of those manuscripts often had good access to various Catholic Holy Scriptures.[194] Full access to the Holy Scriptures often caused 'localization of Christianity' among the Christian flock.

As will be discussed in the next chapter, the Japanese of the nineteenth and twentieth centuries had full access to the Holy Scriptures, although available translations did not cover all Christian writings. Nevertheless, certain Japanese attempted to create their own Christianity. Why did they do so?

Even if one reads a full version of the *Bible* in his or her own language, for example, the issue of the Trinity often becomes controversial as it did to the Chinese of the seventeenth and eighteenth century, because Jesus Christ never claims himself to be God. He only says that he is a son of the Lord. This question already existed in the ancient Roman Empire, as the Emperor Julian wrote, "... *if God wished that no one should be adored but himself, why do you adore this son* [=Jesus], *whom God never thought, nor ever will think to be his own?* "[195] This question was continuously raised by almost all pagan cultures, and it often led

---

[194] The *Books of Chilam Balam of Kaua* is a good example. As to a recent translation of it, see Bricker and Miram (2002).
[195] Julian, 361-363:47.

people to the conclusion that what the Westerners taught was not always a proper understanding of the Gospel. It also led the people to consider the great possibility of Western distortion of the original *Bible*. Consequently, they initiated an effort to reinterpret the *Bible* from their own local perspective in order to restore its true meaning.

When a dual religious (Maya religions and Christianity) texts such as the *Books of Chilam Balam* are considered, researchers have tended to consider them evidence of Maya hidden resistance to Christianity (*e.g.* a prudent way of hiding old Maya faith from the Spaniards). Yet, the fact is that the exact intention of the authors of those manuscripts is not known. Although there is plenty of circumstantial evidence that the colonial Maya showed hostility to Christianity, it is also true that there is no solid evidence to deny those authors were a faithful Chritsian flock. When we consider the relationship between Christianity and the Maya and other pagan religions, it must be understood that there have always been certain Maya converts who willingly became Christian. We should not eliminate the possibility that religious 'reconstruction' found in colonial Maya texts may have been made by faithful Maya converts. In Japan, in spite of the dominant pagan society, some Japanese converted to Christianity. The important point is, nevertheless, that those faithful converts often created their own version of Christianity due to their anti-Western feeling.

In the case of the colonial Maya, precise reconstruction of their views towards Christianity is virtually impossible. No doubt there was considerable anti-Spanish feeling, not only among the traditional Maya pagan priests, but also among the Maya converts. Although some mendicant orders worked hard for the Maya, the *encomenderos* exploited the Maya, and it is also true that there were certain friars cooperative with the Spaniards. In addition, like Diego de Landa, the bishop of the Yucatan, some friars used violence to evangelize the Maya.

In Guatemala, it is well known that the Dominicans led by Father Bartolomé de Las Casas, who practiced evangelization by peaceful methods, gained a certain credit from the Native Guatemalans in the sixteenth century. In their supervised area, the Maya traditions were usually tolerated. However, it is also true that there were notable numbers of the friars, including the Dominicans, who exploited the Guatemalan Maya.

Tomas López Medel, who acted as a *visitador* in Guatemala, in his letter of 1557[196] stated that the Spaniards were the worst example to the Native Americans and argued the necessity of increasing the number of friars as a remedy.

In another of his letters to the Spanish king on 20 April 1556, he expressed an urgent remedy for corruption among not only the Spaniards, but also the clergy:

> *La clerecía deste obispado y aun de todo el distrito tiene necesidad de especialísima reformación porque su codicia es mucha y muy sin rienda, y su recogimiento y compostura exterior disoluta y muy desbaratada, y en alguna manera retardan y impiden la conversión destos pobres naturales entre quien andan, con el mal ejemplo de pestilencial codicia y con otras disonancias de vida. Sería yo de voto y parecer que V. M. mandase dar orden cómo hubiese un visitador general para acá, persona de grande autoridad y bondad, con suficientísimo salario para reformación destos abusos.*[197]
>
> (The clergy of this bishopric and of all the districts even have a necessity of the most special reformation because their greed is extreme without a rein, their collective, outer composure dissolute and very ruined; and in some way they delay and prevent the conversion of poor Natives with whom they walk, with their bad example of pestilential greed and with other dissonances of life. I would wish that Your Majesty would issue an order that there be a general *visitador* here, a person of great authority and kindness, with sufficient wages for reformation of these abuses.)

His letter clearly suggests that not only ordinary Spaniards, but also certain of the friars, provoked anti-Spanish sentiment among the Maya. It is not strange to consider that among those who were already converted, the desire to be independent from the Spanish friars had increased.

Moreover, another important point must be made. Although various writings by Tomas López[198] suggest that he showed sympathy to the Native Americans and

---

[196] *Carta al Real Consejo de Indias* [Reformas que debían hacerse en Guatemala, Yucatán y en el Nuevo Reino de Granada] *20 de diciembre de 1557.* in Pereña et al., 1990:124-140.

[197] This letter, *Carta al Rey*, is printed in Pereña et al., 1990:114-118. The quotation with some modernizations cited from *ibid.*:116.

[198] Pereña et al. (1990) is a published collection of his reports.

continued insisting on the necessity of defending them from abuse from the Spaniards, his humanistic attitude does not mean that what he was to create in Guatemala was desirable for the Guatemalan Maya, because his humanistic view was based on a self-righteous Christian view. In his letters, he always suggests that more effective evangelization of Christianity was the best remedy to save the mistreated Native American. While insisting on the equal treatment of the Maya, however, he cautioned against the religious commitment of the Maya. In his order issued on the Yucatan peninsula in 1553 (see Appendix III), his humanistic but also lopsided view of Maya traditions is clearly observed. One of the problems of his policy was exclusion of Maya from controlling ecclesiastical matters two years before the ecclesiastical council's decision of prohibiting the creation of a native priesthood, in spite of the inadequate quality and number of the Spanish friars. Moreover, due to his excessive desire to spread the Gospel in a pure (from a Spanish view) form, he intervened in every aspect of Maya life. Let us look at the text:

31. En Jesucristo todos somos libres, y en cuanto a la ley temporal también lo son los que nacen de padres libres. Y no obstante esto, en esta dicha provincia los caciques y principales de ella y otras gentes de los naturales de esta dicha provincia se apoderan de indios e indias libres, pobres y débiles huérfanos que quedan sin padres, y so color que son sus esclavos se sirven de ellos, y a veces los llevan a vender a otras partes. Por remedio de esto mando que ningún indio ni india ni otra persona alguna de cualquier estado o condición que sea de esta provincia, de aquí adelante no tome ni tenga por esclavo indio o india alguna de ella ni haga siervo alguno por vía de rescate ni compra, ni en otra cualquier manera, so pena, etc. Y so la misma mando que todos los indios de esta dicha provincia, que tuvieren esclavos al presente, dentro de la data de este mandamiento los pongan en su libertad y alcen mano de ellos. Pero bien se permite que los caciques y principales e otros indios poderosos puedan alquilar y recibir a soldada indios e indias para servicio de sus casas e para entender en sus haciendas e milpas, pagándoles en su debido trabajo e alquilándose ellos de su voluntad y no por fuerza ...
32. Costumbre es también de esta dicha provincia de hacer largos convites los indios y naturales de ella, en que convidan a todos los del linaje y a todo el pueblo y otros comarcanos, y de ellos resultan grandes desórdenes y pasiones, ...
33. Otrosí mando que no se hagan mitotes de noche, si no fuere de día y después de los divinos oficios, y en ellos no canten cosas sucias ni de su

gentilidad, y cosas pasadas, si no cosas santas y buenas y de la doctrina
cristiana y ley de Dios...[199]
(**31**. In Jesus Christ, all of us are free, and as for the temporary law also the
ones who are born of free Fathers, are free. And in spite of this, in this
province, the lords and principal people of this province and other peoples of
the Natives of this province seize free and poor Indians and Indian women and
weak orphans who remain without parents, and under pretext that they are
their slaves, they use them, and at times they carry them to sell to other parts.
By remedy of this, I command that from now, neither Indian and Indian
women, nor another any person of any state or condition which would be this
province; neither take nor consider slave of Indian or of any Indian women of
this province. Make any [Indian] servant neither through redemption, nor
purchase, nor in any other way. I am grieved by it, etc. And under the same
order, all the Indians of this province who have had slaves to the present, upon
issue of this commandment, give them their liberty and raise hand of them.
But it is properly permitted that the lords, principal and other powerful Indians
can rent and can receive Indian soldiers and Indian women for service in their
houses and to deal with their estates and maize fields, on paying them for their
proper work, they being rented of their will, and not by force...
32. Custom of this province is also to make many invitations to the Indians
and natives of this land, in which they invite all of the lineage and all the town
and other neighboring peoples, and this results in great disorder and passion
from them...
33. Moreover, I order that dances must not be done at night, only in daytime
and after the divine duties, and in them, they must not sing dirty things or
things of their paganism, and old things, apart from holy and good things, and
of the Christian doctrine and law of God.....)

Certainly, these regulations issued by Tomas López suggest his serious
concern for the welfare and other human aspects of the Maya. Although some of the
rules were useful to enhance the lives of the Maya, however, the fundamental
problem was a denial of Maya traditions. Even though the significance of religion
in our present society is somewhat declining, religion is still strongly associated
with numerous aspects of our culture, such as political ideology. On the other hand,
in the past, religion was often life itself. The influence of religion was more closely
related with the daily life of the people in the sixteenth century, as we found in the
instructions issued by Tomas López. The Maya people were the same. In that case,
an introduction of a very exclusive religion, Christianity, meant a total destruction

---

[199] *Ordenanza de Yucatán, año de 1533.* published in Pereña et al., 1990:100-114. Cited from
ibid.:112-3. I include some extractions of this document and their translations as Appendix III of
this volume.

188

of the daily life of the Maya which had been based on their own religious traditions. *Reducción*, a forced resettlement of the Maya into a new 'ideal' Christian town to receive the Gospel, was one example. By removing the Maya from their own land, numerous traditions were destroyed. This was practiced in various parts of New Spain. In spite of some noted friars, such as Las Casas and Acosta, proposing the necessity of tolerating indigenous cults to a certain degree, actual policies issued by the Spanish administrators were frequently intolerant of numerous aspects of Native American life.

The writings of Tomas López clearly prove that his 'proper' evangelization of Christianity was to intervene in every aspect of the Maya as if he were a schoolmaster teaching children. In spite of continuous efforts to defend the intellectual capability of the Native American made by Las Casas, the majority of Spaniards tended to underestimate the Native Americans. For example, Fray Gerónimo de Mendieta wrote in his book of 1595 that although permitting the Native American to take the habit as a priest was an excellent means to promote Christianity, they were by nature made to be disciples rather than masters, and thus it was not appropriate to appoint a Native American as a priest.[200] His view towards the Native Americans may be said to be slightly better than an extremely discriminative opinion, such as the theory of the natural slave defined by Juan Ginés de Sepúlveda, but it is true that Mendieta also treated the Native Americans as lesser human beings.

We do not have historical evidence to know how individual Maya reacted to and felt about this assertive instruction imposed by the Spaniards. As I have persistently mentioned, neither did the Maya of that period leave us their private documents, nor did the Spaniards preserve a personal view of the Maya, and thus no solid assumption can be made. Nevertheless, I believe that the Spanish policy of imposing a Christian lifestyle on the Maya must have created a somewhat difficult feeling towards Christianity, even among the Maya who willingly received it. The

---

[200] Mendieta, 1595:lib.IV, cap.23, p.85-6.

fact is, that because of the inadequate number of Spanish administrators, their control over the Maya (and of the other peoples of New Spain) was not well established until the end of their colonial rule. In numerous rural areas, traditional Maya authorities retained their political power to a considerable degree.

Though it is hypothetical, it is very likely that in some specific cases, the colonial Maya received the 'Spanish Christianity' with disapproval and must have felt a necessity to eliminate 'Spanish- originating elements' from Christianity. In the case of the Aztec, as discussed in the next chapter, the personal reaction was very negative and led a person who was once converted into Christianity, to oppose it. Also, the case of Japan discussed in the chapter tells us that Western over-intervention in Japanese traditions resulted in a movement to be independent from Western missionaries.

No doubt (though there is a lack of solid documentary evidence), some Maya may have opted for a secret resistance to Christianity, but there must have been a certain number of the Maya who attempted to accommodate Christianity in their daily lives without sacrificing their old pagan traditions. The fact is that in spite of being Christians, numerous Spaniards in Latin America were religiously corrupted. Nevertheless, the Maya were forced to live according to the Christian moral code. In this case, what did happen?

There is a possibility that some of the Maya converts attempted to consider Christianity and the Spaniards as separate entities. It is quite possible to hypothesize that even if they loved Christianity, it was not so unusual that they hated the Spanish-dominated atmosphere within the church. Together with the traditional religious dualism concept of the Maya, this aspect should be included in our consideration of the relationship between Christianity and the Maya religions. Due to a lack of solid documentary evidence, this is merely hypothesis at this moment. Nevertheless, bearing this in mind is necessary when we analyze some difficult points of the colonial Maya religious notions.

Chapter III: Christianity from a World Perspective of the Confrontation between Dualism and Monism: Process of Its Localization.

"Japan is not a Christian country...Because Japan does not believe Jehovah as the god, it is the country of the devil."(The testimony of Junzo Akashi. A Japanese Christian as the accused in a Japanese trial. 7 April 1941)

> *"The Sky as father and the Earth as mother, men are born in the middle of them. Sky, Earth, and Man become settled in this order. Japan is originally a country of KAMI* [=Gods]. ... *The Christian's cliques unexpectedly visited here in Japan. They not only trade through merchant vessels, but also propagate an evil teaching* [=Christianity] *without a good reason, confuse the true teaching* [Buddhism], *and by doing these, they tried to change Japanese political order, and to possess Japan. This is just a sign of a serious evil. Suppression of Christianity must be applied...The faction of those Christians is against the entire government ordinance mentioned above. Moreover, they have suspected Shintoism* [the Japanese Native religion], *and have libeled the true teaching* [Buddhism], *and have ruined the justice and the good. When execution of the Christians is practiced, these Christians are pleased to see it, do run about, and make a bow* [to them as the martyrs] *of their own accord. Such behaviors are the essence of the teaching of them.*
> *If Christianity is not a heretical religion, what is it? It is just the enemy of Shintoism and Buddhism. If it is not forbidden at once, it will surely become a serious illness of the state of Japan in the future"*
> (A document of A.D. 1614, in which the Tokugawa Shogunate demonstrates its policy to oppress Christianity within Japan. Translation by the author from the original Chinese writing in "誹切支丹" "排耶書" 491-492)

The purpose of this chapter is to examine how Christianity was dualistically relativized with pagan religions outside the Maya area. The process of the dualistic

191

relativization of Christianity with a native pagan religion, which will be discussed in this chapter, often offers a quite useful perspective for understanding the relationships between Maya religions and Christianity, though the perspectives obtained from the non-Maya region cannot be directly applied to the case of Maya. It is neither the aim of this chapter to investigate the evangelization of each area, nor is it to discuss these examples from non-Maya areas as direct evidence for Maya studies. Nevertheless, I believe that this chapter is particularly advantageous for non-pagan people to comprehend and to be familiarized with the general nature of pagan religions based on dualism. Various types of dualism (often in the form of the religious trinity) discussed in this chapter are often observed as variations in the case of the Maya. As in the case of the colonial Yucatec Maya and present-day K'iche Maya, examples taken from non-Maya pagan areas suggest that Christianity was not often treated as the only cosmos, but as a part of their cosmovision.

When investigating Christian expansionism from the sixteenth century, it is often useful to understand that the process of evangelization that took place in Asia and America.[1] However, there is a negative view. In his criticism of a French historian, Robert Ricard, Antonio Sisto Rosso once wrote: "... *in order to explain their approach to Chinese cults, there is no need to explore the attitude of the Friars in Mexico in connection with the native cults. In fact, the problem of Mexico were substantially different from those of China (for one, the problem of human sacrifices) was not as simple, drastic and unreasonable as pictured by second hand historians.*"[2] Certainly, Rosso is quite correct when considering the various different cultural, political, and religious circumstances that surrounded the 'European' mendicant friars. Readers of my book may still have the same opinion. The religious battle in China was chiefly raised between Confucianism and Christianity. Although Confucianism is generally regarded as a religion, its fundamental character is that of a moral teaching, rather than a religion. This could

---

[1] Vogeley, 1997

be a reason to treat the case of Christian evangelization in China and that in other pagan regions as separate issues. Nevertheless, it must be noted that such views are often generated by bias. Although comparative studies of the activities of mendicant friars would not produce a good result, from the view of pagan cultures, as long as issues of dualism are primarily considered, this view cannot be acceptable. Unless the essential conceptual difference between dualism = polytheism and monism = monotheism is comprehended, there can not be a substantial understanding of conflicts between pagan religions and Christianity. Indeed, Rosso did not argue the issue of the anti-Christian movement from a perspective of religious conceptual differences.[3] In terms of a dualistic perception of Christianity, it is quite worthwhile to investigate the evangelization of the non-Maya regions.

Although Chinese and Japanese religious philosophy often differs from that of the Native Americans, it has several quite similar notions. For example, like the colonial Maya, the Chinese have not had the concept of the '*religious sin,*' of the Europeans.[4] In spite of the fact that both Europeans and Asians left us a considerable number of documents concerning the evangelization process of Catholic Christianity of the sixteenth and eighteenth centuries, it has been rare to see works in the form of a dialogue between Asian religions and Christianity.[5]

I initially considered making this chapter a comparative study of the reaction to Christianity in various dualistic cultures of the sixteenth and seventeenth centuries. The period covering these two centuries is often called the Christian Century. However, because I have found the case of the Japanese Christians of the early twentieth century to be a fascinating one in considering a dualistic understanding of Christianity, in the case of Japan a study of anti-Christianity in the twentieth century will be made.[6] In Japan, the majority who remained pagan

---

[2] Rosso, 1948:108.
[3] Rosso, 1948:224-229.
[4] Gernet, 1996:68, also see *ibid.*:309.
[5] Gernet, 1996 is one of the exceptionally good works.
[6] Another reason is a lack of fund.

tried to place Christianity into the Japanese cosmovision, as was the case with other pagan peoples. However, there was an interesting factor in the case of Japanese Christians. In spite of strong opposition from Japanese nationalists, a small number of the Japanese became stoic, uncompromising Christians. Nevertheless, as will be argued, because of anti-European feeling and Western domination of the Japanese church, not all the Japanese Christians were satisfied with the Western version of Christianity, and considered the Gospel as taught by the West not true Christianity. Thus, they tried to find evidence from the Holy Scriptures that Christianity originated in Japan.

Although this is the case of Japan, when we take into account the origin of a localized version of Christianity, this kind of observation can also be pointed out in the case of colonial New Spain. In all pagan cultures of the 'Christian Century' mentioned in this chapter, unlike the pagan peoples of the Roman Empire, the grasp of the context of Christianity was far from adequate. Although this phenomenon was once considered evidence of intellectual inferiority of the people in the New Worlds, it was largely because of the European Catholic missionaries' policies.

The noted Roman pagan philosophers, such as Celsus, Porphyry, and the Roman Emperor Julian, were fully aware of the content of the Christian Holy Scriptures, because they had easy access to them. Their fragmental, surviving texts suggest that they carefully read the Scriptures, and often efficiently attacked several important contradictions existing between the *Old Testament* and the *New Testament*. However, the cases of the Maya, Aztec, Inca, and Chinese were different. The European friars generally prevented them from studying the full Holy Scripture. Therefore, in the New Worlds, due to a lack of precise knowledge of the Gospel, some confused ideas about Christianity were inevitable.

The reason for the Native Americans' acceptance of Christianity while they kept their faith in ancient pagan deities, as has repeatedly been argued, is that the Native Americans, because of Spanish military success, came to attach importance

194

to the spiritual power of Christianity.[7] On this point, Enrique Dussel mentions, *"the Indian was attracted to Christianity. It was the logical result of his primitive and mythical cosmovision. It could not have been otherwise."*[8] I am not in favor of this view. First, as will be discussed in this chapter, there is no solid documentary evidence that the Native American showed an attitude of dismissal towards the Christian God in their first encounter with the Spaniards. In most cases, their anti-Christian sentiment was occasioned by the brutal acts of the Spaniards. In Japan and China, where military conquest did not occur, Christianity's divinity was not initially dismissed, though it was often regarded as a lesser belief.

The Maya's religion and their cosmovision are an explanation of the natural and supernatural phenomena within their cosmovision. So when the Maya encountered a previously unknown kind of people, the Christian Lord and the Spaniards, the Maya had to make an addition to their own cosmovision. Of course, such additions were most probably generated within their dualistic understanding. Therefore, it is likely that without any military success, Christianity and its doctrine would have been recognized as one of the various ways of understanding the universe among the Maya, even though they regarded it as negative teaching.

I have mentioned the Asian trinity consisting of Buddhism, Confucianism, and a local religion. The case of Japan is interesting.[9] When a Buddhist idol was first sent to Japan as a gift from the king of Paekchein (a kingdom in Korea, allied with Japan in that time) in 552AD (or 538), although the Japanese Emperor, Kinmei (欽明), and some conservatives were pleased with the gift, they were also very confused, because they could not be convinced of this new religion due to the possibility of angering the existing Japanese gods. Because the Emperor declined to express his decision on this issue, his vassals were divided into two groups and struggled with each other. Interestingly, both the supporters of the new religion and its opponents recognized the Buddha as a divine god. Although the idol was

---

[7] For example, Dussel, 1981:67.
[8] Cited from *ibid.*
[9] The following story and analysis is based on Masaki, 1996:45-7.

eventually put into a river by those who opposed Buddhism, a later record suggests that in spite of the fact that the idol was considered a rival of Japanese gods, it was 'deified' by the Emperor. Therefore, it is suggested that the Buddhist idol was not simply thrown away as a figure of a devil, but sent back to Korea by being put into the water with considerable respect. As will be discussed, this concept can commonly be found in China, and in Native American states. The reason is clear: none of their pagan Holy Scriptures or oral traditions defines a foreign deity as 'Satan' or 'Devil.' It can be said that the divine nature of the Christian Lord was recognized from the first, though the brutal military action of the Spaniards provoked an anti-Christian reaction.

In this chapter, this hypothesis will carefully be examined. As there is little information about the first encounter between the Spaniards and the Maya, this issue will be argued as the first confrontation between major pagan and dualistic cults of the world and Christianity. None of the pagan cults is an exact equivalent of the Maya religious culture of the sixteenth century.

In the case of the colonial Maya, they were not allowed to read the entire Holy Scripture, and they were under the control of intolerant Catholic Christians. In the case of Japanese Christians of the twentieth century, on the other hand, the Protestants were more dominant than the Catholics. Also, the Japanese Christians had a full knowledge of both the *Old* and *New Testaments* and their religious ideology received a certain influence from Unitarianism, which allowed them to take a theologically relaxed position towards Japanese traditional religions. By adopting the ideology of Unitarianism, the Japanese managed to justify their localization of the Gospel.

Therefore, researchers must always avoid overgeneralizations. Nevertheless, as will be shown, it is clear that as all these cases have the concept of dualism, and treated Christianity as homogeneous with their own native beliefs, since numerous common reactions to Christianity are found among them. Therefore, summarizing reactions to Christianity within the pagan world should be a good comparative

196

study for understanding Christianity within a dualistic culture. In most cases there is no good evidence that Christianity was dismissed as a religion, but its exclusiveness and anti-European feeling generated hostility towards it.

Some critics may feel that my attempt in this chapter is in vain. However, understanding the dualism concept can be a great help for Westerners to understand not only the Maya, but also the '*mysterious*' culture of my country, Japan. Also, as a example of a cultural conflict between the Christian cultures and the Mongoloid pagan ones, the introduction of Christianity during the sixteenth and seventeenth centuries should provide the readers with several important keys to overcome the difficulties of conceptual differences.

I: Nahuatl Discovery of Christianity[10]

> *They* [=the Europeans] *came there initially simply to trade, and then, with insane pretexts of trade, they subjugated all the country. I, your subject, when I consider all the cruel Kingdoms beyond the seas, it seems to me that the Kingdom of Japan exceeded all the other Kingdoms in force and power... however, the people of Japan always made their trade with us peacefully...Thus, only the Europeans have to be feared; they are the most malicious and more intractable over all the* [barbarous] *people. Hûng Mao* [=the European] *is a common name of all the barbarians who live in the land located between the North and the East.* (a part of a petition of Ching-Mao (陳昂), the superintendent general (碣石鎮総兵) submitted to the Chinese emperor, Kang-hsi （康熙帝） in 1717. Translated from a French translation made by Father Mailla, a French Jesuit, attached to his letter dated on 5 June 1717 in Pekin (in Querbeuf 1780-83: vol.19, p.9-10))

While the colonial Maya provided us with scattered information on their first encounter with Christians, the colonial Nahuatl people, such as the Aztec and Tlaxcalan, left a relatively rich amount of documentary evidence about their discovery of Christianity. Although such materials also often contain a strong Spanish cultural bias, as in the case of the Maya, they are still useful. This chapter will examine their discovery of Christianity.

---

[10] My argument presented here is an expanded version of Yamase, 2005:23-27, 149-154, 282-3. León-Portilla (1990), (1993), and Klor de Alva (1993) are a concise summary of the Náhuatl concept of religión and Christianity.

197

There is a concession that the Spaniards were initially considered gods by the indigenous people due to their 'strange and amazing' equipment. The so-called best authorized Aztec source, the *Florentine Codex*, records that Hernán Cortés was treated by the Aztecs as a god (*Quetzalcoatl*) who was predicted to return to Mexico in order to restore his rule. It also narrates how Cortés pacified Mexico without much resistance, because the Aztecs considered that the time to hand over their rule to *Quetzalcoatl* had come, and they lost their vigor to fight with the divine people, the Spaniards. In that source, from the first, *Montecuhzoma* II (=Motecuhzoma Xocoyotzin. He is often called Montezuma II), the Aztec emperor, was depressed by the news of the arrival of the white people, and was scared of Cortés as a living *Quetzalcoatl* and timidly treated him as his master. As this kind of narrative was convenient for the Europeans to elaborate the conquest as a miracle war made possible by the Christian Lord, and to insist upon their military and religious superiority over the Native Americans, various Spanish and European historians later exaggerated the myth about the Spanish conquest considerably.

Although some scholars still favor this half-mythic narrative of the Spanish conquest of the Aztec,[11] some scholars began to reevaluate this view.[12] In fact, the Spanish sources written by the *Conquistadors,* who actually fought with the Aztec, tell us the opposite. For example, Hernán Cortés, the *Conquistador* of Mexico, wrote in his second letter of 1522 to Carlos V that the Aztec emperor told him that 'he is a human like the Spaniards,'[13] though he treated Cortés as a legatee of the natural lord of the Aztec.[14]

As to the conquest of the Aztec, the works of Hernán Cortés and Bernal Díaz del Castillo are particularly rich in context and provide us with a considerable amount of information about the Aztec's initial reply to Christianity. These texts

[11] *E.g.* León-Portilla, 1974, Carrasco 1982.
[12] *E.g.* Gillespie, 1989.
[13] Cortés, 1986:86-7.
[14] Cortés, 1986:85-6.

mention that when in the land of the Maya, they were often confronted with strong hostility from the inhabitants.

For the indigenous peoples, calling the foreigners 'gods' did not mean an acceptance of the supernatural power of the Spaniards. In the case of the Aztecs, for instance, they named Pedro de Alvarado, who was the bravest commander of Cortés, '*Tonatiuh*' = the Sun God. Yet, it must be noted that this name was given because of Alvarado's hair color, and he was regarded as a human being. In fact, it is recorded that Motecuhzoma II just used the term of *Tonatio* to show his personal affection for Alvarado.[15]

The term, *teul* (=god) which was a nickname for the Spaniards among the Aztecs, was also used in a similar manner. Bernal Díaz del Castillo, one of Cortés' footsoldiers, notes that as a result of several efforts propagating the Spaniards as immortal people, the indigenous people came to call them *teul*. Nevertheless, this term *teul* was only used as a nickname for the Spaniards. Although they were initially shocked by the emergence of the white people, the Aztec people soon recognized them as humans. In fact, what Bernal Díaz tells us is that the Aztec continued regarding and treating Cortés and his fellow Spaniards as mere human beings.

In spite of the fact that a Spanish Franciscan friar, Bernardino de Sahagún, was chief editor of the *Florentine Codex*, it has often been used as the authentic Aztec Nahuatl source, because it was believed that he and his Nahuatl students carefully collected Aztec traditional tales and history from the surviving Aztec old sages of that time. Of course, the Spanish translation by Sahagún accompanying the original Nahuatl text, shows that he contributed a type of religious propaganda, including omissions and intentional mistranslations (e.g. native gods translated as devils). Similar attempts to identify Aztec deities as demons can be seen in the pictorials of this codex. Nevertheless, because it was considered that Sahagún did not modify the Nahuatl original text of the *Florentine Codex*, the Nahuatl text

---

[15] Díaz del Castillo, 1989: Cap.XCVII, p.281.

199

found in this codex has been considered the authentic view of the Aztec people. However, scholars of the twentieth century became suspicious of this view. They considered that even in the original Nahuatl text, there were some important fabrications, modifications, and propaganda concerning the original story taken from the elder Aztec informants, in order to degrade the Aztec tradition and history.

It cannot be made clear whether such 'fabrication' was done on Sahagún's order or by his Nahuatl students' will. For the Spaniard, associating Cortés with *Quetzalcoatl*, an indigenous deity, was quite useful to propagate Christianity in New Spain, because it became possible to insist that the Aztec previously knew about the handover of their rule to the people of *Quetzalcoatl*, the Christians. In my opinion, not only Sahagún,[16] but also Sahagún's Aztec assistants and their informants, made fabricated myths about 'the Spaniards = the Gods' of this codex, such as Cortés being a God.

Even though the Spaniards may have principally propagated the myth of the Spaniards as *Quetzalcoatl*, this myth seems also to have been convenient for the Aztec in explaining their miserable defeat. As to the origin of 'the Spaniards = returning *Quetzalcoatl*' tales found in Nahuatl chronicles, Susan Gillespie proposed that they were an attempt by the Aztec to explain their defeat as a natural consequence within their cosmovision.[17] There was a notion among the Aztec that as the ruling deity of the world was been changed at certain periods, their gods rule for a certain period only. They considered the end of the Aztec rule could happen every 52nd year. As principal gods of the Aztec once expelled *Quetzalcoatl*, who dominated the world, when *Quetzalcoatl* restored his power, the domination of the

---

[16] Of course, identifying Sahagún's possibly modified part of the original Nahuatl text is difficult. My view is merely hypothetical and is based on the fact that when Sahagún later "revised" a part of the Spanish Conquest, Book 12 of the *Florentine Codex*, his revision was concentrated on glorifying Cortés' achievement as the symbol of the Spanish conquest. By regarding Cortés as a prophet like *Moses*, he tried to justify the conquest. Based on this point, it is suggested that the original text of the book 12 of the *Florentine Codex* contains a certain bias of Sahagún, though it is not beyond my personal speculation.
[17] Gillespie 1989.

Aztec supported by his rival deities also had to be ended. Therefore, as the Aztec wished to consider that their defeat was a result of the emergence of the new world, they needed a theological explanation. By identifying the Spaniards as the returning *Quetzalcoatl*, they explained their collapse as an unpreventable incident. As I have argued in Chapter I, this type of logic, 'Native deities as the gods of the previous time cycle and the Christian Lord as that of the present cycle,' was used in the *Book of Chilam Balam of Chumayel* of the Yucatec Maya.

I am largely in favor of this explanation. Nevertheless, it must be pointed out that although the story of Cortés as returning *Quetzalcoatl* is found in some 'native' chronicles, those who support these texts often overlook another type of Nahuatl source. The *Proceso inquisitorial del cacique de Tetzcoco Don Carlos Ometochtzin (Chichimecatecotl),*[18] a famous colonial inquisitional record of 1539 against a wealthy Nahuatl royal family of Tezcoco, is a good example. After the Spanish victory over the Aztec, Don Carlos Ometochtzin, who was a son of Nezahualipilli, a King of Tezcoco, and a grandson of Nezahualcoyotl, known as the great king of Tezcoco and the father of the Aztec law, became a very rich cacique under Spanish rule. As were many others, Don Carlos was baptized, yet as he secretly continued his faith in ancient Mexican deities by keeping idols and an ancient codex, and discouraged his people from believing in Christianity, he was later sentenced to death. This record has been often regarded as one of the principle origins of the colonial Mexican inquisition. Nevertheless, a number of scholars have practically ignored an important testament of Don Carlos found in this record when considering the myth of *Quetzalcoatl*.

---

[18] *Proceso inquisitorial del cacique de Tetzcoco Don Carlos Ometochtzin (Chichimecatecotl)* (1980). Although I have previously argued this, it was based on partial English quotation in León-Portilla 1990:76-9.(Yamase 2002b:228) Since I was able to obtain a copy of *Proceso inquisitorial...* in 2004, a more systematic analysis of Don Carlos was made for this research. Kobayashi (1995) is a fairly useful summary of this record for me, though the level of editing and proofreading (e.g. error of citation) of his book is impoverished.

Don Carlos was critical of the introduction of Christianity to the native people. In order to deny its divinity, he used his father and grandfather as authorized evidence.

>...*el dicho Don Carlos llamó á este testigo y le puso delante de sí é le dijó á este testigo: Francisco ven acá, oye hermano; dirás por ventura ¿qué hace Don Carlos? Mañana me iré á Tezcuco; mira, ove, que mi agiielo [=abuelo] Nezahualcoyotl y mi padre Nezahualpilli ninguna cosa nos dixieron cuando murieron ni nombraron á ningunos ni quienes habían de venir; entiende hermano que mi agiielo y mi padre miraban á todas partes, atrás y delante como si dixiese, sabían lo pasado é por venir y sabían lo que se había de hacer en largos tiempos y lo que se hizo, como dicen los padres é nombran los profetas -que de verdad te digo que profetas fueron mi agiielo y mi padre que sabían lo que se había de hacer y, lo que estaba hecho; por tanto hermano, entiéndeme, y ninguno ponga su corazón en esta ley de Dios é Divinidad"- como si dixiese que no amase ninguno á Dios ni á su ley- y dixo: "¿qué es esta Divinidad, cómo es, de dónde vino? qué es lo que enseñas, qué es lo que nombras?:...*[19]*
*
>(...this Don Carlos called this witness, and put this one in front of him and said; "Francisco, see here. Hear, brother. You may say, "What does Don Carlos do?" I will go back to Tezcoco; Look! Hear! My grandfather Nezahualcoyotl and my father Nezahualpilli spoke of nothing to us when they died. They mentioned neither anybody nor those who were to come. Please understand, brother, that my grandfather and my father watched all parts, back and ahead. That is to say, they knew what passed and what was to come. They knew what it had to be done in the long period, and what was done, as the parents say and the prophets mention. I really say to you that prophets were my grandfather and my father who knew what had to be made, what was done; therefore brother, please understand me. Nobody must put his heart in this law of the [Christian] God and its Divinity. As if he said that nobody loves God and his Law, and [Don Carlos] said: "what is this Divinity, how is it, from where did it came? What is what you learn? What is what you mention?

The above quotation can be considered Don Carlos' denial of the existence of myth of Cortés and the Spaniards as the returning god, *Quetzalcoatl,* or the natural lord before the Spanish arrival. This also suggests that the tale of the returning *Quetzalcoatl* = Cortés was chiefly propagated by the Spaniards and it was widely believed true among the Aztec until 1539. Of course, there is no evidence that this statement is more reliable evidence than the others. Since Don Carlos'

---

[19] Cited from *ibid.*:40.

anti-Spanish sentiment was provoked by the consequence of the decline of the Native elite's status after the Spanish conquest[20], it is possible to consider that he deceitfully invented a 'fact.'

It is true that the colonial Nahuatl chronicles edited by the Spanish friars tend to glorify Cortés as if he were a prophet like Moses. This tendency became stronger as the time passed. On the contrary, Aztec sources with less influence from the missionaries seemed to not be seriously concerned with Cortés, and they did not treat Cortés as an important person for them. For example, one of the Aztec codices, the *Codex Telleriano-Remensis,* illustrates a curious issue. In this codex, in spite of the fact that the death of the bishop Zumagara in 1548 is painted as an important event, the death of Cortés of the previous year, is not painted at all.[21] Although the fact that part of this codex was painted more than twenty years after the conquest, this fact questions a view of Cortés = *Quetzalcoatl* among the Aztec of the period of the conquest.

Don Carlos strongly criticized Christianity. He insisted that the Nahuatl people must believe what their ancestors believed = traditional Mexican deities instead of the Christian Lord. However, his 'rejection' of Christianity should not be considered as the same as that of the Christians. It is not known whether Don Carlos was willingly baptized or not. Although we do not have any verification, Don Carlos might also have been impressed with the Gospel during the first decade of the Spanish colonial domination. In the process of denying the Spaniards as the predicted return of divine people, a denial of the divinity of Christianity was also necessary for Don Carlos. It was recorded that he openly ordered his fellows not to believe Christianity and not to follow the instructions given by the friars. He told Francisco Maldonado: "...*te digo que eso que se enseña en el colegio, todo es burla.* (I tell you what is taught in the [missionary's] school. All is a hoax)."[22]

---

[20] *Ibid.*:48-49.

[21] Yamase 2005:266-268. See a photographic reproduction of this codex, Quiñones Kebler, 1995. The death of Cortés is recorded in Spanish on a separate page.

[22] Cited from *Proceso inquisitorial del cacique de Tetzcoco Don Carlos Ometochtzin (Chichimecatecotl),* 1980:40.

Nevertheless, it must be understood that he did not actually reject Christianity as a religion. Fernando Cervantes argues that anti-Christian tendencies among the Native Americans should not be regarded as evidence of their denial of Christianity, because even if the Nahuatl found a negative deity like the Christian lord, any negative deity was considered a part of their pantheon.[23] In fact, although Don Carlos called Christianity 'false,' he did not call it 'evil.' A further careful reading of the record will reveal that the origin of his attitude of dismissal towards Christianity was at least partly originated from the Catholic policy of rejecting pre-Hispanic life traditions, such as the banning of mistresses. A testament of Cristóbal, a resident of Chiconaute, mentions that Don Carlos said that they must guard their old pagan gods and must have women as their parents did.[24] This suggests that, for him, not only old pagan deities, but also old traditions of Nahuatl life style had to be restored at the same time. It is evident that both occupied an important position in his mind. Therefore, it may be said that one of the reasons for his anti-Christian stance was generated by the Christians' over-intervention in every aspect of the Nahuatl traditional life.

As Cervantes and Miguel León-Portilla have already pointed out, Don Carlos was not to dismiss Christianity completely.[25] Although their arguments are quite useful, however, it is questionable that they tried to understand the relationship between Christianity and the Nahuatl religions as an incorporation of Christianity within their pagan pantheon. This opinion is commonly observed in any writing of Mesoamerican scholars to date.[26] I also did not critically consider this issue in the past, because this explanation is applicable when a foreign deity, which is of the same nature as indigenous deities, is introduced. Indeed, Aztec religions are a pantheon of pagan deities of other Mexican people. However, since I have noticed

[23] Cervantes, 1994:45-7.
[24] *Proceso inquisitorial del cacique de Tetzcoco Don Carlos Ometochtzin (Chichimecatecotl)* 1980:49.
[25] Cervantes, 1994:45-7, León-Portilla 1990:78-9.
[26] E.g. see Klor de Alva, 1993:175.

the importance of the dualism concept in pagan cultures, I am not in favor of this idea now.

It must be pointed out that this kind of idea makes a serious controversial point in the relationship between Christianity and Mesoamerican (and Asian) pagan religions. Unlike Christian culture, for these pagans, a religion is often a mere part of the universe. Therefore, if a religion whose concept is extremely alien, like Christianity, was introduced into a pagan culture, another conceptual world for Christianity was frequently created. As each of those two worlds was interchangeable in pagan people's minds, an outsider often observed these conceptual religious worlds as if they were merged together. For example, the Japanese treat their native religion (=Shinto) and Buddhism as if they are a single religion. However, the fact is, that each of the religions constitutes a different conceptual world in the Japanese mind. In other words, in the Japanese mentality (of course, some Japanese believe in only one religion), there are two different worlds. This perception should not have been an alien one to the colonial Maya. As I have discussed in Chapter I, the authors of a colonial Maya text used the dualism concept of the past and the present. The Maya placed Christianity in the present world. Although different, the Japanese used a similar dualism when conflict with Christianity was raised. Although less clear, this concept seems to have existed among the colonial Nahuatl.

The text suggests that Don Carlos clearly separated Christianity from Nahuatl religions. The *Proceso inquisitorial* says:

> *Pues oye hermano, que nuestros padres y aguiielos dixieron, cuando murieron, que de verdad se dixo que los dios que ellos tenían y amaban fueron hechos en el cielo y en la tierra, por tanto hermano sólo aquello sigamos que nuestros agiielos y nuestros padres tuvieron y dixieron cuando, murieron; oye hermano Francisco ¿qué dicen los padres? ¿qué nos dicen? ¿qué entendéis vosotros? Mira que los frailes y clérigos cada uno tiene su manera de penitencia; mira que los frailes de San Francisco tienen una manera de doctrina, y una manera de vida, y una manera de vestido, y una manera de oración; y los de Sant Agustín tienen otra manera; y los de Santo Domingo tienen de otra; y los clérigos de otra, como todos lo vemos, y así mismo, era entre los que guardaban á los dioses nuestros, que los de México*

205

tenían una manera de vestido, y una manera de orar, é ofrecer y ayunar, y en otros pueblos de otra; en cada pueblo tenían su manera de sacrificios, y su manera de orar y de ofrecer, y así lo hacen los frailes y clérigos, que, ninguno concierta con otro; sígamos aquello que tenían y seguían nuestros antepasados, y de la manera que ellos vivieron, vivamos, y esto se ha de entender así, y lo que los padres nos enseñan y predican como ellos nos los dan á entender; que cada uno de su voluntad siga la ley que quiere y costumbres y ceremonias; hermano, no digo que quizá entenderéis esto y quizá no, y lo recibiréis ó no como yo os lo digo.[27]

(Then, brother, hear! Our parents and grandfathers spoke when they died. It was really said that they had Gods and loved them; the Gods were made in the Sky and the Earth. Therefore, brother, we only follow what our grandfathers and our parents had and spoke when they died. Hear! Brother Francisco, what do the parents say? What do they say to us? What do you understand? We see the friars and clergymen! Each one has its way of penance; we see that the friars of the Franciscan have a doctrine, that of life, that of dress, that of oration. In addition, those of the Augustine have another way. Also, those of the Dominican have another one; and the clergymen have another one, as all we see it.

There was the same [difference] among those who maintained our Gods. Those of Mexico had a way of dress, and a way of praying, of offering, and of helping, and [those] in other towns of another [region had their own way]. They had their way of sacrifices, and their way of praying and of offering in each town. Thus, what the friars and clergymen do is nothing coincident with others. We continue what our ancestors had and they followed, and in the way that they lived. Let us live [as they did]. This is what must be understood and what the parents teach us and preach, as they make us understand. Each one of his will follows the law that he wants, customs and ceremonies. Brother, I do not say that you will perhaps understand this, and perhaps you do not, and that you will receive it or not as I say to you ...)

In the above quotation, he told Francisco the importance of their own traditions. He insisted that the Nahuatl must live with their own gods and that preaching could be different, because each group of the Christians also has a different tradition. From this, although ambiguous, it may be suggested that Don Carlos did not reject the whole of Christianity. As León-Portilla suggests,[28] in spite of his strong opposition to Christianity, Don Carlos essentially insisted that Nahuatl religions must have a place along with the various factions of Christianity. Therefore, some scholars argue that the anti-Christian Nahuatl, like Don Carlos,

---

[27] *Proceso inquisitorial del cacique de Tetzcoco Don Carlos Ometochtzin (Chichimecatecotl)* 1980:40-1.
[28] León-Portilla, 1990:78.

206

did not completely deny Christianity.[29] Some may feel that Don Carlos's view is self-contradictory. It is generally considered that there was a necessity of introducing certain useful elements of the Christian culture.[30] Yet, a question remains. While criticizing Christianity as vain and false, why did he accept it as divine?

Yet, if we try to understand his concept dualistically, it is clearly analyzed. Although Don Carlos mentioned that none (of the Spaniards and the friars) must intervene in their traditional religions and affairs of daily life as long as the Nahuatl people are in their own land, he said at the same time that if all of the Nahuatl died, the Spaniards and Christians may do anything as they wish.[31] From this statement, as I have previously mentioned,[32] it is clear that Don Carlos considered that the rule of Christianity could be allowed if the Nahuatl people died out, and if Christianity only existed for the Spaniards and their land. In this case, his understanding of the relationship between Christianity and the indigenous religions was slightly different from the case of the *Book of Chilam Balam of Chumayel* argued in the previous chapter. Although the Maya authors of the *Chumayel* accepted the rule of Christianity, Don Carlos did not. Therefore, contrary to the case of the Maya in which a compound of the past and the present was used to constitute their logic of religious dualism, Don Carlos used another type of dualism compound. This is a set of one world for the Spaniards and Christianity and one for the Nahuatl. He psychologically divided the present cosmos into two worlds, one for the Spaniards and another for the Nahuatl and other indigenous people (or possibly one cosmos and two worlds). By dividing this world into two, he made a world for monotheistic religion. In his logic, although the God is only one in the world of the Spaniards, as there is another world for the Nahuatl, the Nahuatl deities can exert their supernatural power within that world. It

---

[29] *e.g.*, Kobayashi, 1995:182-3.
[30] See *ibid.*
[31] *Proceso inquisitorial del cacique de Tetzcoco Don Carlos Ometochtzin (Chichimecatecotl)* 1980:49.
[32] Yamase 2002b:228.

appears that both worlds are clearly separated from each other. Based on this hypothesis, I think that a traditional understanding of the Nahuatl perception of Christianity, incorporating it with the Nahuatl gods' pantheon, seems not to be suitable for the case of Don Carlos, because this type of idea considers the issue of the relationships between two religious systems within a single world only.

Is this idea unique to Don Carlos? If we go back to the period of the Spanish conquest, a similar concept can be found in the Spanish chronicles. Let us look at writings of the *Conquistadors*. When we investigate in this context, care must be taken. not to exaggerate. For example, it is known that in order to justify their military action, the Spaniards tended to overstress the scale of human sacrifice practiced among the Native Americans. Contemporary historians, such as Francisco de Gómara, did more. Bartolomé de Las Casas criticized the work of Gómara. He wrote that although Gómara mentioned the frequent practice of human sacrifice and cannibalism among the Yucatec Maya, he himself neither heard of nor saw any human sacrifice or cannibalism practiced on the Yucatan Peninsula.[33]

Apart from this, there is another question. Although all the surviving documents tell us there was perfect communication between the Spaniards and the Aztec, the reliability of the interpreters accompanying Cortés must be considered. It is well known that they were a Spanish sailor, Gerónimo de Aguilar, and a Nahuatl woman called Marina (or *Malinche*). Later historians often mentioned that Aguilar was very fluent in the Maya language. For example, Fray Gerónimo de

---

[33] Las Casas, 1986: tomo III Cap.117, p.427. Of course, although he stated that he was also informed from Cortés (*ibid.*), it is likely that he also might have modified the fact, as the Franciscans of the later period reported several human sacrifices practiced among the Yucatec Maya. Gómara (1553: tomo I, p.32) wrote that Géronimo de Aguilar testified to the existence of human sacrifice. Tomas López Medel wrote in his *De los tres elementos: aire, agua y tierra* (presumably written about 1570? The portion of Cap.XIV-XXII of this unpublished text is published in Pereña et als. 1990:374) that although there was some practice of human sacrifice in some parts of the Yucatan, the Maya of the rest of the peninsular did not have that tradition (*ibid.*:cap.4, 331 [in the original cap.20 see *ibid.*:14-5]). Although the scale cannot be known and may have well been exaggerated by the Spaniards, it is certain that human sacrifice was practiced on the Yucatan Peninsula.

208

Mendieta wrote that finding him was a true miracle.[34] However, Las Casas, who criticized Cortés and his fellows during his lifetime, ironically pointed out Aguilar's deficiency as an interpreter. He wrote it in his *Historia de las indias*;

> *Hallóse una india, que después se llamó Marina y los indios la llamaban Malinche, de las veinte que presentaron a Cortés en la provincia de Tabasco, que sabía la lengua mexicana, porque había sido, según dijo ella, hurtada de su tierra de hacia Xalisco, de esa parte de México que es el Poniente, y vendida de mano en mano hasta Tabasco, ésta sabía ya la lengua de Tabasco, y aunque aquella lengua era diversa de la de Yucatán, donde Aguilar había estado, todavía entendía algunos vocablos. Visto Cortés que la india entendía los mexicanos, dióla a Aguilar, que comunicase mucho con ella, tratando de hablar y aprender vocablos para que se entendiesen y pudiese por medio della entender los secretos de la tierra, y poder dar noticia a los indios de lo que deseaba. Con esta india comenzó a hablar con el gobernador de aquella provincia-, Cortés hablaba a Aguilar y Aguilar decía a la india, según él podía declarar por algunos vocablos, puesto que con mucha falta, dello por palabras, dello por señas y meneos,...*[35]

(An Indian woman was found. She was later called *Marina* and the Indians called her *Malinche*, she was of twenty years. She was presented to Cortés in the province of Tabasco. She knew the Mexican language, because, according to her, she was stolen from the land near Xalisco, in that part of Mexico in the West. She was sold from hand to hand as far as Tabasco. This one knew the [Maya] language of Tabasco already, and although that [Maya] language was different from the one of Yucatan, where Aguilar had been, he still understood some vocabularies. Cortés saw that that Indian understood the Mexicans, he gave her to Aguilar. He communicated much with her, trying to speak and to learn words so that they were understood, and by means of that they could be understood the secrets of the Earth, and were able to notify to the Indians which Cortés wished. With this Indian, he began to speak with the governor of that province, Cortés spoke to Aguilar, and Aguilar said to that Indian, according to [what] he could declare by some words with many mistakes, by words, and by signs and movements...)

Of course, it is possible that Las Casas also may have exaggerated the deficiency of Aguilar. Even if Las Casas is correct, moreover, it must be considered that by the time of Cortés' arrival in the capital of the Aztecs, no doubt, Tenochititlan, their language abilities were improving. It is recorded, moreover,

---

[34] Mendieta, 1595:lib.III, Cap.1, p.55.
[35] Las Casas, 1986: tomo III Cap.121, p.441.

that in addition, there were several interpreters[36] and several Spaniards who became capable of making conversation with the Aztecs.[37]

However, to what extent they managed to explain the complicated religious issues within the Gospel, such as the Trinity, remains extremely questionable, because even at the time of the fall of the Aztec, Cortés still needed both Aguilar and Malinche in order to communicate. This suggests the limitation of their language improvement by that time.

Even later, the infant level of communication caused serious trouble. For example, the *Historia de Tlaxcala* tells us that after the conquest of Mexico, the missionaries initiated their propagation in Tlaxcala.[38] Although the text does not mention it, they must have had an interpreter. Otherwise, they would not have been traveling in the unknown land. Yet, it is clear that that an interpreter was not able to translate what the friars said. Their preaching resulted in an unfortunate reaction. The first friars looked so miserable that the Tlaxcan first considered them to be beggars. The source says that the Tlaxcalan simply ignored them as insane.

In addition, a Mexican historian, José Luis Martínez, wrote about Aguilar as a poor intellect in his commentary on Aguilar's testimony against Cortés. [39] Therefore, there is a question whether Motecuhzoma II could understand when Cortés spoke about the Gospel. Although a noted historian and writer, William Prescott, once wrote in the nineteenth century; *"But the doctrines were too abstruse in themselves to be comprehended at a glance by the rude intellect of a barbarian,"*[40] it is not difficult to consider that the quality of Spanish interpreters must have been problematic.

---

[36] Fernando Ramírez, 1847:36-8.
[37] Such as Orteguilla. According to Díaz del Castillo (1989: Cap.XCV, p.276), because Orteguilla had already learnt Spanish, he became a page of Motecuhzoma II upon his request.
[38] Camargo, 1986: 177-178.
[39] Martínez, 1990-2:tomo I, p.72, nota7
[40] Cited from Prescott, 1843:book 3, chap.IX.

210

Based on these points, let us read the conversation recorded by Bernal Díaz del Castillo. Díaz, a foot soldier of Hernán Cortés, recorded a conversation about the Aztec divinities and Christian God between Cortés and Motecuhzoma II.

> The next day Cortés decided to go to Motecuhzoma's palace, ... Then Cortes began to make an explanation through Doña Marina and Aguilar ...we told them then that we were Christians and worshipped one true and only God, that we believe in Him and worship Him, but that those whom they look upon as gods are not so, but are devils, which are evil things, and their looks are bad, their deeds are worse, and they could see that they were evil and of little worth, for where we had set up crosses such as those his ambassadors had seen, they dared not appear before them, through fear of them, and that as time went on they would notice this
>
> He also told them that, in course of time, our Lord and King would send some men who among us lead very holy lives, much better than we do, who will explain to them all about it, for at present we merely came to give them due warning, and so we prayed him to do what he was asked and carry it into effect...
>
> Motecuhzoma replied: "Señor Malinche [Cortés], I have understood your words and arguments very well before now, from what you said to my servants at the sand dunes, this about three Gods and the Cross, and all those things that you have preached in the towns through which you have come. We have not made any answer to it because here throughout all time we have worshipped our own gods, and thought they were good, as no doubt yours are, so do not trouble to speak to us any more about them at present. Regarding the creation of the world, we have held the same belief for ages past, and for this reason we take it for certain that you are those whom our ancestors predicted would come from the direction of the sunrise. As for your Great King, I feel that I am indebted to him, and I will give him of what I possess, for as I have already said, two years ago I heard of the Captains who came in ships from the direction in which you came, and they said that they were the servants of this your great King, and I wish to know you are all one and the same. "[41]

As the credibility of Díaz's narrative remains questionable, it is often argued to what extent the above citation from his work is accurate.[42] There is no evidence that Motecuhzoma II exactly understood what Cortés told him. Based on this, if we trust his narrative as a true one, two important points about his dualistic understanding of Christianity may be pointed out.

---

[41] Díaz del Castillo, 1989: Cap. XC, 245-246. The English translation was cited from Bernal Díaz 1956:Cap.LXIII, p.205-6.
[42] Wagner, 1944:XIX-XXIV. See also Brook 1995.

211

As a Christian of that era, Cortés denied that Aztec gods were devils based on the Christian concept that God is only one. That concept was to categorize the Aztec religion as inferior. On the other hand, Motecuhzoma treated Christianity as homogeneous with his own religion. Since Motecuhzoma II invited Cortés as a special guest to his capital, he must not have had a negative view of Christianity at that time. The view of Motecuhzoma II was by no means an attempt to incorporate Christianity into his own religion. For Motecuhzoma II, Christianity and his own religion must exist in parallel.

The problem is; *"Regarding the creation of the world, we have held the same belief for ages past."* Did Motecuhzoma II mean, 'We have the same story of the Creation of World as that of Christianity?' The original Spanish text says, *"...en esto de la creación del mundo, así lo tenemos nosotros creído muchos tiempos pasados..."*.[43] Unlike the English translation, the original text does not actually tell us that the Aztec belief of the creation is the same as that of Christianity. How do we understand this? It must be postulated that although the creation of the world occupies the central part of Christian theology, it did not have the same emphasis in the Aztec cosmovision because the creation of the world took place several times. In this respect, for the Aztec, two different stories of the creation of the world could co-exist at the same time. Therefore, Motecuhzoma II at that time may have considered, 'We have our own quite similar, **but our own different,**' narrative of the creation of 'our' world.'

The idea of Motecuhzoma II is quite similar to that of Don Carlos, although the former was positive about Christianity, unlike Don Carlos. They both considered the existence of two different conceptual worlds within a single physical world. Some may consider this kind of idea chaotic. On this point, however, apart from the existence of several previous worlds in the Aztec cosmovision, it must also be considered that the Aztec concept of the 'world' was different from the Spanish one. For them, their territory was often the world. For

---
[43] Díaz del Castillo, 1989: Cap. XC, 246.

example, the term '*mundo*' in colonial Nahuatl, such as *cemanauac, cemanauatl, tlalticpa,* and *tlalli,* often simply means a particular '*tierra* (=land)'. This concept is also found in the classic Maya. *Caban* in Maya generally refers to 'earth,' but it is also often employed to signify a territory of a ruler.

The '*mundo*' which Motecuhzoma II referred to, could simply have been 'my land.' By using this logic, two different conceptual worlds (one for the Christian, another for the Aztec) could co-exist perfectly in the single physical world. Therefore, it is not surprising that the Aztec understood the existence of two contradictory beliefs within their dualism between the Christian land and the Aztec land. Perhaps, I think, Motecuhzoma II did not manage to comprehend the fundamental nature of the Christian God on that occasion, but through numerous subsequent contacts through which Cortés tried to abolish Aztec deities, it is likely that he did gradually come to understand that Christianity was a religion rejecting all gods apart from the Lord. Within sources written by the *conquistadors*, there is no evidence that Motecuhzoma II spoke ill of Christianity, though his vassals often derided it. This suggests his acceptance of the divinity of the Christian Lord. Nevertheless, he did not accept the Christian Lord as the unique God of the world.

One of the Spaniards, Andrés de Tápia, recorded an incident when Córtes tried to remove principal pagan idols from Tenochititlan. It is recorded that as a reply to Cortés' naming of Aztec idols as the symbol of vain and devilish cults, Motecuhzoma II said to Cortés, "*No solamente esta ciudad; pero toda la tierra junta; tienen a éstos por sus dioses; y aquí está esto por Uchilobos... e toda la gente no tiene en nada a sus padres e madres e hijos, en comparación deste ... quieren morir por sus dioses.*"[44] (Not only this city; but all over the land; they have these as their Gods; and here he is this as Uchilobos [=*Huitzilopochtli*]... and all

---

[44] Cited from Tápia 1934:69. I modernized the spelling. Although Tápia claimed that Cortés successfully removed the idols and built two altars of Christianity, the reliability of this record remains questionable. A similar conversation was recorded by another conquistador, Bernal Díaz (1988:1989: Cap.XCII, p.261-2). Cortés suggested that Motecuhzoma II replace his pagan idols with Christian images. Yet, contrary to the text of Tápia, this source says that by seeing the anger of Motecuhzoma II, Cortés apologized for his rude attitude toward Aztec idols and went back.

people have nothing to their parents and mothers and children, in comparison with this, ... they want to die for their gods).

Although some time had passed since the first meeting with Cortés, there is no clear evidence that Motecuhzoma II fully understood Christian monotheism. Various sources written by the Spaniards suggest that Cortés spoke of Aztec deities as a satanic cult every time, nevertheless it is likely that Aztec king understood Christianity as a denial of his pagan deities. If we assume this hypothesis to be true, how did he manage to tolerate Christian people's opposition to the Aztec gods? Of course, his fear of the Spanish military technology or his political strategy of incorporating the Spaniards as one of the Aztec allies may have been reasons for his crafty tolerance of those who believed in, for the Aztec, a disgusting religion like Christianity. Yet, if this matter is considered from a perspective of dualism, a different opinion may be presented. I have argued that his dualistic conception of the cosmos probably consisted of two different *tierras* (=worlds): one for the Aztec, another for the Spaniards. In this case, it may be considered that he likely considered that there was only one god in the world of the Spaniards (Christian). There is no good direct supporting evidence in the case of Motecuhzoma II, but because Don Carlos used this logic, this notion may have been quite common among the Nahuatl people. This concept is not unique to the Aztec, because a similar notion is commonly seen in many dualistic cultures. For example, anti-Western Japanese classic scholars argued that there are two kinds of humans in the world, since the ancient Japanese sacred text refers to the Japanese as the descendants of Gods and the *Bible* records that the Westerners are a mere product of the God.[45]

Based on the points discussed up to here, I suggest that the case of the relationship between the early Aztec religions and Christianity could be understood by the dualism of two different worlds. After the Spanish Conquest,

---

[45] Yamase, 2002b:240-1. Although ambiguous, this concept should have existed among the colonial Yucatec Maya. See Chuchiak, 2000:445-6 and Yamase 2002b:228. The case of China will be discussed in this book; see Yamase 2002b:252.

although some of the elite like Don Carlos continued to resist Christianity, the majority had to compromise with it by incorporating some Christian elements. Fray Diego Durán, who evangelized Christianity in the Mexico of the early colonial period, provides us with a famous example:

> Después de los quince días, volvieron y dijeron que no querían a San Pablo, ni San Agustín. Pues preguntados qué santo querían, dijeron que a San Lucas. Yo, notando la petición y el ahínco con que la pedían advertí en qué podía haber algún mal, y fui al calendario de sus ídolos, y miré que fiesta y signo era en el que caía San Lucas,...[46]
>
> (After fifteen days, they returned and they said that they did not love Saint Pablo or Saint Augustine. Then I asked them which saint they wanted; they said Saint Lucas. As I noticed the request and the zeal with which they requested it, I was warned of what he could badly want, and I went to [see] the calendar of his idols, and watched that celebration and sign fell [on the day of] Saint Lucas...).

By the middle of the sixteenth century, as the Spanish authority was established elsewhere, it became virtually impossible for the Nahuatl to refuse Christianity. Therefore, as in the above text, they tried to discover some equivalent elements from Christianity in order to hide their ancestral religious beliefs.

However, this phenomenon should not be considered evidence of their rejection of Christianity.

Durán also records:

> Me dijo que, como no estaban aún bien arraigados en la fe, que no me espantase; de manera que aún estaban neutros, que ni bien acudían a la una ley, ni a la otra, o por mejor decir, que creían en Dios y que juntamente acudían a sus costumbres antiguas y ritos del demonio, y esto quiso decir aquel en su abominable excusa de que aún permanecían "en medio y eran neutros".[47]
>
> (He said to me that, as we were not still well rooted in the Faith, I should not be afraid. They were still neutral. They neither went to the Law [of Christianity], nor to the other, or better said, they believed in God and at the same time, they went to his old customs and rites of the demon, and this [is] what this one wanted to say by his abominable excuse of which they still remained in the middle and were neutral".

---

[46] Cited from Durán 1984.
[47] cited from *ibid.*

Although I have omitted it, Durán records that the native man used the term *nepantla* in order to express his neutral position. For Father Durán, what the native people were doing was no more than a deception. However, as seen in the text, a native person told him that although they still believed in their old religions, they also had faith in the Gospel. On this point, it can be said that they were struggling with two religious systems, and their attempt was by no means to hide old religious customs from the Spaniards, as they were looking for interchangeable elements from both religions. Based on these points, it is clear that the colonial Nahuatl people considered both Christianity and the Nahuatl religions a part of their dualistic cosmovision. Unfortunately, they were deprived of their religious freedom and thus the unique solution was of establishing a new religion from them.

As the time passed, due to the growing pressure from the Spanish authorities, the old pagan religions gradually decreased. The pagan priests who held knowledge of their ancient rites disappeared. Without a proper knowledge of the old religious traditions, they were not able to maintain them.[48] This was the beginning of their religious confusion = syncretism. Some in urban areas completely abandoned their old pagan beliefs, while farming villagers continued developing their new religion consisting of Christianity and their ancestral religion, albeit in a more confused form, a syncretic one.

However, even among the converted Nahuatl, there seems to have been a strong desire to be independent from the Spanish religious authority. From my point of view, this was practiced as a new dualistic concept of 'Spanish Christianity and Nahuatl Christianity.' Since reviving ancient religions under Spanish rule was difficult, their passion was represented in the form of creating a Nahuatl's own version of Christianity. This seems to show that the Nahuatl had had their own Christianity born in Mexico, or that, as they did not want

---

[48] Of course, it must be pointed out that the abuse of the Spanish caused the destruction of numerous indigenous communities, which resulted in collapse of the pre-Columbian traditions. For example,see Mendieta 1959:Lib.III, Cap.50, Lib.IV, Cap.33)

216

Christianity through the Spaniards, they tried to show that Christianity was directly given to them by the Lord. Although this hypothetical view is peculiar for some readers, as I will mention in this chapter, this kind of example also existed in Japan.

In my opinion, the so-called Our Lady of Guadalupe (or the Virgin of Guadalupe), which appeared in Mexico soon after the Spanish conquest, may have been an example of their desire to separate Christianity from the Spaniards.[49] Indeed, this type of religious phenomenon was frequently reported in New Spain during the colonial period. Of course, what I have argued here is not based on solid research, and thus it is merely hypothetical. Although I initially wanted to discuss this issue more carefully, due to the ambitious scale of this research, it has become impossible to make an adequate analysis. This point may be argued on another occasion in the future.

II: Inca Discovery of Christianity[50]

> The eyes of the Indian monarch [Atahualpa] flashed fire, and his dark brow grew darker as he replied, - "I will be no man's tributary. I am greater than any prince upon earth. Your emperor may be a great prince; I do not doubt it, when I see that he has sent his subjects so far across the waters; and I am willing to hold him as a brother. As for the Pope of whom you speak, he must be crazy to talk of giving away countries which do not belong to him. For my faith," he continued, "I will not change it. Your own God, as you say, was put to death by the very men whom he created. But mine," he concluded, pointing to his Deity, - then, alas! sinking in glory behind the mountains, - "my God still lives in the heavens, and looks down on his children.""[51]

As the Inca did not leave much information about their ideology, it remains unclear as to what extent they developed dualism. Yet, it is evident dualism was an important cultural element in their society. It is known that the Inca society

---

[49] Our Lady of Guadalupe may not have been a product of the colonial Nahuatl, as it attracted the Spaniards more than the Natives (Burkhart, 1993:207). Our Lady of Guadalupe was often considered a representation of the disguised Aztec female deity Tonantzin, but Burkhalt (*ibid.*:209) suggests that it is unlikely. Although there are numerous works examining this phenomenon, Burkhart (1993) is a useful and concise work to grasp the whole figure.

[50] As to the history of the Spanish Conquest of the Inca, see Hemming, 1993. For the Japanese readers, see Yamase, 2004.

[51] Prescott, Chapter V.

217

consisted of two elements. For example, their capital Cuzco was divided into two parts, *Hanan* (Upper) Cuzco and *Hurin* (Lower) Cuzco. Each community had this system. The Inca royal family was also categorized according to this rule. Some such as Franklin Peace G.Y. argue that the Inca empire was ruled by two Inca emperors at the same time.[52] Therefore, there is good reason to believe that this dualistic concept of *Hanan* and *Hurin* was represented in other social, political and religious aspects of Inca belief.

As in the case of other Native Americans, the majority of colonial documentary sources were written by the Spaniards. Even if the authors of those documents claim that they faithfully transcribed what their Inca informants told them, there must be some European bias. Therefore, there is a limitation to reconstructing a history by using such materials.

Unlike the Maya and the Aztec, the Inca had a very clear concept of the single creator of the world. His name was *Viracochan*. Therefore, the early colonial Inca tended to identify the Christian Lord as equivalent to *Viracochan*. Nevertheless, the position of *Viracochan* in the Andean world is not as the absolute ruler of the universe, as in Christianity. Marzal pointed out that other deities also had similar power.[53] It is almost certain that the Inca also had a concept of religious dualism before the Spanish conquest.[54]

The Inca Empire was placed under the control of the Spaniards soon after the arrival of Francisco Pizarro. At Cajamarca, the Inca Emperor, Atahualpa, was arrested in spite of the fact that numerous soldiers guarded him. Atahualpa was later killed, and his rival, prince Manco Inca, ascended the throne as the Spanish puppet Inca Emperor. Although this Inca Empire found benefit in an alliance with the Spaniards for expelling the remaining forces of Atahualpa, due to the continuous demands for gold and the mistreatment of the Inca nobles by the Spaniards, Manco Inca decided to initiate his *reconquista* of Peru. After his failure

---

[52] e.g., Pease and Masuda, 1998.
[53] Marzal, 1993:88-89.
[54] e.g., see MacCormack, 1993:109, 118.

218

to capture Cuzco and Lima, Manco retreated to Vitcos in the Vilcabamba religion, and the Inca built a new capital called Vilcabamba and refused to accept Spanish rule and Christianity. The Inca Empire continued to resist the Spaniards until 1572, for nearly forty years. Because the Inca managed to sustain their state and religious system, it could be suggested that their resistance to Christianity was far more organized and systematic than the Maya, at least until 1572. During this period, it can be said that the religion of the Inca became a symbol of resistance not only to the Spaniards, but also to Christianity. From their colonial records, therefore, more direct hostility towards Christianity is expected than from the Aztec or the Maya.

When Francisco Pizarro landed in the territory of the Inca, the Spanish became more brutal than they had been in the previous expedition. Nevertheless, Atahualpa did not seriously consider the arrival of the Spaniards, nor their power. He was not scared of a Spanish horse approaching him directly, and talked with Hernándo Pizarro, a brother of Francisco Pizarro, without any respect. Rather, it is more likely that the Spaniards were terrified of Atahualpa.[55] Therefore, it seems true that Atahualpa did not consider them divine people from the first. Nevertheless, his attitude towards the religion of the Spaniards, Christianity, remains uncertain.

According to records written by the *Conquistadors* at the meeting with Pizarro at Cajamarca, Atahualpa had some conversations about Christianity with Father Valverde through an imperfect interpreter. Although I quoted a paragraph of the Spanish writer cited in Prescott at the beginning of this section, it is very unlikely that Atahualpa managed to understand exactly what Valverde told him. Since colonial Spanish writers often questioned the ability of this interpreter, and Valverde did not leave in writing what he talked about on this occasion, to what extent he could exactly transfer the words of Valverde to Atahualpa is unknown. Almost all records confirm that Atahualpa threw away the *Bible*. Yet, it cannot be

[55] Spanish soldiers' records, such as Estete 1534:322, Marquina 1533, narrate that all of the Spaniards were terrified of being killed by Atahualpa's troop.

219

known whether his anger was caused by the Christians' attitude, or because he did not understand the importance of the *Bible* for the Spaniards.

At the meeting of Cajamarca, one of Pizarro's two principal interpreters (Felipe or Martín) translated what Father Valverde told Atahualpa. All Spanish witnesses and historians wrote as if there were a perfect oral communication between the Spaniard and Atahualpa.[56] However, as in the case of Cortés' conquest of the Aztecs, exaggeration of the efficiency of interpreters must be considered. Indeed, a half-Inca man, el Inca Garcilaso de la Vega, criticized the ability of Pizarro's interpreter in his book.[57]

Moreover, there is a book based on Inca informants. A colonial Spaniard, Juan de Betanzos, who acted an official interpreter of the Quechua language in Peru of the sixteenth century, wrote a book on history of the Inca.[58] Since he married an Inca royal princess, he was able to obtain information on Inca history from the Inca royal family and her people. It is said that he transcribed what his Inca informants told him, with minimum interference. Although this book must contain his bias, the detail of Atahualpa's reaction at Cajamarca is also mentioned. Because there is no solid evidence that his Inca informants actually witnessed the historical incidents mentioned, or directly heard what Atahualpa said, the reliability of the context of his book remains uncertain. Nevertheless, as Betanzos' book is based on Inca views towards the Spaniards, it can be suggested that although what his book narrates may not be Atahualpa's actual reaction to Father Valverde, it should contain the first view of one of the 'Inca nobles' towards Christianity. Therefore, the narrative of the meeting between the *Conquistadores* and Atahualpa at Cajamarca in his book is quite interesting.

Betanzos' book says:

---

[56] Cieza de Léon, 1998:Chap.XLV, p. 211, Xerez, 1992:111, Pedro Pizarro, 1984:Cap.8, pp.59-60.
[57] Garcilaso de la Vega. He wrote that Felipe was the interpreter at Cajamarca.
[58] Betanzos, 1996.

When he entered the square of Cajamarca, he asked if his lodgings had been vacated. They should take him directly to them. They told him that those men were staying in them. Then he commanded that they take him to his father, Huayna Capac's, house. They told him that those men were also occupying them. Then he said that they should take him to the houses of the Sun. He was told that they, too, were occupied by those men.

When he heard this, he said:---There is no place where I can stay. All has been filled.---While he was engaged in this conversation, Fray Vicente de Valverde approached him. He brought with him an interpreter. I fully believe, because of what those lords said who were right next to the Inca's litter, that the interpreter did not know how to relate to the Inca what the priest Fray Vicente told him. They said what the interpreter told the Inca when the priest took out a book and opened it. The interpreter said that that priest was the son of the Sun, and that the Sun had sent him to tell the Inca that he should not fight, he should obey the captain who was also the son of the Sun, and that was what was in that book and the painting in the book said that.

Since he said painting, the Inca asked for the book and, taking it in his hands, he opened it. When he saw the hues of letters, he said: "This speaks and says that you are the son of the Sun? I, also, am the son of the Sun." His Indians answered this and said in a loud voice all together: "Thus is Capa Inca."

The Inca repeated in a loud voice that he also came from where the Sun was. Saying this, he hurled the book- away and again all his people answered him: "Yes, he is the only lord."

When Fray Vicente do Valverde saw this, he went to where the marquis was. What he said to the marquis, the conquerors who were present will have to say. When the marquis had heard out Fray Vicente about that turn of events, he made his signal to the artillerymen. When they saw it, they fired their cannon and the harquebuses. Then everybody cattled out at once and fell upon the Inca's men. The horsemen lanced them and the foot soldiers cut with their swords without the Inca's men putting up any resistance.[59]

The Inca Empire practically collapsed when Francisco Pizarro captured Atahualpa, the Inca emperor. The emperor offered a great amount of his treasure to Pizarro, but he was later forced to convert to Christianity, and was finally executed. Before this, there is no strong evidence that the Inca initially rejected Christianity. It is certain that this execution created a strong feeling of hostility toward Christianity among Atahualpa's faction.

The Spaniards also arrested the most important general of the Inca emperor, Chilichuchima. On marching to Cuzco, Francisco Pizarro became suspicious that the Inca general may have been keeping in touch with Quizquiz, another important

Inca general, and sentenced him to death. Like Atahualpa, Chilichuchima was asked to become a Christian. He rejected this proposal and chose to be burnt alive. Sancho Pedro who served as a secretary of Francisco Pizarro at that time records the last of Chilichuchima, as follows:

> *The religious tried to persuade him to become a Christian, saying to him that those who were baptized and who believed with true faith in our savior Jesus Christ went to glory in paradise and that those who did not believe in him went to hell and its tortures. But he* [Chilichuchima] *did not wish to be Christian, saying that he did not know what sort of thing this law was, and he began to invoke Paccamaca* [Pachacamac] *and captain Quizquiz that they might come to his aid.*[60]

However, for those who supported Huascar, Atahualpa's brother and the former emperor of the Inca, the arrival of the Christian people and the execution of Atahualpa were just what they wanted. It is said that Huascar's faction in Cuzco was pleased with the news of the death of Atahualpa, and they even considered that the Spaniards might be sons of *Viracochan*, an Andean god. Among the anti-Atahualpa faction, the anti-Christian feeling was not raised.

One of the princes of Wayna Capac the great Inca emperor, Manco Inca, went to Pizarro's camp, and offered his future military cooperation. Manco tried to use Spanish force to establish himself as an Inca, and to destroy the remaining force of Atahualpa led by Quizquiz. Because Francisco Pizarro also realized he necessity of allying with some Inca royal families and nobles in order to gain complete control of the territory of the Inca, the relationships between Manco and Pizarro were good at least until Quizquiz's army eventually collapsed in Ecuador.

There is no evidence that Francisco Pizarro forced Manco Inca to convert to Christianity. Since Francisco Pizarro received a rebuke for his execution of Atahualpa from Carlos V in 1534[61] and he needed Manco's aid to defeat Quizquiz, Pizarro must have acted in a very friendly manner with the Inca. Consequently, there is no solid evidence that Manco had a negative view of Christianity. At least

---

[59] Quoted from Betanzos, 1996: Part II, Chap.XXIII, p.263.
[60] Cited from Sancho 1917: 97.

in the first few years, Francisco Pizarro seems to have treated Manco Inca fairly well. In fact, it must be noted that Manco's son, Titu Cuci Yupanqui, never castigated Francisco Pizarro in his *Instrucción del inga Don Diego de Castro Tito Cussi Yupangui,* in 1570.[62] Although the superiority of the Spanish king as their master had to be accepted, the Inca were allowed to continue and to practice their old religious customs.

In Cuzco, pagan religious practices were tolerated to some extent. The colonial Spanish chronicles record numerous facts supporting this. Manco celebrated his accession according to the Incan religious tradition. The people continued worshipping mummies of dead people as they had done before the arrival of the Spaniards. Miguel Estete, one of the *conquistadors,* records that the Spaniards and the Inca of Cuzco celebrated their victory against Quizquiz with Inca mummies.[63] Moreover, the traditional religious posts, such as the priest of the Sun God, Villa Oma, continued to act as the second most influential post within the Inca Empire. Later, when Manco Inca revolted against the Spaniards in 1536, Diego de Almagro made Paullu Inca, one of Manco's brothers, a new puppet Inca emperor. After the defeat of Almagro, Paullu Inca remained a pagan, though he finally became a Christian in 1543.

However, although the Inca were not forced to be Christian, it is almost certain that Manco and other Inca novices were occasionally instructed in Christianity by the Spanish friars. To what extent did they manage to comprehend the Christian doctrine? Some colonial chronicles suggest that Manco initially tried to understand the Christian God as homogeneous deity with *Viracochan,* the Creator of the Andean world.

Although the relationships between Manco and the Spaniards went well, as Francisco's brothers were young and not prudent, they began to mistreat Manco. After Francisco Pizarro left Cuzco in order to build Lima as a new Spanish base,

---

[61] CP:66-9.
[62] Yupanqui Inca, 1570:183.
[63] Estete, 1919:334.

223

Gonzalo and Juan Pizarro were responsible for the administration of Cuzco. In order to accumulate their own properties, they began to abuse their power and mistreated Manco Inca in order to obtain more precious metal. As a response to such treatment, Manco decided upon a rebellion against the Spaniards. This rebellion is often called 'The Great Rebellion' or 'the Inca *Reconquista* of Peru.'[64] Several documents tell us that religious conflict was not the main cause of this *Reconquista*. Let us look at several texts.

Before he raised action against the Spaniards, Manco Inca assembled his people in Cuzco and told them:

> *Remember that the Incas, my fathers, who rest in the heaven with the Sun, ruled from Quito to Chile, treating those whom they received as vassals so that it seemed they were children who had emerged from their own entrails. They did not steal and killed only when it served justice when it served justice... these bearded ones* [the Spaniards] *entered our land, theirs being so far away from here. They preach one thing and do another, and they give us so many admonitions, yet they do the opposite. They have no fear of God or shame...*[65]

Manco referred to the Spaniards' saying one thing and doing the opposite. It is almost certain that what the Spaniards said to the Inca was mostly Christian teachings. Therefore, it is suggested that Manco received a certain part of the Christian teachings in a positive light before he decided to revolt against the Spaniards. No doubt, the main reason for his revolt was his eventual mistreatment by the Spaniards.[66]

It is recorded how Manco Inca later complained furiously of mistreatment received from Gonzalo and Juan to Pedro de Oñate and Juan Gómez, messengers of Diego Almagro, as follows:

[64] "*Reconquista*" is preferred among Peruvian Scholars, because "rebellion" sounds as if Spain had originally been the sovereignty of Peru.
[65] Cited from Cieza de León 1998:Cap.XC, p.407-8.
[66] E.g. Yupanqui Inca, 1570:143-191, Zárate, 1968:lib.III, Cap.3, p.163, Murúa, 1987:Lib.I, Cap.LXV, p.230-1, Enríque de Guzmán, 1543:Cap.XLIV, p.99, Cap.XLVII, p.106, Anomynous, 1539:1-10.

Cómo el grande Apo de Castilla manda que me tomen á mí mujeres y me tengan preso con una cadena al pescuezo y me meen y cager en la cara ... "(How did the Great Apo [King] of Castilla [Carlos V] order them to take my women, and to make me a prisoner with a chain tied to my neck, to piss on and to make shit on my face...?). [67]

Although some religious conflicts may have existed between the Inca and the Spaniards, at least in the 1530s, the religious factor seems not to have been the primary reason for Manco's *Reconquista* of Peru.

Nevertheless, as long as Christianity was a symbol of the domination of the Spaniards, his anger was also directed toward Christianity. Christianity gradually and inevitably became a symbol of the enemy, the Spaniards. However, as will be seen, unlike Motecuhzoma II of the Aztec, Manco seems not to have considered the Christian Lord an alien deity.

Although Manco Inca twice mobilized large forces, he did not gain any final victory. After the failure of his attempt to recover control of Peru, Manco Inca decided to retreat to Vitocos, a place in the Vilcabamba region. Titu Cusi Yupanqui, a son of Manco, recorded his father's speech to his people at that time.

...en lugar de hacer bien, nos han hecho mal tomándonos nuestras haciendas, nuestras mujeres, nuestros hijos, nuestras hijas, nuestras chacaras, nuestras comidas y otras muchas cosas que en nuestra tierra teníamos, por fuerza y con engaños y contra nuestra voluntad , y a gente que esto hace, no les podemos llamar hijos del Viracochan, sino como otras veces os he dicho, del supai, y peores" (instead of doing something good, they [the Spaniards] have done bad to us. They have taken our properties, our women, our children, our daughters, our *chacaras*, our meals and many other things that we had in our land, by force and with fraud and against our will, and we cannot call those who do this children of the *Viracochan*, but as I have said to you on other occasions, they are children of *supai*, and worse...) [68]

From the above quotation, it appears that Manco had initially confused the Christian God with *Viracochan*. After he raised the *Reconquista*, due to his hostility towards the Spaniards, he seems to have changed his view towards

---

[67] *Pedro de Oñate y Juan Gómez de Malaver al Emperador, Cuzco 31 de Marzo de 1539.* in CP 337-8, quoted from p.337. My own translation.

[68] Cited from Yupanqui Inca, 1988:208. The original Spanish text is modernized by me. My own translation.

225

Christianity and recognized the Christian Lord as a very negative alien deity, like *supai* of the Andes. Nevertheless, let us look at another piece of Titu Cusi Yupanqui's narrative.

> *Lo que más habéis de hacer, es que por ventura éstos os dirán que adoréis a lo que ellos adoran, que son unos paños pintados, los cuales dicen que es Viracochan, y que le adoréis como a guaca el cual no es sino paño, no lo hagáis, sino lo que nosotros tenemos, eso tened; porque como veis, las vilcas hablan con nosotros y al sol Y a la luna vérnoslo por nuestros ojos, y lo que esos dicen no lo vemos bien. Creo que alguna vez, por fuerza o por engaño, os han de hacer adorar lo que ellos adoran, cuando más no piéredes, hacedlo (sic) delante dellos, y por otra parte no olvidéis nuestras ceremonias (sic), y si os dijeren que quebrantéis vuestras guacas, y esto por fuerza, mostradles.*" (What you have to do more, is that these [Spaniards] will probably say to you to adore what they adore, a painted cloth, and they say that a piece of cloth is *Viracochan*, and they say to you to adore it like *huaca*. It is not [*huaca*] but a piece of cloth. Do not do it. What we have [=*huacas*], is that you have; because as you see, *vilcas* speak with us, and the sun and the moon are seen by our eyes, but we do not see well what those [Spaniards] say. I believe that by force or deceit, they must sometimes make you adore what they adore, when you cannot [refuse to do], do it (*sic*) in front of them. On the other hand, do not forget our [traditional religious] ceremonies (*sic*), and if they say to you to destroy your *huacas* by force, pretend to do these).[69]

What Manco insisted upon was to encourage the Inca to continue a hidden resistance to Christianity under Spanish domination. Although to what extent Titu Cusi exactly remembered what his father said remains uncertain, this speech of Manco is interesting. Some may argue that Manco's learning of Christianity from the Spaniards was in its infancy, because he equated *Viracochan* with the Christian lord, and he did not understand the concept of Christianity that 'the Christian God is invisible.' In the above text, it appears that he rejected the Christian God as a divinity, because he mentions that the cult of the Christian God is merely a vain and useless piece of cloth. However, when this text is considered carefully, it can be conjectured that Manco considered the god of the Spaniards a negative and vain god for the Inca, because *Supai* is not the equivalent of Satan in Christianity, but simply a god of negative aspect. Therefore, it is suggested that in spite of his

---

[69] Cited from Yupanqui Inca, 1988:208. The original Spanish text is modernized by me.

hostility, Manco recognized the Christian Lord as a supernatural power. On this point, Manco seems to have insisted that the Christian Lord did not have any supernatural power over the Inca. Because neither is the Christian God visible to the Inca, nor does it speak to them, nor does it appear in physical form in front of them, he considered that it is not a deity for the Inca, but for the Spaniards. It seems clear that there was a solid belief among the Inca that a deity must appeal to man's conscience. Of course, this view is not beyond conjecture. A more careful analysis must be made, therefore.

After the death of Manco Inca, his sons continued their resistance at Vilcabamba. It is known that this 'new' Inca continued rejecting Christianity. The resistance of the Inca to the Spaniards was not always one of monolithic solidarity, nevertheless. For example, although one of Manco's sons, Sairi Topac, became the Inca emperor after Manco, he sought peace with the Spaniards. He left Vilcabamba and became a vassal of the Spanish king. He promised to be a Christian. On this point, there is an interesting record.

Garcilaso de la Vega, a half-Inca Spanish historian, met him in Cuzco in his childhood, and later left a record of that occasion. This author unveiled Sairi Topac's lack of faithfulness to Christianity. In spite of being a Christian, Sairi Topac called the Blessed Sacrament '*Pachacámac*! (=an Andean deity)', and called the image of Our Lady 'Mother of God.' In addition, he did not stop worshipping his father, the Sun, and his ancestors.[70] That is, his mind was still that of a pagan. From the brief account recorded by Garcilaso de la Vega, it is impossible to know what Sairi Topac actually believed. Yet, a hypothesis may be suggested. Did he deceive the Spaniards as if he had faith in Christianity? Alternatively, did he consider *Pachacámac* the Christian Lord? In the Inca religion, the most important God was *Viracochan*. The second one was the Sun. Although the shrine at Pachacáma was very important, *Pachacáma* was merely one of the

---

[70] Garcilaso de la Vega, 1966:Book 8, Ch.XI, p.1445.

subordinated Gods to the Sun. [71] If he considered the Lord to be the same deity as the Andean Creation God, he would have used the name *Viracochan*. Why did he use '*pachacámac*'?

As in the Aztec concept, the Creator in the Andean conception does not embrace the whole universe, but often a territory. Therefore, apart from *Viracochan*, there were other divine Creators in the Andes. As the etymology of the word *pachacáma* means creator of the world, the common people believed that creation took place at Pachacáma. [72] It may be said that Sairi Topac simply used the term '*pachacáma*' as a synonym of the 'Creator = Lord' of Christianity. Yet, it may be also suggested that because Sairi Topac still had strong faith in the Sun and *Viracochan*, calling the Christian Lord '*pachacáma*' was his attempt to avoid identifying the Lord of Christianity as the same divinity as the God of the Sun and *Viracochan* of the Inca. If this view is correct, he identified the Lord as the second most important Creator next to *Viracochan*, and was prudently hiding his faith in the Andean deities. Otherwise, as in the case of the Aztec, by metaphorically calling the Christian Lord '*pachacáma,* he may have assigned him to be the creator of the 'Spanish' world, different from that of the 'Inca' world. Of course, as this view is very hypothetical, there is no answer for his action.

Although Sairi Topac left, the Inca at Vilcabamba chose Titu Cusi Yupanqui as Sairi's successor and continued their resistance. While Sairi, the former Inca, was near the Spanish, the Inca at Vilcabamba kept their peace. Yet, when Sairi Topac died for an unknown reason, they restarted their military assaults into the Spanish territory. It is almost certain that the new emperor, Titu Cusi, who was once baptized when he lived in Cuzco, refused to accept Christianity. Nevertheless, since the Inca leaders at Vilcabamba knew that the Spanish friars quite often acted for them, churches were often excluded from their attacks. [73] It is often argued that the reason for the neo-Inca adoption of Spanish symbols and religion was their

---

[71] Cobo, 1990:89.
[72] *ibid.*:12.
[73] See Rodríguez de Figueroa,1565.

228

need of improving their military effectiveness.[74] However, this kind of traditional interpretation of the Inca's attitude toward Christianity lacks a perspective on the dualistic nature of the pagan cultural concept. The Inca perception of traditional Andean deities and Christian ones seems not to have been the same as the relationship between the Lord and Satan of Christianity.

When we talk about the anti-Christian movement in Andean history during the sixteenth century, *Taki Onqoy* is perhaps the best-known case. Because several scholars have presented detailed analyses of *Taki Onqoy*,[75] I will not argue this phenomenon in detail here. Because surviving documentary sources concerning this movement were Spaniards, it remains questionable as to what extent these biased texts record a precise picture of *Taki Onqoy*. Also, they offer little information. By accepting this, only the main points of this curious social and religious movement will be discussed.

During the 1560s, the *Taki Onqoy* (dancing sickness) movement arose in Peru. Messengers of the indigenous Andean gods, the *taquiongos*, insisted that the power of Andean deities would be restored and they would vanquish the Christian god and kill the Spaniards by causing disease and other calamities. It was claimed that since *huacas* (Andean deities) would restore their power, unless the people returned to worship idols of the *huacas* and abandon their Christian faith, they would face the same fate as the Spaniards. In their version of events, after the catastrophe of Christianity and the Spaniards, the revived *huacas* would generate a new world for the Andean people.[76] Thus, it can be said that *Taki Onqoy* was a kind of separatism of the Peruvian people from the Spaniards and Christianity. This *Taki Onqoy* was soon widespread in Peru. A Spanish friar of the sixteenth

---

[74] Stern, 1982:69.
[75] *e.g.*, Stern, 1982:51-71. Some are suspicious of this as a real historical incident. See Mumford 1998. The record of Spanish investigation of this religious movement was published in Millones 1990, See Molina 1570.
[76] Molina, 1573:59-64.

229

century, Cristobal de Molina, believed that Titu Cusi Yupanqui at Vilcabamba maneuvered *Taki Onqoy*.[77]

Because this movement was spread among tribes who had been cooperative with the Spaniards and hostile towards the Inca, the *Taki Onqoy* movement probably originated because of the Andean people's disappointment in the consequences of the Spanish conquest. The statement of the *taquiongos* was, of course, a challenge to Christianity and the Spaniards. Yet, a question remains. Did the *taquiongos* treat Christianity as a heresy?

As Steve J. Stern argues, the supernatural power of Christianity was recognized.[78] According to Cristobal de Molina, the Andean people believed that the Christian Lord conquered *huacas* when Francisco Pizarro arrested Atahualpa, but, as the rule of the Christian Lord would be over, the people had to renounce Christianity and had to return to the old religion.[79] From Molina's explanation, a strong anti-Christian movement is suggested. Although the *taquiongos* accepted the Christian Lord as a divinity of a certain time in their dualistic understanding of two religions, they did not believe its power to be permanent in the Andes. On this point, Christian readers may consider this issue as if the statement of the *taquiongos* was a challenge, as in the uncompromising battle between the Christian Lord and Satan. In spite of the fact that the *taquiongos* predicted the end of Christianity, however, some of them were feted as Christian saints rather than as *huacas* in the midst of an anti-Christian war.

According to the *Información de Servicios* written in *Huamanga* of 1570, some native women named themselves '*Santa Maria,*' '*la Magdalena*' (*Santa Maria Magdalena* =the Mary Magdalene) and other saints' names. The source mentions that these women committed several crimes against Christianity.[80] In this case, the information about the precise background of those who feted Christian

---

[77] Molina, 1573:60. Varón Gabai (1990:404) concludes that although it is likely, there is no substantial evidence.
[78] Stern, 1982:66.
[79] Molina, 1573:61.
[80] Molina, 1570: 69, 99.

230

saints in the anti–Christian movement is limited to just a few sentences. Therefore, what we can say about this issue is also extremely limited. Concerning the 'questionable' favor of some Christian saints among women who participated in *Taki Onqoy*, Steve J. Stern suggests that because their attempt to gain the favor of some of the lesser Christian divinities exposed a crisis of confidence in the capacity of Andean *huacas*, this anti-Christian movement was diluted by the Spanish suppression.[81] Perhaps his view (=a religious war must be fundamentalist) is a quite usual one for a Western researcher. However, anti-Christianity in a pagan culture does not always mean an exclusion of Christianity. In fact, the history of the world proves that anti-Western movements often have involved some important Christian elements. A pagan religious movement similar to these *Taquiongos* in *Huamanga* of 1570 was reported in colonial Chiapas in 1584 (see Chapter IV of this volume). A Japanese pagan theologist of the nineteenth century, Hirata, incorporated some important theology of the Gospel with the Japanese native pagan religion in order to expel Christianity from Japan. The Imperial Japanese Government of the twentieth century encouraged the 'Christianity for Japanese pagan' movement in order to expel 'Anglo-Saxon or Jewish Christianity.'

In fact, it became an important religious force as a part of the Japanese state pagan religion. In the case of the *Taquiongos*, all were female and the name of Maria, the mother of the Christian Lord, and *la Magdalena*, another female who ministered to Jesus Christ, were proclaimed. They are the mother and servant of Jesus Christ. Why did not the male *taquiongos* do the same? Female deities have often been considered the mother and origin of the supernatural. The *taquiongos* allying with female Christian saints was an attempt by the native Andean

---

[81] Stern, 1982:66-7.
[84] Murúa, 1987: libro I, Cap.LXXVI, p.272, CLDRHP, 1ser. Tomo2, p.134, Ocampo 1610: 210-5. See also Levillier 1935: 343-4.

Christians to create a 'new' Andean religion allied with some Christian female saints and the *Huacas*, although this point is not clear.

We should go back to the neo-Inca emperor, Titu Cusi (ruled 1557-1571), who made the treaty of Acobamba with Spain in 1566, in which the residence of the Spanish *corregidor* and Catholic friars of the Augustinian order within Vilcabamba, his capital, was allowed. During his rule, the military power of the neo-Inca was gradually declining and the possibility of the recovery of their land from the Spaniards became impossible. Under such circumstances, accepting Christianity may have been a political tactic of Titu Cusi to keep the independence of his state within the Spanish empire.

Titu Cusi Yupanqui Inca was later baptized as a Christian again in 1568 in the process of peace negotiations with the Spanish crown. Nevertheless, several records suggest that he did not abandon the old gods of the Inca. Whether he actually hated Christianity or simply wanted to keep his ancestral gods together, cannot exactly be known. Some of the Inca still hated Christianity, because the successor of Titu Cusi was Topac Amaru, who had rejected Christianity and remained a believer in the Inca gods. But, because of the mysterious death of Titu Cusi in 1571, the majority of the Inca became hostile towards Spain and Christianity. It must not be forgotten that the Inca ordered a Spanish friar to revive Titu Cusi.[84] What was their intention? If Topac Amaru rejected the divine power of Christianity from the first, such a 'test' of the supernatural power of Christianity would not have been necessary. Perhaps, although there is no supporting documentary evidence, because there were certain numbers of the Inca who believed in some supernatural power of Christianity, Topac Amaru needed a 'test' to deny that divine power. Since the Inca emperor was also regarded as a god, Inca converts at Vilcabamba dualistically worshipped both the Christian Lord and the Inca's living God. Unfortunately, the friar failed to revive Titu Cusi, and was brutally killed. However, it is also true that Topac Amaru, the priest of the Sun, did not manage to revive Titu Cusi. On this point, he did not succeed in his denial of

232

the supernatural power of Christianity. He only confirmed that Andean deities were as powerless as the Christian Lord. Therefore, what he attempted to prove on the death of Titu Cusi may have been the fact that the Christian Lord was not superior to the Inca and Andean deities.

In 1972, Francisco de Toledo, the viceroy of Peru, destroyed all the remaining forces of the Inca at Vilcabamba. The purpose of his conquest of Vilcabamba was to eliminate the influence of the Inca emperor from Peru. In fact, in spite of the steady progress of evangelization, the Inca was still adored as a kind of god among the Andean people, so position of the Inca among the Andean people was still above that of the Christian Lord. Francisco thought that the traditional native authority, such as the Inca royal family, would become an obstacle to constructing a new paradise for Christianity. Yet his crude policy towards the Inca was remembered by the Andean people. He also introduced *reducción*, a policy to order the native people to reside in newly-built Spanish-style towns. By separating the native people from their traditional residential areas, Toledo expected an end to the old religious beliefs they held. In this he was wrong. Although worship of the Sun God disappeared soon after the final collapse of the Inca, other religious traditions remained.

Before the Spanish conquest, the Inca allowed the conquered people to continue worshipping their native deities. The new master, the Spaniards, required the subordinated Andean people to accept the Christian Lord as the only God of the world and all other deities had to be treated as demons. This caused a religious trauma among the native Andean people.

A Quechua document, the *Huarochili Manuscript* of the colonial Andes of the late sixteenth century, tells us of this feeling:

> We've already heard that Locally Huancupa was an evil demon and
> Don Cristóbal defeated him...Don Cristóbal began to speak: "Listen,
> Locally Huancupa!... 'Is not Jesus Christ the son of God? Shall I revert to
> this one, the true God...'... "Or am I mistaken? Then tell me now! Say, 'He is
> not the true God; I am the maker of everything!' so that from that moment on
> I may worship you"...but the demon stayed mute...Then he woke up. From

*that exact time on, right up to the present, he defeated various huacas in his
dreams the same way. Any number of times he defeated both Paria Caca and
Chaupi Ñamca, telling the people all about it over and over again, saying,
"They are demons!" This is all we know about this evil demon's existence
and about Don Cristóbal's victory.*[85]

The above quote is an interesting and witty one. The author of this text
apparently suggests that even after Christianity was widespread in Peru, existence
of the old Andean gods, *huacas,* never disappeared from the Andean people's
minds. It also tells us that the Christian-converted people were frustrated by not
knowing how to treat old Andean deities under the Christian rule. In the text, the
huacas appearing in front of Don Cristóbal spoke nothing. They neither insisted
that they were true gods, nor did they reject the divinity of Jesus Christ. What does
this suggest? Some may think that victory of Christianity over the *huacas,* which
only took place in the dreams of Cristóbal, is ironically implied in the text. It may
also be said that the text made fun of those who converted as betrayers. Don
Cristóbal was not confident of his faith in Christianity, in spite of the fact that he
claimed to be. Indeed, the majority of the Andean peoples did not forget the sacred
power of the Andean *huacas.* Andean deities were not defeated in the minds of the
indigenous people.

Another part of the *Huarochili Manuscript* says:

> ...*Doctor Francisco de Avila, a good counselor and teacher, it may be
> that in their hearts they don't really believe. If they had another priest they
> might return to the old ways. Some people, although they become Christians,
> have done so only out of fear... Although they say the Rosary, they still carry
> some pretty illa [small sacred objects] amulet elsewhere; although they
> themselves might not worship these native divinities, they contact some old
> people to worship in their stead. Lots of people live this way.*[86]

This text seems to suggest that the colonial Andean people were unwillingly
converted to Christianity in most cases. For them, the true gods were still the
huacas. However, it is not clear how these people regarded the Christian Lord. Did

---

[85] *Huarochiri Manuscript* 1598: 107-110. Also see *ibid.*:103.
[86] *Huarochiri Manuscript* 1598: 74.

they hate Christianity? As Durán mentioned *Nepantla* in the case of the colonial Nahuatl, did they struggle with two very different religious systems? In the case of the Inca, it is difficult to know the answer. At least, I can say now that the divine power of Christianity was not dismissed by the Inca, in spite of their hostility to it.

III: In Defence of Christianity: Chinese Discovery of Christianity

Having read the papal proclamation, the emperor wrote the following comment: "Reading this proclamation, I have concluded that the Westerns are petty indeed. It is impossible to reason with them because they do not understand larger issues as we understand them in China. There is not a single Westerner versed in Chinese works, and their remarks are often incredible and ridiculous. To judge from this proclamation, their religion is no different from other small, bigoted sects of Buddhism or Taoism. I have never seen a document which contains so much nonsense. From now on, Westerners should not be allowed to preach in China, to avoid further trouble."(Chinese Emperor, Kang-Shi (康熙帝) made his comment on the papal bull which prohibited participation of Chinese Christians in Confucians' rites and made a decision to ban Christianity. Cited from Li 1969:22)

The history of China and Confucianism are not my specialized subjects.[87] I do not discuss the details of the ideological conflicts between Confucianism and Christianity, because I have not specialized in Confucianism and it requires a considerable knowledge of the Chinese civilization. Therefore, I rely much more on secondary sources than on primary sources in this chapter. As some curious issues concerning the Chinese dualistic understanding of Christianity can be observed in French Jesuits' reports from the sixteenth to the late eighteenth centuries, these will receive most attention.

First, a brief history of the European evangelization of China of that period will be summarized. A noted historian, Lewis Hanke's, works remain an indispensable reference for colonial Latin American history to date. However, some of his writing concerning the China of the sixteenth century clearly shows his ignorance of the diplomatic relationship between Asia and Europe. After the

---

[87] For those who are interested in the Christian history of China of that period, see Dunne, 1962, Gernet, 1996, Minamiki, 1985, Rosso, 1948, Young, 1983, and Yazawa, 1972b. For the different concept between Confucianism and Christianity, see Yao, 1997.

conquest of Latin America, by the Spanish crown, there were several opinions that Spain must wage war against China because of its tyrant emperors and practice of pagan religions and sodomy. Yet, the Spanish King, Philip II, who in 1573 issued a royal instruction that 'future discovery and subordination of new land must be done with peaceful methods', rejected this, and decided to send diplomats to China. Hanke mentions that when the letter of Philip to the Chinese emperor is one day discovered, it will be proof of the total abolition of the Spanish *requerimiento* policy.[88]

Regrettably, it is most likely that the Spanish diplomatic corps were neither allowed to enter the Chinese emperor's palaces, nor to meet the emperor, as expected by Hanke, because concept of 'diplomacy' did not exist in China. All messengers from outside China had traditionally been treated as barbarous tribute-payers and were often received by the Chinese governor of a local province only. Indeed, almost all Western and Islamic diplomats from the late sixteenth century were recorded as coming to pay tribute to China. Of course, a part of Japan, the Ryukyu Kingdom (presently the Okinawa prefecture, it was then still an independent state), and other Asian and Muslim kingdoms were treated as such. Therefore, the Chinese Imperial Office was generally less concerned about the relationships with Western and the Islamic states, and did not have much information on them. Most likely, the gifts from Philip II were treated as a tribute from a vassal.

China was not conquered by the European. Rather, the Chinese continued regarding the rest of the world as a land of barbaric people until early in the nineteenth century. This feeling in China is quite similar to that of the Byzantine (East Roman) emperors who claimed to be the 'unique and true Roman emperors.' By the eighth century, when the Frankish Western Roman emperor was created by the Pope, any sense of belonging to the Byzantine 'Roman' Empire disappeared in Western Europe. However, the Byzantine emperor did not cast his pride away. The

---

[88] Hanke, 1941:85-6.

Byzantium never accepted the revived Western Roman emperor as a Roman emperor of the former western part of their territory, but as the emperor of the Franks. Moreover, although the Byzantine Empire gradually lost its former territories, its authority as 'the true Emperor of the Romans' still remained among the Western Europeans until the eleventh century. It is well known that when Otto I requested of the Byzantine Empire permission to use a title, (Holy) Roman Emperor, in 968AD, the Byzantine emperor at that time, Nicephorus II (reigned 963-969), scornfully rejected his proposal. Later, the crusaders of medieval Western Europe who came to Constantinople at the request of the empire, were forced to submit an oath as vassals to the Byzantine emperor before going to Jerusalem. Yet, there was a big difference between the Byzantine empire and China. While the Byzantine emperors claimed to be true rulers of the Roman world only, the Chinese emperors claimed to be rulers of the entire world until the nineteenth century. This latter claim is called Sinocentrism. Also, unlike the way in which the Roman Empire finally collapsed in the fifteenth century, the Chinese had steadily expanded their gigantic territory over time. Although some Arabian chronicles record several magnificent gains against China, the core of China had been steadfast.

Although it is true that China had been conquered by foreigners several times in their history, all such invaders were finally 'spiritually' conquered by the Chinese civilization. Due to the superiority of the Chinese civilization, all alien invaders were inevitably forced to become a part of the 'Chinese civilization' as time passed. Except for a very few points, they had to make their best effort to respect and to preserve almost all the Chinese cultural and religious beliefs. Unless they did so domination of China was impossible. With such a history, it is not surprising that the Chinese people were accustomed to looking down on the cultural standards of the West.

Although Christopher Columbus, officially recognized as the first discoverer of the Americas, believed what he discovered to be Asia (Japan and China) until

237

his death in 1504, Asia was finally re-discovered by explorers from Portugal. Based on their military success in America, the early Portuguese and Spanish considered that even if the Chinese had an uncountable number of soldiers, they would be able to conquer a large part of the coastal area of China with a small number of troops, as they had already done in many parts of the world. Indeed, Portugal had already managed to occupy an important coastal area of India, and Spain had already conquered Mexico, Peru and the Philippines. What is more, Chinese battleships of that time were still not equipped with cannons. It is not surprising, therefore, that in China they expected to repeat Francisco Pizarro's success in Peru on 16 November 1532 when less than 200 Spanish soldiers defeated the Inca Emperor who was guarded by 80,000 Inca warriors.[89] The fact is, however, that according to China the Europeans were merely people from barbaric states in China andthey were never able to read their *requerimiento* in front of the Chinese emperor.

Early Spanish and Portuguese reporters underestimated the military power of China. Early Europeans reported on the weakness of Chinese military units stationed in South China, because they suffered from Japanese pirates who came to the coastal area of China in small numbers. By observing the weak Chinese army, the Europeans considered China easily conquered.[90] However, it later transpired that Chinese military units of the coastal area were troops with the lowest morale and most insufficient training in the Chinese army. In the late sixteenth century, when the *Taiko* (the supreme minister of Japan), Hideyoshi Toyotomi, invaded Korea and China, the Portuguese and Spanish realized the true military power of China. This Japanese invasion, whose ultimate aim was to conquer the world, was

---

[89] The number of Incan soldiers guarding Atahualpa at Cajamarca is apparently exaggerated by the Spaniards. Also, when the meeting between him and Francisco Pizarro took place, it is almost certain that the majority of the guards of Atahualpa did not carry arms. Therefore, it can be said that what happened in Cajamarca was simply a "massacre," not a "battle." Nevertheless, due to the propaganda by Pizarro's colleagues done in Spain, numerous Spaniards believed in a miraculous victory over the Inca in Cajamarca.

238

attempted twice. The military power which the Japanese army mobilized is said to have been 300,000 or more soldiers. They were well equipped with firearms introduced from the West, and their soldiers were highly trained from a long period of civil war. Even the Spaniards admitted that except for the Japanese navy, the Japanese army of that period was skillful in war and extremely brave. Nevertheless, the Japanese army did not manage to defeat China.

Like the early Portuguese, Hideyoshi Toyotomi had underestimated the power of China. Although his large army expelled the Korean army within a short period and put the whole of the Korean Peninsula under the control of Japan, they did not know that the majority of the powerful and well-trained, large army of China was arranged in the northern area of China. Although the Chinese army was only equipped with primitive firearms, it always outnumbered the Japanese army. In addition, its soldiers were heavily armored and their morale was high. In spite of the fact that the Japanese troop was well equipped with firearms (especially matchlock) and sharp swords, the huge force of China troubled them. Although due to the advantage of firearms, there was a famous battle in which a Japanese corps of 12,000 soldiers gained a victory over a Chinese corps of 200,000 soldiers, in spite of such a great victory, it did not do serious damage to the whole of the Chinese army. Moreover, due to their bitter experience with the Japanese army, the Chinese quickly introduced firearms during that war. In addition, the Korean marine army and people's resistance increased and seriously damaged the supply routes of the Japanese army. In the overall war situation, the Japanese army gradually became inferior in strength, and finally had to withdraw.[91] Although Taiwan was colonized by the Netherlands, it was later attacked by a small Chinese army and finally surrendered and withdrew from Taiwan. By seeing this situation,

[90] José de Acosta who was in Peru, left two writings in 1587 (Acosta 1587a, 1587b). These tell us the details of opinions concerning the possibility of waging war against China which were widely argued by the Spaniards.
[91] Of course, Korean marine's activities and the Korean people's resistance to the Japanese invasion are equally an important reason for the Japanese defeat. The Japanese navy of that period was considerably weak.

the Europeans came to understand that three or four thousand European soldiers would not be an enemy of China.[92]

Thus, although one of the New Worlds was conquered by the Europeans, the core part of another New World, Asia, remained unconquered. Therefore, as I have argued, the history of Christianity in Asian countries provides us an opportunity to present a hypothesis: '*If the Native Americans had not been conquered by the Europeans, what would the relationship between Catholic Christianity and Native American religions look like?*' In fact, while the Catholic friars largely ignored the pre-Columbian cultural and religious traditions in Latin America, they had to make great efforts to adapt to Chinese political and religious philosophy.

Although the Chinese of the sixteenth and seventeenth centuries accepted that the Europeans were superior to the Chinese on some points, such as astronomy, firearms and navigation systems, they were not impressed by them, as on many other points, the China of that era was still far superior to Europe. The classic works of Western philosophers and civilization did not impress the Chinese either, because they thought that Chinese philosophers had produced a better philosophy much earlier. It is not an exaggeration that among the Chinese, the Europeans were considered the most barbarous people in the world. Since China could mobilize a gigantic army, they were not afraid of military invasion from Europe. It is true that Macao became a colony of Portugal. However, unlike the story of Hong Kong, the last colony of Britain in Asia, the European colonization of Macao was not due to European superiority. Macao had been a Chinese pirates' base, because its caves were suited for their activities. It was thought that if the Chinese emperor gave Macao to the Portuguese, they would have to deal with the pirates. It was also

---

[92] The Ming dynasty was taken over by the Ch'ing dynasty in 1644. However, it is noted that several large and important military units of the Ming dynasty revolted and joined Ch'ing's force. In the late nineteenth century, Western countries managed to half-colonize many parts of China during the Ch'ing dynasty with a relatively small number of soldiers, because of their superiority of firearms and the fact that the Ch'ing was already weakened by several internal revolts and the morale of its soldiers had much declined. Destructive power of the firearms of the late nineteenth century could not be compared with those of the sixteenth century. Although the Chinese emperors

convenient to assemble the Europeans in one place for the security of China.

Under such circumstances the propagation of Christianity within China had to be done very differently from the Americas, because most of the European friars served as vassals of the Chinese emperor. And in the China of that period the deputy of the supreme divinity was not the Pope, but the Chinese emperor.

It is not surprising that the European monks were forced to make considerable compromise with Chinese traditions. Perhaps, during the sixteenth and seventeenth centuries, China was unique where the Christians practiced extensive cooperation with native pagan religions. Had they appeared in sackcloth rags, no doubt the Chinese would have considered them 'crazy beggars'. By this time the missionaries in Japan had already begun to wear Buddhist costumes, and so the first Portuguese Jesuits to land in China wore the costume of Buddhist priests. However, Buddhism was not as respected in China as it was in Japan, although it gained considerable popularity among the common people.

As Jacques Gernet points out, it may be true that if the Catholic Church had accepted 'chaotic' religious practices, which consisted of Confucianism, Buddhism and Christianity, among the Chinese people, many would have welcomed Christianity. [93] Indeed, Chinese Buddhists welcomed those first Catholic friars with Buddhist costumes, as they considered them to be a sect of Buddhism.

China had traditionally treated foreign religions with patience, [94] albeit barbaric in origin. In fact, in China, the Islamic religion was officially permitted despites its stronger rejection of paganism than Christianity. However, it was never counted as one of the principal Chinese religions, because none of the ancient Chinese philosophers refers to any individual mentioned in Islamic writings. The Islamic religion in China was localized as 'Chinese Islam' in the centre of China,

---

were interested in Western technology, they did not make it a policy to utilize it to develop industries and weapons.

[93] Gernet, 1996:103.
[94] Yazawa ,1972b: 278.

and the Muslims in China were commonly allowed to build a mosque in any part of China. Christianity had been allowed in China before the arrival of Ricci.

Why was Christianity of the seventeenth and eighteenth centuries rejected in China? When Christianity was banned in China, it was also ordered at the same time that Catholic friars must not be maltreated. In China, for example, although there was often hostility toward Catholic Christianity after its introduction by Matteo S. Ricci in Canton, China, in 1587, it is generally considered that these attacks on Christianity were raised as a reply to the Catholics' exclusive attitude towards Chinese traditional religious beliefs and practices.[95]

Ricci realized that Confucianism was the most influential religion among the political elite, while Buddhism and Taoism were more popular among the common people. The political elite were always the target of the evangelization process of the sixteenth-century missionary, because it was considered that the subordinated people would easily be baptized if the politically important people ordered or recommend it. Moreover, the first of those missionaries considered that allying with the most influential religion of China was important, as they would not be able to cope with all three major enemies (Confucianism, Taoism and Buddhism) of Christianity at the same time.

In 1592, Ricci decided to change this policy. In 1594, the Jesuits began to wear costumes of Confucianist style. He tried to attract the educated people who usually had a good position within the Chinese government, and since those who had high rank in China were all educated as Confucians, he sought common ground between Confucianism and Christianity, and treated Taoism and Buddhism with disfavor. However, while he placed Confucianism above Taoism and Buddhism, Ricci wisely avoiding attacking Taoism and Buddhism as devil pagan cults.

---

[95] As to the evangelization activities in China of Matteo Ricci, Cronin (1957) still remains the most readable account. On the theological difference between Confucianism and Christianity in this period, Yao, 1996:53-66.

Let us cite a part of Ricci's book, the *True Meaning of the Lord of Heaven,*
first published in 1603:

65. The Chinese scholar says: ...
*66. In our China there are three religions, each with its own teaching. Lao
Tzu* [of Taoism] *said: "Things are produced from nothing," and made
"nothing" the Way [of Life]. The Buddha taught that "the visible world
emerges from voidness," and made "voidness" the end [of all effort]. The
Confucians say: " In the processes of Yi there exists the Supreme Ultimate"
and therefore make "existence" the basic principle [of all things] and
"sincerity" the subject of the study of self-cultivation. I wonder who, in your
revered view, is correct?*
*67. The Western scholar says: The "nothing" spoken of by Lao Tzu and the
"voidness" taught by the Buddha are totally at variance with the doctrine
concerning the Lord of Heaven; and it is therefore abundantly clear that they
do not merit esteem. When it comes to the "existence" and "sincerity" of the
Confucians, however, although I have not heard a complete explanation of
the meaning of these words, they would seem to be close to the truth.'*
*68. The Chinese scholar says: The superior men of my country too are
vehement in their dismissal of Buddhism and Taoism and have a deep hatred
of them. Mistaken Views About the Lord of Heaven*
*69. The Western scholar says: It is better to refute [the teachings of Buddhists
and Taoists] than to hate [the men who hold these opinions]; and it is better
still to use clear reasoning than to refute them merely with many words; for
Taoists and Buddhists are all produced by our great Father, the Lord of
Heaven, and we are therefore all brothers. For example, if my younger
brother goes mad and falls to the ground, should, as his elder brother, pity
him or hate him? What is most important is that we should employ reason to
explain the truth and make things clear to them.*
*70. I have read a great number of Confucian books and have noticed that
they never cease to express animosity towards Buddhism and Taoism. They
are condemned as being barbarian, and the rejection of them is described as
attacks on heresy; nevertheless, I have never seen anyone expose their errors
with any overriding principle. The result has been that if one says the other is
wrong, the other says his opponent is wrong, and so they have attacked one
another, neither party being willing to yield, for one thousand five hundred
years; and they are still unable to reconcile their different points of view. If
they were able to argue with each other in a rational manner they would
naturally be able to distinguish between truth and falsehood; and the three
schools would be able to return to the one and only correct Way. There is a
Western proverb which runs: "Strong rope can tether the horns of an ox and
rational speech can subdue men's minds."* ... [96]

---

[96] Cited from Ricci, 1985: Chap.II, pp.99-100.

243

It appears that Ricci used the same logic as Bartolomé Las Casas. Unlike other contemporary Europeans; he treated pagan religions as innocent errors. By presenting this idea to the Chinese, Ricci tried reducing hostility toward the Chinese.[97] Furthermore, Ricci argued that as in Christianity, Confucians also realized the existence of one god over the world. In this period of China, neo-Confucianism scholars in China regarded the Supreme Ultimate (太極) as the most important divine existence within Confucianism. This concept is a principle based on dualism. As the Supreme Ultimate is not considered self-existing like the Christian Lord, but a symbol created by *Ying* and *Yang*, therefore, Ricci suggested that a mere symbol could not be the supreme deity who created the world.[98] By pointing out the fact that the concept of the Supreme Ultimate did not originally exist in Confucianism, moreover, Matteo Ricci attempted to persuade the Chinese that original Confucianism had a quite similar concept to the Christian Lord. He established a logic of the concept of *the Sovereign on High* (*Shang-ti* 上帝) in the Sky (*t'ien* 天 In this case, the 'sky' is not a physical one, but refers to a conceptual one. (Nowadays *t'ien* is usually translated as heaven. I will follow this convention in this manuscript) of China is the equivalent of the Christian Lord (it was written as 天主 in Chinese).

Ricci wrote:

104. Our Lord of Heaven [=the Christian Lord] *is the Sovereign on High* [上帝] *mentioned in the ancient* [Chinese] *canonical writings [as the following texts show]: Quoting Confucius, the Doctrine of the Mean says: "The ceremonies of sacrifices to Heaven and Earth are meant for the service of the Sovereign on High." Chu Hsi comments that the failure to mention Sovereign Earth [after Sovereign on High] was for the sake of brevity. In my humble opinion what Chung-ni intended to say was that what is single cannot be described dualistically. 41 How could he have been seeking merely for brevity of expression?"*[99]

---

[97] As will be mentioned, he often expressed an opposite idea to the Europeans.
[98] Ricci, 1985: Chap.II, p.106-7.
[99] Cited from Ricci, 1985: Chap.II, p.123.

By stating that the sky is often used as a synonym of *the Sovereign on High*, Ricci argued that the sky (Heaven) of Confucianism was the Christian Lord. Indeed, although Ricci does not refer to it, it was once considered in China that the Heaven had its own will and metes out justice like the Christian Lord. Under the Sung dynasty (960-1127AD), especially after the eleventh century, this interpretation was questioned and it was concluded that the Heaven is a natural reality, and the relationship between the Heaven and the human is tied through *Li* (理), a law of nature. Also, the position of Heaven became placed under the Supreme Ultimate. In this respect, it may be said that the original Chinese concept of the Heaven was quite close to Christianity.

In this way, he tried to persuade the people that Christianity was the last goal of Confucianism. He explained that Christianity was close to original Confucianism, and that Christianity sustained much of the ancient teachings of Confucius' ideas in a purer form than Confucianism in China. According to Ricci, Confucianism in China was somewhat corrupted, because it had wrongly been developed by misinterpretations of neo-Confucian Chinese scholars of the late period. Concerning the Chinese rites practiced among the former Confucianists who were converted to Christianity, Ricci insisted on approval of their continuous practice, because they were not pagan cults, but civil ceremonies. After a debate, the Jesuits decided to allow Chinese converts to continue Confucian rites which used tablets and incense.[100] This decision allowed Christianity to be widely accepted in China.

The early success of Christianity in China was because some noted Confucianists welcomed it, since the Catholic friars' attacks on Buddhism and Taoism were considered preferable. Buddhism was occasionally perrosecuted by emperors in Chinese history, though those persecutions never lasted for long. Such persecutions were made because Buddhism was not a true Chinese religion. Some Chinese elite thought that declining morals among the Chinese were caused by the introduction of Buddhism. Gernet pointed out that the Confucianists considered that if the friars had not worshipped the Christian God = Creator, they would have been perfect Confucianists.[101]

Ricci made great efforts to teach science, because it attracted many people to his talks, and he praised the Chinese civilization. In fact, the majority of early Chinese converts initiated their interest in Christianity through science taught by the friars. When he made a map of the world, for example, Ricci never failed to locate China in the center of the world. Although the Jesuits openly called Confucius and other Confucian saints devils in Macao, which had become a territory of Portugal, Ricci considered that they must be rescued from blame, and tried to put them into the heavens.[102]

However, the fundamental concept of the Lord of Heaven differed between two cultures. In China, the relationship between the Heaven and the human is interdependent (=more humanism, in short, it is dualism), while Christians regard the Lord as the Lord of human beings (=more theism = monotheism). Naturally, the Chinese had no concept of sin. Although the view of human nature as fundamentally depraved was proposed by a faction of neo-Confucianists, their aim was to suggest enhancing virtue by their own efforts to acquire proper knowledge to be wise, not to ask the Lord for salvation; as was the case in Christianity.

Consequently, the Europeans had to reject several important aspects of Confucianism, and what the Catholic friars practiced was different from Ricci's hope. In the middle of the seventeenth century, the Jesuits invented '*An Old Holy Place*' to rescue noted old Chinese saints from hell.[103] Although they claimed that all old Chinese gods and Buddha must be placed in hell, as they were demons, noted figures of Confucianism were respectable enough, and thus they could be

---

[100] For the early controversy on the Chinese rites among the European, see Dunne, 1962:282-302, .

[101] Gernet 1996:58. While heaven is considered a place of Christian god to control everything, heaven 天 of China cooperate with land in order to create livings. See *ibid.*:253-261.

[102] Gernet, 1996:228-9.

[103] Gernet, 1996:229-231.

placed in a place better than present world, but below heaven, as they were a kind of demon.[104] As time passed, the Chinese came to understand that 'The Old Holy Place' was one of four hells, 'a bit better place than the real Hell.' On hearing this, criticism of Christianity began in China.[105] What the majority of Chinese converts had wanted was the co-existence of Christianity and Confucianism.[106] Also, it was ill-fated for the Jesuit that his rivals, the Franciscans and the Dominicans, had also initiated their evangelization in China, and forbade the practice of Chinese rites. Consequently, prosecution of Christianity was initiated. Some Chinese intellectuals also came to see that there were several fundamental contradictions within the Christian doctrine, which Matteo Ricci published.

It is true that some of these Chinese converts became Christian fanatics and began to destroy idols of Chinese traditional gods, Buddhist and Confucian. Yet, there were far more Chinese who refused the policies of the European missionaries. Moreover, although the Chinese elite often hated Buddhism and Taoism, they did not intend to expel them. The exclusive nature of Christianity was becoming a serious issue for the Chinese elite.

They began to question the Christian doctrine. Gernet summarized several of the Chinese critics on the Christian concept of sin. Commonly found criticisms are: the Christian God is so imperfect and incapable. If he created everything as the Catholic monks insisted, he could have avoided making the devil or Satan which was also created by him. The fact is that he cannot control his own creation. Also, he did not make perfect human beings who do not have any desires. What must really be criticized is his own failure.[107]

As a natural consequence, the anti-Christian movement was observed in Nanking only six years after the death of Ricci. This was not simply occasioned by

---

[104] A few like Francisco Furtado considered it a potential salvation of Confucius (see Dunne 1960:274), as Juan Ginés Sepúlveda did in the case of the Greek sages.

[105] Gernet, 1996:230-231.

[106] Many of the Chinese converts continued worshipping idols, while they criticized Buddhism and Taoism. See Gernet, 1996:87-97.

[107] Gernet, 1996:300-309.

247

Chinese anti-European feeling. By that time, many neo-Confucians who had once been fascinated by the Gospel, had noticed that Christianity essentially expounded a very different ideology from Confucianism.[108] Anti-Christian sentiment in China gradually increased. Nevertheless, in general, Christianity was still tolerated in China. In the seventeenth century, the Ming dynasty in China, the Ming emperor (1644-1661AD) told a Catholic monk who suggested that he be converted to Christianity, that he did not understand why all moral codes of Christianity must be practiced.[109] He added that if two or three difficult codes could be removed, the rest of the codes might be practicable. While the Chinese were always ready to compromise with this new faith, the Catholics refused.

While the Portuguese Jesuits met with some success, the Spanish Franciscans and Dominicans' first attempt to establish a base in China in the late sixteenth century failed. The Dominicans were shocked with the news of the Jesuits' success in China. Therefore, the Dominicans sent friars to China in 1630 and began to develop their evangelization, and the Franciscans followed. However, unlike the Jesuits, the Dominicans and Franciscans did not allow the Chinese converts to worship their ancestors and other idols. As a natural result, the situation for Christianity became worse. It is said that they had over ten thousand converts and twenty churches in South China in 1665.[110] Therefore, they had many problems with the Chinese. The Dominicans were expelled from China in 1637. They were also the first to be persecuted by Chinese officials between 1647 and 1648. Since the Dominicans considered that their expulsion from China in 1637 was a Jesuit plot (the reason was, in fact, the Dominicans' hostile attitude towards Chinese rites and other religions), they accused the Jesuits of tolerating the continuous practice of the Chinese 'pagan' cult among Chinese Christians. They and the Franciscans criticized the practices of the Jesuits in China to the Pope, and serious controversy was raised in Rome.

---

[108] Argument found in Young (1983:59-76) is useful on this incident.
[109] Gernet, 1996:89-90.
[110] Yazawa, 1972b: 71.

248

In this debate, the Jesuits gained a victory. Pope Alexander VII issued a decree in 1656 in which it was stated that the Chinese converts should be allowed to participate in these rites, because they were instituted for an exclusively civil cult.[111] This allowed a decrease in anti-Christian sentiment among the Chinese. After the collapse of the Ming dynasty, the Ch'ing dynasty succeeded. In the early period of this dynasty, its attitude towards Christianity was very negative. The Chinese Emperor of the Ch'ing Dynasty, K'ang-hsi, initially prohibited building churches and propagation of Christianity.[112] By then, neo-Confucian scholars formed a strong opposition to Christianity. They often attacked the Europeans effectively by pointing out several contradictory theories and ideas found in the Christian doctrine. The Jesuits were forced to consume much time in order to defend themselves from their attacks. A historian, John D. Young, summarizes the course of the missionary efforts in a chapter titled 'In Defense of 'Christianity in China'' in his book, *Confucianism and Christianity*.[113]

In spite of the strong anti-Christian feelings among the Chinese intellectuals, because of an interest in Western science, especially in astronomy, the Kang-hsi emperor employed several talented Jesuits friars. The Jesuits greatly contributed to him as diplomats and scientists in order to gain official approval of propagation of Christianity in China. As a result of their efforts, the K'ang-hsi finally allowed the Jesuits to propagate Christianity in China in 1692.

A French Jesuit, Joachim Bouvet (1654-1730), who served the Chinese emperor K'ang-hsi, and who was also trusted by the emperor for many years, published a book for King Louis *Le Grand* (1643-1715) in France in 1697. He wrote that the emperor was satisfied with the fact that Christianity had numerous similarities with Confucianism and the latter was virtually the same as

---

[111] See Minamiki, 1985:29-32.
[112] For Christianity under this Emperor's reign, see Rosso, 1948:122-211..
[113] Young, 1983:Chap.VI, p.97-108. This part of his book deals with several important issues of the controversy between Confucianism and Christianity at the Chinese palace in the eighteenth century.

Christianity.[114] In addition, he emphasized that the Chinese imperial family was interested in Christianity and China might be converted into a great nation of God.[115]

However, the fact is that what was important for K'ang-hsi was that the Christianity introduced by the Jesuit order would not cause religious struggles with Chinese religions. It must be noted that the Christian book which the Emperor was shown by Joachim Bouvet was a copy of Matteo S. Ricci's *True Meaning of the Lord of Heaven*.[116] His version of the '*Bible*' includes numerous citations from Chinese classical works.

Now, we should look at the Chinese imperial document concerning K'ang-his's permission for evangelization China in 1692. On 20th March 1692, *Li Pu* [= the Imperial Council of Religion] of Ch'ing submitted the following context for K'ang-hsi's approval:

> The Europeans managed a calendar method. They manufactured arms and firearms for our military strategy. They went to Russia, where they made a sincerity [diplomatic] effort [for the Ch'ing dynasty of China], and succeeded in their mission. Thus, their distinguished services [to Ch'ing] should be regarded as a great one.
> The European who are residing in each province, are neither performing wrongdoing, nor living a debauched life. Moreover, they do not confuse people and do not perform heresy. Offering incense in Lamaist, Buddhist and Taoist temples is allowed by them. The Europeans are never doing the illegal thing. It can be said that it is not very appropriate to continue prohibition [of Christianity].[117]

In reply to this report, Emperor K'ang-hsi approved it on 22 March 1692. By using only two Chinese characters, he wrote '*Carry out as proceedings.*' It must be pointed out that one of the important reasons for the official imperial approval of Christianity was that it did not cause a conflict with other religions.

Moreover, as the emperor used only two letters to write this approval, it appears that he was not very interested in Christianity. In fact, Christianity was not

---

[114] Bouvet, 1971: 111-112, 141-149.
[115] Bouvet, 1971: 111-112, 141-149.
[116] Matteo S. Ricci, 1985.

counted as one of the major Chinese religions even after this approval. This means that his approval of Christianity was issued as evidence of the Chinese emperor's open-minded attitude to the 'barbarous' European. The reason for his approval of Christianity was its supposed similarity with Confucianism and Kang-hsi's personal friendship with European friars. Christianity was only understood within that Confucian ideal. The fundamental aim of Confucianism is principally to enhance the virtue of the individual in the present world. On the other hand, that of Christianity is to gain the salvation of the soul after death, although enhancing the virtue is also important in Christianity. In other words, Christianity was only accepted as one of many moral codes constituting the Chinese universe.

However, Kang-hsi's attitude towards Christianity was drastically changed soon after his approval of it. In Rome, Clement IX stated that the Decree of 1656, which allowed the Chinese converts to continue rites of Confucianism, was invalid and issued a notice that the Chinese rites must not be practiced by the Chinese converts, because he saw worship of tablets as evidence of a pagan cult. The Chinese never understood the reason why the Catholic Church prohibited worshiping of plates or tablets and figures of Confucius on which ancestors' names were written. Although food was offered to them, they thought that they were simply memorials and soulless objects.[118]

No doubt, Kang-hsi was a good person. He did not forget the French missionaries with whom he had established personal friendships. In the Imperial Instruction of 1707, given to all missionaries, he promised to allow only some French Jesuits who promised not to return to Europe and to accept the Chinese rites,

---

[117] My own translation from the original Chinese text cited by Yazawa in Bouvet, 1967.

[118] Due to influence from Chinese Confucianism, the Japanese also worship the tablet of ancestors on which the names of parents and other ancestors are written. However, although worship of ancestors is commonly observed among the Chinese and the Japanese, contrary to China, the use of the tablet was adopted by 'Japanese' Buddhism in Japan (in Japan, Buddhism has been the most influential religion), it is used in Buddhist rites, and it is considered that the souls of ancestors exist in the tablets.

by issuing a license called *p'iao*.[119] The Franciscans and Dominicans were expelled from China.

In the imperial instruction, Kang-hsi claimed his friendly French Jesuits, who received the license, were the 'same' as Chinese.[120] He added, if they wished to go back to Europe, they would be sent beheaded.[121] This meant that the Catholic friars in China became subjects of the Chinese emperor and he would act as a pope within China. In a sense, it may be said that the intention of Kang-hsi was to create a Christianity suitable for the Chinese.

Like other Chinese, Kang-hsi did not see the reason for the banning of worshipping tablets employed in Confucian rites, because they were regarded as soulless objects. Rites honoring Confucius were the same. Although Confucius had been respected as the highest intellectual, as if he were a divine human, he was not regarded as a god. Father Pedrini and Ripa wrote a report to Clement XI in 1714, in which they recorded what the Emperor Kang-hsi told them.[122]

> The ancestral tablet in China has no significance other than keeping the memory of one's father and mother by writing their names on the tablet, merely lest they be forgotten. The custom of writing that the soul was contained in the tablet has never existed. It is just the same idea as when you draw the portrait of your parents to preserve their memory. But as a portrait may be crudely drawn, it cannot be compared with the written name which would be without error...[123]

After a long debate, in 1715, Pope Clement XI announced an instruction (*Ex Illa Die*) which banned the practice of rites relating to Confucianism. The Roman Catholic Church tried to negotiate with the Emperor, Kang-hsi, by sending Carlo Ambrogio Mezzabarba as a Legate of Pope Clemence XI.[124] Since it was

---

[119] This imperial instruction was translated into English and published by Rosso, 1948:Document 5, p.242-4. Also see *Decrees of 1707 and 1708*, Document 6 in *ibid.*:245-283.

[120] Rosso, 1948:244.

[121] *Ibid.*:243-4.

[122] An English translation was published in *ibid.*: Document 11, pp.298-301.

[123] Cited from *ibid.*:301.

[124] The detailed record of their meeting from 24 December 1720 to 24 January 1721 originally written Chinese was translated into English and was published by Rosso (1948:342-374). Also see *ibid.*:202-211, Young 1983:117-123.

considered by the Chinese that the mandate of dominating everything (including the universe, religion and time) in the world had been given to the most appropriate individual, the Chinese emperor from heaven, this decision from Rome naturally provoked the anger of the emperor. At the same time, he ordered an investigation into whether it was really issued by the Pope.[125]

For Emperor Kang-hsi, it was puzzling why the Christians had suddenly revoked their early acceptance of Chinese rites. The fact is that since Matteo Ricci decided to allow the Chinese converts the rites, there had been no serious problem in China. On 17 December 1720, the emperor issued an instruction to the European missionaries. In that text, he wrote:

> *From the time Li Ma-tou [Fr. Matteo Ricci, S. J.] came to China, for over two hundred years, you Westerners, have in no sense indulged in luxury or heterodox activities, but undoubtedly you led the ascetic life in perfect peace, and never violated any Chinese laws... As the Religion you preach is without any harm or benefit to China so also it is of no consequence whether you go or stay. To-lo [Card. Carlo T. MAILLARD DE Tournon], however, from the time of his arrival mistakenly listened to YEN Tang [Bishop Charles MAIGROT, M. E. P.], an illiterate ecclesiastic who has wantonly bred criticisms. If the latter had an insufficient understanding of the principles of Chinese literature, he might still be forgiven. He, however, not only did not know the principles of literature but could not even recognize (the simplest) characters. How could such a person presume to discuss the truth or falsity of the Chinese system?*
> *Take for example his contention that Heaven is a material thing and should not be worshipped. To speak my mind in simile, when one renders homage and gratitude to the Throne, one must address the Emperor as Pi-hsia or Chi'eh-hsia " under the steps to the Throne," and similar terms And when one passes the Imperial Throne one most certainly hastens to pay proper reverence toward the ruler. It is the same everywhere. Could one take Pi-hsia as a "seat under the steps," something made by artisans, and fail thus to show proper respect to it? The same idea underlies China's worship of Heaven. If one follows YEN Tang's assumption, one must invoke nothing but the name of the "Lord of Heaven" to show proper reverence. That is very much opposed to the Chinese idea of Heaven worship,*
> *According to you Westerners, you practice asceticism, with the primary idea that the soul has to return to the Lord of Heaven; thus You mortify yourselves during your lifetime Oil account of the eternal affairs of the soul. In China ancestral tablets are exhibited and revered so that the sons of men may remember their parents who brought them up. We may find a similar*

Rosso, 1948:337.

253

example even in the young of the animals: they cry for many days when their mothers die because they remember their parents. How much more then will Mall, the most spiritual creature of the universe, express without what lie feels within. Even you who practice asceticism must also mourn and grieve should your parents depart. Should you treat their passing with indifference, you would not be equal to animals; how then can you be compared to the Chinese?

Why do we venerate Master K'UNG [=Confucian]? The Saint Sage by the great doctrine of the five constant Virtues, the many kinds of conducts, and the cardinal relationships of ruler and minister and of father and son, handed down a system, for the education of posterity, and inculcated thereby in the people the great duties of love for their superiors and ancestors. This is why the most holy Sage should be respected and venerated. You Westerners also have Saints, and venerate them because their actions:...When To-lo came, he listened entirely to lesser ecclesiastics, shameless false speaking people; with the result that truth and falsity were interchanged.

Now the Pope sends a Legate to the Capital... Should he question you on the method of spreading your Religion, all of you are bound to answer in unison thus: "In spreading our Religion we all follow the practice of Li Ma-tou, as His Majesty was thoroughly informed many years ago ... "

You must not each one express his own views and answer nonsensically after his own fancy, so is to confuse once again truth and falsehood.

Everyone must strictly obey these instructions, expressly given for the foregoing object.[126]

From this text, it is evident that Kang-hsi is addressing the Europeans and stating that none of them was qualified to discuss issues within China, because of their lack of reading the writings by the Chinese sages. In his analysis of conversation between two persons, Toshihiko Yazawa points out that on hearing the reason for the banning of Chinese rites, the emperor concluded this controversy was an outlandish one.[127] When Mezzabarba met the emperor as a messenger from 'a vassal of China,' the King of Propagation [the Papal] on 31 December 1720, the emperor asked him why angels were painted with wings in some Western paintings. The record narrates:

...The ceremony ended CHIA Lo [=Carlo Ambrogio Mezzabarba], he was commanded to sit with First Rank Grandees on the west side, where he was offered food from the Sovereign [= the Kang-hsi emperor]. The Sovereign ... asked CHIA Lo thus: I have seen in your Western pictures men

---

[126] Cited from Document 22 in Rosso (1948:338-341).
[127] See Yazawa, 1972b:229.

with wings. What does it mean?" CHIA Lo answered: " This is to suggest the idea that the Angels are spiritual and swift as though they had -wings, but in reality there do not exist persons with wings." Then the Sovereign continued: "The Chinese do not grasp the purport of Western -words, hence they do not find it appropriate to dispute about your Western Customs and doctrines. As you Westerners do not grasp, the purport of Chinese characters, how do You presume to discuss the right or wrong of the Chinese doctrine? This is what I had in mind when I asked the question. [128]

Yazawa considers that the emperor, Kang-hsi, had criticized numerous arguments about the practice of Chinese pagan rites that had been raised by the Catholics. While the Europeans criticized the worship of the tablets of parents among the Chinese as superstition, they made paintings of angels, which were believed not to have a carnal body.[129] Based on this paradox of the Christians, the emperor asked how Messabarba and the pope, who did not know the Chinese traditions at all because of their illiteracy in Chinese script, managed to conclude the Chinese rite was a superstition. The reason why Kang-hsi declined to attack the paintings of angels is clear. In the text, he says: *"The Chinese do not grasp the purport of Western -words, hence they do not find it appropriate to dispute your Western Customs and doctrines."* The emperor implied that because the Chinese are more mature than the Europeans, the Chinese did not raise a controversy against Christian customs such as painting 'invisible' angels.

On 14 January 1721, the emperor again raised the same idea with Messabarba; *"If you want to discuss the doctrine of China, you must necessarily penetrate deeply into Chinese literary style, and study Chinese literature thoroughly: only then will you be able to argue. I, the Emperor, do not know any Western tonguage [sic], and therefore I do not discuss any things Western."* [130] In short, what the emperor insisted was that unless a foreigner precisely understood the cultural and religious background of China, it would be no more than harebrained for him to judge whether issues and traditions within China were false or not.

---

[128] Cited from Rosso, 1948:353.
[129] Yazawa, 1972b:230.
[130] Cited from Rosso, 1948:357.

255

It is recorded that after the Emperor K'ang-hsi had several conversations with the Pope's legate and read the concise Chinese translation of *Ex Illa Die*, he concluded that Christianity was a childish superstition and issued a vermilion endorsement on 19 January 1721, as follows;

> *In perusing this Manifesto one but wonders how the Westerners, mean men as they are, can talk about the Great Way of China? None of the Westerners understand Chinese literature thoroughly and many of them when speaking and discussing make people laugh. The Legate's Manifesto which I have just seen after all is akin to Buddhist mid Taoist adepts' superstitions and mean teachings; but no wild talk surpasses this. Hereafter the Westerners need not practice their religion in China. It must indeed be prohibited to avoid troubles.*[131]

In addition, the emperor promulgated another Imperial Decree on the same day:

> *I, the Emperor, must collect the Decrees I gave at various times together with your arguments, have them printed, as before, in form of a Red Manifesto, and delivered to the Russians and the vessels of Kung-tung to be carried to the West and published in the various Western countries, so that they must discuss them publicly.*
> *Respect this.*[132]

Messabarba was terrified by this decree, and begged the emperor for permission to return to Italy in order to discuss the issue with the Pope. On the same day, the emperor issued another imperial mandate in which he said:

> *Your Sovereign Pontiff* [=the Pope] *in the Constitution* [=*Ex Illa Die*] *charges that to revere Heaven and honor Master K'ung has a superstitious purport...There is no book* [on Chinese Classics] *that I, the Emperor, do not read; hence I can discuss these things. As you Westerners do not know a single character, nor understand a single sentence...How, then, do you charge that K'ung's principles are superstitious? This is extremely unreasonable...I, the Emperor, must have the whole case written down clearly, printed as Red Manifesto, and delivered to the Russians to carry it over and publish in all Western countries.*[133]

---

[131] Cited from Rosso, 1948:376.
[132] Cited from Rosso, 1948:365.
[133] Cited from Rosso, 1948:368-9. Although "Sovereign Pontiff (of course, this is also a proper noun representing the pope)" is used in his translation to refer to the pope as if both are of

It is clear that his attitude towards Christianity was not hostile, but rather he just despised it as meaningless and childish. In fact, although he was strongly provoked by the exclusive character of Christianity, he never called it evil. In his mind, as long as religion, including Christianity, aimed to improve human virtue, having a respect for all of other religions at the same time, it was not an unnatural thing. From this viewpoint, this Chinese emperor assumed that in spite of their ignorance of the basic concepts of Chinese civilization, the Westerners caused trouble by emphasizing the trivial differences between each religion, and thus they were just like selfish and naughty children.

On hearing the context of that mandate, Messabarba had no option but to accept his incapability of understanding Chinese issues. It is said that he knelt down and accepted his total illiteracy in Chinese.[134]

Can we call this historical evidence the '*Anti-Christianity Movement in China?*' As the quoted text suggests, the emperor did not have an intention to criticize Christianity. Contrary to the Europeans, the emperor kept his stance not to argue any fundamental issue of Christianity, because he had not fully read Christian scriptures. By doing so, he tried to show his fairness in the controversy. He treated the Westerners as 'immature,' and simply talked about the necessity of showing evidence based on their comprehension of Chinese philosophy before they could raise controversy concerning Chinese rites, as this was believed to be the behaviour of mature and educated people.

On this point, the emperor's perception of Christianity on that occasion must be considered. The Emperor Kang-hsi had learnt Christianity from the Jesuits. The Jesuits followed the policy of Matteo Ricci. Although there is no direct evidence, it is evident that the emperor and his fellows regarded the *True Meaning of the Lord*

---

equal status, the original Chinese text says "教化王 = King of the Propagation" to express the inferior position of the pope to the Chinese emperor.
[134] Rosso, 1948:371.

of Heaven compiled by Matteo Ricci as a reference, and they bore in mind its context in the controversy over Chinese rites.

Here, I will again quote a part of Ricci's book:

> **69.** *The Western scholar says: It is better to refute [the teachings of Buddhists and Taoists] than to hate [the men who hold these opinions]; and it is better still to use clear reasoning than to refute them merely with many words; for Taoists and Buddhists are all produced by our great Father, the Lord of Heaven, and we are therefore all brothers. For example, if my younger brother goes mad and falls to the ground, should I, as his elder brother, pity him or hate him? What is most important is that we should employ reason to explain the truth and make things clear to them.*[135]

At least in front of the Chinese, Ricci continued to say that if someone tried to reject the religious ideas of others, reason must be employed, and also he insisted that because their beliefs were an innocent error, a hostile attitude must not be employed. Nevertheless, the fact was that the legate from the pope who appeared in the Chinese palace failed to justify the banning of Chinese rites among Chinese converts. It is not surprising, therefore, that Kang-hsi found a self-contradiction in Christianity and thus decided to allow only those who followed Matteo Ricci to continue Christianity in China. Although Kang-hsi finally treated Christianity as a childish superstition, it must be noted at the same time that he did not deny it. I have mentioned in the previous chapter that the true virtue was considered a creature harmoniously generated by various religions in Asian cultures. By this logic, even though Christianity was not desirable, it was not appropriate to reject it.

As John D. Young points out, the emperor may have considered that because the existence of God was known in China from ancient times, as ironically proposed by Matteo Ricci long ago, it was possible for him to consider that the idea of the one Lord was originally introduced from China to Europe.[136] If so, there was no need to introduce Christianity from Europe, because it was merely one variation of the Chinese Confucian tradition. The successor of Emperor Kang-hsi,

---

[135] Cited from Ricci, 1985: Chap.II, pp.100.
[136] Young, 1983:122-3.

Yung-Cheng, later frequently expressed this view. Surviving historical texts concerning Emperor Yung Cheng provide us with more useful information clarifying the substantial difference in the concept of religion between the Europeans and the Chinese.

By the end of the seventeenth century, it had become widely known among the Chinese officials that Christians regarded the old Chinese sages of Confucianism as devils. This meant that Christianity would destroy the Chinese social order. As a natural consequence, frequent persecutions of the Christians were practiced by officials.[137] In 1724, a French Jesuit, Mailla, wrote a letter to his friend in Pekin, in which he records what they were told by the Chinese emperor:

> *Voici en substance ce que Sa Majesté leur dit:*
> *«Des Européens, dans la province de Fokien, voulaient anéantir nos lois, et troublaient les peuples; les grands de cette province me les ont déférés; j'ai dû pourvoir au désordre; c'est une affaire de l'empire, j'en suis chargé; et je ne puis ni ne dois agir maintenant, comme je faisais lorsque je n'étais que prince particulier*
> *Vous dites que votre loi n'est pas une fausse loi, je le crois; si je pensais qu'elle fût fausse, qui m'empêcherait de détruire vos églises et de vous en chasser? Les fausses lois sont celles qui, sous prétexte de porter à la vertu, soufflent l'esprit de révolte [...]. Mais que diriez-vous si j'envoyais une troupe de bonzes et de lamas dans votre pays pour y prêcher leur loi? Comment les recevriez vous?*
> *Ly-ma-teou (nom chinois du P. Ricci) vint à la Chine la première année de Ouan-ly. je ne toucherai point à ce que firent alors les Chinois; je n'en suis pas chargé. Mais en ce temps là vous étiez en très petit nombre, ce n'était presque rien; vous n'aviez pas de vos gens et des églises dans toutes les provinces; ce n'est que sous le règne de mon père qu'on a élevé partout des églises, et que votre loi s'est répandue avec rapidité; nous le voyions, et nous n'osions rien dire; ...*
> *Vous voulez que tous les Chinois se fassent chrétiens; votre loi le demande, je le sais bien: mais en ce cas là que deviendrions nous? les sujets de vos rois. Les chrétiens que vous faites ne reconnaissent que vous ; dans un temps de trouble, il n'écouteraient point d'autre voix que la vôtre.*
> *Je sais bien qu'actuellement il n'y a rien à craindre; mais quand les vaisseaux viendront par mille et dix mille, alors il pourrait y avoir du désordre...*[138]

---

[137] Father Mailla's letter dated on 16 October 1724 (Yazawa 1971:3-64) is particularly useful. See next note.

[138] A lettre ; *Du P. de Mailla, missionnaire de la Compagnie de Jésus, au père ***, de la même Compagnie, 16 October1724, Pékin.* The French text cited from an abbreviation reprint found in Vissière (2001:138-139). Since this reprint omitted a considerable part of the original text,

259

(Here is the context of what His Majesty says to them:
The Europeans in the province of Fokien wanted to destroy our laws, and disturb the people; the high officials of this province submitted them to me; I had to cater for the disorder; it is a business of the empire, I am charged with it; and then I should not act now, as I did when I was only a particular prince.[139] You say that your law is not a false law which I believe. If I thought that it were false, who would prevent me from destroying your churches and driving you out? The false laws are those which, under pretext of carrying the virtue, blow the spirit of rebellion [...]. But what would you say if I sent a troop of bonzes [=Buddhist priests] and lamas [of the Lamaism] to your country in order to preach their law there? How would you receive them?

Ly my teou [Matteo Ricci] came to China in the first year of Ouan ly [万 曆初年=1582]. I will not touch what the Chinese made [a permission of the evangelization of Christianity] at that time; I am not charged with it. But at this time, you were very small in number, it was almost nothing; you did not have your people and churches in all the provinces; it is only under the reign of my father that churches were made everywhere, and that your law was quickly spread; we saw it, and we did not dare have anything to say...

You want to make all Chinese Christians; your law requires it, I know it well: but in this case what would we be? Subjects of your kings. The Christians recognize only them [=the same Christian]; in time of disorder, they would not listen to other voices but only to yours [=the Christian].

I know well that there is currently nothing to fear; but when the vessels come by thousands and ten thousands, then there could be disorder...)

The thinking of Yung-Cheng is clear. He clarified that the reason for banning Christianity was to maintain the social order of the empire, because he was held publicly responsible for it as an emperor, and no personal bias towards Christianity was involved. He blamed the Europeans. In spite of the fact that China had never imposed their religions on the Europeans and perhaps the Europeans would not allow it, the Europeans came to China to dismiss Chinese traditional religions without a good reason. This theory was frequently used during his time.

In 1725, the emperor sent a letter to Pope Benedict XIII, in which was written:

"*The* [Chinese] *Emperor, appointed by Mandate of Heaven, addresses the*

I have also consulted a complete Japanese translation of it made by Yazawa (1971:3-64). The full French text can be seen in Querbeuf (1780-83:vol.19, 262-328)

[139] When he was a prince, he often acted for the Jesuits. The emperor reminded the French friars that he did not personally have an objection to Christianity (as long as it would remain within the Europeans), but as a Chinese emperor, he was not able to overlook the situation in which the Christians ignored and denied the fundamental concept of the Chinese civilization.

Sovereign Pontiff, in Italy."[140] Although the superiority of the Chinese emperor, as the deputy of Heaven, over the Pope is emphasized in this sentence, another fact is that he neither questioned the authority of the pope within Europe nor defined Christianity as a creed. Although he treated converts in his royal family heartlessly, he ordered the European friars who were arrested and ordered to leave China to be treated with respect and guarded from potential harassments by the people at the same time. It must be noted that the Europeans were never punished according to their faith in Christianity.[141] This was partly his policy to show the Europeans that the Chinese emperor was a humanitarian.

In 1727, Yung-Cheng expressed his view towards Christianity as a reply to the Third Portuguese Embassy, as follows:

> ...the *Emperor decreed: "Today is the birthday of the Buddha* [the founder of Buddhism]; *coincidentally the ambassador from Europe (Hsi-yan-kuo, Portugal) presents Us a memorial of congratulation...It was long, long ago that the Buddhists and the Taoists severely attacked the Westerners' religion and the Westerners in turn severely attacked the errors of the Buddhists and the Taoists. They calumniate each other and denounce each other's religions as heresies. They regard their own doctrine as the only orthodoxy, and other religions as heresies. The so-called heresy, however, is not the heresy of the precepts of our sage Confucius said, 'It is useless to attack sectarianism.' Does Confucius regard the other's opinion as a heresy? In this Middle Kingdom it only when the adoption of a foreign religion harms the heart of the people and the normal way of life, that it is regarded as heresy; for example the Westerners' worship of the Lord of Heaven.*
> *"However, Heaven (nature) creates the ten thousand things [everything on earth] by the interactions of the Yin and Yang and the five elements. Therefore, We say that the ten thousand things originated in Heaven [the Creator] is the Almighty God (Chu-tsai). From ancient times down to the present, have you heard of any one who does not worship Heaven? Or of any religion which does not respect Heaven? Are there any differences between our worship of Heaven and the idea of the worship of Heaven of the Western religion? If they say that God the Creator, for the sake of saving the people, transformed himself into a human being on this Earth, they lie wantonly. They use the name of Heaven to seduce and enchant our foolish people into following their religion. This must be the heresy of the European religion! In Our opinion it may mean simply that at first when the Western religion was*

---

[140] Cited from Rosso, 1948:401.

[141] Contrary to China, in Japan of the sixteenth and seventeenth centuries, numerous friars were cruelly executed.

261

being founded, the people respected their founder as reverently as they worshipped Heaven. But to say that the founder of their religion himself was the Lord of Heaven is unreasonable nonsense....

"China has her Chinese religion, just as Europe has a European religion. The European religion does not need to be practiced in China; similarly how can European countries practice Chinese religion?... European theology, which claims that the Lord of Heaven was himself transformed into a man, is particularly ridiculous. Since the Lord of Heaven can rule human destiny supernaturally, it is unnecessary for him to transform himself into a human being. To say that the believers in the religion of the Lord of Heaven will themselves become transfigured into the likeness of the Lord of Heaven [=the Trinity of Christianity], is the most unreasonable nonsense!

.... In short, people under Heaven do not possess impartial hearts. They do not see the truth clearly and usually regard only those who are like themselves as right and those who are different as wrong. Therefore, they criticize each other as if they were enemies. They ignore the fact that since the nature and quality of each individual varies, the customs and traditions which these individuals like and in which they are interested cannot be the same. We cannot change them (these traditions) by force nor can we make them the same by force. Moreover, all religions have their own advantages and disadvantages. In other words, we must know the defects but we should not be blind to the merits. Then we can all get along peacefully. [142]

The above citation expresses a common Chinese understanding of Christianity. The emperor cited an absurdity in the Christian insistence that the communication between god and the human had always been done through a physical human existence, while the invisible and non-physical existence of the Supreme Deity with no emotion was also argued by the Christian. In Confucianism, there is no such existence. Although the above citation does not mention it, the Supreme existence in the Heaven of Confucianism was regarded as invisible and un-communicative, and His mandate from the Heaven was considered unseen in China. Therefore, believing the logic of the existence of the prophet and the son of God was ridiculous. In this respect, the emergence of god in the form of a human is highly improbable in Confucian logic, and the Chinese were also negative about the idea of a prophet appointed by the supreme deity. Therefore, there was a belief that the throne of the Chinese emperor was made upon an invisible intention of

---

[142] Cited from Fu, 1966:155-156.

Heaven. Based on this traditional view of Confucianism, Yung-Cheng caustically criticized the contradictory theory of the Trinity within the Christian doctrine.

At least in the above text, it is suggested that this Chinese idea of the supreme deity differentiated their concept of religion from that of the Christians. That is, by recognizing that any religion is an ideology created by the human rather than divine law. In this idea, as none has contact with the Lord of Heaven, no religion can be beyond a work of human interpretation, and thus it is quite natural that each religion has a particular merit and disadvantage. Consequently, all religions have been regarded as moral codes in China, at least among the ruling class. In a sense, any religion is a part of the universe for the Chinese, as I discussed in the case of the Maya in Chapter II.

It should be noted that Yung-Chen purposely mentions the name of Buddha of Buddhism, which was treated as a somewhat inferior philosophy to Confucianism among the ruling elite in China, in order to show his tolerance of different types of religion within his empire. The emperor addresses a question to the Westerner as to whether some defects found in Confucian ideology could be a reason for abandoning the honoring of god. While openly damning Christianity as a heresy, the emperor did not reject Christianity as one of the interpretations of heaven.

By emphasizing the supreme deity as a creature of interaction between Yin and Yang, the emperor argued the essential principle of the universe based upon dualism. What the emperor wrote is based on the neo-Confucian idea of the Supreme Ultimate, consisting of the negative and the positive. The emperor implies that as the supreme deity is also subject to dualism, a permissive attitude towards various differences is a path to true virtue.

His view of religions is also substantially the same as that expressed long before by Matteo Ricci. Ricci wrote: "*It is better to refute [the teachings of Buddhists and Taoists] than to hate [the men who hold these opinions]; and it is better still to use clear reasoning than to refute them merely with many words; for*

Taoists and Buddhists are all produced by our great Father, the Lord of Heaven, and we are therefore all brothers."[143]

If this issue is considered from the perspective of dualism, it is clear that the conflict between China and the Europeans was caused by the difference between monism and dualism. While the emperor regarded the heaven as the supreme deity, his mind was actually occupied by the principal concept of neo-Confucianism, the Supreme Ultimate. In other words, various ways of worshipping the supreme deity must be tolerated according to neo-Confucianism's Supreme Ultimate. Since it is the symbol of harmonious relationship between two opposing elements, showing gratitude to a hated heresy like Christianity was a duty of the emperor. Yung Cheng talked about the necessity of embracing several defects to maintain a positive aspect, according to the positive and the negative principle. In short, the human cannot avoid certain mistakes, and thus defects are also an indispensable part of virtue. Therefore, the Chinese were not essentially interested in correcting their religious 'faults,' because faults are a part of successful virtue in their ideology. The emperor also implies that virtues ought to be created through interactions of various interpretations (=religions) of Heaven. Because it is impossible for humans to communicate with Him, it is quite natural that each nation has a different way of understanding the supreme deity, and thus no religion can claim its absolute rightness over others.

In Chinese ideology, both Taoism and neo-Confucianism insisted upon the idea that virtue was to be created through the interactions of various ideas. On the other hand, the Christians persisted with the orthodox Christian doctrine that the way to reach virtue was ordered by the Lord, and thus eliminating defects from the human society was a path to salvation.

Although simple, the barrier of this conceptual discrepancy between both sides was never overcome. Matteo Ricci talked about the necessity for religious

---

[143] Cited from Ricci, 1985: Chap.II, p.100.

reconciliation with the Chinese; the fact is, that his mind was never altered. Let us compare the previous extract with one of Ricci's letters:

> *At this time the commonest opinion among those who are considered wisest, is that all three sects are similar and can be professed simultaneously. This they utterly deceive themselves and others into thinking that the more religious doctrines there are, the better it is for the nation. But, in the end, this turns out contrary to expectation. For, wishing to follow all laws, they remain without any, since they keep none in their heart.*[144]

Although Ricci describes religious practice among the Chinese as 'deception,' as I have mentioned before, for the Chinese, harmonizing various religious concepts was a path to true virtue. It is not surprising, therefore, that this Chinese concept was not understandable for the European Christians. As Christianity is often the universe itself in Christian belief, there was no room for other religions.

Yung-Cheng's persecution of the Chinese converts continued. The insistence of Matteo Ricci that the Heaven of China was the same as the Christian Lord was effectively used to suppress the converts in the Chinese royal family. The emperor insisted that because every nation had worshipped the same divinity according to its own traditions since the ancient times, those who belong to a region must obey its local tradition. The fact is that the same context of Moses' Ten Commandments and the *Bible* had already existed in Chinese sages' writings before the time of Jesus Christ. It is not unusual that each nation that had lived under a different climate, and developed its own way of preaching about the supreme deity differently. Such differences should be regarded as natural consequence. Therefore, the emperor concluded that there was no need to introduce Christianity from the West.[145] Although in 1811, Christianity was eventually labeled officially as a false creed in China, the Chinese took 96 years to do this after the ban on Christianity issued by Emperor Kang-hsi .

---

[144] Cited from a translation published by Rosso (1948:74-5).

[145] See a Jesuit report dated on 26 September 1727, which was wholly translated in Yazawa (1971:216-305). The original French text is published in Querbeuf (1780-83:vol.20, 107-238). I have not consulted the original French version.

In China, religion tended to be considered a moral code rather than religious conviction. Although Chinese sages were respected as if they were divinities, they were not actually regarded as gods. Confucian rites were essentially to 'honor' parents and ancestors as the origin of the present humans, but not to 'worship' them. The Christian Lord was identified as the Heaven of Confucius' idea. In addition, unlike the Japanese emperor who claimed to be a living god, the Chinese emperor remained the supreme human deputy of Heaven, and thus his authority was never questioned by the existence of the Christian Lord. Although the missionaries continued their evangelization even after the ban, it remained on a small scale. Consequently, as Christianity was practically expelled from China, it may be said that there was no struggle between two different pantheons on the same level as in other pagan cultures.

Although historians working on these issues have traditionally looked at the political reasons for the Chinese compromise with Christianity, I think that the true problem between the two cultures existed in the different concepts of the dualism of Confucianism (partly influenced by Taoism) and the monism of Christianity. For the Chinese, the principal concept rested on dualism. The Supreme Ultimate in Confucianism and the *Tao* in Taoism explain that the supreme principle can harmoniously embrace both positive and negative aspects at the same time. In the Chinese dualism, negative aspects were considered a necessary opponent of the positive aspects. It is said that true virtue can embrace any opponent. Therefore, in spite of the intolerance of the pagan cults of other monotheistic religions, Islam and Judaism, they had been tolerated in China with certain restrictions upon their acceptance of Chinese rites. In this type of belief, no religion can monopolize the cosmos. At the same time, no religion is rejected unless it directly challenges the ruling authority of the emperor as the deputy of Heaven.

In the initial stages, Christianity was also accepted because it was expected to interact peacefully with other religions. Until it unveiled its intolerance of other religions and became a serious threat to the Chinese order, which was based on dualism, the persecution of Christianity did not take place. However, Christianity challenged dualism. When the Emperor Kang-hsi received a questionable request from the Pope, and cited the Christian insistence on the superiority of their doctrine over the others as merely based on their bias, Christianity could not avoid being banned.

Lastly, a curious issue must be mentioned. As I have discussed, through various communications with the West, the Emperor Kang-hsi finally concluded that China as the origin of perception of the one Lord of Heaven existed in the writings of ancient Chinese sages before the emergence of Christianity. This may be viewed as an attempt to place the origin of Christianity in China. This attempt is commonly seen in the pagan cultures which I discuss in this volume. It must be noted that in colonial Latin America, similar attempts were also practiced in the form of the emergence of another Moses and Virgin. This will be argued at the end of this chapter.

IV: Japanese Discovery of Christianity and the Development of "Christianity Made in Japan": The Christian Lord as a Vassal of the Living God = the Japanese Emperor 1873-1945

> *"Since there is no doubt that the people of this Empire* [Japanese] *are the posterity of God, I do not ask you a question on this issue. However, I am not certain about the origin of foreign people. Are they the posterity of OHNAMOCHI and SKUNABITO* [Japanese gods]*? If they are, it might be an error that only the people of this Empire are considered to be the posterity of God?*
> [Answer:] *Since there is no old record of the Empire* [Japanese] *recording how foreign human beings were created, the origin of those beings cannot be known. However, compared with Japanese people, foreign people have a strange appearance and look very low. When this point is considered, a hypothesis can be presented. ...Possibly, those old traditions* [of various religions] *tell the truth of the beginning of foreigners. Now, it is clear, possibly, that foreigners are not the posterity of God."*[146] (Atutane Hirata, an anti-Christian Japanese pagan nationalist of the early nineteenth Century)

---

[146] Hirata, 1813:101-102.

Unlike New Spain, the native religious authority, the Japanese Emperor, was regarded as the superpower of the world. Some Japanese Christians hesitated to accept the Christian Lord as superior to the Emperor, and they often struggled between two religious authorities, though there were exceptions. Therefore, when we consider the issue of religious dualism, the case study of Japan is quite curious.

What must be discussed is how Christianity was recognized in the Japanese dualism concept. My initial plan for this part was to discuss the anti-Christian movement in Japan of the Edo era, such as the issue of *Kakure Kirisitan* (the underground Christian) under the suppression of Christianity in Japan, or to further argue the ideology of the Japanese anti-Christian scholar Atutane Hirata.[147] However, I found the ideology of the Japanese patriot Christian from the late nineteenth to the early twentieth century to be particularly useful in considering a case of localized Christianity in a dualistic culture. Therefore, Japanese Christian ideology held by the Japanese patriot Christians from the late nineteenth century to the middle twentieth century, observed through two local incidents, will be examined.

The purpose of this book is not, of course, to summarize the history of Christianity in Japan, and there are already numerous academic studies published. Yet, for those who are not familiar with the history of Japan, a short account will be given.

From the seventeenth century, the Tokugawa Shogunate had banned Christianity. The Tokugawa family adopted Buddhism as the state religion in order to unify Japan. When the domination of the samurai class was ended in Japan, the Japanese emperor was restored all political power within Japan.

At the beginning, although the new Japanese imperial government allowed the Western Christians to live in Japan, it did not have a plan to accept Christianity

---

[147] In my previous book (Yamase 2002b), I made an error. The name of the author of the *Sandaiko* is not Chuo Hattori. His name is Nakatune Hattori (1754-1824).

268

except in the foreigners' residential area.[148] In fact, the policy of suppressing Christianity among the Japanese was inherited from the Tokugawa Shogunate and thousands were sent into exile to a remote island. The main reason was not only their anti-Christian feeling, but also because it was necessary to place the other religions under the control of Shinto to establish a state centered on the Japanese emperor, the supreme priest of Shinto. In order to restore the prestige of the Japanese emperor, who had been a mere puppet for more than one thousand years, it was considered that Shinto must be recognized as the sole state religion, and other traditional religions including Buddhism must be excluded. Therefore, the traditional Japanese religious concept of a harmonious relationship between Shinto and Buddhism had to be changed. As a result, numerous Buddhist idols and other holy materials were destroyed and Buddhist priests were persecuted. However, as Buddhism had taken deep root in Japan and its followers cooperated with the new government's policy of eliminating Christianity, this attempt failed within a short period.[149] Suppressing Christianity was also short-lived. Persecuting Christians aroused political pressure from France, England, and the USA, which claimed religious freedom as evidence of a civilized country.[150] It was also demanded that the new government make the Western countries remove 'the national disgrace' of one-sided treaties, which the former Japanese samurai government had made with West. The Japanese were seriously shocked by the defeat of China by Britain in the First Opium War (1839-42), and the reason being that China had not actively introduced enough technology so that the Chinese army that once terrified all the world could not oppose the United Kingdom. Therefore, a rapid Westernization was considered an urgent task in Japan. In order to invite Western instructors and technicians, certain guarantees of religious freedom were necessary.

---

[148] As to the history of the Christians of the late nineteenth century, see Ebizawa, 1968, Gonoi, 1990:261-303, Kishimoto, 1954:253-280, Sumiya, 1975, Mullins, 1998. Mullins' work is a useful summary on indigenous Christianity in Japan for English speakers.
[149] See Ebizawa, 1968:293-338, Kishimoto 1954:67-126..
[150] Kishimoto, 1954:126-7, see *ibid:* 281-8.

269

Under such political circumstances, Japan virtually abandoned its initial plan to eliminate Christianity in 1873. Since that time, although it was not officially sanctioned, the government removed the ban on Christianity, and its propagation was openly practiced.[151] Nevertheless, hostility to Christianity remained. The Japanese tended to feel an aversion to Christianity, and in fact, noted intellectuals at Tokyo Imperial University and Yukichi Fukuzawa (福沢諭吉 the founder of Keio University) made a campaign attacked Christianity in campaigns between 1881 and 1882[152], though certain ceremonies of Christianity, such as Christmas, did gain popularity among the Japanese.

However, when Hirofumi Ito (伊藤博文) who investigated the political systems of various counties, came back to Japan in 1883, the situation was changed. He insisted that a rapid Westernization of Japan was necessary in order that Japan gain an international reputation. The Imperial Government adopted his idea, and every aspect of Western culture was encouraged and introduced. Christianity was also considered a necessary part of that policy. By seeing this change of governmental policy, all of a sudden, Professor Kato at Tokyo Imperial University, who had previously shown an open hostility towards Christianity, praised it as the most effective religion to enhance the national prestige of Japan. Another Japanese nationalist, Yukichi Fukuzawa, insisted on the necessity of Christianity as the Japanese state religion.[153] As a result, the Christian population in Japan rapidly increased (ca. 4.400 in 1882, 11,000 in 1885, 32,000 in 1890), though the majority of them were attracted to fashionable aspects of Christian culture only.[154]

However, in spite of the policy of rapid Westernization, progress in abolishing the unfair treaties with the Western countries was not satisfactory. This provoked an anti-Western movement in Japan. Yukichi Fukuzawa changed his mind and

---

[151] As to the activities of the early Christians in Japan, for example see Kishimoto, 1954:281-345.
[152] Ebizawa, 1968:423.
[153] Ebizawa, 1968:425-6.

once again attacked Christianity. Ito fell from power in 1887 and the conservatives regained power. Christianity became a target of the Japanese nationalists again.

The Japanese Imperial Constitution of 1889 confirmed religious freedom among the Japanese. Christianity was officially accepted as one religion. Nevertheless, there was concerned that a Japanese Christian and the minister of education, Arimichi Mori (森有道, was stabbed to death on the day of official announcement of this imperial constitution. Although religious freedom was proclaimed, there were two problems. The constitution defined the Japanese emperor as the absolute inviolable authority. The government set up its strategy to consolidate its ideology of 'the emperor as a living god.' Since orthodox Christianity is monotheistic, accepting another divine existence such as the divinity of the emperor was not possible. Although the government established the logic that the one Lord mentioned in the Bible meant that of the Western world only, by creating two different psychological worlds as was discussed in the case of the Aztecs, some of the Japanese converts did not respond positively to this. Consequently, hostility from Japanese traditional religion never ceased.[155]

On 30 October 1890, the emperor's instruction on education (the Prescript on Education) was issued. It was distributed with a picture of the emperor. Afterwards, worshipping the picture of the emperor as if it were a god became a common practice in Japanese schools.[156] Naturally, the exclusive character of the Christian religion caused several serious conflicts with this pagan practice. There was a famous incident in 1891. A Japanese Christian, Kanzo Uchimura (内村鑑三 1861-1930), a junior high school teacher, did not worship the signature of the emperor on the emperor's edict on education (the Rescript on Education).[157] Because by that time the concept of the Japanese emperor as the living God was well established, anything created by him was considered divine, and thus

---

[154] Kishimoto, 1954:344-5, Ebizawa, 1968:426-7.
[155] See Sumiya ,1975:414-9.
[156] Kishimoto, 1954:353-4.
[157] An English translation of the Rescript can be found in Minamiki, 1985:113-4.

Uchimura's action was taken as a lese majesty to the God=Emperor. Once this news was widely known among the Japanese, persecutions of Christians occured in many parts of Japan. Some Christian teachers were expelled from school and, in Kumamoto Prefecture, students were forbidden to go to church by the order of the local governor. Consequently, in the same year, the minister of education ordered all schools to worship the picture of the emperor and his instruction on education, and further banned the admonitory lecture of Christianity in schools in 1892. Placing Christianity under the control of the Imperial Government was reinforced. In 1899, the ban on Christian education was also applied to private schools.

In general, although the Japanese Christians did not have an objection to accepting the emperor as the ruler of the present world, because of the monotheism of the Gospel, it was hardly possible for them to accept any god apart from the Christian Lord. On the other hand, although struggles among factions were frequent, neither Buddhism nor Shintoism discouraged its believers from worshipping a deity of another religion. Therefore, for the majority of the Japanese, the idea of Christianity was totally incomprehensible. Moreover, the fact is that the Christians called all deities apart from the Christian God, Satan. This attitude naturally provoked a strong hostility towards the Christian religion among the Japanese, whose majority was pagan. Although I do not think it proper that the Japanese nationalism of that period imposed upon the people to worship the emperor as the God, at the same time the exclusive nature of Christianity was no doubt one of major reasons for its isolation within Japan.

Due to the increasing persecutions in Japan, the majority of Japanese Christians decided to adopt a Japanese pagan element. For this purpose, the idea of new groups of Christians such as Unitarians or Universalists, who first arrived in 1890, was convenient. Unitarianism and Universalism, which were called the Free Theology, were known for their rationalism. Unlike the Catholics and the Protestants, Unitarians neither define Jesus as the God nor insist on the absolute perfection of the *Bible*. One of leading figures of Unitarianism, Arthur M. Knapp, made a speech at a Japanese school in 1888. On that occasion, he stated that even if Christianity is far more excellent than Japanese traditional religions, the Japanese first must give allegiance to those traditional religions. By his logic, no one who despises his ancient traditional religions would be able to utilize the context of the Gospel in his country.[158] This kind of opinion comforted Japanese nationalists. As he also denied the Trinity and insisted on the necessity of appropriating Christianity for the Japanese, an anti-Christian Japanese intellectual leader, Yukichi Fukuzawa, wrote an article to praise his speech.[159] This doctrine was ideal to localize the context of the Gospel as 'Japanese Christianity 日本的キリスト 教'.[160] Father Danjyo Ebizana（海老名弾正 1856-1937）is known for his adoption of the Free Theology concept.

Because adopting Universalism was considered a cause of syncretism, confusing the context of the Gospel, some fundamentalists, such as Masahisa Uemura（植村正久）, strongly criticized it and continued their uncompromised faith in Christianity.[161] There were several debates between Danjyo Ebina and Masahisa Uemura from 1901 to 1902. In 1902, the traditionalists gained a victory over the Free Theology, and the *Bible* was officially recognized as the perfect discipline.

Although Unitarianism and Universalism did not succeed in establishing themselves well in Japan, due to increasing hostility from Japanese traditionalists, their ideologies continued to be used to defend Christianity by a considerable number of the Japanese Christians.

In addition, it must be pointed out that the majority of the Japanese Christians were of the intellectual elite, and they lived in an Age of Reason in which the

---

[158] Sugii, 1984:364.
[159] Kishimoto, 1954:376-7.
[160] Kishimoto, 1954:381-3, Sugii, 1984:353-364..
[161] For example, see Kishimoto, 1954:380, Ozaki, 1892:66.

273

development of science threatened the value of all religions.[162] As a result, the people of this age of science began to suspect the mystical nature of Christianity. Phenomena which were once considered miracles of the Lord began to be denied by new scientific discoveries. In fact, a US friar, J.T. Gulick, pointed out that the new materialism of modern Europe was the most rigorous enemy of Christianity.[163] This trend assisted people to consider a religion a moral teaching rather than a divine code (except for the emperor). Therefore, even though they may have been faithful Christians, it was not always easy for the Japanese to believe the whole of the Gospel as truth.

Consequently, the Japanese Christians noticed that Japanising Christianity was necessary to popularize Christianity in Japan by using the ideas found in Unitarianism and Universalism.[164] In order to pander to Japanese imperialism, the exclusion of Western friars and missionaries from Christian organizations in Japan was practiced in order to create a 'Christianity for the Japanese.'[165] As a result of this Japanese mentality, although the friars generally remained faithful to orthodox Christian doctrines, the ordinary flock sought a path to merge Christianity with Japanese traditional religions.[166]

Some may argue that this movement of compromising with Japanese nationalism was a defeat for the Gospel in Japan.[167] In fact, Danjyo Ebina, who adopted the Free Theology, was criticized as an apostate.[168] Certain of the Japanese Christians continued their open or hidden resistance to the Japanese Shinto religion, the others only passively accepted Japanese state Shinto. However, the conflict between the fundamentalist Christians and the Japanese government is sometimes over-emphasized.

---

[162] Kishimoto, 1954:373-376. Although the number of people at Christian schools increased, because the majority of them simply used it as an educational place of Western knowledge and culture, they left Christianity after their graduation (*ibid.*:385-394).
[163] Cary, 1909:143.
[164] Kishimoto, 1954:382-3.
[165] Kishimoto, 1954-368-373, Sumiya, 1975:422.
[166] Sumiya, 1975:422. See also Ebizawa, 1968:454-66.
[167] E.g., Ebizawa,1968:461, Sumiya, 1975:422-3.

It is also true that a considerable number of the Japanese Christians of that period did not essentially oppose Japanese patriotism, as many of the Japanese Christians belonged to the middle class and were essentially nationalistic, valuing Japanese religious traditions as well as the Gospel. Since they generally had grown up under the strong ideological influence of the Confucian doctrines of Wang Yang-ming or the Orthodox Neo-Confucianism, as children of the former lower samurai class, denying fundamental Japanese traditions partly based on Chinese culture was difficult, as in the case of the Chinese Rite Controversy discussed already. Even though they believed in the Gospel, they often detested the Western-dominant atmosphere within Western mission churches. As their contact with the Western friars became close, there was increasing mental conflict between their ethnic pride as Japanese and Western culture. Unlike Justin Martyr of the early Roman Empire, who regarded Roman deities as demons soon after his baptism, a Japanese becoming Christian was not always able to dismiss the ancient religions as vain and devilish cults.[169] Even the Saint Justin Martyr accepted certain elements of Platonism as Platonist Christianity of the early Christians, therefore, the emergence of Confucian or Shintoist Christianity was a natural course.

Even Kanzo Uchimura, who is often said to opt for a stoic fundamentalist Christianity based on the *Bible*,[170] surprisingly accepted a kind of holiness of Buddha or Buddhism, although the superiority of Christianity in his mind was not changed.[171] It must be pointed out that his motivation for creating a Buddhist Christianity is not fundamentally different from the early Christian Platonism of the Roman era. This devoted Christian-rejecting worship of the Japanese emperor began to eliminate Western elements from Christianity to establish Japanese

---

[168] Sumiya, 1975:433.
[169] Ebizawa, 1968:419, 424, note 4, 5.
[170] It is often argued that Uchimura aimed to sublimate Christianity, which was corruptly practiced in Japan. For example, see Kishimoto, 1954:422-6, Sumiya, 1975:423.
[171]Uchimura also valued Confucianism. Mullins, 1998:60-67.

Christianity.[172] It must be noted that what Uchimura wanted was to create his version of Christianity for Japan differently from that proposed by the Free Theologians.

A noted Japanese Christian and an important critic of Unitarianism, Hiromichi Ozaki (1856-1939), wrote in his autobiography that he became a Christian in order to complete the teachings of Confucianism, in spite of the fact that he often criticized Confucianism.[173] In general, the development of Japanising Christianity was more frequently observed in non-mission Christian schools, of which Japanese Christians chiefly took leadership. Although they were critical of the view of human beings held by Orthodox neo-Confucianists, they valued it as excellent moral teaching.[174]

For the majority of the Japanese Christians, it was impossible to place the Lord of Christianity above the Japanese Emperor. What did they do? There were numerous contradictory struggles among the patriotic Christians. For example, one of the best-known Christians of that period, Danjyo Ebina, known as a noted leader of the Free Theology of his period, tried to explain Christianity as the final form of Japanese State Shinto, while criticizing the vanity of the idolatry practiced in Shinto at the same time.[175] In 1906, he published an article, which said:

『神儒佛の國民教育に於ける功蹟は、 日本史のあらん限り、 永久
没すべからざるのみならず、 その幾多の訓戒は生存競争して、 戰勝す
るものもあれば、 戰敗するものもあり、 時代的なるものもあるべく、
永久的なるものもあるべく、 等しく日本魂の滋養となりて、 これを育
成する方便となりたらんは疑ふべからず。
　　然りと雖も國民の倫理的教育は、従来のものを以て滿足すべから
ず、こゝにまったく新しき理想を要すべきは、國民の發展上亦已むべ
からざるものあり。新しき理想とは何ぞや、吾人は是れ即ち基督教の
主張する倫理なりと憚らざるなり』[176]

(As long as the history of Japan exists, the contribution of Shinto, Confucianism, and Buddhism to our national education will remain forever.

---

[172] See *ibid.*
[173] Sumiya, 1975:422.
[174] Ebizawa, 1968:419.
[175] Ebina, 1903, 1906.
[176] Ebina, 1906:177.

Numerous admonitions [of these religions] will compete with each other. Some admonitions may win over others in that battle. Others may be defeated. Some of them may be temporal, yet others should be permanent. I do not doubt that all of the admonitions [given by Shinto, Confucianism, and Buddhism] will equally become a nutrition of the Japanese [nationalistic] Spirit and will become an expedient to create it.

Nevertheless, for the ethical education of our Nation, we should not be satisfied with traditions. Here, a new ideology is inevitably necessary to develop our Nation. What is the new ideology? I do not hesitate to mention that the ethic argued in Christianity [should be the new ideology].)

In Ebina's argument, it is evident that the superiority of Christianity over Japanese traditional religions is argued. Nevertheless, it is also clear that he neither argued Christianity as the divine law nor dismissed traditional religions, but defined the former as excellent moral teaching. The idea that makes Christianity merely a code of ethics was often proposed by some of the Japanese Christians of those days.[177] Apart from this point, it must be noted that Ebina used the term 'Japanese Spirit,' and this 'Japanese Spirit' was often used to refer to a kind of 'Godhood,' like the K'abawil of the contemporary K'iche Maya. He insisted that a certain element of the Christian moral teaching should be incorporated into the Japanese Spirit [= a kind of religious Trinity], which consisted of three traditional religious moral codes. In another book, he also argued that he was not particular about any one religion in order to find the principle of religion (of course, in his thinking, such a reconstruction must largely be based on Christian doctrines).[178] It is interesting that they were to deny partly the Christian godhead, to take up only its ethical teaching, and to have tried to locate a point of compromise with the other religions in Japan.

On this point, a question may arise: 'What did happen to the Christian Lord?' What Ebina attempted was to identify the Christian Lord and the Japanese divine Creator as the same divinity that ought to be worshipped. He suggested that other major Japanese deities must not be worshipped, but must be 'respected' [like angels or saints, though he did not directly mention them]. In this way, by using

[177] Kishimoto, 1954:379-81.
[178] Ebizawa, 1968:424 note 5.

Christian doctrine, he tried to reform Shinto from polytheism into monotheism. Because this kind of logic proposed by the Free Theologians was officially criticized and was regarded as a heresy by the Orthodox Japanese Christians, their influence has tended to be ignored in the history of the religious ideologies of Japan.[179] In fact, a study suggests the influence of the Free Theology was very much limited to the educated class.[180] Nevertheless, as will be shown, except for their view of 'The Japanese Creation God = The Christian Lord', variations of their view of Christianity were later used by the Japanese 'patriot' Christians.

In spite of numerous efforts made by some leading Japanese Christians, Christian persecution continued within Japan. For example, as the Japanese army was suspicious of Christians as spies because of their strong ties with Western states (especially the USA and Britain), they often forced Christians to move from important strategic regions. In order to reduce hostility, Japanese Christians aggressively supported the war policies of the Japanese government. They also stopped donations from foreign missionaries and later excluded foreign friars. By these practices, they tried to avoid being regarded as a religious colony.

The fact is that the Japanese Imperial Government also had to make a certain compromise with Christianity due to Japan's relationship with Christian countries. As I have mentioned before, although it was initially planned to forbid Christianity as an evil, because religious freedom was proclaimed in the Japanese constitution, no official banning of Christianity was possible, as Japan prided itself as a civilized country.

Moreover, there was another important reason why completely banning Christianity was impossible. The answer is simple, because it meant a banning of all Western science. Since the science and technology of Japan of that time was still far behind that of the West, this had to be avoided. Therefore, a policy "integrating Christianity into the Japanese cosmovision" was gradually developed as a political necessity. Although it was not directly mentioned, it is obvious that

---

[179] Sugii 1986:355.

278

the idea of the Free Theology was conveniently used to distinguish the 'patriot' Christians from the non-Japanese Christians. The government tolerated the Christians who adopted a Japanised Christianity. Some of the Japanese Christians were against visiting Shinto shrines and continued refusing to pray to the emperor because they were considered pagan cult practices. Among them were the Catholics. Therefore, the prejudice towards Christianity never ceased among the Japanese traditionalists. The fact is that authorized prayerbooks and Catholic catechism in Japan continued to mention the practice of Buddhism and Shinto rites as sins, although the Catholics were cooperative with the policies of the Japanese Imperial Government.[181]

However, for the Japanese government, expulsion of the Catholics was practically impossible. Because in 1930, Italy became an important ally of Japan, the Japanese Government had to avoid a fatal conflict with the Catholics. Not only the Catholics, but the Protestants also had to be accepted to a certain degree because of Japanese ties with Germany. In spite of numerous persecutions of Christians, because the Japanese government maintained its policy of 'religious freedom' defined in the constitution and due to the necessity of its diplomatic relationship with Western countries, Christianity was never categorized as a banned religion, at least in official records. Therefore, because under any circumstance, the government had to avoid prosecuting Christianity as a creed, integrating Christianity as a part of the Japanese religious Trinity was a solution. Although, the core concept of Christianity, monotheism, was an obstacle, the Japanese government used two kinds of logic to localize Christianity as a part of Japanese society.

The equal status of Christianity to Shinto and Buddhism in Japan was not practically recognized until 1912 when the Japanese government invited representatives of Shinto, Buddhism, and Christianity to an official meeting. The intention of the Japanese government was to use these three religions as a united

---

[180] See *Ibid.*:353-404.

religious force supporting the living God, the Japanese Emperor. Although it was said that the Christians in Japan were pleased with this governmental invitation, it also meant that Christianity was integrated within the new Japanese Trinity = the Japanese Spirit centered on the state Shinto as a part of it. [182] A noted fundamentalist Christian, Kanzo Uchimura ironically called the Japanese religious Trinity a politically-made new religion; like a monstrous bird.[183] However, since the religious meeting of 1912 confirmed the recognition of Christianity in Japan, former enemies of Christianity began to hold more respect for the Gospel and thus the social status of Christianity was greatly improved. Therefore, with the authorization of the government, orthodox Christian parties, especially the Catholics, tried to follow the governmental policy. Nevertheless, although Christianity became one part of the state religion in Japan, a serious issue was raised. How to accommodate the Christian concept of the one God in the polytheism of other religions? It became necessary to establish a theological justification overcoming the fundamental difference between Christianity and Japanese traditional religions, monotheism and polytheism. Also, during that period, because the Japanese policy of establishing the Japanese emperor as *Arahitogami* (the living God, 現人神) had been consolidated, that 'new Japanese Trinity' of 1912 consisting of four religions meant that the Japanese Christians had to regard the emperor as a god superior to the Christian Lord. The Japanese people were taught that all Japanese were the descendants of gods, and that Japan was the state of the Gods.

In order to validate the absolute religious and political authority of the Japanese emperor more effectively, furthermore, the Japanese government issued

---

[181] Minamiki, 1985:123-129.
[182] Kishimoto, 1954:418-422. Precisely, Christianity was given a status equal to "folk" Shinto. During the process of restoring the prestige of the emperor, Shinto was divided into two parts. The former is the State Shinto to worship the emperor, and in theory, the governmental invitation of Christianity in 1912 meant Christianity to become a vassal religion of the state Shinto.
[183] Cited in Kishimoto, 1954:421.

a notice ordering every Christian student to visit a shrine of Shinto as a duty of the nation.

Because this decision would raise trouble with Christian countries, the Japanese government had to avoid disputes with these countries.[184] Japan therefore identified Japanese Shinto temples as non-religious places. Although the government ordered Christian students to make a visit to Shinto shrines as a part of their 'moral' education, the official view towards Shinto shrines expressed by the minister of education was that Shinto shrines were not religious places. By this logic, although the minister of education supervised all religions, including Japanese Shinto, the Interior Ministry supervised Shinto shrines, and thus the buildings of Japanese Shinto were not treated as religious places. Therefore, it was stated that Christian students were not forced to 'pray' to Japanese gods, but were merely required to pay 'homage' to Japanese traditions as evidence of their devotion and patriotism towards the Japanese Empire.

Under the social circumstance of the Shinto- and Buddhist-dominant climate, therefore, refusing to visit Shinto shrines became impossible for Japanese Christians. Because the forced visiting of Shinto shrines practiced in Japan meant a denial of Christianity, the pope in Rome sent a diplomat to Japan in order to verify his serious concerns in 1928. As the answer of the minister of education to him was the same as what I have mentioned the above, the Catholic Church concluded that the visiting of Shinto shrines was an acceptable non-religious act for Japanese Christians.[185]

---

[184] Japan of that time (even now) did not officially reject the divinity and the supreme position of the Christian Lord within Western countries.

[185] Although the controversies continued in 1932, the official directive of the Church concerning the approval of the Shinto shrine visit by Christians as a tolerance was not issued until January 1933. An English translation of this directive is found in Minamiki, 1985:148-9. Minamiki (1985:146-148) found a Latin document in which "tolerance" of shrine visits is argued based on a canon issued in 1258. He also published an English translation of it (*ibid.*:146-8). The position of the Japanese Ministry of Education was that although ordinary citizens have a right of refusing to visit shrines, students have to obey the decision of the ministry as a part of their duty, as they are under the Japanese educational policy.(Mino Mission, 1949:374, Yanase, 1933:64)

However, although the diplomatic matter with the Roman Catholic Church was solved, the official government comment did not satisfy either the Japanese traditionalists or the 'patriot' Japanese Christians, because the Catholics were only a portion of the Christian population. For the former, including the Japanese Imperial Special Secret Police, it was not acceptable that the Christians did not accept Shinto shrines as houses of God.[186] On the other hand, many of the latter continued regarding Shinto shrines as temples of idols=devils, while making a bow to Shinto shrines due to their fear of persecution and potential arrest by the Imperial Special Secret Police. Discussing the religious resistance of the 'fundamentalist Christians' to Shinto, the Japanese imperial religious cult of this period may be an interesting subject for scholars of Christianity. Yet, as the aim of this chapter is to discuss the dualistic concept of the Japanese religious mind, the view of Christians who attempted to identify themselves as more 'moderate Japanese Christians' who created 'Christianity for the Japanese,' will be examined.

Some 'patriot' Christians tried accommodating Christianity with Japanese traditions. How did they manage to integrate a polytheistic ideology with their monotheistic mind dominated by the Gospel? A series of persecutions of the Mino Mission, a Christian mission (of an independent party not belonging either to the Catholics or the Protestants), which happened in Ogaki City of the Gifu Prefecture, is quite an interesting case in which to examine this issue.

The brief history of the persecution of that mission school is follows.[187] On 24 September 1929, four Japanese junior school students refused to make a visit to a Shinto shrine in Ogaki city. Although three students were allowed to go back to their homes, only Tokiko Kuwana, a daughter-in-law of a Ms. Weidner, was

---

[186] For example, see the report of the arrest and status of religious crime by *Tokko Keisatu* (the Japanese Imperial Special Secrete Police) 1943:1203-1284 (reprinted in Wada 1972:234-258), and a contribution to the *Mino Taisho* Newspaper by Sho Nisino, a citizen of Ogaki city, 1933.

[187] The references treating this incident are Library of the Mino Mission (1949) and Yanase (1933). Yanase (*ibid.*) collected numerous articles published by several newspapers about the argument and commented on each of them.

forced to go to the shrine. As a Christian, Ms. Weidner was embarrassed by this fact. On 6 November, she met with the president of the school, Toyonosuke Ohno, to inquire the reason. While refusing to provide the reason why only her daughter-in-law was forced to make a visit to the shrine, Ohno insisted that although he did not have the right to limit the rights of Christians, it was not necessary, because Japanese shrines are not religious.[188]

Unlike some fundamentalist Christians, as Ms. Weidner did not order ·her followers and students to call Japanese pagan deities 'devils,' it may be said that her religions belief was less of concern as an issue in this controversy. Yet, she clearly denied the divine nature of the shrines. Although she considered that those at her mission could afford to respect them, they could not pray to them.[189] This point became a cause of trouble with the non-Christian Japanese. After this, Ms. Weidner ordered her students not to go to the school on the day of visiting to a Japanese Shrine. In March of the next year, when her policy was reported in the assembly of Ogaki City and a local newspaper, the *Mino Ogaki Shinbun*, made the story public. Her decision was taken as a betrayal and was openly criticized. Nevertheless, the persecution of Christians was still moderate.

In 1933, a refusal to visit a shrine by a Christian student happened again. In the previous year, the a student from Sophia University, a Jesuit school, who had once refused to visit a shrine, participated in a state celebration held in Yasukuni Jinja [Shrine]. Since his mother was a member of the Mino Mission, two local newspapers took up this refusal as a sensational case. The local police visited his mother. This resulted in large-scale, open hostility to the Mino Mission in Ogaki City.[190] On 23 July 1933, the Mino mission was attacked by the citizens. A mob broke into the mission, and a witness later reported that they were given tacit permission by the police officers.[191]

---

[188] Mino Mission, 1949:344-5.
[189] Yanase, 1933:37. Mino Mission 1949:362-3.
[190] Mino Mission, 1949:347-349.
[191] *Ibid*.:361-2. This part is based on a surviving witness. A Japanese local newspaper, *Mino Taisho Shinbun* reported this incident differently (cited in *ibid.*).

The persecution of the mission by the civil authorities of Ogaki city was extended to a children's garden managed by the mission. The conservative citizens of Ogaki City forced parents of its pupils to leave the children's garden. It was eventually closed.

From 23 June to 28 July 1933, in a local newspaper, the *Mino Taisho Shinbun*, there was a debate on the refusal to make visits to Shinto shrines between the Japanese nationalists and Japanese Christians. I have made partial translations of some of the contributors' articles in Appendix II.[192]

In analyzing their opinions, a process of localizing Christianity by using various types of the dualism concept can be observed. Although the Christian religion of the Mino Mission was accused of being a heresy, Japanese nationalists did not essentially deny the divine nature of the Christian Lord (Appendix II, A, B), because Christianity was one of the emperor's approved religions in Japan. It is interesting that they insisted on visiting shrines from a view of ethnic identity rather than religion.

A more interesting reaction can be observed in the case of Japanese Christians with regard to the considerable difference between the Western view of the Japanese religion and that of the Japanese Christians. Although the European Catholics tried to solve the shrine visit issue by defining it as a civil issue (=non-religious), no 'patriot' Japanese Christian agreed with such a view, because the emperor must also be the supreme for them at the same time. Some of the Japanese Christians justified it by inventing another type of religious divine existence comparable to the Christian Lord (Appendix II, D, G).[193] By using this logic, some Japanese Christians justified the co-existence of Japanese gods and the

---

[192] Almost all contributions from the readers are reprinted in Mino Mission (1949:350-361) and Yanase (1933). There is no complete set of this *Mino Taisho Shinbun* newspaper preserved in public libraries. Only a few copies of a few remaining back numbers of this local newspaper are now preserved at such institutions as Tokyo University. Therefore, although there may be a good private collection, I did not unfortunately have access to the texts originally printed in this newspaper.

Christian Lord. This can be said to be an example of the Japanese parallel perception of Christianity with Japanese religions as a part of their dualistic culture. As proposed in the case of the colonial Yucatec Maya text in Chapter I, the pair of the Stone and the Christian Lord mentioned in that Maya document may have been generated on similar grounds.

In the case of Appendix II-G, the Japanese ancestors, and the belief in worshipping them, were treated as a comparative deity to the Christian Lord. According to this logic, although the *Bible* forbids Christians from worshipping other gods, it only means prohibition of worshipping the same type of divinity as the Lord. Therefore, the purveyor of this argument was able to conclude that because Japanese *Kami* (gods) are a different type of supernatural power, worshipping them together with the Lord does not cause any problem.[194]

Moreover, it can be noticed that Christianity is divided into Jewish Christianity and 'true' Christianity in Appendix II-D, which was written by Nobuo Sato. In his writing, the elements found in the *Old Bible* were often considered negative because the Jews had not well been received in Europe. Also, the portrait of the God between the *Old Testament* and the *New Testament* is totally opposed. In the former, He is very negative. According to Vine Deloria, the Lord mentioned in the *Old Testament* is '*a psychopath like Saddam Hussein*' of Iraq.[195] On the other hand, the same Lord is portrayed as very friendly in the *New Testament*. This

---

[193] The author of Appendix II-D, Mr. Nobuo Sato, told of the same context three years before he wrote Appendix II-D to Nohara. (Nohara 1930:46-7) Although he was a Christian, he put the Shinto altar in his house and prayed to it every day.(*ibid.*:46).

[194]Another Japanese, Shigeru Ishida (石田繁), had already presented the same logic on the *Mino Taisho Shinbun* on 19 March 1930.(cited in Nohara 1930:51-3) According to him, the beginning of the conflict between Christianity and the Japanese Shinto religion was caused by translating "God" in English as "*KAMI* (神=God)" in Japanese, because it gave an impression that both gods are the same in the nature. He argued that in order to clarify the different nature between Japanese gods and the Christian Lord, it is necessary to call the Christian Lord GOTTO (ゴット =GOD). As an example, he cited the history of the introduction of Buddhism into Japan. He argued that the reason for the success of Buddhism was based on a fact that its deities were recognized as a different type of supernatural power from those of the Japanese Shinto religion. Therefore, he concluded that there were far fewer conflicts between Buddhism and Shinto than those between Christianity and Shinto.(*ibid.*:52)

[195] Deloria, 1993:151-22

difference seems to have allowed some to consider anti-nationalistic characters found in Christianity as evidence of a Jewish fraudulent distortion of the original Gospel. Indeed, the author of Appendix II-D insisted that the negative aspects found in the *Bible* concerning Japanese cults must be ascribed to the Jews. Indeed, it must be noted that while the *Old Testament* was received badly, Sato never criticized the *New Testament*.

Sato did not accept the *Bible* as the word of God, but as an ancient record containing some fables.[196] Interestingly, the Japanese nationalists who argued with this author never criticized his view that 'The Japanese sacred texts contain similar fables to the *Bible*.' This suggests that because they lived in a so-called age of reason, some miracles of the context found in the religious scriptures were sometimes mere myths, and thus the position of religion could often not be beyond a moral code.

Although, like those at the Mino Mission, some orthodox Christians who remained faithful to the context of the *Bible*, continued refusing to visit shrines,[197] the intention of the Japanese nationalists was not to expel Christianity, but to indigenize Western Christianity in order to integrate it as a part of the Japanese cosmovision. Therefore, they were satisfied with the movement among a considerable part of the Christian community in attempting to justify the superior authority of the Japanese Emperor over the Christian Lord. As the result, in 1935, Dr. Tetujiro Ioue (井上哲治郎), a known critic of Christianity, favorably commented on the decline of anti-nationalistic ideology within 'well-Japanised' Christianity of that time.[198] Japan was to establish a close tie with Germany and

---

[196] Among the Japanese "patriot" Christians, there was a consensus that because the *Bible* was edited hundreds of years after the death of Jesus, the authenticity of some of miracles mentioned in it are questionable. For example, see Yamane, 1994:80-1.

[197] As to the continuous refusing of visiting shrines practiced by the Mino Mission, see Yanase (1933:147-228). Although Ms. Weidner continued propagating Christianity in spite of continuous pressure from the citizens of Ogaki City, due to her cerebral hemorrhage, she decided to go back to the USA for treatment in 1939. She left Japan in December 1939, and died on the returning ship on 24 December 1939. The Mission was dissolved in 1939 and its activity was restored after the Second World War.

[198] Kishimoto, 1954:356.

Italy. On the other hand, the relationships with the USA and Britain were becoming worse. Therefore, while the Catholics and some parties which maintained strong ties with Germany and Italy, were more tolerated, the Protestants and other parties were increasingly cautioned. It was often said that the religious intolerance of Christianity was a product of the USA and Britain, and that Christianity of the USA and Britain (mostly Protestant) became a target of police persecution. Although the open resistance of some Christian parties against Japanese nationalistic religious views still existed, even after Japan waged a war against the USA and Britain in 1941, the majority of the Japanese Christians found compromising with Japanese traditional rites to be a unique way of keeping their Christian faith. For example, it was reported in 1941 that a church decided to place a Japanese Shinto altar in front of its entrance.[199]

While a strong fundamentalist Christian faith was observed in Protestant and independent churches (of course, some Catholic as well),[200] there was a considerable number of Christian people who thought that the Westerner (in this case, those of the USA and of Britain) interpolated Jesus Christ's original teaching to make it convenient for their propaganda. There was an idea that Jesus Christ's original idea must have fit with the traditions in Japan. As the Japanese Imperial Secret Police (=*Tokko Keisatu* 特高警察) continuously watched the movements of Christian leaders, the ideology held by the Japanese patriot Christians can be seen in the monthly reports of *Tokko Keisatu*. I translated some important points of the patriot Christian, Mr. Horiuchi's, logic in Appendix I of this book. In reading it, it must be pointed out that Horiuchi treats both the *Bible* and the *Kojiki* (The Sacred Text of Japan) as an authentic, homogenous, ancient historical record. In short, it is said that he justified their compromise with ancient pagan religions by using interactive dualism. Indeed, the prototype of his logic was used in the case of the Mino Mission. More importantly, Horiuchi, a Japanese 'patriot' Christian, tried to

---

[199] Tokko Keisatu, 1941:171.
[200] Based on a statement published by the Japanese Imperial Secret Police of 1942 (Tokko Keisatu 1942:147).

287

prove that the origin of the anti-Japanese nationalistic character of Christianity was a religious ideology generated by the Puritans in the USA. By his logic, although the original Christianity did not essentially contradict Japanese pagan traditions, the USA spread a distorted version of Christianity as a type of propaganda. This type of logic was commonly used among the Japanese 'patriot' Christians.

The *Tokko Keisatu* recorded various reports of this kind of Japanised Christianity. Their monthly report narrates that refusal to visit Japanese shrines continued among certain groups of Christians even in 1943, two years after Japan joined the Second World War.[201] Although the Catholics generally maintained moderate relationships with other Japanese religions, some continued refusing to visit Japanese shrines. One case was reported in the small village of Rutu Amakusa in the Kumamoto prefecture in 1942,[202] and in 1943.[203] Therefore, the head of the local police invited the Christians to a meeting in order to 'correct' their unpatriotic attitude. It was held at a Catholic Church on 19 August 1943. According to the report published by the secret police, the head of the local police and the head of the volunteer guard of that village talked about the importance of visiting Japanese shrines as the duty of the Japanese.[204] After the talks, there is an interesting and important statement when we consider the idea of a 'Christianity made in Japan'. This report tells us that a reserve duty army captain and Christian of the village, Masuda, said:

『カソリック教の教へにしても先刻私が言ったやうに本当の精神からいえば我が国体に密接な関係のある神社に対しては之を崇拝することを奨励はしても、参拝することを拒むことを教へることはない、それを米英の謀略で本当の精神を教えられず、神社のない外国の其の儘を日本に教へて神社に参拝するな等教へて日本国内の対立を激化させやうと闘っているのである。』[205]
(Concerning the teaching of the Catholics, as I have spoken before, if saying based on its true spirit, it encourages us to visit [Japanese pagan]

---

[201] Tokko Keisatu, 1941, 1942, 1943, 1944:*passim.*
[202] Tokko Keisatu, 1942:148-9.
[203] Tokko Keisatu, 1944:193.
[204] *Ibid.*:193-4.
[205] Cited from *ibid.*:194.

shrines, and it does not teach us to refuse visiting shrines. We were not taught the true spirit by plots of Britain and the USA. [The friars who came from Britain and the USA] tell us to observe [the customs of] foreign countries in which there are no Japanese shrines, just as they are, and tell us not to make a visit to shrines, because they were fighting to provoke internal conflicts in Japan.)

The report mentions the successful results of the meeting.[206]

Up to this point, I have discussed the issue of the indigenization of Christianity investigated by the Japanese academic society. Though it has not been treated as an academic subject, there is an academically ignored local issue in Japan.[207] Although the following case is different from the dualistic perception of Christianity, it contains some useful ideas about localized Christianity.

As I have already mentioned, around the 1930s, due to increasing nationalism in Japan, there were several attempts to separate Christian teachings from the Western society. In order to do so, finding evidence that Christianity was directly given to the Japanese, or that Christianity introduced into Japan had been distorted by the Westerner, was required. Though a small group, some Japanese Christians and Japanese traditional pagan priests considered, therefore, that Christianity must not have been born in a barbaric region like Israel. For such Japanese nationalists, it was necessary to explain Japan as the divine origin of all religions, and the superiority of the Japanese over others. For them, therefore, evidence that Judaism, Christianity, Islam and all other religions must have been initiated in the country of the divine people (=Japan), had to be established.

In 1935, a document called the *Takeuchi Bunsho* (竹内文書), was fabricated and became widely advertised by Takeuchi, who was a priest of a shrine named *Kosokotaigu Shrine*, as a previously unknown, ancient text (originally written more than tens of millions of years ago!)[208]. According to this text, founders of all

---

[206] *Ibid.*:195-7.
[207] A brief account of this cult is mentioned in Mullins, 1998:194-5, although any primary source for it is not mentioned.
[208] The original manuscript was lost. The *Takeuchi Bunsho* consists of various documents. It must be noted that its credibility and authenticity as a historical source is totally denied within the formal academic society, as this text is now used in Occult Studies (=non-academic party). An

religions, such as Moses, Buddha, and Muhammad first came to Japan to lead an ascetic life. As only fragmental texts of this document now survive, the portion of this manuscript referring to Jesus' stay in Japan is not available to us. The surviving portion of the *Takeuchi Bunsho* illustrates that Moses came to Japan in order to worship the Japanese Emperor and he received Moses' ten commandants after forty-one days' training at *Kousokotaigu* Shrine.[209] It also narrated that Moses lived in Japan for twelve years. The purpose of this book was to insist upon Japan as the origin of the world.

A scholar of Japanese classics, Ryoukichi Karino, published an article concerning the *Takeuchi Bunsho* in 1936, in which he rejected its authenticity, because it is written in a very poor style of the Japanese classical language.[210] This text is now recognized as a forged manuscript written by Takeuchi as an act of self-promotion for his religious party, but it is still widely used in occult studies, such as the study of UFOs. Therefore, formal academic researchers in Japan avoid studying this manuscript, because of their fear of being treated as occult researchers in conservative atmosphere of the Japanese academics. Of course, I do not accept it as an authentic ancient text, and reject it as a historical source. Nevertheless, it must be pointed out that from the perspective of ethnological study, the religious influence over some minor Japanese religious sects caused by the *Takeuchi Bunsho* should not be ignored as a formal academic subject. Indeed, investigation of the influence exerted by this manuscript provides quite a curious issue of the indigenous version of Christianity in Japan of the mid-twentieth century.

When the existence of the *Takeuchi Bunsho* was announced, it was strongly criticized by the majority of the Japanese Christians, and they ignored it.

---

interested reader may consult some surviving part of this text published in Takeda 1999. Harada (1989) is an intriguing survey of this text, though it is not scholarly. The Shrine of *Takenouchi, Kousokoutaijingu* (皇祖皇太神宮) is now managed by his successors. See the official HP, http://www.kousokoutaijingu.or.jp/

[209] モーゼの遺言と系圖, in Takeda 1999:246-7.
[210] Karino 1936.

Nevertheless, it attracted a devoted Christian woman, Kiyo Yamane (山根キヨ 1893-1965). Although she was a dedicated Christian, she was also affected by the Japanese emperor and was a Japanese patriot of that period at the same time. She appears to have disliked Christianity introduced from the West, and was preoccupied with the notion of 'Japan as a divine country.' Yet, within the Christian holy scriptures, there is no reference to Japan. Therefore, the existence of the *Takeuchi Bunsho* which was claimed to have been written tens of millions of years before (=much older than any other religious sacred text!), was extremely helpful for her to identify Japan as the divine origin of all religions.

According to Yamane, the *Takeuchi Bunsho*, which was still available in her time, tells that Jesus Christ came to Japan at the age of twenty-two, practiced asceticism for the truth, and initiated Christianity there! Jesus then went back to Israel in order to develop the Gospel when he was aged 33.[211] However, due to the persecution by the Jews, Jesus escaped from there to Japan again while in Israel his brother Isukiri was crucified! Jesus Christ lived in Japan until his death at 106 years old. This text suggests that the tomb of Jesus Christ exists in a small village, Herai (戸来), located in Aomori Prefecture of the Tohoku area, a part of Japan. As a narrative found in the *Takeuchi Bunsho* says, if Jesus and the founders of other religions had come to Japan to gain supernatural power, the ancestor of the Japanese emperor would be the Christian Lord and supreme deities of other religions. Therefore, it is not surprising that this story narrated in the *Takeuchi Bunsho* led Yamane to an investigation of Herai Village. After her 'careful' investigation in that village, she claimed she had discovered the tomb of Jesus Christ and other related sites. She concluded that the story found in the *Takeuchi Bunsho* was verified as historical fact. She published a book in which she identified Japan as the origin of Christianity.[212] The person, who released the *Takeuchi Bunsho*, Takenouchi, was later arrested for his disrespect to the Japanese

---

[211] Because the part referring to the life of Jesus Christ in Japan originally found in the *Takeuchi Bunsho* is now lost, I have used Yamane (1994).

[212] Yamane, 1937.

emperor. The original text of *Takeuchi Bunsho* was lost during the war.

As is known, Japan accepted unconditional surrender in 1945. In the next year, the emperor declared that he was not a divine existence but a human being. However, the notion of 'the divine Emperor' has remained strong in Japanese society. Kiku Yamane was no exception. She continued regarding the emperor as the best divine authority while claiming to be a faithful Christian. In 1958, she published a revision of her previous book.[213] In that book, Japan is still considered the origin of the all religions, and Jesus Christ is treated as a human being. This is not surprising, because this type of ideology is often seen among the Japanese born before the Second World War.

The level of her argument is not so much different from the notion of 'The Aliens as the founders of the Maya Civilization,' a theory that was once popular among non-academic people. For example, while dismissing the authenticity of some stories found in various sacred texts, she did not question the reliability of the *Takeuchi Bunsho* itself. Yet, her effort to define her mother country as the origin of a foreign religion was quite a curious comparative example of indigenous Christianity. Therefore, it is vain to offer a detailed analysis of her theory. What we need to examine is her motivation for revising the context of the *Bible*.

We must consider: How did a faithful Christian manage to reject the *Bible* as the authentic text given by the Lord? As I have already mentioned, as a person of the age of science, she was not able to believe the context of the *Bible* as the word of God. She denied the *New Testament* as the true words of God. Based on her own 'scientific' consideration, she cited several facts of the *Bible*, such as the lack of a complete record of Jesus Christ from the age of twelve to thirty within the *New Testament*, as evidence that several fabrications were added and facts deleted.[214]

---

[213] Yamane, 1994.

[214] Yamane, 1994:5-6. This type of idea had been proposed since the ancient time. "*Except for the episode of Jesus in the temple at the age of 12 in Lk 2:41–50, the NT writings leave a tantalizing gap in the life of Jesus between his birth and his baptism at the beginning of the public ministry. Inevitably, the developing literary tradition, taking its cue from the childhood story in Luke, created a series of incidents that tell of events in Jesus' boyhood. Their main theme is to show Jesus' precocious awareness of his supernatural origin and his power over life, death, and*

Since the *Bible* entirely lacks a record of the life of Jesus during that period, she therefore concluded that the *Takeuchi Bunsho*, which recorded the incidents that happened to Jesus Christ during that period, was a true history.[215]

In 1958, she wrote;

『釈迦は五十二歳にして「カララ仙人」より教えられて、日本に
渡来し、キリストも同じく若くして来り、マホメットも亦た然り、彼
らの一生の秘められた歴史、而もその終焉の地こそ日本であって、
各々天寿を全うして、その墳墓あり、天孫民族の意味、天津国、日の
本の名も、形容詞や一人よがりで名付けたものではなくて、事実の歴
史であり、本家は何処までいっても本家に間違いなく、分家はどう考
えても分家にしかならない証拠が判りとしているではないか。
　従つて本家の当主は天皇であって…本家の当主は分家に対しても、
床柱を背負う立場にあらせられて、貧乏はしていれど、金持の成り上
りものの分家のものからは、如何ともする事の出来ぬ不文律の掟があ
るではないか。世界の乱れはこの席順を誤るからであって、金や学問
位で威張るような分家が、巾をきかす世界である限り、世は乱れるに
定っている。やはりものの願序を正して、正しい席順にもどしてこそ、
世界も国も家も、社会も正しく直く治まるのである。』[216]

(Buddha was taught of Japan by 'Karara Sennin [=a legendary wizard]' at the time of 52 years old. In addition, Christ came to Japan when he was young. Mahomet [=Muhammad] did too. The unknown history of their lifetimes was kept in Japan and the place of their death was in Japan. They fulfilled the natural span of life respectively and there are their tombs in Japan. The meaning of the state of the *Tenson* people [= the descendants of Gods], the name of *Amatukuni*, and the name of Japan were not named as an adjective or for self-claiming, but are an actual history. No doubt, to the end of the world, the head family is the head family. Whatever it may be considered, there is clear evidence that the branch family cannot be more than a branch.

Therefore, the current head of the main family is the [Japanese] emperor and ... There is a regulation of the unwritten law that as the present head of the head family is a position of carrying an alcove post for [=the Japanese emperor carries a responsiblity for] the branch families, although [the Japanese emperor is now] poor, those upstart rich branches cannot do anything [against him]. The disorder of the world was caused because this seating arrangement was mistaken. As long as the branches, which are over proud of their money and academics, have influence, the world will be disordered. Therefore, the seating arrangement [making the Japanese

---

nature."(cited from Barton et als. 2005:Chap.82, THE NEW TESTAMENT APOCRYPHA, L. Jesus' Childhood.)

[215] Yamane, 1994:5-7.
[216] Cited from Yamane, 1994:256.

293

emperor as the top] must be restored by correcting the order of things so that the world, state, house, and society can justifiably be governed.)

The text cited above explains her motive. Although she was a Christian, because of her strong nationalistic character she could not accept the fact that the divinity of the Japanese emperor was not acceptable to Christianity. Unlike other Japanese 'patriot' Christians, she did not use the logic that as the Christian Lord is a different type of divinity, it is not contradictory to worship the Japanese God, another type of divinity, at the same time. For her, the emperor must be the primary important divinity. What she opted for, was to identify ancestors of the Japanese emperor as the Christian Lord. As I have mentioned, a questionable lack of the record concerning Jesus Christ's life during a certain period helped her to create her own version of Christian history by using the 'world's oldest record,' *Takeuchi Bunsho*. By insisting that Christianity was initiated by Jesus Christ, who was instructed in his supernatural power in Japan and was given a title of king from the Japanese emperor[217], in her mind, Japan became the most sacred place in the world.

Although she later published another book in which she argued various ancient remains all over the world were evidence of the Japanese emperor's visit to that place in the ancient times,[218] since it is substantially the same as her previous two books, the context of it is not discussed in this book.

It is quite easy to conclude that the case of Kiku Yamane is a humorous folk tale. Nevertheless, her idea that 'Western Christianity is not a true Christianity' offers us a useful perspective when we consider the indigenization of Christianity in non-Western countries.

---

[217] Yamane, 1994:63-6.

[218] Her attempt was rejected again. Yet, the context of it continued developing as the "facts" among the folk people and enthusiastic sales people. Although this story has not been taken as a fact, due to demands for tourism, a museum was established in the village of *Herai*. (See http://www.marumarushingo.com/densyoukan.htm) The villagers are not Christians, and thus they do not have the *Bible* or the monks. They celebrate, nevertheless, the cross in a churchlike building, according to traditional Japanese pagan tradition. A photograph can be seen in Mullins, 1998:194. In short, they respect Jesus Christ as one of Japanese deities.

In this chapter, I have mainly discussed 'Japanese patriot' Christians. Although there are various useful points for understanding the dualistic perception of Christianity, only two important points are summarized here.

First, these patriot Christians valued their own ancient myths as equivalent to the *Bible*. Because of a substantial lack of reference to Japan in the *Bible*, they did not often question the justification of using ancient Japanese myths to fill the gap of ancient history found in the *Bible*.

Another cause of creating a 'Japanese' Christianity was considerable anti-Western (especially against the USA and Britain) sentiment. These people tended to conclude that most of the Christian traditions opposing Japanese traditions were made as political propaganda of the Europeans in order to conquer other ethnic groups, or that what the Westerners taught was not the original Gospel, but a much distorted one. It must be noted that this movement was not restricted to Japanese 'patriot' Christians. As I have mentioned, even among faithful Japanese Christians, there have been some like Uchimura who tried eliminating Western elements from Christianity in order to establish his true path to the Lord, while he remained a critic of Japanese imperialism.[219]

In some extreme cases, consequently, it was considered that Christianity was not originally initiated in Israel, but in Japan. In the case of Kiku Yamane, by moving Christianity's sacred place from Israel to Japan her version of Christianity was completed. In her mind, Christianity was originally developed as a branch of the Japanese Shinto religion. Although this is a case specific to Japan, bearing her view in mind may be useful when a localization of Christianity in other non-Western areas is considered.

Finally, as in the majority of the pagan world, it is noted that the concept of sin and salvation after death were not always a prime concern for the Japanese 'patriot' Christians. They tended to see the Christian scriptures and teachings as a

---

[219] See Mullins 1998:137-9.

moral code. Indeed, it is suggested that there is a general lack of the concept or notion of sin in the writings of the Japanese 'patriot' Christians.

V: Summary

> *If, by chance, we should sin against God and His commandments, and if He did not help us, we would remain forever the slave of the devil and in Hell.* (cited from Córdoba 1970:105)

In this chapter, localization of Christianity in various pagan-dominant situations has been considered, though the case of the Inca may not have been sufficiently argued.

In the case of colonial Mexico, Fernando Cervantes argues that although it is not difficult to observe anti-Christian tendencies among the colonial Mesoamerican people, this should not be interpreted as evidence of a conscious native opposition to Christianity.[220] He ascribes the reason for his view to a general lack of authentic writing among the Nahuátl, which allowed them to adapt the Christian doctrine. He is partly correct if we speak of an illiterate people who often confuse the Christian theology. Moreover, contrary to Christianity, most of the pagan religions do not have a concept of religious opposition, and thus although Christianity often faced strong hostility, certain parts of it were often taken as positive.

This type of phenomenon is also observed in Japan and China where the people were literate and have had several holy texts since ancient times.

Because Christianity was usually perceived in terms of its own religious concepts, it was, for example, received as a moral code, like Confucianism. Also in other states, Christianity was received as one homogenous variation of their pagan cults, and thus it can be said that its original meaning, the *Bible* as mandate of the Lord, was not taken seriously by the pagan peoples. Moreover, the Gospel was usually understood under the pretext of dualism. As a result, the existence of the

---

[220] Cervantes, 1994:46.

Christian religion was only allowed to be a part of the pagan dualism religious concept. As the negative aspect is an indispensable part of dualism, in spite of the existence of negative feeling towards Christianity, this negativity was taken as a part of religious dualism or as a kind of religious trinity (one cosmos and two or more religions) in all pagan regions. These indigenized Christianities are, of course, considered a heresy by the orthodox Christian. Yet, should we call them a product of their poor intellectual ability, or of their primitive cosmovision, as Enrique Dussel mentioned?[221] It appears that although there were confusions about the context of the Gospel due to the lack of full access to Christian sources, Christianity was generally localized with a reason based on various types of dualism in many cases. For example, in spite of being Christian, pagan sacred texts or traditions were frequently treated as a source homogenous with the *Bible*.

In the pagan cultures, a religion is often a part of the cosmos, while Christianity embraces the whole of the cosmos. Although it may not be an appropriate explanation, this conceptual difference allowed the pagan peoples the existence of a hostile religion, Christianity, together with their ancestral deities, because each religion forms its own independent mental world. Unless Christianity failed to remain in its own world, there was no need for the pagans to attack it. The example was discussed in the case of the colonial Aztec. Don Carlos and Motecuhzoma II spoke as if there were two different worlds in their universe, and this their reaction is not unusual in other pagan cultures. Because of this conceptual difference, the pagans have generally felt no contradiction in the co-existence of Christianity with their pagan cults.

As has been discussed, some process of indigenizing Christianity found in non-Maya pagan regions is quite similar to the colonial Maya in some points, although ostensibly more complicated. All pagans perceived Christianity in their own dualism. Because much of the process of localizing Christianity among the colonial Maya can be universally found in the pagan cultures, 'Christianized Maya

---

[221] Dussel, 1981:67.

religions' found in their colonial sacred texts are not always necessary to define the result of their confusion, but their systematic integration of Christianity by using various types of dualistic logic can be seen.

In the case of Japan, in spite of the fact that there were strong religious and political pressures from the dominant Japanese pagans, and although a certain number of Japanese converts remained as faithful believers in the Gospel, the majority chose to establish a religious dualism consisting of the Japanese Shinto religion and Christianity. Since the purpose of this book is to argue religious dualism, the latter case was discussed. In the case of Japan, why did the majority of the Japanese converts betray the *Bible* on some important points? The Japanese converts were born and educated in the Age of Reason; their scientific knowledge prevented them from putting faith in the *Bible*. Consequently, they tended to regard the *Bible* as one ancient mythic and moral narrative among their native pagan texts. Of course, the colonial Maya and other pagan people of the pre-modern period were not living in the age of science. Yet, there is a point in common among them.

That key point is the existence of anti-Western sentiment. Abuse and exploitation of the Native American by the Spaniards can be considered the primary reason. Yet, another important factor must be pointed out. Accepting Christianity often meant dismissing not only pagan religions, but also cultural traditions based on daily life, and an evangelization process and monopoly of ecclesiastical matters by the Westerner naturally aggravated the anti-Christian mind. Some converts reverted to their old pagan faith, as in the case of Don Carlos of the Aztec, while pretending to be Christians at the same time, and some chosen to remain Christian. The latter, who usually accepted Christianity as one of his/her religions, often cited some incompatible aspects of Christianity as an intrigue of the West, and felt a necessity to eliminate 'Western elements' from Christianity (of course, there were a certain number of the Japanese Christians who remained orthodox followers of Western Christianity).

Consequently, anti-Christian emotion among the Japanese often led them to separate Christianity from the Westerners. As I have discussed in this chapter, some Japanese converts concluded that the true history of Christianity is different from what the Westerners taught, and some anti-nationalistic characteristics, such as the denial of the Emperor's divinity found in the *Bible,* did not originally exist. In order to verify their logic, therefore, the Japanese pagan texts became important documentary evidence as a historical source. As I have mentioned in this chapter, a document of Appendix I of this book is a good example of this.

In the case of Japan, in order to accommodate Japanese deities within the cosmovision of a monotheistic religion like Christianity, a new concept of 'although the Christian Lord is unique, as the Japanese gods are in nature different from Him, worshipping those different types of Gods does not contradict the Gospel' was invented by some Japanese Christians. The reader may find the idea found in Document G of Appendix II to be a very peculiar concept, unique to Japan.

If the motive of the Maya authors of the *Chumayel* was quite similar to the author's Appendix II-G, however, it would suggest that the colonial Maya cleverly avoided a contradiction with one of the most important principles of the Gospel, 'the Lord as God is unique over the world'. It should be remembered that a variation of this logic was possibly used by the authors of the *Books of Chilam Balam of Chumayel* discussed in a previous chapter. Although it is based on my own interpretation of its context, my analysis suggested that while the colonial Maya authors of the *Chumayel* treated their old deities as dead ones, and accepted the rule of Christianity, another Maya divine element, 'the precious stones,' was mentioned as a superior (or possibly equivalent) supernatural power to the Christian Lord. Since the prohibition of worship of other deities is mentioned in the Gospel, the colonial Yucatec Maya who accepted the rule of Christianity in the present world rejected their old deities as gods of the present world.

Yet, it seems that the authors considered a non-God deity an exception to the Christian theological rule of 'no god apart from the Christian Lord.' In my view, because the stones were considered a different category of supernatural power by the Maya, they were not dismissed from their divine role in the era of Christianity. The Maya managed to continue regarding the stones as the superpower in their cosmos, and placing them above the Christian Lord was not a problem for them. Of course, as this view is hypothetical, it is possible that the authors of the *Chumayel* may essentially have had a different idea.

It is interesting that among some of those who opted for compromise with a traditional pagan religion, there were several movements to identify Japan as the origin of Christianity. Although the case of Kiyo Yamane mentioned before is extraordinary, similar phenomena have been observed in the Japanese Christian society to a lesser degree. Such people tended to consider that although Christianity was primarily given to the Japanese, because the Westerns had distorted the true context of the Gospel, current Christianity had become incompatible with numerous Japanese traditions. By thinking so, they were to create (or to restore?) a new Christianity for the Japanese only. A careful consideration of this case reveals that it is not an extraordinary one. In the case of China, it was discussed that the emperors ultimately considered that the European-distorted Confucianism was Christianity. The hint of this idea was ironically provided by the European who first insisted that heaven in ancient Chinese writings was the Christian Lord.

Possibly analogous cases can be pointed out in the case of the colonial Maya. For example, it was recorded that a Maya, Andres Chi, claimed another Moses in the Yucatan Peninsula in 1597.[222] In colonial Chiapas, virgins appeared in order to take the controlling power of Christianity from the Spaniards in the early eighteenth century.[223] These cases were often considered a hidden revival of old Maya pagan religions, or an expression of discontent with Spanish control of the

---

[222] López de Cogolludo, 1971:II:91-2.

Catholic Christianity, as proposed by Victoria R. Bricker.[224] Although Bricker's view is quite acceptable, it remains questionable that the colonial Maya simply opted for Catholic Christianity.

Because the details of their religious practices are little known, it is quite difficult to reconstruct their true intention. Nevertheless, if we pay attention to the fact that an emergence of virgins and Moses was claimed, a different view might be presented.[225] Why did they need them? It must be noted that another *Moses*=a Prophet meant a messenger of the Lord, and thus what he was ordered by the Lord, would be a new code of Christianity. Virgin = the mother of God can also be said to be a justifiable tool to create another type of Christianity.[226] Therefore, it may be suggested that what the colonial Maya intended was the creation of 'Maya' Christianity which was directly given from the Lord. 'Another son of the Christian Lord' was not claimed during the Spanish colonial period. Why did they not claim another Jesus, but only a Moses or virgin? The reason for the substantial lack of 'another son of the Christian Lord' in the colonial Maya history may have been that because they accepted the divinity of Jesus Christ, creating another son of the God had the possibility of becoming a challenge to Jesus. It may be said that as they could not claim another Jesus without a proper reason, claiming a prophet or virgin was a radical alternative. By these justifiable tools, they were able to separate their own Christianity from the Catholic Christianity. This case should not be considered a peculiar example of the Maya cultures. The same logic was used by Joseph Smith (1805-1844) to establish the Mormon religion of the USA.

On this point, one of the mysterious issues found in several colonial Guatemalan texts is the parallel existence of Tulan and Babylon as the place of the

---

[223] For these incidents, see Bricker, 1981:55-69, Gosner 1992.
[224] Bricker, 1981:69.
[225] To my best knowledge.
[226] Of course, regarding Our Lady of Guadalupe, I do not deny the idea presented by Burkhart (1993:211) that Mary was selected by those who lived in surrounding area of Guadalupe, because Mary only offered sympathy and mercy while the Lord was the harsh taskmaster. Also in the case of the Maya, my discussion is not to deny the previous traditional view of some apparitions of

Maya's origin.[227] How can two different cities, one of Maya myth and another of Christianity, co-exist? Although they are treated as if the two cities were one, a careful reading suggests that each of them is mentioned as a separate city in the texts. This suggests that contrary to the Chinese and the Japanese who attempted to identify their country as the origin of Christianity, the Guatemalan Maya gave a dual identity to the birthplace of Christianity and did not completely move it to their homeland. The issue of Tulan and Babylon in those Guatemalan Maya texts may simply be summarized as an example of the Maya dualistic perception of their myth and a Christian one. However, it is not always correct to consider this phenomenon as a representation of Maya dualism. Although my previous work cannot sort out this issue well[228], another hypothesis may be presented.

Unlike Japan and China, Christianity was the dominant religion among the colonial Maya. Traditional pagan deities were losing power in the Maya area and there was no religion to rival Christianity. In my opinion, under such religious and social circumstances, the indigenous religious movement had to be made in the form of a new Christianity which was theoretically justified by the Christian doctrine, rather than by reviving their old deities. While accepting the superior power of Christianity, nevertheless, they could not totally abandon their ancient traditions. In that case, it is possible to consider that a parallel link between Tula and Babylon was necessary for their avoidance of challenging the context of the *Theología Indrum*, their sole reference material on Christianity. Tulan was not superior to biblical places found in the *Theología Indrum*, but equivalent.

For the Maya, expulsion of Christianity became less of an issue of concern as time passed. As recorded in colonial Chiapas, the rebellious colonial Maya during the anti-Spanish religious movements reported in the early eighteenth century

Christian subordinated deities (such as the Virgin and the saints) on the Yucatan Peninsula during the colonial times as disguised Maya female deities (e.g. Gutiérrez Estévez, 1993:267).
[227] Such as the *Historia Quiché de Don Juan de Torres* of the K'iche Maya published in Recinos (1984:25-70), and the *Historia de los Xpantzay of the Kaqchikel Maya* published in *ibid.*:120-9.
[228] Yamase, 2002b.

worshipped the Catholic saints, though this new Christianity did not completely exclude ancient Maya deities.[229]

Based on these points, it is suggested that what the Maya were to create might have been a new form of Christianity for the Maya only. If this view is correct, this type of colonial Maya did not reject Christianity, as Bricker suggests.[230] The case of the Christianized leaders of *Taki Onqoy* of colonial Peru may also be analyzed from this perspective, though the currently available information is far from sufficient.

Of course, analyzing social and religious beliefs is by no means simple. The above discussed interpretation cannot be applied to all Maya. For example, my analysis of the *Chilam Balam of Chumayel* mentioned in the previous chapter yields a different result. In the *Chumayel*, the origin of Christianity was still recognized as being of the Spaniards. In that document, as in the case of the Japanese 'patriot' Christians of the early twentieth century, it is suggested that the emergence of Christianity was interpreted within the Maya traditional cosmovision based on the context of their old sacred texts. It is evident that the *Bible* was not received as the word of the Lord but as one among the ancient records. The authors of the *Chumayel* attached more importance to their old writings than to the *Bible*.

Therefore, I do not insist that my hypothesis should apply to all cases of the relationships between Christianity and the colonial Maya. It is quite possible to consider that a considerable part of the Maya secretly resisted Christianity. Nevertheless, it must be pointed out that such Maya resistance to Christianity was also based on their own dualism.

---

[229] Bricker, 1981:55.
[230] Bricker, 1981:68.

Chapter IV: Maya Perspective of Christianity

"For this reason, we can believe that the ancient philosophers [Greek pagan, such as Plato and Aristotle], [Greek pagan] *followers of the justice, and the other* [Greek pagan] *virtuous men educated by them, had a faith in Christ, and they could be saved by the natural law before his* [=Jesus'] *arrival.)"* (Juan Gines de Sepúlveda, a fanatic Christian and prominent Spanish nationalist of the sixteenth century)[1]

I: The Popol Vuh

"In the old days the beasts, birds, fishes, insects, and plants could all talk, and they and the people lived together in peace and friendship. But as time went on the people increased so rapidly that their settlements spread over the whole earth, and the poor animals found themselves beginning to be cramped for room...They [all the animals] *began then to devise and name so many new diseases, one after another, that had not their invention at last failed them, no one of the human race would have been able to survive."* (On the origin of disease, found in the Cherokee's myth. Cited from Mooney 1897-8: 250-1)

A: It's Authenticity

"We also have a religion which was given to our forefathers, and has been handed down to us their children. It teaches us to be thankful, to be united, and to love one another! We never quarrel about religion. " (A speech of the Great Seneca (a tribal people of the North Native American) orator cited from Eastman 1911)

There are several sorts of religions, not only in different parts of the island, but even in every town; some worshipping the sun, others the moon or one of the planets. Some worship such men as have been eminent in former times for virtue or glory, not only as ordinary deities, but as the supreme god. Yet the greater and wiser sort of

---

[1] Sepúlveda 1984:52-3.

them worship none of these, but adore one eternal, invisible, infinite, and incomprehensible Deity; as a Being that is far above all our apprehensions... (Thomas More. *Utopia*, 1516)

The *Popol Vuh* is one important source material when we consider Maya dualism, it is quite important to argue several issues of this manuscript.

The *Popol Vuh*, the most famous of Pre-Columbian Native America literature, is often regarded as the *Bible* of the Americas. Yet, the use of the terminology '*Bible*' may be controversial, when the character of it is considered. Contrary to the Christian *Bible*, this text is not a mandate given by Maya gods. This text narrates the creation of the World and ends the K'iche dynasty at Utatlan. In terms of structure, this manuscript shows a similarity to the Japanese mythological book, the *Kojiki*.

No doubt, the *Popol Vuh* was largely written on the basis of the Pre-Columbian tradition of the K'iche Maya. Some argue that it was directly transcribed from ancient Maya hieroglyphic texts, while the others consider that the context of this text had been orally recorded until the Spanish Conquest.

The authenticity of this manuscript as the source of Pre-Columbian Maya tradition has frequently been questioned since its 'rediscovery' in the nineteenth century.[2] The surviving *Popol Vuh* was written in Spanish scripts after the Spanish Conquest, perhaps in the middle of the sixteenth century. Those who taught Spanish to the Maya were Catholic friars. In order to learn Spanish letters, the author(s) of this text undoubtedly had a close contact with the Catholic friars and must have known Christian doctrine to a certain degree. Therefore, it is generally suggested that the *Popol Vuh* must have received unconscious influence from Christianity.[3]

A British scholar, Lewis Spence once wrote;

"The cosmogony of the "Popol Vuh" exhibits many signs of Christian influence, but it would be quite erroneous to infer that such influence was of a

---

[2] As a short summary, see Recinos 1954:16-19.
[3] Spence 1908:237, Rivera Dorado 2000.

305

> *direct nature; that is, that the native compiler deliberately infused into the original narrative those outstanding features of the Christian cosmogony, which were undoubtedly quite familiar to him. The resemblance which is apparent between the first few chapters of the "Popol Vuh" and the creation-myth in Genesis is no more the result of design than was the metamorphosis of King Arthur's Brythonic warriors into Norman knights by the jongleurs. The inclusion of obviously Christian elements was undoubtedly unconscious. A native Guatemalan, nurtured in the Christian faith, could, in fact, quite be expected to produce an incongruous blending of Christian and pagan cosmogony such as is here dealt with."*[4]

In spite of numerous publications which have appeared since his book, his view has not substantially been changed until today.

For example, even if the following myth of the Cherokee of the North America contains an apparent influence from 'the world was created within seven days' found in the *Old Testament*, its context cited below is apparently suggesting that its core concept is of the Cherokee.

> *"When the animals and plants were first made--we do not know by whom--they were told to watch and keep awake for seven nights, just as young men now fast and keep awake when they pray to their medicine. They tried to do this, and nearly all were awake through the first night, but the next night several dropped off to sleep, and the third night others were asleep, and then others, until, on the seventh night, of all the animals only the owl, the panther, and one or two more were still awake. To these were given the power to see and to go about in the dark, and to make prey of the birds and animals which must sleep at night. Of the trees only the cedar, the pine, the spruce, the holly, and the laurel were awake to the end, and to them it was given to be always green and to be greatest for medicine, but to the others it was said: "Because you have not endured to the end you shall lose your hair every winter.""*[5]

Is there anybody who could call the above text the product of a Protestant? The internal mind of the author(s) of the *Popol Vuh* cannot be known. Concerning the surviving text of this mythological and chronological narrative, academic arguments, such as '*To what extent it received the influence of Christianity?*', '*Was it really written by the K'iche? Or, it may have been a fabrication product of the*

---

[4] Spence 1908:237.
[5] Cited from Mooney 1897-8:240.

Spaniards', have been presented and have continued from the nineteenth century to date.[6] Those who produce the majority of Maya studies tend to identify it as a source almost entirely copied from an old Maya hieroglyphic text, and have tried to minimize the possible influence from the Christian concept.

On the other hand, some scholars insist that the *Popol Vuh* also contains a strong influence, and consider that such Christian elements were added by the Spanish Catholic friars. Some argue that there are strong influences from Christian doctrine in the *Popol Vuh*. A Mexican scholar, Rene Acuña even argues that a Dominican friar, Domingo de Vico or an anonymous Dominican, wrote it.[7] Since his first article dealing with this controversy, René Acuña, who has continuously raised the question of the authenticity of the *Popol Vuh* as a K'iche Maya source, wrote in 1998:

> "*Y es obra, a mi juicio, que merece ser estudiada a fondo. No como "el compendio de los mitos, leyendas e historias de El Quiche"; no como "un tesoro de información etnográfica < que > .... fundamentalmente aborigen.... expresa y documenta experiencias históricas del mas grande y poderoso de los pueblos mayas de Guatemala"; no como "una de las mejores introducciones a la cultura que lo produjo", porque nos de "una visión de la civilización de Mesoamérica, mas clara que ninguna otra fuente que conozcamos";" sino como uno de los mas grandes y extraños poemas épicos que el mestizaje produjo en nuestra América Indo-hispana.*"[8] (And it is a work, in my opinion, that deserves to be studied thoroughly. Neither as "the compendium of myths, legend and histories of the K'iche"; nor as "a treasure of ethnographic information < that >.... fundamentally native.... it express and documents historical experiences of the great and the powerful Maya towns of Guatemala"; nor as "one of the best introductions to the culture that produced it", because it gives us "a vision of the civilization of Mesoamérica, much clearer than any other source which we know"; but as "one of the great and strange (note: unusual may be a better translation) epic poems that the mixed raced people produced as [works of] our Hispanic Indian America.")

Acuña's view represented his pride of Ladino (=mixed) culture in Mexico which is often found in works of Mexican scholars. By emphasizing several

---

[6] Quiroa (2002:105-119) is a good summary on this controversy.
[7] Acuña 1975, 1983, 1998.
[8] Acuña 1998:94.

potential issues concerning the influence of Christianity within the narrative, he concluded that the *Popol Vuh* is not an authentic K'iche Maya narrative but is derived from new ladino culture created from Spanish and Maya cultures.

However, there is a fact opposing his theory. Although Francisco Ximénez, the discoverer of this text made his Spanish translation as a tool for terminating Maya pagan religions by associating several K'iche divine terms with the devil,[9] he was unlikely to have modified the majority of the original text, because he considered it a source containing error of devilish fables.[10] Therefore, the hypothesis 'the *Popol Vuh* as a fabricated product of the Spanish missionary' is unlikely. Yet, a possibility cannot be denied that Ximénez omitted several parts or sentences when he made the unique surviving transcription of the *Popol Vuh*.

The works which question the K'iche authenticity of the *Popol Vuh* have not generally been appreciated. Quiroa points out that the identification of the Biblical subject and the Dominican authorship theory only served to reassure existing prejudicial attitudes towards the indigenous population, and thus denying the K'iche authenticity of the *Popol Vuh* is a prevailing attitude in Guatemala and other Latin American societies even today.[11] In short, there is an unspoken policy to make the *Popol Vuh* a symbol of resistance to Spanish Christian civilization. Therefore, there is a dominant belief that if the Maya integrated some Christian element within their religious cosmovision, all of them were employed in order to hide the practice of Maya religions.

This idea has created a contradiction. For example, a US scholar, Dennis Tedlock, is noted for his insistence that the *Popol Vuh* is the surviving authentic copy of Pre-Columbian tradition (he believed it to be a Maya hieroglyphic codex).

Nevertheless it is noted that at the same time, he also wrote; "*To this day the Quiché Maya think of dualities in general as complementary rather than opposed...the realms of divine and human actions are jointed by a mutual*

---

[9] Quiroa (2002) is a work of investigating this matter.
[10] Quiroa (2002) suspects this view and examines several possible modifications made by Francisco Ximénez within the *Popol Vuh*.

308

attraction."[12] This clearly suggests his full comprehension of the positive and negative principle of the Maya dualism. Nevertheless, the term 'dualism' is not employed by him, and he has never attempted to consider the relation between Christianity and the Maya during the colonial period from this perspective. The fact is that there are not small numbers of the contemporary K'iche Maya who interpret the relationships between two different religious traditions by employing their version of dualism, often called *K'abawil.*[13]

The most recent English translator of the *Popol Vuh*, Allen J. Christenson writes:

> *The authors of the Popol Vuh were anonymous. In the text they refer to themselves only as "we" (p. 64), indicating that there were more than one who contributed to its compilation. The anonymity of the authors is unusual since most Colonial period highland Maya documents were prepared for some official purpose, and were duly signed by their authors as testimony of their veracity. For whatever reason, those who were responsible for compiling the Popol Vuh did not wish their identities to be known.*[14]

Later, he concludes that the authors of the *Popol Vuh* did not wish to be named in that manuscript because of their fear of potential harassment by the Spanish authority.[15] Contrary to the case of Japan and China, those who became the subject of Christian countries have been the subject of fundamentalist Christianity, and thus there was no room for indigenizing Christianity, at least in public. Therefore, the argument of Christenson has a certain plausibility.

In these arguments, it must be noted that those who emphasized the authenticity of the *Popol Vuh* as a Pre-Columbian Maya source consider syncretism negatively. As I have frequently mentioned, there is a strong ideological belief to regard 'religious mix' as evidence of confusion or as that of a primitive cosmovision of paganism.

---

[11] Quiroa 2002:110.
[12] Cited from Tedlock 1996:59.
[13] Sanematu 2000:248-9. See Yamase 2002b:248-9.
[14] Cited from Christenson 2003:35.
[15] *Ibid.*:36.

Even in the case of Rene Acuña who has continuously argued the possibility of the *Popol Vuh* as a product of the Spaniards, moreover, it is clear that he maintains the same stance as those favoring the *Popol Vuh* as a pure Pre-Columbian literature. This kind of idea, 'apart from the unconscious one, if any possible Christian influence is found in the *Popol Vuh*, it must not have been by the K'iche Maya but by the Spaniards,' has also been popular among the K'iche Maya, Hispanic, and North American scholars.

These ideas seem to be based on an inattentive hypothesis 'the Maya never willingly added noticeable Christian elements to the *Popol Vuh*, unless they were forced to do by the friars or unconsciously blended them.' Yet, it must be noted that such previous studies are a product of a Christian (monism) biased view, and they tend to ignore an important element of the Maya and other pagan religions -- an 'incorporative nature based on their dualism mind.' The lack of dualism perspective is also found in those who considered that the Christian influence within *Popol Vuh* was added by the author(s) of it.[16]

As I have repeatedly argued, this kind of logic tends to ignore an important character of Maya cultures, that of incorporating cultural and religious elements. On this very point, it must be clearly understood that pagan holy scriptures, including those of the Maya, are not essentially the mandate from God as in Christianity and the Islamic religion, but an explanation of the universe. In pagan cultures, in general, their chief interest has often been a precise reconstruction (or appropriation) of the universe. Therefore, there was always room for adjustment of their Cosmovision when a significant event, such as the Spanish conquest took place. This type of example within Maya cultures has been discussed in a section dealing with the *Book of Chilam Balam of Chumayel* in Chapter I of the present volume.[17] In any analysis of Christianized Maya religion, the K'iche Maya's own will to incorporate Christian elements with their ancient belief must also be

---

[16] *e.g.*, Similox Salazar 1999:90-1.

310

considered at the same time, because any conceptual idea presented in the colonial Maya texts is a representation of the Maya dualism. Within dualism, a total omission of an undesirable element cannot be made, and thus both Maya religions and Christianity are a single homogeneous religion. In a sense, one of the major features of the Maya religions, their incorporative character, can be said to be a kind of dualism. Therefore, an analysis of Maya texts from a view of dualism is required. The case of the *Book of Chilam Balam of Chumayel* of the Yucatec Maya which I have discussed in Chapter I, is a good example. My analysis has suggested that the aim of the authors of the *Chumayel* was to explain the situation of the Cosmos of the sixteenth century, and the result of it is that Christian deities are systematically integrated within their Cosmovision to explain the emergence of Christianity. In this case, although there is strong influence from Christianity, it is treated as a part of the Maya Cosmos, and thus the colonial Maya authors simply explained the existence of Christian religion in their Cosmos. In this respect, as long as Christianity is treated as a part of the Maya Cosmos, therefore, whatever elements of Christianity may exist in the *Chumayel*, it is an authentic Maya source.

Of course, the specific political, economic, and religious circumstances surrounding the Maya since the Spanish Conquest, in effect, the Spanish and Ladino (=Christian) dominant society must always be considered. No doubt, this created a strong hostility to Christianity, a religious symbol of the Spaniards. Nevertheless, their hostility against Christianity is not necessarily a total rejection or exclusion of it. In this respect, so-called 'syncretism' does not have such a negative meaning in Maya cultures, because it is not confusion but a reconstruction of their cosmovision based on dualism, as I have argued in the previous chapters.

We should examine one example of the Maya reconstructions of cosmovision practiced in colonial Chiapas. It is true that after the Spanish conquest, Maya

[17] Another example of a reconstruction of pagan cosmovision with Christian elements practiced by a noted anti-Christian Japanese scholar and other examples from the Maya were discussed in Yamase (2002b:234-250).

311

traditional rites were still secretly practiced among the Maya, and that the Maya used Christian elements to hide their traditional religious rites.[18] However, a fundamental Maya religious movement was not always seeking to preserve Maya religions. Historical evidence sometimes provides negative evidence against a total rejection of Christianity among the Maya. Indeed, such secret Maya religious meetings did not always take place as a total resistance to Christianity.

When this issue is considered, we tend to be preoccupied with 'a strong resistance against Christianity' practiced by the Peten Itza who were based on Tayasal. They fought to the last with the Spaniards and refused to accept Christianity. It is known that they occasionally burnt churches. Nevertheless, it must be noted that even the Peten Itza did not wholly reject Spanish culture. For example, while rejecting Christianity, they worshipped a horse of Hernán Cortés as a god. This case suggests that Maya hostility towards Christianity was not always aiming to exclude it completely.

There is a curious colonial record in Chiapas. In Chiapas of the late sixteenth century, a Spanish friar, Fray Pedro de Feria, reported his visit to a Maya village in 1584. He wrote:

> "Visitando el pueblo de Chiapas de los naturales el setiembre del año pasado de 1584, y poniendo el Edicto general, que se suele poner en semejantes visitas acudieron algunos yndios á denunciar de otros naturales de el dicho pueblo de Chiapas, y de Suchiapa sujeto suyo, delitos muy graves, señaladamente de que en el dicho pueblo de Su-chiapa habia una cofradia de 12 indios que se intitulaban los 12 apostoles, y que estos salian de noche, y andaban de cerro en cerro, y de cueva en cueva, y hacian sus juntas, y consultas, donde debaxo, y so color de religion trataban cosas de sus ritos, y culto del demonio, contra nuestra religion cristiana, y que traian consigo dos mugeres, á la una llamaban Santa Maria, y á la otra Magdalena con las quales usaban muchas torpedades, hacen ciertas ceremonias diciendo que con ellas se trocaban, y hacian otros, y otras, y se espiritualizaban, y se convertían en Dioses, y las mugeres en Diosas, y que ellas como Diosas habian de llevar y enviar los temporales, y dar muchas riquezas á quien quisiesen, y que tenian otras muchas supersticiones, y vanidades que parece frizar con la secta de los alumbrados.

Item denunciaron de Juan Atonal (que es como V. P. sabe, uno de los mas principales yndios de aquel pueblo que debe hacer mas de 40 años que se bautizó,..."[19]

(When I visited the town of Chiapas of the Natives in September of last year 1584, and gave the general Edict, that is usually done in similar visits, some Indians came to denounce other natives of the said town of Chiapas, and of Suchiapa of your subject, very serious crimes, especially of those in the said town of Chiapas who made a guild of 12 Indians who entitled themselves the 12 apostles; these went out at night, and they walked from hill to hill, and from cave to cave, and in which, they carried out their meetings, and consultations, under the pretext of religion, they perform their rites, and worship of the devil, against our Christian religion, and they brought two women whom they called Holy Mary, and the other one Mary Magdalene, with whom they used many dishonest ceremonies saying that they exchanged themselves, and did other, and other, and spiritualized themselves, and they became Gods, and the women become female Gods, and they as Gods had to carry and to send the temporary [=perhaps rainy weather etc.], and to give much wealth to those who wanted, and that they had other many superstitions, and vanities that seem to be close to the sect of the drunk people.

Item: They denounced Juan Atonal (who is, as V. P. knows, one of the most important natives of that town who must have been baptized more than 40 years [ago], ...)

This report mentions that the Maya of Chiapas still believed in their old gods even after being converted into Christianity. This may be said to be an example of hidden Maya resistance to Christianity. Yet, in spite of the fact that this text has been used by some scholars, an important point has been overlooked. By reading the above text carefully, it is suggested that their aim was not a simple challenge to Christianity.

It is noted that the Maya of Chiapas were accompanied by two women called Holy Mary and Mary Magdalene. Naming them Christian female deities may have been a strategy to hide their ancient faith from the Spaniards by using these 'disguised' Maya female deities, or it may have been to attract Maya Christian converts.

However, as was discussed in the case of *Taki Onqoy* of the colonial Andes, the example found in colonial Chiapas might suggest that the Maya tried to ally with some noted Christian deities. Why? It may be considered that the Maya of

---

[19] Cited from Feria 1584.

Chiapas were trying to: (1) create another Christianity for them; (2) attempt to generate a hybrid religion; or (3) create a new Maya deity and religion as an offspring of an old Maya god and Christian female deities, in order to oppose Christianity.

As is known, the *Bible* does not clearly deny the possibility of a new prophet in the future. This fact allowed the emergence of Islam initiated by the last prophet of the Lord. Yet, even Mohammad, the last prophet of *Allah* (=the Christian Lord), placed Jesus Christ into a special position as a half divine person especially made by *Allah* (on the other hand, Mohammad is treated as a human), although the logic of the Trinity and the concept = Jesus as the last Messiah was practically denied in the *Koran*. In this way, even Islamic religion avoids a direct challenge to Christianity.

Yet, on this point, it must be noted that the possibility of another son of the Lord is not denied by the *Bible*, because it does not refer to it. In this theory, creating another son of the Lord becomes possible, provided that there is 'another' Mary.

Since the colonial report from Chiapas does not refer to the name of the Maya deity, the exact detail of the god which they worshipped is unknown. Though the reporter mentioned it as a devil, nevertheless, it is almost certain that that deity was one of Maya gods of Chiapas. On this point, if we hypothesize that Holy Mary, and Mary Magdalene were not named to trick the Spaniards, their secret attempt may have been to create a new Maya deity who would be authorized by both their Maya god and the Christian female deities.

Therefore, it is possible to consider that the case mentioned in the above cited colonial report may have been a Maya attempt to create 'Maya Christiany' in order to challenge the Christianity of the Spaniards. Yet, it is important to point out here that this challenge seems not to have been directed at Jesus Christ, because although the record mentions that they became gods, a careful reading of the text suggests that they simply claimed themselves to be apostles. Although this view is of course hypothetical, as I have discussed in the summary of Chapter III, there was another attempt to create a new Christianity for the Maya, Moses was claimed by a Maya on the Yucatan Peninsula, as recorded in a colonial book.

Another possibility may be considered. The attempt of the colonial Maya of Chiapas may have been an attempt to regenerate a completely independent Maya religion from Christianity with the support of Christian female deities.

These examples suggest that the colonial Maya did not always simply resist Christianity, but often attempted to reinforce their old pagan pantheon by using certain elements of Christianity to surpass Christianity. This phenomenon should not be regarded as 'confusion' or 'proof of primitiveness of Maya cosmovision' compared to the monotheism concept, because the fundamental concept of pagan religions is a continuous expansion by interacting with elements of other religions. These new partners did not always have to be positive influences for them. In the dualism cosmovision, reconstructing a cosmovision is often a common creative activity.

I do not deny a possibility that certain of the Maya opted for preserving more fundamentalism in Maya religion in order to oppose the whole Christian religion. In this case, it is quite possible that those Maya rejected any element of Christian religion. However, since we do not know the personal identity of the authors of the *Popol Vuh*, both dualism and fundamentalism positions towards Christianity must be considered when considering the influence from Christianity.

Based on this view, regarding the issue of *Popol Vuh*, its potential influence by Christianity should be considered. Since the author of this text remains unknown, we have not obtained any answer as to whether the K'iche Maya author(s) purposely integrated some elements from Christianity or not. As I have mentioned in my previous work, it is extremely difficult to investigate the true feelings of Maya for Christianity in the early colonial period from the Maya texts. With the exception of the *Popol Vuh*, there is no other identifiable remaining

315

document written by them, and thus our knowledge of the personality of those authors is virtually nonexistent.

The context of the *Popol Vuh* was widely known in early colonial Guatemala. Moreover, there must have been several direct or indirect copies of it. The *Título de Yax*, another K'iche colonial text, which was discovered in the late twentieth century, is a good example.[20] It is known that the context of it is quite close to the last part of the *Popol Vuh*. Rene Acuña calls it another copy of the *Popol Vuh*.[21]

The fact is that the other colonial K'iche Maya texts, such as the *Título de Totonicapán* and the *Título de Yax*, are strongly influenced by Spanish culture, but they still maintain much of their ancient religious traditions.[22] Should we consider this remainder of Maya traditions in those texts evidence of Maya hidden resistance to Christianity? In the *Título de Yax*, indeed, there is an attempt to identify Carlos V of the Holy Roman Empire with their legendary authority in the east, *Nacxit* in Tulan.[23] This K'iche text actually identifies Spain as their mythic original place, Tulan.[24] This story was not found in the *Popol Vuh*. In the *Popol Vuh*, on the other hand, the legendary political authority in Tulan is *Naxit*, and there is no reference to Carlos V. Why was the original story of the *Popol Vuh* altered in the *Título de Yax*? In my opinion, although the use of 'Carlos V' in that part of the *Título de Yax* is confusion, it is evidence that the K'iche authors attempted to explain their origin and Cosmovision within both Christian and K'iche Maya traditions.

As I have discussed, the concept of 'a hidden resistance' is a typical character of monotheism. In the world of paganism, although strong hostility against Christianity which often resulted in a total expulsion of the Christian population

---

[20] It was published with a Spanish translation, in Carmack and Mondloch (1989).
[21] Acuña 1998:49-51.
[22] See Yamase 2002b:210-212.
[23] The *Título de Yax*, in Carmack and Mondloch 1989:79-80. Carmack (*ibid.*:98 nota 66) explains that there is a historical fact that one of K'iche cacique went to the court of Carlos V in Spain few years before the Spanish Conquest, and that the K'iche were confused that fact with their ancestors' legendary visit to *Naxcit* in Tulan presumably around in the 12th century, as this kind of mistake can be seen in other colonial K'iche text. See Yamase 2002b:108-9, Acuña 1998:50.

was commonly observed, it is rare to see even in such a case that some elements Christianity were not reconstructed to reinforce the logic of pagan religions.

In many cases, Christianity was considered an element of the Cosmos. In the case of Japan and China, moreover, although Christianity was banned, 'Christian ideas and science' were often appreciated.

Based on the above mentioned idea, my early works suggested that a portion of the *Popol Vuh* may have been 'reconstructed' with the Christian source by the colonial K'iche. It was also suggested that the author(s) of the *Popol Vuh* might have attempted to create a new cosmovison consisting of K'iche Maya religion and Christianity. Of course, what I identified as Christian influence within the *Popol Vuh* in my previous work is somehow controversial[25], but I still believe that such a perspective is also necessary in considering Christian influence in the colonial Maya culture.

There are several examples that suggest the *Popol Vuh* is almost written as a Maya dualism concept. Although some argue that there is a story of punishment of *Xibalba* by the K'iche Hero Twins, *Hunahpu* and *Xbalanque*[26], this narrative by no means reflects a Christian concept of the conflict between Satan and the Christian Lord. *Xibalba* was treated as a negative but necessary component of the Maya universe.[27] Also, as I have mentioned in Chapter I, the *Madrid Codex* of the Yucatec Maya suggests that the Lord of Death of the Maya is not an enemy of other 'positive' deities. These examples suggest that even if there are several Christian elements in the *Popol Vuh*, it was treated as a part of their dualistic cosmovision.

Christian influence within the *Popol Vuh* may be problematic when it is treated as the authentic Pre-Columbian Maya source. From a perspective of the Maya cosmovision, however, as long as the tale found in the *Bible* is treated as an

---

[24] The *Título de Yax*, in Carmack and Mondloch 1989:80.
[25] Yamase 2001, 2002b.
[26] e.g, Acuña 1998.
[27] Yamase 2002b:231-2.

element within their dualism concept, it may be said that even if there is a considerable influence of Christianity, it is still an authentic Maya source.

B: Conceptual Difference among Translations of the *Popol Vuh*

【廿一章】子貢曰、君子之過也、如日月之食焉、過也、人皆見之、更也、人皆仰之。 *CHAP. XXI. Tsze-kung said, 'The faults of the superior man are like the eclipses of the sun and moon. He has his faults, and all men see them; he changes again, and all men look up to him.'* (Cited from the *CONFUCIAN ANALECTS* 500BC in Hare 2004).

> *By the destruction of Ignorance, Conformations are destroyed, by the destruction of Conformations, Consciousness is destroyed, by the destruction of Consciousness, Mind and Material Form are destroyed, by the destruction of Mind and Material Form, the six Organs of Sense are destroyed, by the destruction of the six Organs of Sense, Contact is destroyed, by the destruction of Contact, Sensations are destroyed, by the destruction of Sensations, Desire is destroyed, by the destruction of Desire, Attachment is destroyed, by the destruction of Attachment, Being is destroyed, by the destruction of Being, Birth is destroyed, and by the destruction of Birth, Decay, Death, Sorrow, Lamentation, Pain, Grief and Despair are destroyed. Thus the whole mass of suffering is brought to an end.* (*The Udâna* of the Southern Buddhism. Cited from *Udâna* 1902:Chap, I. "The Enlightenment.": p.3.)

Although academic arguments about potential Christian influences in the *Popol Vuh* are still popular and will continue to be, I do not intend to present more discussion on this issue in this volume. What will be discussed here, is today's Christian Guatemalan Maya understanding of the *Popol Vuh*.

In this chapter, a comparison of several modern translations of the *Popol Vuh* with its original text will be made.

New translations of the *Popol Vuh* have continuously been published in numerous countries. Although there are several translations published by the Maya, the works by North American and European scholars or writers have nevertheless gained popularity and have been widely used among academics. Among the latter, although the German and French translations were once commonly used by Academics, due to the spread of the English language as the standard academic

318

language since the mid-twentieth century, works written or translated in English have become dominant. This volume is not a place to argue this issue, but there is a fact that works written in other European languages have tended to be ignored.

This situation has created an over domination of English in Maya studies. It is not surprising, therefore, that while the work of Eduard Seler (1849-1922) has remained invaluable on Mesoamerican culture and has been cited in the English speaking world, his German translation of the *Popol Vuh* has practically been forgotten by academics for many years.

A German scholar, Leonhard Schultze-Jena wrote in 1944;

> "*Eine streng auf den indianischen Text Brasseur's zurückgreifende deutsche Obersetzung* [=Übersetzung] *des Popol Vuh hat EDUARD SELER vor rund dreißig Jahren unternommen und handschriftlich hinterlassen; sie wurde mir in einer Abschrift Walter Lehmann's zugleich mit einer Wörtersammlung des Quiche in 27 Zettelkästchen* [=Zettelkasten] *übergeben.*"[28]
> (rigorous one [=study] on the Indian [=Maya] text of Brasseur falling back to a German translation of the *Popol Vuh*, was undertaken and left as a handwritten work by Eduard Seler approximately thirty years before; a copy was transferred to me and to Walter Lehmann at the same time with a text collection of the Quiche delivered in 27 slip boxes.)

Later, the second copy of Seler's translation, given to Walter Lehmann, was published in 1975.[29] Nevertheless, this work had not been referred to in the English and Spanish speaking world at least until 2001.

Because Seler's translation of the *Popol Vuh* appears to be at the draft stage, it is not necessary to use it as an indispensable reference. However, the translation of Schultze-Jena is still important, as he had a close contact with the living K'iche who were not yet as Westernized as they are today.

Although numerous translations of the *Popol Vuh* have been published to date, there are two unusual and often "dismissed" translations.

One of them is by the famous Adrián I. Cháves's *Pop Wuj*, which has been ignored as an off the mark work. HLAS once commented;

---

[28] Cited from Schultze-Jena 1944:XIV.

A new and "unusual" translation of the Popol Vuh, which employs geometrically shaped orthographic symbols invented by Chávez (not found in conventional printing). Includes a comparison of both Ximénez's original Quiché and Spanish texts with Chávez's transliteration and new translation. The translation lacks linguistic, literary, and cultural perspective and is off the mark when compared to others"[30]

Based on the above-cited view, Chávez's work has been ignored. Indeed, Chavez's translation is very subjective in many places. Though it often appears as one of the source references of numerous works, only few discuss the context of it. Yet, the fact is that the influence of Chávez's *Pop Wuj* among the K'iche Maya is often significant. Although it has been suggested to be a work without a proper analysis of *cultural perspective*, the living Maya do not always agree with that comment as it is presented by 'formal' academia. For those who support Chávez's work, works written by non-Maya scholars and their followers are out of question, because there is a belief that they are not Maya and thus it is impossible for them to comprehend the fundamental concepts written in the *Popol Vuh*.[31] In other words, some K'iche Maya consider that the translations made by non-Maya lack a Maya conceptual perspective. Of course, those Maya accept some defects in Chávez, but yet they ascribe the defects found in Chavez's *Pop Wuj* to his fear of accusation from the Church.[32] His translation and transcription have become popular and the standard text of the *Popol Vuh* among certain of the K'iche Maya. Also, his interpretation of *K'abawil* as *DobleMirada* (Double Looks = the dualism concept) is supported by them.[33] Lastly, it must be pointed out that the second international congress of the *Popol Vuh* was entitled *Memorias del congreso sobre el Pop Wuj* in 1999. Should we consider this phenomenon solely as a type of Maya nationalism based on the fact that Chávez was a native K'iche?

[29] Seler 1975.
[30] Cited from HLAS Item#: re831544
[31] Victoriano Alvarez, in Sanematu 2003:53-4.
[32] Sanematu 2000:308-9. see Yamase 2002b:224. Chávez was a Catholic.
[33] *e.g.*, López Mejia 1999:136.

320

In this chapter, examination of Chávez's *Pop Wuj* will be made by comparison with translations of 'outsiders.'

There is another translation of the *Popol Vuh* published by two Kaqchikel Maya of the twentieth century, Carlos Rolando de León Valdós and Francisco Lopez Peren, who identified the *Popol Vuh* as *'Libro universal de la renovación del tiempo'* (The universal book of the renovation of time) and also as *'Libro Nacional de Guatemala'* (The national book of Guatemala).[34]

This work is also categorized as a peculiar one. HALA mentions;

> **"Popol vuh: libro universal de la renovación del tiempo.** *"Completely new translation" of the **Popol** Vuh of the Quiché (Maya), which "has nothing to do with earlier translations," made by two **Cakchiquel**-speakers, based on 10 year's work with microfilm copy of original text. They see the **Popol** Vuh as the "Tree of the Life of Light," which is the "invisible universe," formed by the solar system. Contains their Spanish translation (which will be found strange by many specialists) and their retranscription of original Ximénez Quiché text."*[35]

The above-mentioned two translations have been considered off the mark by academic society for many years. However, it is true that they are one of important academic sources for understanding Maya religious conception. As I have mentioned before, there has been an interesting general contradiction in Maya studies for a long time. While ethnographic data collected from the living Maya of the twentieth century has been treated as precious information for Maya studies, their ideas appearing in the form of writing have been dismissed. Although I have read Tedlock's popular translation of the *Popol Vuh* and have recently purchased a copy the *Popol Vuh* translated by Allen J. Christenson[36] to finalize this chapter, I was amazed at a virtually total ignorance of works presented by Maya scholars in such interpretations. Is there any evidence that K'iche Daykeepers, who were personally selected by non-Maya scholars, have better understanding of the *Popol Vuh* and its ancient tradition than other Maya scholars, such as Adrián I.Chávez

---

[34] León Valés et al. (1985).
[35] cited from HLAS Item#: bi 89000207
[36] Christenson 2003.

and Victoriano Alvarez? The fact is that the latter is also a K'iche Maya shaman priest.

The reason may have been due to a popular academic myth 'those works by Maya authors are peculiar and do not appear in good peer reviewed journals.' If so, those Maya shamans who assisted modern translators of the *Popol Vuh* with their interpretation of the *Popol Vuh* would be required to have a Ph.D. in the future!

It is true that some of the Maya works lack a careful academic orientation, and often their analyses are subjective. A living K'iche Maya shaman, Victoriano Alvarez, insists on *Libertad de culto* (Freedom of worship), as the uniqueness of the Maya[37], yet he fails to recognize that it is a common concept of the majority of pagan religions in various countries. He also published his interpretation of *Popol Vuh* (he calls it *Pop Wuj*) in Japan with the aid of his Japanese friend.[38] The publisher advertised this book with the following sensationalized sales message; '*The origin of the Maya Civilization was much older than we thought!*,' which helped to spread the biased view of the 'Maya as one of the Occult cultures' in Japan.

As Katuyoshi Sanematu, Alvarez's friend, comments[39] that his view is strongly influenced not only by Chávez but also a classic work of Raphael Girard, a French anthropologist who attempted to give an esoteric character to the *Popol Vuh*,[40] yet while based on Girad, Alvarez's theory found in that book contains a strong personal bias which can be called 'his nationalism.' By his logic, the part of the mythology found in the *Popol Vuh,* which he calls *Pop Wuj* according to Adrián I. Chávez, does not reflect ancient Maya astronomic observation, but is a source of their wisdom, and records historical events which narrate the whole

---

[37] Alvarez 1999:55.
[38] Sanematu 2003. Although this author relatively fairly records the idea of Alvarez in that volume, there are some obviously incorrect facts and translations (e.g., *ibid*.:43, 253-4), and it must be noted that it is not primarily written as an academic book. Also, Sanematu attempted to restore the meaning of the original text of the *Popol Vuh* without good authentic linguistic materials (*ibid*.:46-7). Those who can read Japanese and want to use this book, must do so with caution.
[39] Sanematu 2003:257-261.
[40] Girad 1979.

history of Mesoamerica since the creation of the universe.[41] In some points, such as in terms of nationalistic view, his view resembles that found in the work of Kiyo Yamane which was discussed in the previous chapter. Therefore, the use of Maya shamans' works must be done with the utmost caution. At least, serious academic beginners should read their works after consulting 'noted' academic sources.

Nevertheless, they provide a native Maya interpretation of the *Popol Vuh*, which cannot be observed in works written by the Western academics. Indeed, in spite of dismissal by 'formal' academics, Victoriano Alvarez and Adrián I. Chávez correctly understood the strong necessity of understanding Maya dualism in order to comprehend the context of the *Popol Vuh*. In spite of numerous problems presented by the living Maya shamans' views, it is a fact that I could not manage to grasp the fundamental nature of the books of Chilam Balam as long as I was following noted 'academic' books.

The majority of works on the *Popol Vuh* presented by accredited Western scholars are also subject to their own personal subjective interests.

Nestor Ivan Quiroa, a Guatemalan born US scholar, makes several comments on the works of several noted North American scholars, such as Michael D. Coe, Munro S. Edmonson, and Dennis Tedlock who worked to support the theory of the *Popol Vuh* as an authentic copy of a lost Pre-Columbian source.[42] For example, Edmonson insisted that the original of the *Popol Vuh* was first used in ritual performance at Utatlan, the capital of the K'iche.[43] Yet, the fact is that apart from the *Rabinal Achí*, there is no solid evidence that the surviving colonial Guatemalan texts were originally used for that purpose. Furthermore, Quiroa cites the voices of several critics who question Edmondson's theory that the *Popol Vuh* could only be comprehended in poetic form.[44]

---

[41] Alvarez's view is summarized in Sanematu 2003. A brief account of Alvarez's theory is also found in Alvarez (1999).
[42] Quiroa 2002: 110-119.
[43] Edmonson 1971:vii.
[44] Quiroa 2002: 112-114, Edmonson 1971:xi.

Yet, Edmondson's assumption is also based on his own interpretation rather than on solid evidence. I must add my own question to Edmonson's theory. Edmonson was not familiar with dualism, he simply considers that the text of the *Popol Vuh* is composed in the parallelistic form[45]. More recently, Allen J. Christeson follows this 'the *Popol Vuh* as a poetry' proposal of Edmonson. Although Christeson's understanding is much better[46], both of them cite parallelism found in this manuscript as evidence that the *Popol Vuh* was originally composed in elegant poetry. As an oral tradition (even if the *Popol Vuh* was originally written in Maya hieroglyphic, I think that the role of oral transmission was equally important), the *Popol Vuh* should have been prepared in a poetic form. Yet, there is a question. Is the parallelism found in the *Popol Vuh* evidence of its poetic character? It may simply reflect the Ancient Maya dualism concept.

For example, parallelism is also found in ancient Confucianist writings of China, such as the *Confucian Analects*. Also, poetic tradition has been one of essential elements of Confucianism, and the *Confucian Analects* also partly reflect its tradition. Nevertheless, it is difficult to say that we treat the *Confucian Analects* as poetry. Indeed, it is different from Chinese poems written by noted Confucianists and it has been regarded as academic writing.

On this point, it should be considered that a total ignorance of the ideas presented by Maya scholars -- 'the *Popol Vuh* as a reflection of Maya dualism' -- is very questionable. Indeed, although such works of Maya scholars appear in lists of references, it is rare to see them seriously considered and discussed. On the other hand, opinions of Maya Daykeepers (often their own assistants) are taken seriously without showing much evidence for their reliability. In other words, the studies of the *Popol Vuh* have created a paradox, as they have been dominated by Christians who appear to have numerous connectional difficulties and prejudices from their monistic culture. This trend has sometimes produced incorrect assumptions, though it must be accepted at the same time that the Western contributions to the

---

[45] Edmonson 1971:xi.

understanding of the *Popol Vuh* have been significant. But parallelism does not fully explain the conceptual character of the *Popol Vuh*.

There is a significant distinction between parallelism and dualism; the former is independent, and the latter interdependent. As I have argued before, each element of the *Popol Vuh* is closely associated with another; they are not independent, but interdependent. The over-use of the term 'parallelism' only gives us an improper interpretation of the true context of the *Popol Vuh*, as the K'iche Maya scholar, Victoriano Alvarez, argues[47]. In fact, parallelism simply reflects the style of writing, but does not explain to us the concept and idea behind it. As I have argued in Chapter I of the present volume, in the case of the *Book of Chilam Balam of Chumayel*, which Edmonson also argues has parallelism and poetic structure; it is impossible to decipher the meaning of that text from the perspective of parallelism because it is written in interacting dualism.

Quiroa also points out several curious issues based on a translation of the *Popol Vuh* published by Dennis Tedlock. Tedlock's translation of the *Popol Vuh* reflects his personal interest in astronomical matter. It is almost certain that because the main theme of the surviving Maya hieroglyphic texts is astronomical matters, the *Popol Vuh*, which many North American scholars have attempted to assume to be a copy of old Maya hieroglyphic text without physical archaeological evidence, must be the same for a scholar like him. Based on his subjective belief, the narrative of the *Popol Vuh* largely reflects Classic Maya astronomical observation; and he relied on the interpretation of the 'contemporary' K'iche Maya Daykeeper as reliable.[48] However, as reported in the early twentieth century, the narrative of the *Popol Vuh* was already entirely strange to the K'iche Maya.

Of course, in the future, my present work may be commented as 'a work heavily relying on the perception of dualism.'

---

[46] Christeson 2003:42-49.
[47] Alvarez 1999.
[48] Quiroa 2002: 115. Of course, as in other pagan myths, certain parts of the narrative of the *Popol Vuh* should reflect astronomical movements, because it is quite reasonable to assume that the ancient Maya interest in astronomy became a heritage in that text.

The above examples clearly suggest that even peer-reviewed works written by Ph.D. qualified scholars must also be used with the utmost caution, because they often contain the strong personal bias of authors, even though their personal bias is evident in some aspects, their contributions are solid.

What is important here is that the colonial Maya texts were also written by living people like Chávez. The authors of the colonial Maya texts are by no means scholars of our day.

Let us look at some parts of the translation of the *Popol Vuh*. First, two Kaqchikel Maya, Carlos Rolando de León Valdós and Francisco Lopez Peren translated the first part of the *Popol Vuh*:

> "*Esta es la base fundamental del origen de la Antigua verdad del Quiché: El Arbol de la Vida, así es su nombre.*", (This is the fundamental base of the origin of the Old truth of the Quiche: The *Tree of the Life*, as it is its name)[49]

Then, Chávez's translation of the same part:

> "*Desde antes de escribirse el Pop Wuj, aquí se ha llamado "Los Magueyes*""[50] (Since before the *Pop Wuj* was written, here [, this place] has been called "the Magueys".)

Both of the above translations are amazingly different. So therefore, the original K'iche text will be cited.

Now, the above two translations will be compared with several European language translations of several academically noted Western scholars.

First, the same part of a popular English translation of Dennis Tedlock will be quoted:

> "*This is the beginning of the ancient world, here in the place called Quiché*"[51]

Leonhart Schultze-Jena's translation says:

---

[49] Cited from León Valés et al. 1985:13.
[50] Cited from Chávez 1994:31.
[51] Cited from Tedlock 1996:63.

"Dies ist der Uranfang der alten Kunde von Dem, was hier zu Lande den Namen Quiché hat." [52] (This is the beginning of the old tradition of the land here, which has a name, Quiche)

A work of the giant of Mesoamerican studies of the nineteenth century, Eduard Seler (c.1849-1922):

"Das ist der Beginn der alten Geschichte (des Landes), das Quiché genannt wird." [53] (This is the beginning of the old story (of the country), named Quiche.)

The original K'iche text transcribed by Shultze-Jena is:

"are v xe ojer tzih varal Quiche v bi." [54]

So, a word by word translation of the text will be; *Are* (this) *v* [=u] (its) *xe* (origin) *ojer* (ancient or old) *tzih* (true) *varal* (here) *Quiche* (Quiche) *v* [=u] (his) *bi* (name). Therefore, a simple English translation would be: 'this is the origin of ancient truth of here [this land] called Quiche'. Although the translations of Tedlock, Shultze-Jena, and Seler are not the same, this suggests that these translators are faithful to the original K'iche text.

It is now evident that the translations of Carlos Rolando de León Valdós and Francisco Lopez Peren are free renditions. One may suggest that such a considerable free translation may be a result of their different transcription of the original. However, their transcription of the original K'iche is the same as that of Schultze-Jena. [55]

Chávez's translation is also a significantly free translation. Both works lack academic arguments that justify their translations. In term of linguistic accuracy, therefore, both translations produced by Maya scholars must be used with caution.

---

[52] Cited from Shultze-Jena 1972:3.
[53] Cited from Seler 1975:43.
[54] Cited from Scheltze-Jena 1972:2.
[55] León Valdós et al. 1985:131.

However, were they impostors or merely eccentric people? The answer is surely 'no' to both. Although both works often lack 'academically' orientated analyses, it is also evident that Carlos Rolando de León Valdós, Francisco Lopez Peren and Adrián I. Chávez received a good education and were studying the *Popol Vuh* seriously.

Adolfo Colombres, an Argentine acquaintance of Chávez mentioned that according to Chávez, the previous Western (and Western culturally minded) translators of the text overlooked a simple terminological duality referring the same identity in a dualistic ontology found in the text.[56]

Thus, the purpose of his Spanish translation of the *Popol Vuh* was to reconstruct the Maya dualism within the *Popol Vuh*. Yet, in the process of his translation, for example, his denial of the Hero Twins of the *Popol Vuh* later became controversial even among the K'iche Maya. In his Spanish translation, Chávez identified the Hero Twins as one deity with a dualistic character within a single body. Unfortunately, we do not know the reason for his interpretation of the Hero Twins. As the result of this, although he may have proposed his analysis of Maya dualism in his new Spanish translation, many K'iche Maya observed his interpretation of the *Popol Vuh* as a substantial denial of the Maya concept of dualism because of his fear of condemnation by the Church. In my previous work, I wrote that Chávez denied dualism. It must be accepted that I made a mistake.[57] His Spanish translation of the *Popol Vuh* is a representation of his own understanding of Maya dualism. By reading his translation carefully, I could see that his denial of the Hero Twins is not to dismiss Maya dualism but to emphasize his own beliefs of Maya dualism; duality within one object.

In any case, 'peculiar' translations of the *Popol Vuh* were purposely produced according to the author's mysticism-subjectivity.

Let us compare their translations of another part of the Creation in the *Popol Vuh*.

---

[56] Colombres 1994:11.

"*Are cut xchicacam-vi: v cutunizaxic, v calahobizaxic, v tzihoxic puch euaxibal, zaquiribal rumal tzacol, bitol, alom, gaholom qui bi. Hunahpu vuch, hunahpu vtiu, zaqui nimac tzijz, tepeu, gucumatz, v gux cho, v gux palo, ah raxa tzel chughaxic. Rach bixic, rach tzihoxic rij iyom, mamom, xpiyacoc, xmucane v bi: matzanel chuquenel camul yiom, camul mamon chughaxic pa quiche tzih* "[58]

Are cut (here) *xchicacam-vi* (we shall take): *v cutunizaxic* (declaration), *v calahobizaxic* (manifestation), *v tzihoxic* (relation) *puch* (and or also) *euaxibal* (secret or darkness?), *zaquiribal* (clarity, whiteness) *rumal* (by) *tzacol* (Tzacol), *bitol* (Bitol), *alom* (Alom), *gaholom* (gaholm) *qui bi* (their names). *Hunahpu* (*Hunahpu*=a shooter or a hunter with a blowgun. *Hun*=one, but in this case, general or universal, *Ahpu*=(hunter) *vuch* (Tacuatzín=Opossum), *hunahpu* (Hunahpu) *vtiu* (coyote), *zaqui* (white) *nimac* (great) *tzijz* (Peccary), *tepeu* (tepeu), *gucumatz* (Gucumatz), *v gux* (spirit or soul [=GOD] of) *cho* (lake), *v gux* (spirit or soul [=GOD] of) *palo* (sea), *ah raxa lac* [the lord of green plate] *ah raxa tzel* [the lord of green bowl] *chuqhaxic* (as it was said). *Rach* (together) *bixic* (were nemed), *rach* (together) *tzihoxic* (were told) *rij iyom* (grandomother), *mamom* (grandfather), *xpiyacoc* (Xpiyacoc), *xmucane* (Xpiyacoc) *v bi* (their name): *matzanel* (defender) *chuquenel* (protector) *camul* (twice) *yiom* (grandmother), *camul* (twice) *mamon* (grandfather), *chughaxic* (as it was said) *pa* (in) *quiche* (K'iche) *tzih* (word)

Therefore, my draft English translation is:

Here we shall take declaration, manifestation relation and it was darkness, clarity by *Tzacol, Bitol, Alom, Gaholm*, their names. *Hunahpu* Tacuatzín=Opossum, *Hunahpu* coyote, white great Peccary, tepeu, *Gucumatz*, spirit or soul [=GOD] of the lake, spirit or soul [=GOD] of the sea, the lord of green plate, the lord of green bowl as it was said. They were named and told, grandmother, grandfather, whose names are *Xpiyacoc*, *Xpiyacoc*: defender, protector, twice grandmother, twice grandfather, as it was said in K'iche word.

Seler translated this part as:

---

[57] Yamase 2002b:224, 2005b.
[58] Cited Schultze-Jena 1972:2. Now, the standard orthography of the Maya language is unified. Therefore, the orthography used by Ximénez which Schultze-Jena substantially followed, is no longer used. Although I retain the transcription made by Schultze-Jena, those who are interested a transcription of the *Popol Vuh* in the standard Maya orthography of today, see Sam Colop (1999) or Christenson (2004).

"Hier also warden wir vorbringen die Aufzeichnung und die Offenbarung und die Erzählung, wie es verborgen war und wie es hell wurde durch die Erbauerin, den Erzeuger, die Mutter, den Vater, deren Namen sind: Hunahpu Vuch (Eins Blume Beutelratte), Hunahpu Utiu (Eins Blume Coyote)", Zaki Nim Ak (das große Nabel-schwein), Zaki Nima Tzyis (den großen weißen Nasenbären), den Herrn K'ucumatz, das Herz de Sees, das Herz des Meeres, den Herrn der grünen (neun, bemalten) Schüssel, den Herrn der grünen Kürbisschale, wie er (der Gott) genannt wird. Mit ihm zusammen wird genannt und in den Sagen behandelt die Großvater Xpiyacoc (und) Xmucane heißen sie, die das Verborgene herausfinden und mit ihrer Hilfe eintreten (eigtl. Die Beschützerin, der Helfer), zweimal Großmutter, zweimal Großvater, wie sie genannt werden in der Quiché-Sprache,... "

Here therefore we state the record, the revelation and the story how it was concealed and how it became light by the builder, the producer, the mother, the father, their names are: *Hunahpu Vuch* (a flower bag rat), *Hunahpu Utiu* (a Flower Coyote), *Zaki Nim Ak* (the big umbilicus-pig), *Zaki Nima Tzyis* (the great wise nose bear), *K'ucumatz* [Gucmatz], the heart of the Lake, the heart of the sea, the master of the green (nine, painted) bowl, the master of the green dish shell, as it (the God) is named. Together with it, and handled in the legends, the great father who are called *Xpiyacoc* (and) *Xmucane*, the hidden ones find out and occur with their assistance (actually, The defender, the Helper), twice grandmother, twice grandfather, as it was mentioned in the Quiché language....

Schultze-Jena translated as:

"Damit also warden wir uns befassen: wie Das, was verborgen war, offensichtlich, enrhüllt und kundgegeben wurde, wie es hell wurde durch die Erabauerin und der Shöpfer, durch die Gebärerin und den Söhne-Zeuger, wie ihre Namen lauten. Von Hunahpu-Beutelratte und Hunahpu-Heulwolf, vom weißen großen Rüssel-bären, von der Meister des grünen Tellers, vom Meister der grünen Schale soll die Rede sein.

Auch wird erzählt, auch wird gekündet von jener Greisin und jenem Greis, deren Namen Xpiyacoc und Xniucane sind: Beschirmer und Verberger, doppelt ehrwürdige Greisin, doppelt ehrwürdiger Greis, wie sie in den Sagen der Quiché genannt werden,..."[59]

Therewith, therefore we were concerned: like that, which was hidden obviously, unveiled and announced how it became light by the builder and the creator, by the parturitior and the son-locator, as their names read. The speech should be of Hunahpu-bag rat and Hunahpu-howl wolf, of the wise big trunk-bear, of the master of the green plate, and of the master of the green shell,

Also one tells, also told of that aged woman and that old man, whose names are Xpiyacoc and Xmucane: protector and hider, double venerable old

---

[59] Cited from Shultze-Jena 1972:3.

man, double venerable old man as they are named in the legends of the Quiche, ...

A popular English translation (though the original was in Spanish) of Adrian Recinos is:

> "*And here we shall set forth the revelation, the declaration, and the narration of all that was hidden, the revelation by Tzacol, Bitol, Alom, Qaholm, who are called Hunahpú-Vuch, Hunahpú-Utiú, Zaqui-Nimá-Tziís, Tepeu, Gucumatz, u Qux cho, u Qux Paló, Ah Raxá Lac, Ah Raxá Tzel, as they were called. And [at the same time] the declaration, the combined narration of Grandmother and the Grandfather, whose names are Xpiyacoc, and Xmucané, helpers and protectors, twice grandmother, twice grandfather, so called in the Quiché chronicles*"[60]

After Recinos, the interest in the translation of this manuscript became to restore the conceptual element of the text.

Perhaps, the most popular translator of the *Popol Vuh* in the English speaking world, Dennis Tedlock, rendered the above K'iche text as follows:

> "*And here we shall take up the demonstration, revelation, and account of how things were put in shadow and brought to light by the Maker, Modeler, named Bearer, Begetter, Hunahpu Possum, Hunahpu Coyote, Great White Peccary, Coati, Sovereign Plumed Serpent, Herat of the Lake, Heart of the Sea, plate shaper, bowl shaper, as they are called, also named, also described as the midwife, matchmaker named Xpiyacoc, Xmucane, defender, protector, twice a midwife, twice a matchmaker, as it is said in the words of Quiché.*"[61]

The most recent English translation of the *Popol Vuh* published by Allen J. Christenson is:

> "*Here we shall gather the manifestation, the declaration, the account of the sowing and the dawning by the Framer and the Shaper, She Who Has Borne Children and He Who Has Begotten Sons, as they are called; along with Hunahpu Possum and Hunahpu Coyote, Great White Peccary and Coati, Sovereign and Quetzal Serpent, Heart of Lake and Heart of Sea, Creator of the Green Earth and Creator of the Blue Sky, as they are called. These collectively are evoked and given expression as the Midwife, and the*

---

[60] Cited from Recinos 1950:78-9. See *ibid.*, note 3, 4.
[61] Cited from Tedlock 1996:63.

> *Patriarch whose names are Xpiyacoc and Xmucane, the protector and the Shelterer, Twice Midwife and Twice Patriarch, as they are called in Quiche traditions.*[62]

Only Christenson renders *euaxibal* (hidden, secret or darkness?) as a misspelling of *auaxibal* (sowing). In order to justify his analysis, he argues that there is a parallelism concept of the pair of 'dawning' and 'sowing' in the *Popol Vuh*.[63] He may be correct. Yet, it may be said that it is a result of over-emphasis in his belief that the *Popol Vuh*'s structure is parallelistic. Although parallelism constitutes the rhythm of the manuscript and the Maya languages in general, it is a matter of structure, and it does not reflect the Maya concept. It must be noted that the concept of the *Popol Vuh* is written in the positive and negative dualism rule. If we consider this issue from a dualism perspective, his rendering becomes very peculiar as a pagan text. A coupling of darkness and dawning is a quite common concept in paganism. In fact, the two translations made by the Maya of twentieth century, which are discussed in this research, try emphasizing this concept as an essential notion of the Maya. Therefore, while Christenson's careful analysis of the original text must be valued, if my view is correct, it is a possibility that he denied the fundamental concept of the *Popol Vuh*.

I do not appreciate some translators who replaced the name of four K'iche deities; *Tzacol, Bitol, Alom* and *Gaholm* with their interpretation of K'iche language. In my opinion, their proper names should be retained in the main text. If they like to give readers their understanding of the original meaning of terms used to refer to those gods, putting them into footnote or brackets is more acceptable. For example, *Amaterasuominokami* (天照大神 often written as *Amaterasu*)[64] a Japanese deity found in the Japanese sacred texts, such as the *Kojiki*, can be translated as 'Heaven-Shining-Great-God = The Great (or august) God who shines the Heaven,' yet the fact is that our sacred texts have not been translated into

---

[62] Cited from Christenson 2003:60-3.
[63] Christenson 2003:60, note 9. This rendering was first proposed by Chávez (1979:1-1a), though Chávez does not provide any reason to support his rendering.
[64] The ruling deity of and the sun god of Japanese Shinto. This deity is female.

English in that way. I believe the proper name of gods should be retained as follows:

> "*At this time His Augustness the Male-Who-Invites greatly rejoiced, saying: "I, begetting child after child, have at my final begetting gotten three illustrious children." With which words, at once jinglingly taking off and shaking the jewel-string forming his august necklace, be bestowed it on Amaterasu, the Heaven-Shining-Great-August deity. saying: "Do Thine Augustness rule the Plain-of-High-Heaven [=Takamagahara=高天原]." With this charge he bestowed it on her.*"[65]

However, since brackets were not used in the above translation, it must be mentioned that this translation of *Amaterasuominokami* as "*Amaterasu, the Heaven-Shining-Great-August deity*" gives us an impression that is somehow repetitive and thus it changes the original rhythm of the *Kojiki*. Also, the name of the Japanese heaven, *Takamagahara*, is not retained so that the above translation becomes peculiar to the Japanese.

As to the translation of the *Popol Vuh*, my preferred translation is Recinos. Up to this point, translations of non-Maya scholars have been referred to. Let us compare those with two works presented by K'iche and Kaqchikel scholars.

Cháves translates;

> "*De manera que aquí nos ponemos a enseñarlo, a revelarlo, es decir, a relatarlo, lo dejado*[66] *e iluminado por el Arquitecto, Formador, Creado, Varón creado, cuyo nombres: Un cazador de Tacuatzin, Un Cazador de Lobo, verdaderos cantores; venidos del infinito, ocultador de serpiente; espíritu de lago y mar; verdaderos superiores, hijos mayores se decía; compañero de plática y comentario de la partera, abuelo que se llamaba Shpiyakok, Shmukané; armador y trabajador; dos veces partera, dos veces abuelo se decía en lengua ki-che.*"[67]
> (So that here let us begin to teach it, to reveal it, that is to say, to relate it, the [things] left and illuminated by the Architect, Former, Created one, created great man, whose names are; A hunter of *Tacuatzin*, A Hunter of Wolf, true cantors; came from the infinite, hider of snake; spirit of the lake

---

[65] The *Kojiki* cited from a translation published by B.H. Chamberlain of 1882.

[66] Chávez (1979:1) renders *euaxibal* (secret or darkness?) in the original as *vuaxibal* → *u aweshbal* and translated as *su cultivado* (his cultivated [land]) in his draft translation published with his final translation (*ibid.*:1a).

[67] Chávez 1979:1a, 1994:31.

and the sea; true superiors, older children, as it was said; companion of sermon and comment from the midwife and grandfather who were called *Shpiyakok, Shmukane*; constructor and worker; twice midwife, twice grandfather, as it was said in the K'iche language.)

In the above citation, Chávez is somewhat in denial of the dualism of darkness and light, in spite of the fact that he stressed it as an important part of Maya dualism and claimed to restore the Maya dualism found in the *Popol Vuh*.[68] This 'self contradiction' is another reason why some concluded his actual intention in publishing his translation was to deny Maya dualism.[69] Also, he does not provide an explanation for his rendering of *ah raxa lac* [the lord of green plate] and *ah raxa tzel* [the lord of green bowl] as 'true superiors, older children.'[70] This subjective rendering of Chávez is the chief reason why his translation is ignored by formal academia.

The following is a citation from the translation made by two Kaqchikel Maya. This translation is also subjective:

"*Aquí tomaremos la verdad para exponerla y mostrarla y relatar sin velos su esencia que está en oculto, y que viene en la luz reveladora por obra de Tzacol: la mente creadora universal, y Bitol: la mente formadora universal, que son Alom: el padre y la madre supremos del Universo, la raíz masculina y femenina del Cosmos, y Cajolom: el hijo unigénito engendrador de vida del Universo. Así son los nombres del las fuerza divinas del Universo. Uno solo es el origen de la existencia del a vida: Jun Ahpú Vuch. Una sola es su trayectoria, desde hoy, para siempre: Hun Ahpú Utiú. Así son las cualidades del a Gran Luz Blanca de la Verdad: Zaquí Nimá Tzij. Luz que ha venido del a oscuridad del a poderosa vacuidad del a esfera del espacio vació: Tepeu Cucumatz – Matriz gestante de toda forma de vida del Universo-, que es la que está en la oscuridad profunda impenetrable del fondo del Corazón del Lago U:[sic] Cux Chó, y del fondo del Corazón del Mar: U Cux Paló, en las profundidades insondables de su prístino origen: Aj Raxá Lac. Del espacio negro vacío que llena la esfera del Universo salió la luz; ese oscuridad es la Madre, origen de la Luz: Aj Raxá Tzel. Así cuenta la tradición oral, que se trasmite de padres a hijos. Y la cual narra la Historia de la Creación dictada por aquellos que se llaman Iyom: La Abuela Superma del Universo, Mamom: El Abuelo Supremo del Universo, llamados también Ixpiyacoc: El Espíritu de Vida que viene del vacío de la esfera del Universo,*

---

[68] Chávez 1979:2 note 2.
[69] Yamase 2005b, Sanematu 2003.
[70] He transcribed them as *ah raxa la, ah raxa tzel*.(Chávez 1979:1)

Ixmucané: El Espíritu de vida que viene en oculto a tomar forma. Ellos están presentes ocultos en todas partes del Universo: Matzanel Chuquenel. Dos Veces Abuela Suprema del Universo: Camul Iyom. Dos veces Abuelo del Universo: Camul Mamom. Ellos pensaron y platicaron en lo oculto insondable e impenetrable de su morada, la Idea y la Concepción de la realidad del Árbol de la Vida: Quiché[71]

(Here, we will take the truth to expose it and to show it and to relate without veils, its essence is hidden, and comes in revealing light by work of *Tzacol*: the universal creative mind, and *Bitol*: the universal maker mind, who are *Alom*: the supreme father and the mother of the Universe, the masculine and feminine root of the Cosmos, and *Cajolom*: the only begotten son, breeder of the life of the Universe. So, these are the names of the divine forces of the Universe. A single is the origin of the existence of the life: *Hun Ahpú Vuch*. A single is his trajectory, from today, for always: *Hun Ahpú Utiú*. Thus they are the qualities of the Great White Light of the Truth: *Zaquí Nimá Tzij* Light that has come from the dark of the powerful vacuity of the sphere of the drained space: *Tepeu Cucumatz* – matrix expectant mother of all forms of life of the Universe, that is one who is in dark deep impenetrable of the nature of the Heart of the Lake *U Cux Chó* and of the nature of the Heart of the Sea: *U Cux Paló* in the bottomless depths of his perfect origin *Aj Raxá Lac,* from the empty black space that fills the sphere of the Universe, the light left ; that dark is the Mother, origin of the Light: *Aj Raxá Tzel*. So, the oral tradition tells, which is trasmited from parents to children, and which narrates the History of the dictated Creation by whom they are called *Iyom*, Supreme Grandmothers of the Universe, *Mamom*, the Supreme Grandfathers of the Universe, also are called *Ixpiyacoc*, the Spirit of Life that comes from the emptiness of the sphere of the Universe, *Ixmucané*, the Spirit of life that comes in hidden to take shape. They are hidden present in all parts of the Universe: *Matzanel Chuquenel* Two Times Supreme Grandmother of the Universe: *Camul Iyom* Two times Grandfathers of the Universe: *Camul Mamom*. They thought and practiced in hidden secret and impenetrable of its dwelling, the Idea and the Conception of the reality of Tree of the Life: Quiché)

In the above translation, Kaqchikel translators attempted to emphasise the duality (darkness is the mother of light) of the Maya cosmos. In terms of restoring the dualistic nature of the K'iche Maya language, it may be said that they did a good job with a 'free' translation though the accuracy of their interpretations, such as 'the *Popol Vuh* = the Tree of Life' remain controversial. While it is acceptable, the problem is that their over-intervention in the original text is frequently found. For example, regarding a part of the *Popol Vuh* where the original K'iche text

[71] Cited from León Valés et al. 1985:13.

simply says, *ah raxa tzel* [the lord of green bowl] *chuqhaxic* (as it was said), they translated as: 'So, the oral tradition tells, which is transmitted from parents to children.' Adding numerous interpretations of their own of the terms and the concepts of the *Popol Vuh* without using brackets to the main text is against the basic rules of translation.

By comparing the original K'iche text with various translations, a general trend among them may be clarified.

Maya scholars' works may simply be called a free translation, and those of the Westerners 'an academic work.' As Tedlock obviously relied more on the interpretations of the K'iche Maya shamans (especially of Andrés Xiloj) than other culturally Western minded people, his translation may be placed between Seler and Chávez. Nevertheless, it is evident that Tedlock attempted to be faithful to the original text. Although every translator produced a different result, it can be pointed out that while the academically educated translators tend to restore the exact meaning of the text with their knowledge of Maya languages, Maya scholars tend to restore their own Maya vision of the Creation based on their lifetime experience, which they believed to be true, by using the text of the *Popol Vuh*. Yet academic researchers also relied on information obtained from the living Maya in order to comprehend the meaning of the *Popol Vuh*.

Let us compare the next part of the *Popol Vuh*. As to the so-called Creation Myth in the *Popol Vuh*, it has often been argued that the opening part of this manuscript tells us the narrative of world creation. However, an important issue has not seriously been argued. That is, whether the Maya deities created the world or the world gave birth to them. Unlike the Christian God, Maya deities are not the Lords of Nature. They are, rather, an essence and partner of supernatural and natural phenomena (= Nature). If so, it is likely that from the beginning the world had already existed. If not, K'iche Maya Gods could not exist. Of course, in a later part of the *Popol Vuh*, there is a story of the Creation of the World, and an analysis of the opening part of this text will be made.

The first part of the *Popol Vuh*, which I have quoted with several translations, tells us there are at least a Lake and a Sea at the beginning of the world. If a lake existed at the beginning, the land must have existed together with that lake. Therefore, although the precise meanings of *ah raxa lac* [the lord of green plate] and *ah raxa tzel* [the lord of green bowl] cannot be determined, at least, they seem to be a pair. I think that these may refer to a primitive idea of the universe = the sky and the earth, as Christenson argues.[72]

Yet the *Popol Vuh* actually says that the surface of the earth was not visible at first. On this point, Carlos Rolando de León Valdós and Francisco Lopez Peren try to understand the relationships between *ah raxa lac* [the lord of green plate] and *ah raxa tzel* [the lord of green bowl] as that of darkness and light. That is, the relation between the night and day.[73] Contrary to non-Maya scholars who tend to render this part as a type of parallelism, they translated 'the Light is the mother of the Darkness' in order to express the relationships between them mentioned in the *Popol Vuh* as a product of interactive dualism of the Maya.

Another comparison should be made. There is the following text in the *Popol Vuh*:

> *ARE V TZIHOXIC, VAE cacatzinin-oc, cacachamam-oc, catzinonic, cacazilanic, cacalolinic, catolona puch v pa cah.*
>
> *Vae cute nabe tzih, nabe vchan: ma habi-oe hun vinac, hun chicop, tziquin, car, tap, che, abah, hul, zivan, quim, quichelah, - xa vtuquel cah golic.*
>
> *maui calah v vach vleu, xa vtuquel remanic palo v pa cah, ronohel. ma habi naquila camolobic, cacotzobic, hun la cazilobic, camal caban tah, cacotz caban tah pa cah : xma go-vi naquila golic, yacalic. xa remanic ha, xa lianic palo, xa vínquel remanic, xma go-vi naquíla lo golic.*
>
> *xa cachamanic, catzininic chi queεum, chi aεab.*
>
> *xa vtuquel ri tzacol, bitol, tepeu, gucumatz, e alom, e gaholom yo pa ha zactetoh. e go-vi, e mucutal pa cuc, pa raxon: are v binaam-vi > ri gucumatz. < e nimac etamanel, e nimac ahnaoh chi qui goheic.*
>
> *quehe cuí xax go-vi ri cah, go nai puch > v gux cah <, are v bi ri cabauil, chughaxic.*[74]

---

[72] Christenson 2003:62 note 22.
[73] León Valés et al. 1985:13.
[74] Cited from Schultze-Jena 1972:4.

Word by word translation should be;

ARE (There is) *V TZIHOXIC* (account, narration, story), *VAE* (*va* = this, *e*=suggesting plural =these) *ca ca tzinin-oc* (all are in suspect), *ca ca chamam-oc* (are in calm), *ca tzinonic* (are silent), *ca ca zilanic* (are immobile), *ca ca lolinic* (are peaceful), *ca tolona puch* (all empty and) *v pa* (in) *cah* (Sky).

Vae (*va* = this, *e*=suggesting plural =these.) *cute* (are) *nabe* (first) *tzih* (word = a story), *nabe* (first) *vchan* (practice): *ma* (no) *habi-oe* (there is) *hun* (one) *vinac* (people), *hun* (one) *chicop* (animal), *tziquin* (bird), *car* (fish), *tap* (crab), *che* (tree), *abah* (stone), *hul* (hole, grave), *zivan* (ravine), *quim* (grass), *quichelah* (forest), - *xa* (only) *vtuquel* (only) *cah* (sky) *golic* (exist).

maui (no) *calah* (is displayed) *v* (its) *vach* (face) *vleu* (land), *xa* (but or only) *vtuquel* (only) *remanic* (peaceful) *palo* (sea) *v pa* (in) *cah* (sky), *ronohel* (all) .

ma (no) *habi* (there is) *naquila* (nothing) *ca* (is) *molobic* (together), *cacotzobic* (is noisy), *hun* (one) *la cazilobic*(is stirred), *camal* (is invisible) *caban tah* (is made), *cacotz* (is anxious) *caban tah* (is made) *pa* (in) *cah* (sky): *xma* (no) *go-vi* (there is) *naquila* (nothing) *golic* (exist), *yacalic* (on foot = standing = living and moving thing). *Xa* (only) *remanic* (silent, peaceful) *ha* (water), *xa* (only) *lianic* (silent) *palo* (sea), *xa* (only or but) *vinquel* (only) *remanic* (silence, peaceful), *xma* (no) *go-vi* (there is) *naquila* (nothing) *lo golic* (exist).

xa (only) *cachamanic* (is calm), *catzininic* (is silent) *chi* (in) *queεum* (dark), *chi* (in) *aεab* (night).

xa (only) *vtuquel* (only) *ri tzacol* (Tzacol), *bitol* (Bitol), *tepeu* (Tepeu), gucumatz (Gucumatz), *e alom* (Alom), *e gaholom* (Gaholm) *go* (there is) *pa ha* (water) *zactetoh* (like diffuse light). *E* (this word '*e*' signifies that the following are plural) *go-vi* (there are), *e mucutal* (wrapped, enveloped) *pa* (in) *cuc* (feather), *pa* (in) *raxon* (intense green. In this case, *Cotinga*, a bird with blue wings. This does not mean that they are in a Cotinga bird, but in its feathers): *are* (they) *v binaam-vi* (are named)> *ri gucumatz* (Gucumatz). < *e nimac* (great) *etamanel* (experts), *e nimac* (great) *ahnaoh* (sages).

chi (for, by) *qui* (that) *go-heic* (was) *quehe cui* (as well as) *xax* (certainly) *go-vi* (there is) *ri cah* (sky), *go* (there is) *nai puch* (also) > *v gux* (Heart, spirit or Deity) *cah* (sky) <, *are* (This is) *v bi* (his name) *ri cabauil* (K'abawil), *chughaxic* (as it is said).

Some translators, such as Dennis Tedlock and Allen J. Christenson render the above text by using the present tense, as the text is written in the present tense. Yet, since the above text apparently suggests the incident is in the past, I will follow the majority of the previous translators and use the past tense.

The draft translation is:

There is this story, all were in suspect, calm, silent, immobile, and empty in the Sky.

These are the first stories and the first practice: There was no single people, no single animal, bird, fish, crab, tree, stone, grave, ravine, grass, and forest. Only the sky existed.

The face of land was not displayed, but only peaceful sea in the sky, all. There was nothing. Nothing was made together. Nothing made noise, nothing was stirred, nothing was visible, nothing made concerned in the sky: No moving things existed. There was only peaceful water, only the silent sea, There was only silence and peacefulness. There existed nothing.

There was only calm, silent in dark at night.

There were only *Tzacol, Bitol, Tepeu, Gucumatz, Alom*, and *Gaholm*. There was water like diffuse light. They were wrapped in feather [perhaps of *Quetzal*], in feather of *Cotinga*: they are called *Gucumatz*, who are great experts of knowlege, great sages.

As well as there was certainly the sky, there was also the Heart of the sky. This is his name of *K'abawil*, as it was said.

Even in this small part of the *Popol Vuh*, there are numerous points to be argued. However, on this occasion, only issue of *cabauil* (*K'abawil*) as it appears in the text will be discussed. Identifying the supreme deity within the *Popol Vuh* is not always easy. Yet, among some K'iche Maya, it is believed that *K'abawil*, mentioned in the above cited part of the *Popol Vuh,* is the supreme deity of the K'iche Maya. It is also now used to refer to the Maya dualism concept. The detail of *K'abawil* within the *Popol Vuh* is little known, however, because the text simply refers to it as the Heart of the Sky. Since another Heart of the Sky, *Huracan* is mentioned in following part of the *Popol Vuh* and it says that there are other three hearts of the Sky (*Caculha Huracan, Chipa-Caculha* and *Raxa-Caculha* [*Caculha* =Thunderbolt]), it is possibly considered that *K'abawil* is actually one of the Hearts of the Sky. Because of this problem, it must be remembered that it is not easy to assume *K'abawil* as the supreme deity of the K'iche Maya, though it will be treated as such in this research.[75]

Let us compare a part of the latest (though there may be a new English one at the time of publication of this book) translation:

---

[75] Tedlock (1996:222-3 note 65) argues as a possibility of *K'abawil* mentioned in this part of the *Popol Vuh* as an allusion to Christian teaching.

"This is account these things. Still be it silent. Still be it placid, it is silent, still it is calm, still it is hushed, be it empty as well its womb sky. THESE, then, are the first words, the first speech. There is not yet one person, one animal, bird, fish, crab, tree, rock, hollow, canyon, meadow, or forest. All alone the sky exists. The face of the earth has not yet appeared. Alone lies the expanse of the sea, along with the womb of all the sky. There is not yet anything gathered together. All is at rest. Nothing stirs. All is languid, at rest in the sky. There is not yet anything standing erect. Only the expanse of the water, only the tranquil sea lies alone. There is not yet anything that might exist. All lies placid and silent in the darkness, in the night.

All alone are the Framer and the Shaper, Sovereign and Quetzal Serpent, They Who Have Borne Children and They Who Have Begotten Sons. Luminous they are in the water, wrapped in quetzal feathers and cotinga feathers. Thus they are called Quetzal Serpent. In their essence, they are great sages, great possessors of knowledge. Thus surely there is the sky. There is also Heart of Sky, which is said to be the name of the god."[76]

Christenson translated the term, *K'abawil* simply as god, because he considers it a general concept of god in the *Popol Vuh*.[77] However, as he accepts, *K'abawil* was often used as terminology to refer to the Christian Lord by the early colonial Dominicans[78], which suggests that *K'abawil* was used to refer to a specific high ranked god. Therefore, there is no reason to translate *K'abawil* merely as *Kux* (Heart=God). In terms of language, nevertheless, his translation is preferable. On the contrary, as will be seen, the Maya translators attempted to define *K'abawil* as the supreme deity.

Now, the translation by two Kaqchikel Maya will be cited:

"7) Y esta es la narración de cómo todo estaba en suspenso, cómo todoestaba en calma, en silencio absoluto, inmóvil, extendido, todoestaba desocupado, no existía nada bajo la inmensidad del vacío del Cielo.
8) Aquí aparece la primera palabra, el verbo, el primer sonido de la primera vocalización. No había ninguna gente, ni ningún animal, ya fuesen pájaros, peces o cangrejos, tampoco había ni un árbol, ni piedras, ni hoyos, ni barrancos, ni pajonales, ni selvas, solamente existía el vacío oscuro de la vacuidad del Cielo.

---

[76] cited from Christenson 2004:16-7, also see Christenson 2002:67-9.
[77] Christenson 2002:9 note 57. *Kawil* was commonly used to refer to god in the classic Maya lowland. See also Tedlock 1996:222-3 note 65. This rendering is commonly seen in the works by non-Maya scholars, such as Recinos (1950:82), Schultze-Jena (1972:5).
[78] Christenson 2002:9.

9) No se conocía la superficie de la Tierra, solamente estaba el mar con sus aguas tendidas, reposadas, en calma absoluta, bajo la inmensidad oscura del vacío de la bóveda del Cielo.
10) No había nada que estuviese junto, agrupado, reunido, o algo que se moviese. No había nada que hiciera ruido, o que produjera el más leve roce o fricción. Había ausencia total de movimiento en el Cielo.
11) No había ninguna fuerza que manifestara su existencia, solamente el agua permanecía reposada, quieta, en tranquilidad absoluta. Solamente estaban las aguas apacibles del mar existiendo en quietud. No hab ia todavía ninguna manifestación de vida. Todoestaba en calma, sumido en el profundo silencio de la oscuridad de la noche.
12) Solamente existía la mente creadora universal: Tzacol, y la mente constructora universal: Bitol, contenidos dentro de la potentísima vacuidad oscura de la Esfera del espacio vacío: Tepeu Cucumatz. Ellos son El Padre Supremo y la Madre Suprema, raíz masculina y raíz femenina del Universo: Alom; y El Hijo Unigénito Engendrador de Vida del Universo: Cajolom.
Aquellos dioses se movían sobre la superficie de las aguas rodeados de una luz difusa.
13) Allí estaban los dioses invisibles dentro de la poderosísima vacuidad del espacio vacío de la Esfera: Cucumatz, ese es el nombre del poderoso espacio vacío oscuro que es la matriz gestante formadora de toda forma de vida del Universo. Allí permanecen los dioses ocultos en el interior de la vacuidad del espacio, aquellos grandes sabios: Nimac Etamanel, grandes pensadores de existencia todopoderosa: Nimac Ajnaoj Chi Qui Cojeic. Ellos tres siempre existen allí en el espacio vacio del Cielo, ellos son El Corazón del Cielo: U Cux Caj, y éste es su nombre: Cabahuil, el nombre del Dios Absoluto."[79]

(7) And this is the narration of how all was in suspense, how all was in calm, in motionlessness, in absolute silence, extended, all was idle, nothing existed under the immensity of the empty one of the Sky.
(8) Here, the first word, the verb, the first sound of the first vocalization appears. There was neither any people, nor animal, nor already birds, nor fish nor crabs. There was neither a tree, nor stones, nor pits, nor ravines, nor *pajonales* (=broomsedges), nor forests. Only the empty darkness of the vacuity of the Sky existed.
(9) The surface of the Land was not known. There was only the sea with its laid out water which rested, in absolute calm, under the dark immensity of the emptiness of the vault of the Sky.
(10) There was nothing that was [gotten] together, grouped, reunited, or something to move by itself. There was nothing that made noise, or that produced the lightest graze or friction. There was total absence of movement in the Sky.
(11) There was no power that declared its existence. Only the water remained at rest, quiet, in absolute tranquility. There was only the peaceful water of the sea existing in stillness. There was still not any presentation of life. All was in calm, plunged in the deep silence of the darkness at night.

---

[79] Cited from León Valés et al. 1985:14-5.

341

(12) Only the universal creative mind existed: *Tzacol*, and the universal construction mind: *Bitol*, contents inside the most powerful dark vacuity of the Sphere of the empty space: *Tepeu Cucumatz*. They are the Supreme Father and the Supreme Mother, male root and female root of the Universe: *Alom*; and the Unique[80] Son Engenderer of Life of the Universe: *Cajolom*. Those Gods moved on the surface of the water surrounded by a diffuse light. (13) There were the invisible gods inside the power system vacuity of the empty space of the Sphere: *Cucumatz*, that is the name of the powerful dark empty space which is the original expectant mother former at any rate of life of the Universe. The hidden Gods remain there in the interior of the vacuity of the space, those great sages: *Nimac Etamanel*, great thinkers of omnipotent existence: *Nimac Ajnaoj Chi Qui Cojeic*. They three always exist there in the empty space of the Sky, they are The Heart of the Sky: OR *Cux Caj*, and this is his name: *Cabahuil*, the name of the Absolute God.)

Their translation uses a Christian terminology, *Unigénito*. This suggests the translators' knowledge of the *Bible* as Christian. However, except for this, their translation does not reflect any Christian concept. Rather, although the above translation contains their own biased view, they try restoring the duality of the Maya myth, especially that of the dark and the light. Compared with the above, translations of non-Maya people seem not to make much effort to restore that concept as a fundamental or essential one. Although some may consider that the duality between the dark and the light is only based on the translators' personal subjective expertise of Kaqchikel Maya traditions, the fact is that this is often regarded as an important concept of Maya dualism, as in the case of Adrián I. Chávez.

Lastly, let us look at the translation of Adrián I. Chávez:

"*Esta primera palabra, es la primera expresión; no había ni una gente ni animal, pájaro, pez, cangrejo, árbol, piedra, hoyo, barranco, pajón, bosque; solamente estaba el cielo.*

No se veía tierra en ninguna parte, solamente el mar estaba represado; el cielo, todo quieto; nada había de eso que es cosa, todo era absorción, nada se movía; recién acabábase de hacer el cielo, tampoco había algo levantado. Solamente el agua estaba represada, el mar estaba tendido, represado.

---

[80] Unique is a translation of *Unigénito*. This is a special term in Spanish to refer to Jesus Christ, such as '*the only Son of God, Jesus Christ.*' Although there are several interptations of *Unigénito* in Spanish, *único* (unique) is the most common).

No había eso que es objeto, todo era formation, todo vibraba en la
oscuridad, en la noche.
   Solamente El Arquitecto, El Formador, El Infinito, El Oculta Serpiente,
El Creado, El Varón Creado estaban en el agua despejada, ahí estaban,
estaban ocultos entre el limo, entre el verdor, de lo cual vino el nombre de
Ocultador de Serpiente, grandes sabios, grandes pensadores se originaron.
Así es pues que el cielo estaba etéreo, pero estaba el espíritu del cielo, he
aquí su nombre:---DobleMirada le dicen."[81]
   (This first word, is the first expression; there was neither a people nor an
animal, bird, fish, crab, tree, stone, pit, ravine, pajón (=broomsedge), and
forest; There was only the sky. The land was seen nowhere, only the sea was
dammed; the sky, all quiet; there was nothing, all was absorption, nothing
moved; it was just finished to make the sky, also there was not something
raised. Only the water was dammed. The sea was lying down, and dammed.
   There was nothing that is [in form of] object, all was formation, all vibrated
in the darkness, in the night.
   Only The Architect, The Former, The Infinite, The Hidden Snake, The
Created One, The Created Male, they were in the cleared water, they were
there, they were hidden among the slime, among the greenness, from which
the name of hider of Snake came, great wise, great thinkers were originated.
Thus is therefore that the sky was ethereal, but was the spirit of the sky, I
have here his name: it was said, **Double Looks**)

   It is noted that *K'abawil*, the Heart of the Sky, is translated as Double Looks in
his translation. Like the translation of two Kaqchikel Maya, Chávez apparently
considers *K'abawil*, mentioned in the above cited text, the supreme divinity. As I
have discussed before, although his interpretation of the Hero Twins as a single
deity with two personalities (=heads) is often taken as evidence of his denial of
dualism, the belief of Chávez is that the essential concept of the K'iche Maya
culture is represented by dualism.

   According to Chávez, *K'abawil* signifies; *"mira de noche y de día; cerca y en*
el Infinito (View of night and of day; close and in infinity)."[82] In this case,
although Chávez interprets *K'abawil* as the heart of the Sky, it is difficult to know
whether he considers *K'abawil* a self-existence like the Lord of the Heaven, or a
symbolic divine conceptual phenomenon generated from interaction between two
different elements such as *Tao* of Taoism or the *Supreme Ultimate* of
Neo-Confucianism. I do not know whether Chávez had access to Chinese Classics.

---
[81] Cited from Chávez 1979:2a.

343

Perhaps, in his age of Guatemala, Chinese Classics were little known so that he, as a Catholic K'iche Maya, was unlikely to read any of them. Therefore, it may be said that his concept of *K'abawil* was likely generated without a bias toward Chinese dualism.

If we consider an issue of his translation, the same concept as his denial of the Hero Twins (*Hunahpu* and *Xbalanque*) as two deities may be proposed. As I have frequently pointed out, Hero Twins is treated as a single deity with two personalities by Chávez. If he applied this concept to the nature of the supreme divinity of the Maya which he believes to be *K'abawil*, his concept of *K'abawil* may be that it is a self-existing deity with dual identities. Therefore, it is suggested that his view of *K'abawil* is different from *Tao* and the *Supreme Ultimate*, and thus *K'abawil* is a dual identity in his own view.

There is no solid evidence that the *K'abawil* mentioned in the *Popol Vuh* is the highest divinity of the K'iche Maya according to Chávez, though regarding it as such is very much possible. There is no guarantee that the contemporary K'iche Maya dualism is the same as that of the sixteenth century's K'iche Maya. The *K'abawil* mentioned in the *Popol Vuh* may not have been an entity with a dualistic nature but one part of a dualism (or one part of a quad-ism as the *Popol Vuh* refers to the four hearts of the Sky).

In terms of the 'academic,' non-Maya researchers' works have a great advantage, because they attempt translation of the original text as faithfully as possible, though some subjective renderings exist. On the other hand, Maya translators' works are often quite free translations. Nevertheless, these 'academic' translations are not always appreciated by the living Maya. The reason may simply be ascribed to a kind of Maya 'nationalism' so that Chávez's translation, a work of a native K'iche Maya, is highly valued among a certain section of the K'iche Maya.

---

[82] Cited from Chávez 1979:2a note 1.

344

However, Maya conceptual philosophy reproduced in the 'academic' translations does not often match the religious and philosophical notions of contemporary Maya. That notion is dualism. As I have mentioned before, Dennis Tedlock provides us a fairly good summary of the dualism notion among the K'iche Maya.[83] In spite of this, his translation often lacks this perspective, at least in my view, and the context of the *Popol Vuh* is studied from a monotheistic view rather than with dualism in mind.

On this very point, the Maya translators of the twentieth century seem to believe that the context of the *Popol Vuh* must be coincident with the contemporary Maya conceptual world which they actually experience in Guatemala. Although hypothetical, this view may be applied to the case of the original author(s) of the surviving *Popol Vuh*. There is no evidence that the Pre-Columbian version of the *Popol Vuh* was a single source. There may have been several sources which the colonial K'iche Maya authors used to compose the surviving *Popol Vuh*, because the text tells us that the original one was already lost. In this case, there must have been a certain necessity to edit various sources in order to produce a single volume. How did they manage it? In the sixteenth century, not only the Maya but all scholars were usually very subjective. In this case, there may be the possibility that in the process of recomposing the *Popol Vuh*, the original authors of the current surviving *Popol Vuh* may have considered it necessary to make the concept within the *Popol Vuh* fit with the religious and other beliefs of their own age (=the colonial Guatemala in which Christianity had emerged). In other words, as a type of belief, 'knowledge of ancestors must be coincident with the situation of the current world and thus Christian beliefs and histories must also exist in Maya ancestors' records and knowledge.'[84] If this view is correct, neither is it always necessary to consider that the Christian influence

---

[83] Tedlock 1996:59.
[84] Ideology presented by Victoriano Alvarez a living K'iche Maya (edited by Sanematu 2003) is another example. Alvarez believes that the *Popol Vuh* contains evidence that the ancient Maya had discovered all wisdoms such as the heliocentric Copernican theory much earlier than any other people.

found in some colonial K'iche Maya texts is evidence of fabrication made by the Spaniards, nor is it a prudent way of hiding Maya religious traditions, nor is it unconscious confusion.

For example, a questionable reference to Carlos V as the best political authority of the world in the *Título de Yax* (in the *Popol Vuh*, *Nacxit* is mentioned instead of Carlos V) might be explained by this idea rather than by the traditional view among academics of 'confusion.' Through the fact (Carlos V=*Nacxit*) was confused, this may be evidence that the authors of the *Título de Yax* believed that the ancestors of the K'iche Maya had a contact with Europe well before the Spanish Conquest.

If this view is true and this theory can be applied to the *Popol Vuh*, future discussion on possible influence from Christianity within the *Popol Vuh* may be proposed differently. That is if any Christian influence exists in the text, it may be evidence that the authors of the *Popol Vuh* attempted to consider that the ancestors of the K'iche Maya had already known not only Maya traditions, but also Christianity well before the Europeans became Christians, because the origin of Christianity must be in the Maya area. In short, for the colonial Maya, the *Popol Vuh* must be a source of all wisdom (including Christianity) of the world.

Of course, this view is extremely hypothetical, but yet I think that it is worth considering.

Conclusion

Ye have heard that it hath been said, An eye for an eye, and a tooth for a tooth: But I say unto you, That ye resist not evil: but whosoever shall smite thee on thy right cheek, turn to him the other also. (Matthew 5:38-9, King James Bible)

Love your enemies, bless them that curse you, do good to them that hate you, and pray for them (Matthew 5:44, King James Bible)

"The sage has no invariable mind of his own; he makes the mind of the people his mind. To those who are good, I accept as good one. To those who are not good, I also regard them as good;--and in this way, the virtues are obtained. To those who are sincere, I am sincere; and to those who are not sincere, I am also sincere;--and in this way, the trust is obtained. The sage has in the world an appearance of indecision, and keeps his mind in a state of indifference to all. The people all keep their eyes and ears directed to him, and he deals with them all as his children."(Lao-tzu 580-500BC Chap.49, the English translation was corrected by me with the reference to the original text Lao-tzu 1997:113)

4:23 Or if his sin, wherein he hath sinned, come to his knowledge; he shall bring his offering, a kid of the goats, a male without blemish:
4:24 And he shall lay his hand upon the head of the goat, and kill it in the place where they kill the burnt offering before the LORD: it is a sin offering.
4:25 And the priest shall take of the blood of the sin offering with his finger, and put it upon the horns of the altar of burnt offering, and shall pour out his blood at the bottom of the altar of burnt offering. (Leviticus 4:23-25, in the *Old Testament*, cited from King James Bible)

This research has discussed anti-Christian movements and the process of its localization in Latin America and the Far East. In spite of strong hositility towards the Gospel often observed in those areas, it must be noted that it was treated as one component of the universe. For example, the *Book of Chilam Balam of Chumayel* of the Yucatec Maya, which is usually considered a book prudently hiding old Maya paganism from the Spaniards, actually treats both Maya religions in the past and Christianity in the present homogenously. Although this fact is often mistaken as parallelism by scholars, I have suggested that this phenomenon should be interpreted in terms of dualism between the past and present, so that a more accurate understanding of the religious concept within the *Chumayel* is possible. In fact, Peten Itza, the last Maya kingdom resisting Spanish rule employed this logic (Maya deities for current *Katún* time cycle and Christianity for the future *Katún*). Based on this example, a necessity of interpreting various 'mythic' religious concepts of the Maya by employing several types of dualism concepts, such as day and night, a religion as a part of the universe constituting the supreme deity or symbolic concept, and the negative and positive principles.

In order not assume that these examples from the Maya are extremely unusual concepts in the history of the human beings, various examples from other pagan dualism regions were discussed. The result is that in spite of their cultural, political and social background differences, some fundamental conceptual perceptions of Christianity are often quite similar.

For example, one significant conceptual difference between pagan and polytheistic = dualism and monotheism = monism is that the former tend to identify a religious system as a part of the cosmos while the latter sees it as the whole. This was observed not only in the *Chumayel* of the Maya but also in China of the eighteenth century, and in colonial Nahuatl of the sixteenth century. If one compares the view towards Christianity expressed by Don Carlos discussed in *Nahuatl Discovery* and by Yung-Cheng in *In Defence of Christianity* within this volume, it is noted that both views are based on a kind of dualism, "any religion is a necessary part of the universe even if it is undesirable for a Nation, and thus it is quite natural that each of them is different." The Chinese emperor, Yung-Cheng never questioned the authority of the Pope within Europe as the deputy of the Heaven appointed by an invisible mandate from it (though the supreme deputy of the Heaven in the world was the Chinese emperor), as he banned Christianity in China. The Maya of Peten Itza too, while there was some violent resistance, simply categorized Christianity as a religion of the future. Furthermore, it is noted that Manco Inca, the Inca emperor, considered the basic code of Christianity as a good one.

Also, when we consider 'religious hybridization or syncretism' in pagan regions, it is quite useful to distinguish dualistically anti-Western feeling from anti-Christianity. Due to hostility towards the Westerners, Christian converts in the Far East and Latin America often created another, but 'true,' Christianity for themselves. An attempt to generate a new version of Christianity for the Maya in colonial Chiapas was discussed. Although their attempt seems to be the creation of a new hybrid religion by using Christian female deities, perhaps due to their desire to treat both Maya and Christian deities homogenously, as I have discussed, their aim was not to challenge the authority of Jesus Christ but to gain control over ecclesial matters from the Spaniards by creating a 'proper' Gospel for the Maya. Although the colonial Spaniards saw this movement as a deception against the Lord, the colonial Maya actually opposed only the Spaniards.

This can be said to resemble the case of the Japanese of the twentieth century where some Japanese converts refused to deny the divinity of the Japanese emperor. They concluded the Gospel introduced from the West was a fabricated and distorted product of the US and British, and thus they had to reconstruct it in order to restore true Christianity by eliminating Western elements which opposed Japanese traditions. Works of Kiyo Yamane are a good example.

Of course, there are always exceptions. Even in dualistic cultures, there has always been a passion for eliminating an opponent entirely. The fact is that there were many Japanese Christians who strictly followed the original Gospel and refused any compromise with Japanese traditions. The same phenomenon can be observed in some Buddhist and Shintoist parties of Japan, and in some Maya. Therefore, it is not always proper to investigate religious and cultural phenomena found in pagan cultures from a perspective of dualism. However, it is true that employing this perspective often helps us to understand mythic concepts of pagan cultures, because this perspective has often been ignored by academics.

In this research, I have read several English classics in order to understand the basic concept of religion in the Western world. Most of them suggest that the final goal of the human is to attain a monotheism like Christianity, and monotheism is often regarded as evidence of an advanced civilization. Even a modest person, such as Robert Hamill Nassau wrote on a region of West African in 1904:

> *CIVILIZATION and religion do not necessarily move with equal pace. Whatever is really best in the ethics of civilization is derived from religion. If civilization falls backward, religion probably has already weakened or will also fall. The converse is not necessarily true. Religion may halt or even retrograde, while civilization steps on brilliantly, as it did in Greece with her Parthenon, and in Rome the while that religion added to the number of idols in the pantheon. Egypt, too, had her men learned in astronomy, who built splendid palaces and hundred-pillared Thebes the while they were worshipping Osiris.* [1]

Yet, he did not accept polytheism as a proper religion.

> *The native thought in regard to the origin of spirits is vague; necessarily so. An unwritten belief that is not based upon revelation from a superior source nor on an induction from actual experience and observation, but that is added to and varied by every individual's fancy, can be expressed in definite words only after inquiry among many as to their ideas on the subject.* [2]

In spite of the statement of the Second Vatican Council which claimed a change in its attitude towards various religions, this trend, polytheism as a primitive religion, has continued in Western civilization. In areas which were colonized by Christians or Muslims, moreover, people came to have the same notion. In those areas, consequently, pagan religions like the Maya examples have been regarded as a heathen. Given the relatively low social status of the Maya and

---

[1] Cited from Nassau 1904: Chap.3.
[2] cited from *ibid.*;Chap.IV.

other Native Americans, their religious traditions are unnecessarily considered very primitive and coarse, and they are often castigated by the Christian population even today. Under such social and political circumstances, it is not surprising that they are often forced to make their traditional beliefs resemble those of Christianity.

On the other hand, in the Far East, due to the strong surviving legacy of Taoism and Confucianism, dualism has been regarded as the ultimate goal of human civilization; and a negative view towards monotheism such as Christianity has developed. As I have discussed, it is still not unusual that the intolerant concept presented by monotheism is argued as evidence of the immaturity of that religion. In contrast to its experience in Latin America, Christianity is often forced to make considerable compromises with Asian pagan religions.

Because works on Maya religions have been written by Christian or Christian educated researchers since the re-discovery of the *Popol Vuh*, I felt it necessary to write a book from a pagan perspective. In order to produce a more balanced argument on the relationship between Maya religions and Christianity, I considered that arguing these two different concepts as a comparative study was useful. The result is this book.

The purpose of this book is of course not to provoke anti-Christian sentiment, but to find a reconciliation between Christianity and Maya, and other pagan religions. Although a mixed emotion towards Christianity still exits in Japan, hostility against it has dramatically decreased. In fact, Pope Paul II was well received when he visited Japan in the last century.

Although Christianity is often said to be monistic, it never denies the importance of dualism. The fact is that the *New Testament*, from which I cited *Matthew* above, always tells us of the necessity of tolerating those opposing Christianity and evil, while insisting that the value of monotheism is best. From my point of view, because Jesus Christ realized that both Monism and Dualism each had its own advantages and disadvantages, and noticed a potential danger of excessive passion for self-righteous good which was a hangover of the *Old Testament*, he might have felt it necessary to remind his flock of the reconciliation with the other (=dualism). Consequently, the *New Testament* frequently admonishes the flock for raising conflict with those who believe in other religions. It is suggested that the principle of Jesus Christ was to forgive and to reconciliate his non-Christian opponents but not to destroy or to regard other religions as his enemy. In fact, Jesus Christ never refers to the ancient Roman pagan people and the ancient Greek sages as 'devilish people.' As long as I read the Holy Scriptures, the prohibition of idols in the *New Testament* was created in order to defray the mind of people from materialistic life (materially corrupted mind (spirit)=Satan).

Later Saints, such as St. Augustine and St. Thomas also emphasized the reconciliation. The conflict between the Lord and Satan was later elaborated as propaganda to increase the size of the flock. Nevertheless, this point has virtually been ignored by Christians. Rather, the concept of Christian reconciliation is widely used for self-justification among Christians only. Also, in Islam, in spite of the fact that Jesus Christ is given a very unusual half-divine status in the *Koran* and his teaching is also accepted as that of *Allah*, some fundamentalist Muslims call Christians heathen. When *Allah* has told the Muslims not to provoke anti-Christian sentiment, will they then receive salvation?

In spite of the fact that the Roman Catholics of the twentieth century claimed the necessity to establish nonviolent relationships with all other religions, not all friars follow this policy, and Native American religions, especially in Latin America, are often considered evil.

On the other hand, for the Maya, although there has been an important reinstatement of Maya religion, it is also quite evident that they are also required to reform their religious traditions. Is there a K'iche Maya who thinks reviving human sacrifice to *Tohil* is a necessary part of Maya religions of today? Although Christians still accuse current K'iche Maya of practicing animal sacrifice, it must be noted that this practice is not always called evil in Christianity. In the old *Bible*, it is mentioned that Moses says that a sinner must bring a goat and offer it as animal sacrifice to the Lord to receive his pardon.[3] Also, among the Muslims, there is a festival of Bakri-Id in which animal sacrifices are made, in spite of the fact that Mohammad did not institute it. The practice of sacrifice of any kind of animal, including human beings, for Christianity was not originally sin, because Christianity is not essentially a different religion from Judaism but an adaption of it. The *New Testament* actually implies that because Jesus Christ sacrificed himself as the last human sacrifice for the whole human race, no further sacrifice of living things was necessary. Therefore, in this respect, although they can insist that the Maya practice of animal sacrifice is not proper and should be ended, it cannot be called a sin by Christianity. Simply, it is not required any more in Christianity. The Christians can simply persuade the K'iche shamans instead of calling them witches or wizards. The fact is that there is always a room for both sides to reconcile with each other.

This volume, as a result of comparative study of the indignation of Christianity and its conflicts with pagan religions in several pagan cultures, has a certain limitation as a comparative study, because data collected from one pagan culture cannot be considered evidence for another culture. For example, although the Maya were forced to be Christian under Spanish Christian domination, what I took as comparative examples from Japan, is from those who willingly became Christian under the Japanese Imperial pagan rule. Another is that Chinese Confucianism believes that a communication between humans and Heaven can only be done through *Li*, the law of nature (= in other words, they believe that natural law is the best religion in the world), while the Maya have traditionally communicated with their gods through shaman-priests. Therefore, their political and religious circumstance can be said to be totally different. Moreover, it might be true that I have over-focused on the impact of the dualism concept throughout this research. The fact is that there are not so many among the pagans who

---

[3] Leviticus 4:22-25, see Genesis 6-8.

353

systematically understand the logic of dualism. When we consider 'mysterious conceptual' issues found in pagan cultures, a perspective of dualism is often helpful.[4] The overall impact of dualism in pagan cultures cannot be overlooked when we consider issues of their relationships with Christianity. In order to accommodate their old religion within their faith, both the Maya and the Japanese Christians have used variations of dualism. Some of them are quite similar. As a result, this study has suggested that the Maya share lots of conceptual similarities with other dualistic cultures, and thus a perspective taken from other dualistic cultures can often assist us in understanding certain parts of the 'confused syncretic' of colonial Maya texts.

It was once said that the mixture of Maya religions (and other Native American ones) and Christianity was caused by the Maya's improper appreciation of the Gospel or their hidden resistance to Christianity. This biased view may have been created by the dialectic tradition developed in Europe (by ancient Greek sages). The dialectic method is to solve conflict between two differences by sorting out one single truth. On the other hand, dualism is to seek a harmony between them. A noted difference between both may be a perception of the Lord of Heaven of China and Europe. While the European regards the Supreme deity as absolute good and absent of evil, their view is considered an extremely dwarfed perception of the Supreme existence of the Chinese, because it is considered very permissive and thus never worries about a small difference. In other words, it was considered in China that the Supreme deity of Christianity was 'narrow-minded', while that of Confucianism (=dualism) was 'open-minded.'

This kind of conceptual difference has prevailed in non-Maya scholars whose majority have been Westerners, and blocked them from a proper understanding of the Maya concept. However, the dualism concept was once a Western one. In the case of Celsus, a neo-Platonist in the ancient Roman Empire, there is strong evidence that the ancient Europeans once had a principle concept which was quite

---

[4] In the case of Japan, due to a strong influence of Buddhism, the conception of life as

close to the *Supreme Ultimate*, the best recognized dualism concept of China. The world of dualism, therefore, is not totally alien in the West.

This study has revealed that Mayanized Christianity found in the colonial Maya texts is not essentially a product of their peculiar confusion, but of their reasoned mind. Although the difficulties of some of colonial Maya religious texts, such as the Books of Chilam Balam have been noted, this study suggests that it was not because the colonial Maya had a very complicated mythical religious notion, which is difficult to understand for outsiders, but because the Maya utilized various types of dualism at the same time in order to accommodate Christianity into their own Cosmos.

No doubt, certain elements of the colonial Maya had a negative view towards Christianity. Yet unlike those who live in monotheistic cultures, it was not a complete rejection. This point has made researchers confused for numerous years.

As I have mentioned, the Maya version of dualism is essentially not to provoke conflict between the two (*e.g.*, Spirit and body, individual and the universe, and sensual and practical matters). In this concept, they work together in order to create or sustain. Therefore, even though the colonial Maya considered Christianity to be negative in many aspects, Christianity must have been considered necessary to sustain the balance of the world.

This kind of dualism is commonly found in Asia and among Native Americans. In several points, the dualism of the Chinese is also quite similar to that of the Maya.[5] Among the Chinese, it was considered that everything was created and manipulated by the interacting principles of *Yin* and *Yang*; the positive and negative principles. Various examples of dualistic perceptions of Christianity discussed in this research would make the process of restoring the Maya dualism straightforward.

However, although *K'abawil*, which is now proposed and argued to be the essential divine concept of the *Popol Vuh* among some K'iche shamans, has

---

something transient and empty has also been influential.

several quite close concepts to *Tao* of Taoism and the *Supreme Ultimate* of Confucianism, it is also true that there are fundamental differences. For example, Adrian I. Chávez somehow tried to understand *K'abawil* as a single self existence (=a spiritual power) like the Christian Lord, but one with a dual character. On the other hand, the *Supreme Ultimate* of Confucianism and *Tao* of Taoism are neither a self existence nor a spiritual existence. Moreover, the precise definition of Maya dualism, *K'abawil* has not been yet been solidly defined.

Therefore, my purpose in this research is not to suggest that the Maya should read various classical world pagan texts, such as the *Confucian Analects*, instead of the Christian Bible. The Maya religions are of the Maya. They have a freedom in what they practice. The way of reconstructing their religions is solely dependent upon their choice.

It is now time for the Maya to present their own view, and external scholars also have to read them more carefully than they have done in the past, even though some of these texts present a 'peculiar' interpretation. The purpose of this book is to provide the information and the perspective of dualism from my point of view, in order to facilitate the Native Americans in restoring and constructing their own version of dualism.

In this research, I have emphasized the necessity of reconstructing Maya dualism in order to understand the true meaning of the ancient texts. The fact is that until I knew several opinions of the contemporary K'iche Maya, I had not noticed its importance. There may be some serious difficulties to do so under a dominant Christian cultural influence. The educational system of Guatemala is Western and the majority of the Mayaow belong to the Christian church. Therefore it is not surprising that even Maya scholars' works have a great possibility of influence from Christian ideology.

Although the relationships between Christianity and Native American and Asian religions of the sixteenth century are always considered to be '*The First*

---

[5] Gernet 1996:261. see *ibid*.:261-277.

Confrontation,'[6] historical evidence collected from these two 'New Worlds' suggests that hostility against Christianity was generated by an intolerant attitude towards other religions from the Catholic Church, Catholic exclusion of the converted indigenous people from ecclesiastical control, and brutal conquest and exploitation of native peoples by the Spaniards who justified their actions in the name of Christ. Examples from Asian history suggest that these peoples required a long period to establish a firm concept of Anti-Christianity.

In the last part of this research, I discussed the necessity of understanding the context of the *Popol Vuh* not from parallelism but from dualism. The studies of Maya civilization have been dominated by the Western Academy. Although it is true that their efforts are a substantial help in understanding the numerous mythical parts of the Maya cultures, there is a problem in that the 'trend of this academic field is heavily and exceedingly affected by interest of the West.' Over-emphasis on astronomical and calendaric matters of Maya cultures, appear to have been originally generated by Western academics (to be honest, also by recent Japanese who traditionally simply follow the popular movements of the Western Academy). Curiosity in archaeology of Great Ancient Maya Cities, may be a good example. Another example could be Maya shamanism, which has attracted Christian researchers, presumably due to a lack of that tradition in Christian cultures. The result is that the area of Maya studies has exclusively been dominated by the Christian perception.

Again, I do not deny the fact that the Western academics, notably North Americans, have made numerous contributions to the understanding of the Maya Civilization. Nevertheless, it must be noted that this situation also created an unbalanced understanding of Maya religious concept.

Throughout this work, I may seem ironical about the Christian view of Maya culture, the Spanish Conquest, and the problem of academic influence generated by Western self interest in the Maya cultures. However, this does not mean that

---

[6] Gernet 1996.

dualistic peoples like the Japanese have always been better than Western people. When I finished my BA degree at a Japanese university in the 1990s, it was not so unusual to meet university professors who treated the Maya Civilization as a kind of occult culture, and some extreme examples (one of them is a specialist of Latin American history) openly hurled abuse at me stating (though from behind the door): 'that sort of rubbish cannot be an academic subject.'[7]

Although in Japan, it is now popular to argue the danger and madness of the ideology created in monotheistic cultures, I do not suggest that the people of dualism are always more passive in mind than those of monism. Dualistic cultures have not always been calm. As is known, Japan and China, both of which are major states of dualism and paganism, cruelly fought with each other during World War II. The degree of cruelty of the Japanese army was not so different from the army of Francisco Pizarro. This history has continuously caused serious controversy in Japan, China, and Korea. We also ordered the people of Japanese colonized states to visit Japanese pagan shrines, as the Christians did in the past. The fact is that every country has committed this type of war crime (often with the pretext of propagating its own religion).

In addition, the insanity of dualistic cultures often surpassed that of monotheism. For example, storms of the Japanese systematic suicide attacks (*Kamikaze* 神風) during the Second World War were far more terrifying than suicide attacks practiced by Islamic fundamentalist today in terms of their scale and the mental injury given to the US and British army.[8] Although it may be

---

[7] At Aoyama University, a noted Christian college founded by a US missionary! I remember that several who study Occidental history, were paradoxically shouting; 'this guy [=me] must not be allowed to do anything related to academic. What Westerners do is not academic!' This may be a chief reason why Christianity remains a small religious group in my country. The ironical fact is that they have never presented any work in US or Britain since then. Though the numbers of these people at Japanese universities are decreasing these days, this tendency still remains. Indeed, it is quite usual to hear news in Japan these days that every month, two or three professors at famous (and infamous) universities have been arrested or have been dismissed in disgrace or have been suspended from teaching duty because of their sexual & academic harassment of their students. Yet, it is also true that massmedia of Japan often paradoxly promote those nuts as a leading intellectual.

[8] During the Second World War, all Japanese were ordered to fight until they died. This philosophy created a discriminative attitude towards those who surrendered to the Japanese army,

over-used, a dualistic perspective may explain the concept of *Kamikaze* suicide attacks which the Western world have a serious difficulty in understanding.

One of noted example of such suicide attacks, which the West has had extreme difficulty in understanding was a suicidal sally of Battleship *Yamato*, the world largest battleship, to Okinawa in 1945. The last Japanese navy force, the Second Fleet consisting of Battleship *Yamato* with several escort ships (the number of the soldiers in that fleet was almost 6,000) sat sail from the mainland of Japan to Okinawa island to attack the US and British army, which was landing and attacking that island, which possessed more than 1,500 ships and a force 50,0000 (!) strong in total. The Japanese garrison, 10,0000 strong, arrayed in Okinawa had already been ordered to defend the island to the death.

The council of the Japanese Imperial army did not expect the success of the last remaining battleship from the first, because it understood that the possibility of success was almost zero, and that the last Japanese fleet would be destroyed soon after their departure from base. What they chiefly sought, was to create a new mythical tale of the Japanese Imperial Navy for the next generation of the Japanese: that a lone battleship, *Yamato*, dared to fight for a hopeless victory. The staff of *Yamato* fleet knew the nonsense of such a military operation, and criticized the blockhead generals at the headquarters of the Imperial army, because the headquarters never arranged any escort fighters. How did they manage to reach Okinawa without a sufficient escort? Nevertheless, this Japanese fleet decided to fight a vain battle with several hundred US bombers led by US Vice Admiral Marc Mitcher, and was sunk. Yamato lost almost 80% of its crew.

Although keeping the 'Fleet in being' away from fighting was also considered a shame of army in Europe and in the USA, almost all readers from the West will certainly comment; 'Were the Japanese Imperial Army simple nuts?'

---

and became one of main causes of US and British prisoners being regarded as cowards. They were consequently mistreated as if they were slaves. Yet, mistreatment of war prisoner has been practiced by almost all nations including Christian ones. In this book, the execution of Atahualpa is a good example.

Paradoxically, the majority of the Japanese would agree with such a reaction, and will surely say; 'it was a just waste of precious human life,' if they are asked to make a comment on this meaningless operation. Nevertheless, it is also true that this crazy suicide squad of warship *Yamato* has became a famous and popular legend in Japan although its impact is totally opposite to what the Japanese Imperial Army originally expected. It is not rare to see Japanese movies and dramas that still treat the past Japanese *Kamikaze* suicide squads as a sad but a beautiful story.

I am sure that the majority of the readers are confused now by reading this story, and would say; 'understanding of the Japanese nation is impossible'. However, if we consider this issue from a perspective of dualism, a reasonable answer may be given.

The crew of *Yamato* mentally suffered due to the order from headquarters.[9] Mituru Yoshida, who participated in this operation as a First lieutenant and a crewmember of battleship *Yamato*, later published his experiences in *Yamato*. He records that because nobody in Battleship *Yamato* believed in the success of this suicidal attack, there were numerous arguments among crews as to how to justify it. According to him, due to frustration among the crew, exchanging punches with each other was not unusual in Yamato.[10]

『痛烈ナル必敗論議ヲ傍ラニ、哨戒長臼淵大尉（一次室長、ケップガン）、薄暮ノ洋上ニ眼鏡ヲ向ケシママ低ク囁ク如ク言ウ
「進歩ノナイ者ハ決シテ勝タナイ　負ケテ目ザメルコトガ最上ノ道ダ　日本ハ進歩トイウコトヲ軽ンジ過ギタ　私的ナ潔癖ヤ徳義ニコダワッテ、本当ノ進歩ヲ忘レテイタ　敗レテ目覚メル、ソレ以外ニドウシテ日本ガ救ワレルカ　今目覚メズシテイツ救ワレルカ　俺タチハソノ先導ニナルノダ　日本ノ新生ニサキガケテ敗ル　マサニ本望ジャナイカ」
彼、白淵大尉ノ持論ニシテ、マタ連日「ガンルーム」ニ沸騰セル死生談義ノ一応ノ結論ナリ　敢エテコレニ反駁ヲ加エ得ル者ナシ』[11]

[9] Various writings left by the members of Japanese suicide attacks suggest that the majority were undergoing mental conflict before their departures.
[10] Yoshida 1994:47-8.
[11] Cited from Yoshida 1994:46.

Beside the severe discussion concerning the inevitable defeat [of the Japanese Imperial Second Fleet], the chief patrol & the captain *Usubushi* [The first head of office, the head of young military officers] keeps turning his glasses onto the ocean of twilight, and speaks low as if he is muttering.

The person who doesn't know [the necessity of] improvement can never win.

[For such a person] the best way to make his eyes open to the reality is to experience a [forthcoming predicted fatal] defeat [of battleship *Yamato*].

Japan has too much slighted [the importance of] the improvement.

Japan has been unable to discard [its traditional value of] the private scrupulousness and the morality [this suggests the *Samurai* Spirit], and it has forgotten true improvement.

We are to be [vainly] defeated, and that fact will make [the Japanese] open their eyes [to notice the vainness to continue this hopeless war].

How will Japan be saved apart from this method?

When will Japan be saved unless we make them realize [the reality of this war by showing this silly operation]?

We become the vanguard [of teaching the Japanese the vain defeat of their fleet].

We are to be defeated in order to create a new Japan.

Aren't you just satisfied?"

This is the opinion of the captain *Usubushi*, and it is also the conclusion of the discussion on death and life which boiled up every day in "the gun room".

There is no one who dares add a refutation to this.

In short, the crew of *Yamato* concluded that their vain deaths would generate an opposite effect on the Japanese of the future.

Now, the story of *Yamato*'s suicide attack is generally regarded as 'ridiculous but beautiful' by the Japanese. Indeed, a new movie of Battleship *Yamato*'s suicide attack was released in December 2005! On this point, it must be considered whether the death of the crew of *Yamato* was really a simple waste of human life? There is no question that the suicide attack of Battleship *Yamato* simply resulted in a loss of nearly three thousand soldiers, and it was the worst military operation in the world. Yet, it must be noted that the legend of this 'nonsense' operation in Military History has been one of the strong forces to discourage the Japanese from having offensive weapons, and preparing war again.[12]

---

[12] In logic, there is no army in Japan. What we have now, is the SELF DEFENCE FORCE.

361

There are other examples. If Topac Amaru of the Neo-Inca state had not decided to fight with the Spaniards to the last, would the Peruvian people have nostalgia for the Inca Empire now? The same idea may be applied to the brave resistance of Cuautemoc to Hernán Cortés. Sometimes, a vain struggle can create a thing of beauty.[13]

Monism = monotheism has its own demerit. Those who belong to this culture often act self-righteously. A notable example is the Chinese rite controversy discussed in this volume. Apart from it, there is a famous story in Japan. Between 1980 and early 1990, there was a serious frictional war on Japanese cars eating up a share of the US car market. The US Big Three (*e.g.*, Ford) were irritated with the fact that the marketing share of US cars was extremely low in Japan, while Japanese car were rapidly 'invading' the US market. What did they say to the Japanese?

It became a half-legend among people in the Japanese car industry, that the US claimed that "because the roads of Japan are narrow, and the Japanese Law makes a rule 'Keep To The Right,' our big and left-hand drive cars have not been well received!'", as if it was a duty of Japan to change its road regulations.

It is not difficult to imagine that this story simply resulted in spreading dreadful impressions of the snobbish attitude of the US in Japan.[14] It was rather a natural course. It must be noted that the Japanese did not export automobiles of Japanese specification (right-hand drive) to the US, but they specially built left-hand drive cars for export to the US.

The co-existence of various religions is not always harmonious. This is especially true in the relationships between polytheistic and dualistic religions and monotheistic religions. Even in Japan, there is still a somewhat mixed feeling.

---

[13] Of course, I do not suggest that making the people die in vain is acceptable.

[14] Those who followed BIG THREE, such as Kodak, experienced a severe defeat in Japan. Japan is one of the few countries in which Kodak are forced to discount their products. The British have also done the same in Japan. On the other hand, Macdonalds and Kentucky Fried Chicken succeeded in the Japanese market of that period. The reason was simple. They aggressively adopted Japanese tastes. Some US companies, such as Dell, succeeded without that effort, because their sales strategy matched needs of the Japanese from the first.

Among the Japanese nationalists, the Japanese emperor has virtually remained the 'half-supreme' deity of the world, in spite of the fact the former emperor officially denied this concept after World War II. For example, it is known that because the Japanese Prime Minister of 2000-1, Yoshiro Mori (森喜朗), made a speech '*I want to let the entire Nation know that the state of Japan is just a country of gods in which the Japanese emperor takes a leading part*' in 2000, it later became one of the important reasons for him to give up his position. Although open hostility towards monotheistic religions, such as Christianity has now dramatically decreased in Japanese society since the Second World War, the ideology of monotheism is still often considered an intolerable and radical idea.

Often Christian students refuse to participate in local annual ceremonies of Japanese Shinto, because they are considered pagan rites. Since such ceremonies are now held as seasonal festivals rather than religious rites in most cases, for the majority of the Japanese, this behavior is often regarded as hidebound and immature. In fact, this still becomes a controversy and is picked up as a topic of newspaper stories. Recently, the president of Tokyo prefecture talked in a TV program of Terebi Asahi (=TV Asahi Corporation), that Christians visiting the Yasukuni Shrine, which is used as a war memorial for the dead [Japanese] soldiers, is highly desirable. He somehow thinks of a shrine visit as the moral duty of the Japanese Nation, and argues that although they are now treated as gods by that shrine and may have a religious problem, as the Yasukuni Shrine is a symbol of Japanese identity. It is required that Japanese Christians visit the shrine after the example of a Japanese Catholic Christian and popular novelist, Ayako Sone, who used to visit various Japanese pagan shrines.[15] This kind of opinion sometimes becomes unspoken pressure on the Japanese Christian.

---

[15] The stance of the Catholics is that visiting the Yasukuni shrine is not a religious act, as I have argued in Chapter III. It means that a Catholic visit to that Shrine is not to worship the Japanese war dead but to pay respect to them. It is remembered that Mr. Sone, a famous writer in Japan was apparently inclined to respect the Japanese war dead deified by the Yasukuni Shrine. Yet, it is also obvious that the opinions of the Catholics do not reflect those of all Japanese Christians.

363

Another more moderate example is; my late aunt used to attend Buddhist services for dead relatives in the style of a 'Catholic nun' and used to talk about 'Our Lord' during those services. I remember that I was forced to listen to her talk for more than two hours in a Buddhist temple. Although the chief priests of the temple said nothing of her costume and talks, their stiffened faces clearly suggested that they were troubled by her behavior[16], because there is unspoken agreement in our society that even if a person attends a ceremony of a religion in which he or she does not believe, he or she must decline to praise his or her own religion, and must obey the conventions of that religion. Her effort failed, as I have remained a normal Japanese: opting for all kinds of religion at the same time. For me, each religion is a part of the universe.

I do not know the future of religious concept of Guatemala and other parts of Latin America. I do not propose that they should follow our country, or China. But I would like to believe that a better relationship between two very different religions is by no means impossible, as the examples of my country suggest.

Finally, I will comment on my future research. Because the original plan of this research was much too ambitious, several important arguments are not included in this volume because they are still in progress, such as an analysis of the *Book of Chilam Balam of Kaua*.[17] Also, my discussion on the Inca reaction to Christianity remains somewhat unsatisfactory. Hopefully, I will manage to publish these topics in the near future.

---

[16] Yet, it is true that some of Buddhist operated kindergartens in Japan now have 'Christmas' parties for children. It is not very unusual that some Churches now have a churchyard for Christian within a cemetery park operated by Buddhist temple.

[17] The first English translation of the *Kaua* was published as Bricker and Miram (2002).

364

Appendix I

An example of the ideology of 'Japanese Christianity'. Masataka Horiuchi, a devout Christian of Japanese Christianity, the president of *Dainihonshingakusha*, and a former teacher of Kyoritu Singakkou [a divinity school] presented this new Christianity at his home in Yokohama City (collected by the Japanese Imperial Secret Police in February 1941, reprinted in Wada 1972:51-3). 熱心なキリスト教徒かつ、元共立神学校教師であり、大日本神学社主として日本古典と基督教の比較研究を行っていた、堀内真隆が１９４１年に行ったとされる研究会での発言。

　私は過去三十年間基督教に身を投じ聖書の研究を為すと共に常に日本神道の研究を為し之が比較研究をして来たのでありますが、基督教の教理中には反国体的教理が存する事を承知したので軈て国家より弾圧を受ける時が来る事は明かであり、国家より弾圧を受けてから改革するのは余り賞めたものでないから其れ以前教内に於て大改革を為し、日本的基督教を樹立すべきであり、又皇国は世界に類のない天皇統治の国家であって国家に追随する宗教でなければ発展性は望まれないのであると為し改革説を提出したのでありますが、当時日本基督教会に於ては容れられず私は当時奉職中であった共立女子神学校を辞職し（六年前）、其の後自由の立場に於て日

本神道と基督教の比較研究を続けて来たのであるが、恩師である日本基督
教会の長老たる笹尾桑〔粂〕太郎先生．及毛利寛治先生により正面から基
督教反対をやらないで呉れと頓まれたので、両先生に対する関係から私の
運動は精神的に阻止せられ居ったのでありますが、毛利先生は昨年笹尾先
生は本年一月二十九日死亡されたのであります。

　然して笹尾博士の病気見舞の為私の妻を先月伺はせました…先生は地獄
がありとせば先づ地獄に真先行くものは基督教の牧師だ、其次は基督数の
信者だと申されたそうである、此意味は私には解する事が出来るのであり
ます、即ち博士は良く基督教の反国体性を承知して居たのであります。…

I have devoted myself to Christianity for thirty years. I have been making a comparative study by reviewing the *Bible* and Japanese Shinto. Yet, I have noticed that some [Christian] doctrines oppose the fundamental nature of the state, which will obviously receive suppression from the state in the near future. Therefore, I have submitted my idea of reform [of Christianity], not so much because it is praiseworthy to reform Christianity after oppression from the state, but as a revolution to establish 'Japanese' Christianity, which must be made within churches in advance. This empire is a rare country in which the [divine] Japanese Emperor governs, and unless the [Christian] religion follows the state, the development [of Christianity] cannot be expected. However, it was not accepted in the Japanese Christian society of that time, so I resigned a position at the Kyoritu Divine School six years ago. Since then, I have continued my comparative study of Japanese Shinto and Christianity in a free position. I was asked not to openly oppose Christianity by Mr. Sotaro Sasao, my former teacher and the chief of the Japanese Christian society, and by Mr. Kanji Mori so that my campaign has mentally been interrupted. Yet, Mr. Mori died last year and Mr. Sasao died on 29 January 1941.

I sent my wife to pay a sympathy visit to Dr. Sasao last month.... [According to my wife], my teacher [Dr. Sasao] said that if there is Hell, those who first fall in it are the Christian Fathers and the next are the Christian flock. I can understand this meaning. Dr. Sasao understood the nature of Christianity opposing the [Japanese] National policy well.

二、キリスト教の思想的反国体的な立場に於ける出発

…英国より自由の天地を求め自由に信仰をしたいとて脱出したのがピユーリタン（清教徒）と称し渡米し現在の米国の祖先を為して居るのである。之等の思想こそ神（天の父）と人間の中間には如何なる権威者も認めずとなすもので、之が後日皇の現人神信仰の破壊工作として基督教宣伝の為莫大な投資と努力を惜まなかった所以である。…

2: Their origin of ideological anti-national policy of Christianity

…those who departed from England in order to seek a land of freedom for their faith called themselves Puritans (the Protestants), and they became the ancestors of the United States. This ideology does not accept any authority between God and human beings; thus, this later became the reason that large investments and numerous efforts have been made to develop Christianity as a destructive propaganda against the worship of the Japanese Emperor as the living God....

三、日本的基督数

現在の基督教に於ては天皇の上に基督の神を置くのであるが、皇国に於ては全ての神は天皇の下に於てのみ認められる、即ち臣神としてのみ認められ之に反する神は認められないのである。

基督の神は創造神と主宰神とが同一体の神であるが、創造神たる天御中主の神と主宰神たる天照大神とは区別せられ、天照大神の御出現と同時に造化三神は陰身の神となり、万物の中に分神となられ歴代の天皇に御仕へしたとある如く、皇国に於ける創造神は天照大神の御出現により臣神となられている。故に基督教に於ける創造神も臣神として認められるが天皇の上に置くことは認められぬ、之が我国に於ける基督教の永き歴史と努力の割に発展を見られざる原因である。…又最近までは米国の補助を受けつゝあった点に於て日本的基督に改革を為し能はざる点があったが、現在では大体英米と絶縁したので最も改革の好機会である。

　…兎に角私は之から神学的に大いに基督教の反国体性を爆撃し之を健全なものになすべく力める心算である云々。

3: Japanese Christianity

In the current Christianity, the Christian God is placed above the Japanese Emperor. However, in this empire, all gods are accepted under the Japanese Emperor. That is to say that they are only accepted as subordinated gods [to the Emperor]; any god opposing this rule cannot be accepted.

The Christian God incorporates the creation god and the leading god into one. On the other hand [in Japanese Shinto], *Amaminakanusi* as the creation god and *Amaterasuominokami* as the ruling god are distinguished. When *Amaterasuominokami* emerged, three gods of creation became implicit at the same time and were divided into a god of each part of the creatures who served the successive Japanese Emperor. In this way, the creator god became a subordinated god by the emergence of *Amaterasuomikami* [=the ruling god]. Therefore, although the Christian Creator God can be accepted as a subordinated god, it cannot be accepted for him to take a superior position over the Japanese Emperor. This is the reason for the relative unpopularity of Christianity in my country in spite of its long history and efforts... Also, until recently, because of receiving aide from the U.S., there have been some difficulties in reforming Japanese Christianity. Yet, as we are now insulated from the United Kingdom and the U.S., it is the best opportunity for reform.

...Anyway, now I will theologically bomb the anti-nationalistic character of [Western] Christianity, and I will attend to make Christianity wholesome [for Japan].

Appendix II

Various contributions from both Japanese nationalists and Christians appeared in a local newspaper, the *Mino Taisho Shinbun,* in Ogaki City, from June to July 1933. Some important ones were reprinted in a report made by The Library of Japanese Diet of 1959 (Reprinted in Wada 1972:350-361). Although I tried to collect two contributions omitted in that report, neither the public and university library nor the successive newspaper of *Mino Taisho Shinbun* retains a copy covering that period. Some other articles that originally appeared in the *Mino Taisho Shinbun* are printed on Nohara (1930: *passim*) and Yanase (1933: *passim*). Thanks to the Sagamihara City Library for their assistance.

A: An extraction from an article contributed by the president of Higasi Junior School in Ogaki City, printed in the *Mino Taisho Shinbun*, 22 June 1933 (reprinted in Wada 1972:350-1).
大垣市東小学校校長高木氏による美濃大正新聞への投稿。昭和八年六月二十二日掲載。

　『キリスト教徒の神社参拝拒否問題について我々輩がとやかく議論することは、一顧の価値だに与へられざるものとは信づるものであるが、…尤もこの一文はキリスト教従に対する我々の挑戦でもなく喧嘩でもない. 一或はそうである方がヤソは自分等に対する神の試練であるといつて喜ぶか

も知れんが一我々は真摯なる学究的態度で進みたい事を希ふ．この問題を論議するには、ヤソ教従の立場にも立つてみなければ片手落になる．故に我はこの問題の最も代表的と思はれる海老名弾正氏の「日本国民とキリスト教」を目標とする…比較宗教学上より見れば日本の神道は神人同格教であつた．国家的神道の神髄を成してゐるものは国体神道である．そしてこの具象化が神社である．伊勢神宮、明治神宮の如きこの好典型である．而して国家神道の中心は天皇を神皇として拝するところに存する換言すれば日本の天皇は現人神と見奉るのである．この神皇信仰を宗教心理的にいへば日本人の民族精神である儒教も日本の建国精神日本国体を中心としてその下に信教の自由を獲取してゐたのである．憲法上の信教の自由もこの解釈の立場からすべきである．国体の根源をなす神皇信仰の拒否者が若しあるとすればこれは確に安寧秩序を妨げ臣民の義務に背く最大のものである．』

I think it is worth nothing to discuss the issue of the refusal of the Shrine visit among Christians … Of course, this article is neither a challenge nor a row against the Christians, although it might be that if we challenge them, the Christians are as pleased as if a trial was given by the Lord. We wish to proceed with a sincere academic attitude [towards this matter]. In order to argue this matter, it will not be fair unless we consider it from the standpoint of the Christians. Therefore, we pick up the *Nihonkokumin to Kirisuto Kyo*, written by Mr. Danjo Ebina as a supposed typical example concerning this issue … From the view of comparative religion, the Shinto of Japan was a God-Man equality religion. Shinto of national policy accomplishes the quintessence of the state Shinto. Then, a Shrine is that this idea is exteriorized. The ISE Shrine（伊勢神宮）and MEIJI Shrine（明治神宮）are a good example of this. Therefore, the core of the state Shinto is to worship the [Japanese] Emperor as the Divine Emperor. In other words, we regard the emperor as a Living God. If we speak of this worship of the Divine Emperor from a religious psychological view, Confucianism [came from China], our ethnic sprit, by accepting the Spirit of Japanese Foundation = Fundamental Character of Japan, as the leading ideology, gained its religious freedom under it. The religious freedom mentioned in our Constitution must be treated in this interpretation. If there is one opposed to the worship of the Divine Emperor, which constitutes the Fundamental Character of Japan, this will surely disturb our peace and order and will be the maximum disobedience to the duty of the Vassal of the Emperor.

B: An extraction from an article contributed by the president of *Higasi* Junior School in Ogaki City, printed in the *Mino Taisho Shinbun*, 23 June 1933 (reprinted in Wada 1972:351-2).
大垣市東小学校校長高木氏による美濃大正新聞への投稿。昭和八年六月二十三日掲載。

『神社の神々は神話の人物であつて史実を以て検討すれば雲と消去るものである．今日さういふ神社を信じ得られない（海老名）この言は日本の建国の神々を否定してゐる容易ならぬ言である．神話があつて今日の日本が出来上つてゐるのである．日本精神はこの神話によつて独特の成長をなし来つたものである、今日神話の神々を信じよといふことが妥当でないとするならば、ヤソ自身の聖書は如何、死後三日目に昇天するといふやうなことを唯［誰］が信じ得られるか．然しながらその幼稚なる神話によつて…今日の科学をもつてすれば一文の価値なくむしろ笑止に堪へざる…ヤソ精神は世界に確乎たる地位を占め、あらゆる方面に貢献をなし来つたのである。日本の神社が想像の神であらうとなからうとそれは問題でない…創世記のやうに…要は日本精神の根元をなすところに意義があるのではなからうか（自説）…そこで学校の神社参拝であるが、海老名氏のいふやうに神社に霊魂不朽を認めるか否かそんなことは我々にとつてはどうでもよい…

我々は神前に立つて、祖先の英雄の遺徳を追慕し従って崇拝崇敬の念を起さしむれば足りるのである．（自説）』

"*Gods of* [Japanese] *Shrines are mythical persons. By* [verifying] *historical facts, they will be dispersed as if clouds. Now I cannot believe such Shinto Shrines*" (Ebina). Because this suggests his denial of Japanese gods founding Japan, I cannot easily overlook it. Based on our myth, Japan of today has been made. The Japanese spiritualism has grown in a peculiar progress through this myth. If it is not now proper for us to believe in the gods found in our legend, how about the *Bible*? I wonder if there is anybody who believes the ascension to heaven after three days of death [mentioned in the *Bible*]? However, with such a childish myth ... a worthless and ridiculous myth according to our science of today ... Christian spiritualism has occupied a firm position in the world, and it has contributed to every aspect. [Therefore], whether Japanese gods are a product of our imagination or not is the problem... as the *Genesis* [in Christian cultures] ... It is supposed that [the Japanese Gods] have a meaning because they constitute the basis of the Japanese spirit... With regard to the Shrine visit conducted by the school, Mr. Ebina's view whether it is acceptable that the Shrine has an [immortal] permanent soul or not, is not the matter for us... We will simply be satisfied that by standing in front of [Japanese] gods, we recall remaining virtues of the past heroes to cause our wish of the worship and the reverence [of them].

C: An extraction from an article contributed by the president of *Higasi* Junior School in Ogaki City, printed in the *Mino Taisho Shinbun*, 24 June 1933 (reprinted in Wada 1972:351).
大垣市東小学校校長高木氏による美濃大正新聞への投稿。昭和八年六月二十四日掲載。

『日本人として祖先を崇拝せざるは宗教は断じて奏づべからず。外国人のやうに祖先を忘れて即ち根元を忘れて物事は成就し難く、我等は祖先を忘れて繁栄しないのである. 祖先を忘れたる宗教は到底我らの日本民族の信仰し得ざる宗教である（理博海野三朗）.

…祖先崇拝は祖先の遺物宗教であると片付け、そしてそれを日本民族精神の上に及ぼしたる三千年来の偉大なる力として認めやうとしない、非国民的に等しい言動を我らは黙過し得ない. 今日の日本の地位平和はこの偉大なる日本民族の精神によつて築き上げられたものである. 我らは神社ー祖先英雄ーを崇拝し、そしてその祖先英雄の志を継承して行かねばならぬ。ヤソ教もその条件の下に於てのみ国民教育と相容れ得るのである（自説）』

We [the Japanese] must not believe a religion that defrays the Japanese from worshipping our ancestors. Accomplishing a task is difficult if we forget our ancestors who are [the origin of this country] like [Western] foreigners, and we will not flourish while ignorant of our ancestors (according to Doctor of Science Saburo Umino). We do not overlook the words and deeds of those who dispose worshipping ancestors, which has been the great power influencing the Nation of Japan for over three thousand years, as a vestige of the past, and ignore it. The present position and peace of Japan were established by the spiritual power of the great Japanese people. We must worship the Shrine = ancestors and heroes, and we must preserve them [for the future]. Christianity must be consistent with the Japanese educational system under this condition [=worshiping Shrine] (my own view).

D: An extraction from an article contributed by a Japanese Christian, Sho Sato, printed in the *Mino Taisho Shinbun*, 29 June 1933 (reprinted in Wada 1972:352-3). Although Sho Sato appeared in the original, his proper name is 佐藤信夫(Nobuo Sato), according to Yahara (1930:46). He was a teacher at the local junior school.

キリスト教徒佐藤生による、高木への反論、美濃大正新聞への投稿。昭和八年六月二十九日掲載。

『キリスト教がわが国体に何等違反するものでないことは明治時代に於て殆ど全部の識者によりて認められた所であつて昭和の今日に至つて其蒸返しの論議をすることは恰も捜夷論と開国論の当否を論ずるよりもたわけた気がする。然し近頃東小学校の高木氏が美濃ミツションの神社参拝拒否問題を機として熱心に論議せられてをり世人を誤解せしむる虞ありと考ふるので神社参拝とキリスト教徒の立場についてのみ意見を述べることゝした。第一に高木氏はヤソは耶蘇はと一部の宣教師や欧米心酔の一部キリスト教徒を恰もキリスト教信者全体が然るが如くいはるることは我々日本主義のキリスト信者にとつては迷惑千万である。高橋山本両クリスチヤン大臣の如きは尚更御迷惑の御事と御察し申上げる…成程大垣には美濃ミツションと称する我国体も我国民性も無視して絶へず神社参拝を拒否せんとする団体はあるが彼等に対しては一般キリスト教徒は轟蹙し憤慨してぬるのであつて支持したり、賛成する者は極めて稀であるのである。高木氏は又旧約聖書の創世記などを引照してキリスト教を攻撃してをらるゝが旧約聖書の一字一句も信ずべしといふが如きはユダヤ教徒か美濃ミツシヨン一派のみであらう。我々は旧約聖書は聖典として尊重はするがそれは論語や古事記と同程度である高木氏が仮令古神道尊信者であられても古事記の一字一句残らず真であるとは申されまいと思ふ。次に高木氏は海老名弾正氏の著書より神社に対して穏ならざる語句を探し出して攻撃せられてるるが、もし自分の議論に都合のよい箇所を部厚の本より見付けんとするならば、大抵の外国の宗教書から捜出することが出来る。強いて拾へば論語からでも仏典からでも我国体に違反するが如く見える箇所を捜求むることは困難でない、我語句の末を見ずして全思想を味ふべきである。その一々について論議

をする暇はないが高木氏が主張せらるゝ神社を通じて御祭神の神格に触れ
よとか、写真のみでなく銅像記念物等を通じて聖賢の人格を偲べとかいは
るゝ御議論は我々も御同感である. 建物や器具それ自身を拝するに非ずし
て其等を通じて祖先なり国家に功労のある方々の御人格を敬することは我
らが主張するのである.

　…最後に基督教徒として我々の模範たる松岡洋右氏（氏は即耶蘇信者で
ある）の神社に対する行動を当時の新聞記事を真なりとして掲載するに四
月廿八日宮中の御拝謁終るや直ちに明治神宮に参拝、次いで各皇族邸に奉
伺し総ての歓迎宴を固辞した…』

There is already a consensus that Christianity is nothing against the fundamental nature of this state. This view was recognized by the intellectuals of the Meiji era; thus, it is no more than ridiculous to discuss this matter as if we were to argue the rightness of the exclusiveness of Western barbarians and of opening Japan to them in the past. Nevertheless, as Mr. Takagi recently earnestly argued the matter of refusal of the Shrine visit caused by the Mino Mission, and I think that his opinion may lead the people to misunderstand, I would like to express a Christian point of view concerning the relationship between Christianity and the [Shinto] Shrine visit. First, although Mr. Takagi often treats all Christians like those at the Mino Mission or other small numbers who are fascinated by European and US Christianity, it is a great deal of trouble for us who believe 'Japanese' Christianity. I suppose that two ministers [of the Japanese Imperial Government], Mrs. Takahashi and Yamamoto, will be troubled more than [us by your writing]. It is true that there is a mission called Mino Mission in Ogaki City, which ignores both our fundamental nature of the state and national character. [The majority of] ordinal Christians like us [Japanese Christians] are frowned at and are angered by it, and support is very small in number. Although Mr. Takagi also criticizes Christianity by reading *Genesis* of the *Old Testament*, it is supposed that those who order the people to believe every word found in it are Jews and the faction of that mission only.

Although we respect the context of the *Old Testament*, the degree [of our devotion to it] should be the same as that to the *Rongo* [of Confucianism] and the *Kojiki* [the Japanese sacred text]. Even if Mr. Takagi is a believer of Japanese Shinto, I think that you would not say that there is no error within the *Kojiki*. Mr. Takagi also criticized part of what he found in the book of Mr. Ebina; yet, it must be noted that if somebody tries to discover a part convenient for his purpose from a big volume, it can be done from any foreign religious book. If pressed, some words and phrases opposing the fundamental nature of the state [of Japan] can be found in the texts of Confucianism and Buddhism without much difficulty. We should not be occupied with a piece of mere trifle [found in the *Old Bible*], but we should appreciate the whole idea [found in the Scriptures of the each religion]. Although I do not have time to discuss each issue, I agree with Mr. Takagi that we should feel the essence of [Japanese] Gods through the Shinto Shrine, and should imagine the personality of holy sages, not only through their pictures but also through bronze memorial statues. What we insist is not to worship a tool or building [of shrine temple] itself, but through it to respect the personality of our ancestors and of great patriots and contributors...

Last, supposing that articles found in a newspaper are a reliable source, the actions of Mr. Yosuke Matuoka regarding the Shinto Shrine will be mentioned. On 28 April, after being granted an audience in the place of the [Showa] Emperor, he went to visit Meiji Jingu [= the Shrine of the late Meiji Emperor] and later visited each residence of the imperial royal family. He declined to join any party [note: the author implies that Matuoka did not politically worship at the Shinto Shrine for his personal benefit].

E: An extraction from an article of the president of *Higasi* Junior School in Ogaki City, as a reply to Nobuo Sato, in the *Mino Taisho Shinbun*, 24 June 1933 (reprinted in Wada 1972:351).

大垣市東小学校校長高木氏による美濃大正新聞への佐藤生（信夫）に対する返答としての投稿。昭和八年六月二十九日掲載。

『佐藤氏の私に対する抗議については、私は衷心から敬意を表する．…私がヤソ教徒と呼んだのは勿論神社参拝を拒否する或一部の徒輩を指すのである決して全信徒を意味するものではなかった．…私の書き方がヤソについて無智無理解なる人々にとって全信徒皆然るかの如く解訳されるであらうことを心配し、佐藤氏の言を認める、そして氏の神社に対する態度解訳が氏一個人でないことを私は信じたい．また地位ある多くのクリスチャンが自己の地位上よりする神社参拝でないことを佐藤氏を通じて一派の信者に知らせたい…海老名氏はその著「日本国民と基督教」を読んでもわかる通り熱心なる愛国的クリスチャンであることを私は知つてゐる．しかし乍ら海老名氏の神社観全部を私はそのまゝ容認することが出来ないから、その容認出来ない一部分を採って議論したのである．次にキリストと我国体の問題を論ずることは、たはけたことだと論ぜられてゐるがその通りである。しかしそれは我々に向つて言われる議論ではなくして、一派のヤソ教徒に向つて叫ばなければならぬのではないかと思ふ…最後に佐藤氏のやうな信者は必ずや一派の信者から偽信者、異端者視されるであらうと附言せざるを得ない．』

I sincerely respect the protest against me made by Mr. Sato… Those whom I called Christian, of course, refer to only a certain portion of the Christians refusing the shrine visit. I never intended to include the other Christians… As I am afraid that my writing might be misunderstood by unreasonable people, I accept what Mr. Sato wrote, and I hope that his attitude regarding the Shrine and understanding it are not only his own. Also, I wish to let that faction [of the Mino Mission] know through Mr. Sato that many Christians who possessed this position did not make a visit to the Shrine for their self protection [in Shinto dominant society of Japan]…

No doubt, Mr. Ebiba is a patriot Christian, which can be proved by reading his *"Nihonkokumin to Kirisuto Kyo"*. However, as I cannot accept certain parts of his book containing his personal view of Shinto, I argued that portion only. Next, [Mr. Sato] argued that it is ridiculous to discuss the matter of the relationship between Christianity and the fundamental character of the state [of Japan]. I agree with him. Yet, I think that his argument should not be directed to us, but to that faction of Christianity [of the Mino Mission opposing the Shinto Shrine visit]… Last, I must add my own view that Christians like Mr. Sato will be regarded as false Christians or heretics by those [at the Mino Mission].

F: An extraction from an article of Insei Katura [or Sho Katurakage], a citizen of Ogaki City, as a reply to Sho Sato, in the *Mino Taisho Shinbun*, 1 July 1933 (reprinted in Wada 1972:354-5).
桂陰生の佐藤生の投稿に対する批判投稿。美濃大正新聞昭和八年七月一日掲載。

『神社参拝とキリスト教と題する佐藤君の議論はキリスト教徒のことごとくが神社参拝を拒否するものではないという点のみを例証せられたが、高木君が彼の投稿するに至つた動機は神社参拝拒否児童に対する教育者としての立場と美濃ミツシヨンを如何に見るべきかといふ．緊急な二点を明らかにするために外ならぬと思ふ．然るに佐藤君の議論は自分がキリスト者なるが故に十把一束に評されては甚だしい屈辱だといふ気持ちで人気者の松岡洋右氏まで引張り出されたのであらうが、それでは問題の核心に触れてをらぬ。佐藤君に定見があるなら何故に君はキリスト信者としての立脚点から美濃ミツシヨンの反省を促すべく努力しないのか．…要するに高木君が執筆した動機は何人も神社参拝はなすべきものであるとの論旨に外ならないと思ふ．…我国体の尊厳を冒涜するが如き議論をなす凡ての宗教

も宗教家も粉砕せねばならぬ。キリスト教発展のためにも頑迷たる美濃ミ
ツシヨンの謬見を改めしめ本問題の根幹をして正しからしめねばならぬ。』

Mr. Sato's discussion, entitled *the Shrine Visit and the Christianity*, illustrated that all of the Christians were not refusing to visit the Shrine. I think, however, that Mr. Takagi's motive was to clarify two urgent points. He posted a message as the educator to the children on his refusal to visit the Shrine and how the Mino Mission [which discourages its students from Shrine visitation] should be regarded. Therefore, Mr. Sato's discussion as a Christian stated his vigorous mortification as if he was also regarded as the same [of the Mino Mission]. He introduced the example of Mr. Yosuke Matsuoka as the [Japanese] favorite Christian. If Mr. Sato has a fixed opinion, why couldn't an effort be made to ask the Mino Mission to reconsider [the issue of the Shrine visit] from a standpoint of the [same] Christian.... In my point of view, anyone can make a visit to the Japanese Shinto Shrine...All religions and the men of the divine profession who accomplish the discussion to profane the dignity of the Japanese national policy must be shattered... It is necessary to change the wrong view of the hidebound cask [expressed] by the Mino Mission, and the root of this problem must be made clear because it is for the development of Christianity [in Japan].

G: An extraction from an article of Tomotune Kimura, a Christian citizen of Ogaki City, as his defense of the Mino Mission, 23 July 1933 (reprinted in Wada 1972:354-5). (reprinted in Wada 1972:354-5)
木村知常の美濃ミツシオン擁護の投稿。昭和八年七月二十三日掲載。

『…「大正新聞」の伝へるところによると、美濃ミツシヨンの問題はその後ますます悪化し、大垣市当局はミツシヨン撲滅のために既に委員を文部省に遣はされミツション閉鎖の日も開近に迫ってゐるかの如くである。

私は一個のキリスト信徒としてかゝる情勢を黙視するに忍びず、その任に
非ざるを知りつゝこゝに一文を草する.

　美濃ミツシヨンの神社参拝拒否は徹頭徹尾ワイドナー氏の我か国情の誤
解に基づくものである. …

　一、キリスト教が一神教であって聖跡の教ふる神以外に神を認めないの
ことは勿論である. この場合厳重に区別さるべきことは、この神はキリス
ト教の神であって我国で神と呼ばれてゐるものとは性質を異にする…

　一、しかしながら我国で「神」と呼ばれてゐるものは、神といふ言葉の
示す通り、又われわれの所持する普通の神といふ概念が示す通り必ずしも
単なる祖先の崇拝といふべぎものではない. (神道が文部省の宗戦局で扱は
れ、神社が内務省の神社局で扱はれるといふことだけで、その間の関係が
説明しつくせるとは思へない) こゝにワイドナー氏の誤解の生ずる理由が
ある. 我々はこの点について憲法で信教の自由を許されてゐるとか文部省
は神社は宗教に非ずとの方針であるとかの外面的な事情をはなれて精密に
我々の神社…日本における神の思想…について考慮する必要がある. 日本
人の祖先崇拝といふことはただ先人を偲ぶといふが如き漠然たる感情では
ないのであって、その中には永い伝統と深い郷土的信念があり、それが国
家意識にまで高められてゐるのである. その間の事情に極めて特異であっ
て、外国人であるところのワイドナー氏が其理解を欠いてゐる事は必ずし
も怪しむに足りないと思ふのである.

　一、既に我等の敬神思想、祖先崇拝の観念が非常に複雑な国民意識の上
に立つものであって外国人にその理解が困難であるとするならばキリスト
教徒なるワイドナー氏が神社参拝を宗教的行為なりと誤り信じ、自己の信
仰的立場からそれを首肯しないのは極めて自然であって、我々がそれをも
って直ちに美濃ミツシヨンを伏魔殿とよびワイドナー氏を国民思想撹乱者
と見なすのは実に滑稽であるといはねばならない…我々大垣市民として己

れの半生を大垣市の伝道に捧げたこの善き西洋老婦人に対して十分の尊敬を示すのが、市民としての礼儀であらうと思ふのである…』

According to the [Mino] Taisho Newspaper report, the problem of the Mino Mission has been increasingly aggravated. The Ogaki City official has sent a committee man to the Minister of Education in order to abolish the [Mino] Mission and the day of closing the Mission seems to be in the near future. As a Christian, I cannot overlook this situation, although I am not in the position [to discuss this issue]. Instead, I have written an article.

The refusal of the Shrine visit by the Mino Mission is caused by the misunderstanding of our state condition...

1: It is known that Christianity is a monotheism religion and there is no God apart from the God taught in the Holy Scriptures. In this case, it must plainly be clarified that this God is the God of Christianity who is different in nature from *Kami* [=Gods in Japanese] which we call...

1: However, what is called "*Kami*" in our state, is, as the word of *Kami* signifies, or as the concept of *Kami* possessed by us signifies, it is not always necessarily to consider a mere worship of our ancestors. (I do not think that this relationship [between *Kami* and the Christian Lord] can fully be explained by the fact that *Shinto* [as a religion] is under control of the Department of Education and Shrine [as buildings] is under that of the Department of Interior.) On this point, there is a reason why Ms. Weidner misunderstands the issue. Concerning this point, we should not argue the surface of the issue, such as religious freedom guaranteed by our [imperial] constitution or the policy of the Department of Education. "Shrine is not a religion", but a careful consideration of our shrines...the ideology of *Kami* in Japan... is necessary. The worship of ancestors among the Japanese does not simply mean the vague feeling of recalling the late people. Because it has a tremendously long tradition, and our deep belief and love for home, it was raised to the state consciousness. In this point, [the matter of *Kami* and Shrine] is very [complex and] unique [to us]. Therefore, I think that it is not surprising that Ms. Weidner lacks a proper understanding of it.

1: If the concept of our respect to *Kami* and of our worship of the ancestors is based on a very complex feeling of our nation so that foreigners [Western] cannot comprehend it, it is quite natural that Ms. Weidner, as a Christian, mistakes the Shrine visit as a religious practice and does not accept it from her standpoint. Therefore, it is laughable that we instantly call the Mino Mission a pandemonium and regard Ms. Weidner as someone disturbing our national ideology...In my opinion, to this good Western lady who devoted half of her life to preach the Gospel, paying a full respect is required to the citizens [of Ogaki City].

383

Appendix III

Several articles cited and translated from the *Ordenanza de Yucatán, año de 1533* of Tomas López Medel. (published in Pereña et al. 1990:100-114. cited from *ibid*.: 106-110.)

14. La predicación del santo evangelio y la jurisdicción y autoridad de poner escuela pública para el enseñamiento de él pertenece a la autoridad apostólica y a los prelados y a quien sus veces tienen, por ende mando que ningún indio de esta dicha provincia, de cualquier estado y condición que sea, sea osado de levantar ni tener escuela para enseñar la doctrina cristiana y predicar el santo evangelio, pública ni escondidamente, por sí y de su autoridad, ni funde iglesia de nuevo, ni pinten ni pongan imágenes en ella ni bauticen ni casen ni desposen a ningún indio ni india sin licencia y expresa instrucción del prelado de esta dicha provincia o de los padres religiosos que anduvieren en la doctrina, so pena, etc.

15. Por el santo bautismo profesamos los cristianos la creencia de un verdadero Dios, y renunciamos al demonio y a sus malas obras. Por ende mando que todo indio e india de esta dicha provincia, bautizado y cristiano, que ha recibido la ley de Dios, se aparte y deje sus idolatrías y ritos antiguos y no tenga ídolos, no consientan que otros los tengan y les hagan sacrificios de animales ni de otras cosas, ni con sangre propia horadándoes las orejas, narices o otro miembro alguno, ni les enciendan copal ni les hagan honra, ni celebren ayunos ni fiestas pasadas, que en honra de sus dioses solían celebrar y ayunar, ni consientan que otros lo hagan pública ni secretamente; y si lo supieren, den de ello aviso a la justicia. Y enteramente en todo y por todo dejen sus vanidades pasadas y tengan y confiesen y sigan la creencia de un solo Dios verdadero y de su santo evangelio, como lo profesó en el santo bautismo, so pena, etc.

16. El bautismo es uno de los sacramentos que no se reiteran; y se le hace grande ofensa al Espíritu Santo, que por el santo bautismo se nos da, cuandoes reitera. Y muchos de los naturales de esta provincia dicen que, aunque están bautizados, se tornan a bautizar, engañando a los ministros del evangelio; y aun ellos dicen que bauticen a otros, y consienten que otros lo hagan. Por ende mando que de aquí adelante ningún indio ni india de esta dicha provincia, que una vez hubiere recibido legítimamente el santo bautismo, se torne a bautizar, ni lo consienta, ni bautice de su autoridad a otro alguno, so pena, etc.

17. Otrosí, porque muchos de los naturales desta dicha provincia, ya bautizados, con intención de el demonio dicen que han tomado por agüero que el bautismo mata a los niños chiquitos y que los niños bautizados se mueren luego, y los no bautizados se crían, y con este embaimiento del demonio los dichos naturales esconden sus hijos, cuando los religiosos vienen a bautizar; por ende mando que todo indio e india cristiano bautizado, desechando de sí tan grande error, manifiesten y lleven a bautizar sus hijos y menores, cuando los padres religiosos de la doctrina fueren a bautizar y los pidieren, y no los escondan, so pena, etc.

18. El sacramento del matrimonio es muy usado entre los naturales de esta dicha provincia, porque todos los naturales de ella se casan, aunque en celebrar este santo sacramento cometen grandes errores y abusos. Por remedio de esto mando que se guarden los capítulos siguientes, so las penas en ellos contenidas: ...

23. Ítem, por extirpar toda gentilidad y resabio de entre los naturales, mando que ninguno sea osado de poner a su hijo o hija nombre gentil ni divisa o señal alguna, que represente haber ofrecimiento al demonio, so pena, etc.

24. Otrosí mando que todo indio o india desta dicha provincia hinque las rodillas al Santísimo Sacramento, cuando le encontraren en alguna parte. Y cuando tañeren el Ave María, las manos puestas recen la oración acostumbrada y hagan reverencia a la cruz y en las imágenes de nuestro Redentor Jesucristo y de su bendida Madre; y el que no lo hiciere, por la primera vez, etc.

25. Item mando que todo indio o india (por introducir buenas costumbres en los naturales de ella) sea obligado cada día dos veces, una por la mañana y antes que se ocupen en sus labores y otra a la tarde cuando alcen de ellas, de ir a la iglesia de sus propios pueblos a rezar el Ave María y Paternóster y lo demás, y a encomendarse a Dios; y que siempre que entrare en la iglesia y mientras estuviere en ella rezando y en los divinos oficios y en el signarse y santiguarse y en sus oraciones y en oír de la misa y en todos los demás actos espirituales, guarden y tengan las ceremonias y reverencia e humildad en que los padres que los doctrinaren impusieren y enseñaren, so pena de ser por la primera vez gravemente reprehendido, etc.

26. Y so la misma pena mando a los dichos naturales que sus comidas y cenas las coman y cenen en sus mesas con sus manteles, con toda limpieza, con sus hijos y mujeres; y tengan asientos en que se asienten, y al principio de la comida y cena bendigan la mesa, y al fin della den gracias a Dios, las manos puestas, con las oraciones y ceremonias que los padres religiosos les enseñaren y dijeren; y que al tiempo de acostarse, cuando fueren a dormir y cuandoes levantaren, se signen con la señal de la cruz y se santigüen y encomienden a Dios y recen las oraciones que los dichos padres les enseñaren, y lo mismo enseñen a sus hijos y familiares que lo hagan.

27. Otrosí mando que los indios e indias que fueren bautizados y cristianos dejen (así como lo prometieron en el santo bautismo que recibieron) todas supersticiones y agüeros y adivinaciones y hechicerías y sortilegios, y no echen suertes ni cuenten maíces para saber lo por venir, ni canten ni publiquen sueños como cosa verdadera ni agüeros, ni consientan que otros lo hagan, ni hagan la fiesta del fuego, que hasta ahora en esta dicha provincia se hacía. Y ninguno sea osado de traer insignia alguna de sus gentilidades en las orejas ni en las narices ni en los labios, ni se embigen con color alguno ni críen coleta, sino que en todo dejen sus insignias gentílicas y la costumbre o por mejor decir corruptela que los varones y mujeres tienen de labrarse todos. Lo cual, demás de ser peligroso para la salud corporal, tiene también algún resabio de su infidelidad y gentilidad. Y los maestros y oficiales de labrar quemen y desechen todos los instrumentos y aderezos que para ello tengan, y de aquí adelante no labren a persona alguna ni usen tal oficio, so pena, etc.

(14. The preaching of the Holy Gospel, the jurisdiction and the authority of establishing a state school for the purpose of teaching it, belongs to the apostolic authority, to the prelates, and to those duly authorized. Therefore, I order that no Indian of this province, regardless of status or condition, dare to erect or be in charge of a school to teach the Christian doctrine and to preach the holy Gospel, public or secretly, of his own initiative nor of his own authority, neither plant a new church, nor paint or put images in it, nor baptize, perform wedding ceremonies or betrothals for any Indian, male or female, without a license and the expressed instructions of the prelate of this said province or of the religious father charge of doctrine, on penalty, etc.)

(15. By means of Holy Baptism, all of us Christians profess the belief in one true God, and we renounce the devil and his evil works. Therefore, I order that all Indians both male and female of this said province, baptized and Christian, who have received the law of God, be separated and put aside their idolatries and old rites, abstain from idols, do not consent to others having them and be partakers in animal sacrifices nor other things, nor with their own blood pierce their ears, noses, or any other body part, neither burn incense nor pay them homage, neither observe fasts nor past holidays , which they used to celebrate and fast for in honor of their gods, nor consent that others do so publicly or secretly; and if they are aware of it, report said activities to the proper authorities. And entirely, in everything and by

everything, abandon their past vanities and hold fast, confess, and follow the belief in one true God and its Holy Gospel, as was professed at his holy baptism, on penalty, etc.)

(16. Baptism is one of the sacraments that is not to be repeated; and a grave offence against the Holy Spirit is committed, who is given to us by means of holy baptism, if it is repeated. And many of the natives of this province say that, even though they are baptized, they return to baptize, deceiving the ministers of the gospel; and still they say that others be baptized, and consent to others doing so. Therefore, I order that from henceforth, no Indian whether male or female of this said province, who having once legitimately received holy baptism, return to baptize, consent to it, nor of his/her own authority baptize anyone else, on penalty, etc.)

(17. Moreover, because many of the natives of this said province, already baptized, with devilish intentions say that they have taken as an omen that baptism kills infants and that baptized children die soon thereafter, and those not baptized grow up, and with this devilish imposition the natives hide their children, when the religious come to baptize. Therefore, I order that all baptized and Christian Indians, both male and female, casting aside so great an error, declare and take their children and minors to be baptized, when the religious fathers of the doctrine go to baptize and requests them, and hide them not, on penalty, etc.)

(18. The sacrament of marriage is used frequently among the natives of this said province, because all the natives of this place get married, although in celebrating this holy sacrament they commit grave errors and abuses. In order to remedy this, I order that they safekeep the following chapters, on penalty contained therein: (omitted parts contain narrations such as: having several women, marrying twice, and buying women)

(23. Item, in order to eradicate all gentiles and vices from among the native people, I order that no one dare to give his/her son or daughter a gentile name nor any emblem or sign, that would represent an offering to the devil, on penalty, etc.)

(24. Moreover, I order that all Indians, both male and female, of this province kneel down to the Holy Sacrament, wherever they encounter it somewhere. And when they play the Ave Maria, with hands clasped, pray the customary prayer and do reverence to the Cross and to the images of our Redeemer Jesus Christ and his Holy Mother; and whoever does not do so, for the first time, etc.)

(25. Item. I order that all Indians, whether male or female, (for introducing good morals to the natives of this [land]) be obligated twice a day, once in the morning prior to their being occupied with their labors and once in the afternoon after finishing them, to go to church in their own towns to pray the Hail Mary, Paternoster [Our Father] and the others, and to entrust themselves to God; And that whenever they enter the church, and while praying in it, in the exercise of holy devotions, in crossing themselves and making the sign of cross, in their prayers, and in hearing the mass and all the other spiritual acts, that they keep and hold the ceremonies in reverence and humility in conformity with the Fathers who indoctrinated them, imposed and taught them, on penalty of being seriously reprehended for the first time, etc.)

(26. And on the same penalty, I order the above mentioned natives that their meals and suppers be eaten at their own tables with their respective table cloths, in cleanliness, with their wives and children; and that they'll have chairs to sit on, that at the beginning of the meals they bless the table, and at the end of it, they give thanks to God, with hands clasps, with the prayers and ceremonies that the religious Fathers taught and said to them; and that at bedtime, when they go to sleep and when they get up, they cross themselves with the sign of the cross, and that they entrust themselves to God and pray the prayers that said Fathers taught them, and that they teach their children and relatives to do so likewise.)

(27. Moreover, I order that the Indians, both men and women, who were baptized and Christian, to leave behind (just like they promised at the Holy Baptism which they've received) all superstitions, omens, divinations, witchcraft and sorceries, and neither to engage in casting lots nor count maize as a means of foretelling the

future; Neither sing nor disclose dreams reckoning them to be true or omens, neither consent others to do so, neither do ye the celebration of fire, that was done in this province until now. And none dare to wear any gentile insignia in their ears, noses, or in their lips; neither corrupt themselves with some color or grow a pigtail, but that in everything they leave their gentile decorations and habits, or better said still, corruption that men and women have of carving themselves. A fact which, besides being dangerous to the body's health, it also has some inkling of its infidelity and gentility. And the teachers and officials that work burn and discard of all the instruments and materials that they have for it, and that from now on, they do not carve any person or make use of such craft, on penalty, etc.)

Appendix IV: People against Themselves

By Vincent Stanzione (2008)

On February 24 of 2006, Santiago Atitlan made the cover page of the 'Foreign Service' section of *The Washington Post*. It isn't often that a lakeshore town makes the headlines in such a prestigious paper and it is usually because something is amiss. The only time Santiago Atitlan has ever made the big papers is when something bad happens. In late 1990 Atitlan got into print because of an army massacre in Panabaj. In 2005 a massive landslide wiped out Panabaj and, again, Atitlan was in the news. But in 2006 and 2007 Atitlan was in the press because of a new phenomenon called, "limpieza social' or 'social cleansing', another bad thing.

The *Post* article mentions that Santiago is in Guatemala, a nation still recovering from 36 years of civil war. But it doesn't explain exactly what that means. In Atitlan it means that the people have been left to their own cleverness to solve the problems in their community that have arisen in this complex and overpopulated urban struggle. It takes a lot of work to right the many elements that have gone wrong in those three-and-a-half decades of war. Many people believe that the civil war in Guatemala was a genocidal war of Ladinos against Indians, but that isn't really true. Often times, Guatemalan towns used the guerrillas or the army to solve personal vendettas.

Civil war is always about people against themselves. It is about a society, and its culture, that desires to change in revolutionary and profound ways. Santiago Atitlan is one of those towns where its citizens turned against one another in order to eliminate those on the other side of the ideological fence. In Atitlan, the 'fence' as a dividing line is still there, and people are being killed on both sides of it.

The Washington Post stated that seven members of the 'social cleansing' group were captured after a firefight with the police. What the newspaper did not know at the time was that those seven armed men would be set free within six months. It also didn't mention that those seven men were helped out of jail by a lawyer working for the mayor of Atitlan. Luckily for us citizens of the Guatemala state, another newspaper was able to tell more of the story in September 2007.

In September 24th of 2007, Atitlan made the front page of the reputable Guatemalan newspaper *El Periódico* because of the terror of 'social cleansing'. The paper reported that 35 people in Atitlan, all Tz'utujil speaking Maya, had been killed without any probability of finding anyone guilty of the crimes. *El Periódico* did an outstanding job of naming the various vigilante groups that are active in Santiago. It went so far as to insinuate that the municipality itself was doing its best not to get to the bottom of the homicides. It even said that 'social cleansing acts with the consent of local authorities.'

El Periódico stated that various groups are now working in town through violent means to find a balance of power in the small world of the citizens of Santiago Atitlan where 'might makes right'. The Oficina de Derechos Humanos is working overtime to shuffle its paper up the chain of the High Commission of Human Rights at the United Nations, but can do almost nothing to protect the citizens, at least ten per month, who are threatened by these men with guns.

What the article was not able to do was to look into the plan of the municipality to do away with the Principals or Elders who once had a word as to how the town would be governed. The Principals once were a group of traditionalist Maya-style thinking and praying individuals who were chosen by election to help guide the town through difficult times. These men were once part of a civil-religious hierarchy that once controlled the town. The 'Ten Years of Spring' revolution of Arevalo and Arbenz did its best to take away the power of this governing organization so common to the indigenous municipalities of highland Guatemala. All democracies strive to separate the civil government from religious denominations, but it is a very complicated issue here in Guatemala. All democracies need checks and balances, so without the Principales around to check the civil administration, there is no way to challenge corruption and poor management of the municipality.

When the landslide of October 2005 hit town, it left in its wake a boatload of cash for those individuals who were, or became, the leaders of groups who would supposedly distribute it in the most judicious and honest way possible. The Principals should have been involved in this vital reconstruction process. Instead, they were being killed for being brujos and idolaters. It is now standard in town that if one is a practitioner of the Old Ways, then they are witches and it is open season on witches. It seems the Fundamentalist Christians have made this an accepted reality, as they see it mandatory that these people be eliminated before the second coming of Christ can be made a reality. One day I said to an evangelical youth that it was said that the social cleansers had killed a friend of mine who was a Principal, and all he said was, "But he was a witch." Something is severely wrong in Atitlan; violent death for shamans is a completely normalized concept.

After the land- and mudslide, townspeople, like all people, had to explain why the natural disaster happened. The geologists and meteorologists explained to people over the radio what had happened in an attempt to stifle the inevitable fingerpointing that goes on in such situations, but their good intentions only paved the road to a new kind of ideological hell. The traditionalists said it was because the shamans who were murdered had returned to the mountain as rain warriors. The fundamentalists ordered everyone to become evangelicals in order to keep the rest of the mountain in its place; otherwise a big rain was coming and the judgment day would be upon us all. The Catholics said it was because the Church wasn't Catholic enough and that parish members just needed to go to confession and stop their mixed-up Mayan practices. Everyone had an answer. Social cleansers said it was time to increase the body count, so last year many people were sacrificed in order that the gods be appeased and that religion still be the answer to Atitlan's questions.

Anthropologist Clifford Geertz tells us that 'traditional' societies around the world over the last fifty years have gone through similar transformations. The first change is some type of anti-colonialist Marxist-type revolution that takes people away from their ancient ways of being. After the violence of these wars comes fundamentalist religion and then some type of capitalist free market system. This analysis of 'developing nations' goes a long way in explaining what is going on in Santiago Atitlan. First came the revolution against the oligarchy, and now comes the fundamentalist whiplash, and hopefully we will all enter the vicious world of the free market system. I can't believe I now find myself hoping for the inequities of a capitalist system!

Everybody who lives in and around Atitlan has been negatively affected by the violence and the threat of its actualization in their lives. To find the guilty parties would be a victory for justice in Guatemala, but the realization of that justice seems almost an impossibility for a town where violence is as natural as the surroundings that encapsulate Atitlan. I thought I would shed some light on the violence in Atitlan in order to say goodbye to my many years of involvement as an ethnographer in that town, a town that is now an overpopulated little city.

There is no doubt that the violence that thrives in Atitlan is a legacy of a very frustrating trajectory of social and cultural development. One could look back to 1954 when the Agrarian Reform of Arbenz, known as Decree 900, was ended with the change of government brought about by the U.S.A. and reactionary elements of Guatemalan society. The town of Santiago Atitlan would have received large pieces of land, had the agrarian reform gone through. But it didn't, and in its wake people involved in the reform were killed and from their bones grew the guerrilla movement. The guerrillas were active for many years in Atitlan until they came in from the mountains with the signing of the peace treaty in 1996.

But before those warriors came down off the volcanoes, Atitlan lived through a five-year period without the military's presence in town. Before 1991, when the military was forced to leave town by Vinicio Cerezo, Atitlan was occupied by soldiers who intimidated the indigenous population and used violent means to get whatever they needed. When the military picked up, they left a power vacuum that was soon filled by toughminded townspeople who said Atitlan needed a hard hand to keep the pueblo in order. In a very short period of time, different groups have taken on the work of policing the town and killing people whom they believed need to be 'cleansed' from the face of the earth. The oppressed have taken on the job of the oppressor, and they are doing their best to make a culture and social hell out of their own town.

The town of Atitlan is situated in one of the most beautiful natural settings in this world, but the people are unable to enjoy their place on earth because of the in-fighting that has gone on ever since. Perhaps it is time that the United Nations and other peacekeeping forces should occupy the town in order to begin negotiations between the different fundamentalist mind groups that now reign in town. It isn't enough to just sign peace treaties and expect there to be peace in towns as adversely effect by the civil war as places like Atitlan. It is important to stop the violence in Atitlan by capturing those individuals who perpetrate it, but it is just as important to help Mayan communities reeducate themselves after so many years of 'la mala educacíon' taught in the years of 'la violencia.'

Guatemala is a country of various 'nations of people,' the Tz'utujiles of Santiago Atitlan being one of those 'nations of people.' Those nations were given tremendous power to govern themselves with the signing of the 1996 Peace Treaty. But in order to govern a municipality as large as Atitlan, authorities must be responsible to the country within which they exist. For a country to become an integrated and dynamic system, it must create a citizenry that is protected not only

395

from those who threaten them from the outside, but also from themselves. My question is: when does a country begin to take away the powers of abusive local authority in order to create a more peaceful and democratic society?

The men who have governed Atitlan once were the leaders of the Comite de Seguridad and Desarrollo. Everyone loved them for standing up for the rights of the Atitecos and for denouncing the corruption of previous administrations. But as in George Orwell's *Animal Farm,* the once beloved leaders have become hated tyrants. It is, in no uncertain terms, a sad situation for everyone. It would be very easy to point fingers at the perpetrators of Atitlan's violence, but it would also be a case of blaming the victims. I can't blame the victims of a civil war who simply have become a people turned against themselves.

Over the past twenty years, I have lost many close friends and colleagues to violent deaths. I have been forced to give up my research on shamans, day-keepers, musicians, singers and curanderos because of intimidating violence. With these final words, I leave behind the town of Santiago Atitlan and my participation in town as a foreigner who wanted to know what life could be like in a Mayan town in the highlands of Guatemala. I do hope someday that peace will truly exist for the people of Atitlan, but for my own well being and that of those who are nearest and dearest to me, I must move on, leaving my grief to heal with time after this final departure.

Bibliography

(Primary Sources)

Unpublished Sources

Basseta, Domingo de. (?1698) *Vocaburario en lengua quiché*. I have used a xerographic copy of original Ms.(Americanins 59) in Bibliothèque Nationale de France, Paris.

Vico, Domingo de. (?1555) *Arte de lengua de la lengua Cakchiquel, con advertencia de los vocablos de los lenguas qiché, y Tutohil, de tras...*. I have used a xeographic copy of original Ms. (Americanins 46) in Bibliothèque Nationale de France, Paris.

Published Primary Sources (Including Published Translations of Primary Sources)

Acosta, José de. [1587a] *"Parecer sobre la guerra de la China. Méjico, 15 de marzo de 1587"*, in *Escritos menores*. estudio preliminar y edición del P. Francisco Mateos, Biblioteca Virtual Miguel de Cervantes, Alicante 1999. http://www.cervantesvirtual.com/servlet/SirveObras/12471736544570517087 891/p0000003.htm#I_20_ (Originally published in *Obras del Padre José de Acosta*, Madrid, Atlas, 1954, pp. 250-386.)

[1587b] *"Respuesta a los fundamentos que justifican la guerra contra la China (México, 23 de marzo 1587)"*, in *Escritos menores*. estudio preliminar y edición del P. Francisco Mateos, Biblioteca Virtual Miguel de Cervantes, Alicante 1999. http://www.cervantesvirtual.com/servlet/SirveObras/12471736544570517087 891/p0000003.htm#I_20_ (Originally published in *Obras del Padre José de Acosta*, Madrid, Atlas, 1954, pp. 250-386.)

[1590] *Historia natural y moral de las Indias*. (The author used a Japanese translation by Yoshio Masuda *Shintairiku Shizenbunkashi* 2vols.

397

Iwanamishoten, Tokyo, 1966). For a recent English translation, see Acosta 2002.

(1999) *De Procuranda Indorum Salute.. Predicación del Evangelio en las Indias.* estudio preliminar y edición del P. Francisco Mateos. Electoronic Reprint, Biblioteca Virtual Miguel de Cervantes, Alicante.(Originally in *Obras del Padre José de Acosta*, Atlas, Madrid, 1954, pp. 388-608)

(2002) *Natural and Moral History of the Indies.* Duke University Press, Durham, and London.

Aquina, St Thomas. (1960) *Philosophical Texts.* Oxford University Press, Oxford.

Anonymous [1539] *Relación del sitio del Cuzco y principo de las guerras civiles del Perú hasta la muerte de Diego de Almagro.* en CLERC vol.13, p.1-195.

Arriaga, Pablo José de. [1621] *Exirpación de la idolatría del Pirú.* BAE 209, pp.191-277.

(1968) *The extirpation of idolatry in Peru.* University of Kentucky Press, Lexington.

Aristotle. (*ΑΡΙΣΤΟΕΛΟΓΣ*).(1961) *Seijigaku (Politica. ΠΟΛΙΤΙΚΑ)*. Mituo Yamamoto (trans.), Iwanamishoten, Tokyo.

(1976a) *De philosophia.* Japanese translation in *Aristotelis.* Chikuma Shobo, Tokyo, pp.276-295.

(1976b) *Phisca.* Japanese translation in *Aristotelis.* Chikuma Shobo, Tokyo, pp.300-418.

(1976c) *Eudemus.* Japanese translation in *Aristotelis.* Chikuma Shobo, Tokyo, pp.245-251.

Augustine, Saint. (401) [n.d.] *Confession.* Translated by Albert C. Outler, Harry Plantiga (ed.) http://www.ccel.org/ (1st. MCMLV). Another English Translation can be found in Hare 2004.

[426AD](1998) *Concerning the City of God against the Pagan.* R.W.Dyson (ed.), Cambridge University Press, Cambridge.

Betanzos, Juan Diez de. (1996) *Narrative of the Inca.* Roland Hamilton et al. (trans.) University of Texas Press, Austin.

Bouvet, Joachim. [1697] *Portrait historique de l'Empereur de la Chine présenté au Roy.* Paris, (*Kohkiden.* Sueo Goto (trans.), Toshihiko Yazawa (ed.), Heibonsha, Tokyo. 1970)

Brasseur de Bourbourg, C. O. (ed.) (1869-1870) *Manuscrit Troano.* Imprimerie Impériale, Paris.

Bricker, Victoria R. & Helga-Maria Miram. (ed.& trans.) (2002) *An Encounter of Two Worlds: The Book of Chilam Balam of Kaua.* Middle American research Institute, Pub.68., Tulane University, New Orleáns.

Carmack, Robert M. and James Mondloch. (trans. and ed.) (1983) *El Título Totonicapán.* Universidad Nacional Autonoma de México, México.

(1985) "*El Título de Ilocab*", Tlalocan (10), pp.213-256.

(1989) *Título Yax y otros documents*. Universidad Nacional Autonoma de México, México.

CDI (1989-1900) *Colección de documentos inéditos relativos al descubrimiento, conquista y organización de las antiguas possesiones de Ultramer*. N.S., Real Academia de la Historia, Madrid.

CDIA (1864-1884) *Colección de documentos inéditos relativos al descubrimiento, conquista y colonización de las posesiones españoles en América y Oceanía sacadas en su mayor parte del Real Archivo de Indias*. 42 tomos. Madrid.

Celsus. [ca.178] (1987) *On the True Doctrine: A Discourse against the Christians*. Translated by R.Joseph Hoffmann. Oxford University Press, Oxford and New York.

Chávez, Adrián I. (trans.) (1979) *Pop Wuj (Libro de Acontecimientos)*. Ediciones de Casa Chata, México.

(1994) *Pop Wuj: Libro del Tiempo*. Ediciones de Sol, Buenos Aires. (1st.1987)

Christenson, Allen J. (trans.) (2003) *Popol Vuh: The Sacred Book of the Maya*. O Boks, Hants, UK.

(2004) *Popol Vuh. Vol.II: Literal Poetic Version*. O Boks, Hants, UK.

Cieza de León, Pedro de. (1998) [ca.1554] *The Discovery and Conquest of Peru*. University of Oklahoma Press, Norman.

CLDRHP *Colección de libros y documentos referencia a la historia del Perú*. Carlos A. Romero et al. (eds.), Serie primero 12 tomos (Lima 1916-19), Serie segundo, 10 tomos (1920-34).

Cobo, Bernabé. (1990) [1653] *Inca Religion and Customs*. University of Texas Press, Austin .

Codex Madrid. see Brasseur de Bourbourg (1869-1870).

Colop, Sam. (ed.). (1999) *Popol Wuj: Versión Poética K'iche*. Cholsamaj, Guatemala.

Confucius. (孔子) (500BC) *Confucian Analects*. (論語) In Hare (2004).

Córdoba, Pedro de. [1544] (1970) *Doctrina Cristiana (Christian Doctrine for the Instruction and Information of the Indies)*. Sterling A. Stovdemire(trans.), University of Miami Press, Coral Gables, Florida.

Cortés, Hernán. (1986) *Letters from México*. Anthony Pagden. (trans. and ed.). Yale University Press, New Heaven.

Coto, Thomas de. (1985) *Thesavrvs berborv: Vocabulario de la lengua Cakchiquel v[el] guatemalateca, nueuamente hecho y recopiado*. Universidad Autonoma de México, México.

CP: Porras Barrenechea, Raúl. (1959) *Cartas del Perú, 1524-1543*. Colección de documentos inéditos para la historia del Perú, 3, Sociedad de Bibliófilos Peruanos, Lima.

Cruz, Martín de la. [1552] (1939) *An Aztec Herbal*. An English translation of *Libellus de Medicinalibus Indorum Herbis*. The Maya Society, Baltimore (Reprint: Dover, New York 2000).

Cruz, Frei Gaspar da [1569-1570] *Tractado en que se côtam muito por estenso as cousas da China, cô particularidades, & así do reyno dormuz côposto por el R. Padre frey Gaspar da Cruz da ordern de sam Domingos...* An English Translation is in Bóxer 2004:44-239.

Cupil López, Alfredo. (trans.) 1999*Pop Wuj. El Libro de la Palabra*. Proyecto de Educación Maya Bilingüe Intercultural/Corporación Alemana para el Desarrollo, Guatemala.

Díaz del Castillo, Bernal. (1956) *The Discovery and Conquest of Mexico*. A. P. Maudslay (trans.), Ferrar, Straus and Cudahy, New York.
(1977) *Historia verdadera de la conquista de la nueva españa*. 2 tomos, Editorial Porrua, México, [1st.1960].
(1989) *Historia verdadera de la conquista de la nueva españa*. Alianza Editorial, Madrid.

Diccionario de Motul. (1935) Juan Martinez Hernández (ed.) Talleres de la Compaña Tipografia Yucateca, S.A., Mérida, México.

Diccionario de San Francisco. (1976) Oscar Michelon (ed.) Akademische Druck-u.. Verlagsanstalt, Graz, Austria.

Dotirina-Kirisitan [1590] in Ebizawa et als (1970), pp.14-81.

Durán, Diego. (1984) *Historia de las indias de nueva españa e islas de la tierra firme*. Angel MA. Garibay K. (ed.), Editorial Porrua, S.A., México.

Ebina, Danjyo. (海老名弾正 1856-1937) (1903) *Shin Nihon no Seishin Teki Kokuze*. 「新日本の精神的國是」『新人』(明治三十六年一月所収) reprinted in Takeda 1975:174-6.

(1906) *Kokumin Kyoiku to Kirisuto Kyo*「國民教育と基督教」『新人』(明治三十九年八月所収) reprinted in Takeda 1975:176-8.

Ebizawa, Arimichi et als(eds.) (1970) *Kirisitan Sho Haiya Sho*. Iwanamishoten, Tokyo.

Edmonson, Munro S.(trans.) (1971) *The Book of Counsel: The Popol Vuh of the Quiché Maya of Guatemala*. The Middle American Research Institute, Tulan University, New Orleans.

(1982) *The Ancient Future of the Itza: The book of Chilam Balam of Tizimin*. Austin: University of Texas Press.

(1986) *Heaven Born Merida*. University of Texas, Austin.

Estete, Miguel. [1534] *La relación del viaje que hizo el señor capitán Hernándo Pizarro por mandado del señor Gobernador, su hermano, desde rl pueblo de*

Caxamalca a Parcama y de allí a Jauja. En Xerez 1992:130-148. (An English translation: *A Report on Hernándo Pizarro's reconnaissance of Pachacamac.* Included by Xerez 1872:74-94)

(1919) [ca.1540]*"Noticia del Perú"* en Boletín de la Sociedad Ecuatoriana de Estudios Históricos Americanos, tomo I, no.3, pp.300-350,(Reprint: Quito: Banco Central del Ecuador, 1986, t. 1).

Falcón, Francisco. [1567] *Representación hecha por el licenciado Falcón en concilio provincial* [de Lima], in Pereña 1986:175-187. (Originally in Biblioteca Nacional, ms.3042, fols.220-223v, Madrid).

Feria, Fray Pedro de. [1584] *Revelación sobre la reincidencia en sus idolatrías de los indios de Chiapa después de treinta años de cristianos.* notas, comentarios y un estudio de Francisco del Paso y Troncoso, http://www.cervantesvirtual.com/

Fernando Ramírez, Jose. (ed.). (1847) *Proceso de residencia contra Pedro de Alvarado.* Impreso por Valdes y Redondas: México. (Reprint: Anales de la Sociedad de Geografia e Historia, Guatemala 1930-1933).

Fox, John. (ca.1560) *Foxe's Book of Martyrs.* Edited by William Byron Forbush. Reprint in Hare (2004).

Fu, Lo-shu. (ed.) (1966) *A documentary chronicle of Sino-Western relations, 1644-1820.* compiled, translated, and annotated by Lo-shu Fu. Published for the Association for Asian Studies, II vols. The University of Arizona Press, Tuscon. (I have used a version of single volume published by Rainbow Bridge Book Co. (虹橋書店) in Taipei, Taiwan 1966).

Garcilaso de la Vega, el Inca. (1985-6) *Comentarios reales de los incas.*ガルシアーソ・デ・ラ・ベーガ『インカ皇統記』全二巻 大航海時代叢書エクストラ・シリーズ 岩波書店 一九八五—一九八六年

(1965-6) *Royal commentaries of the Incas and general history of Peru.* Translated with an introduction by Harold V. Livermore. Foreword by Arnold J. Toynbee. 2 v. Texas, Univ. of Texas Press, Austin. (Translation of the 1609 Lisbon (Part I) and the 1616-1617 Córdova editions (Part II).

Gómara, Francisco López de. [1553] (1957) *Historia general de las indias.* II tomos, Editorial Iberia, S.A., Barcelona.

González de Mendoza, Juan. [1585] *Historia de las cosas mas notable, ritos y costumbres del Gran Reyno de la China, sabidas assi por los libros de los mesmos China, como por relación de religiosos y otras personas que an estaban en el dicho Reuno.* Roma

(1965) *Sina Daioukokusi.* A Japanese translation of *Historia de las cosas mas notable,...* by Chunan and Yzawa (trans.) Iwanamishoten, Tokyo

Huarochirí Manuscript (1991) *The Huarochirí Manuscript: A Testament of Ancient and Colonial Andean Religion.* Frank Salomon and Geroge L. Urioste (trans.), University of Texas Press, Austin [1598?].

Joseph-Marie Callery, Melchoir Yvan. (1853) *History of the Insurrection in China. With notices of the Christianity, creed, and proclamations of the insurgents.* Translated from the French, with a supplementary chapter narrating the most recent events, by John Oxenford. Elibron Classics, 2002, 358 pages Replica of edition by Smith, Elder & Co., London.

Julian. (JULIANUS APOSTATA, Roman Emperor (361-363 AD)) [ca.361-363] (n.d.) *Arguments of the Emperor Julian against the Christians.* (A Translation of the Greek texts) Translation by Thomas Taylor, Reprint by Kessinger Publishing's NP, (based on Hermetic Publishing Co, Chicago IL, 1932). This translation was first published in 1793.

(ca.361-3b) *Two Orations of the Emperor Julian: One to the Sovereign Sun and the other to the Mother of the Gods.* Translation by Thomas Taylor, (based on Hermetic Publishing Co, Chicago IL, 1932). This translation was first published in 1793. Reprint in Hare (2004) or at http://www.sacred-texts.com/

Justin Martyr, Saint. *The First Apology of Justin,* in ANF-01.PDF, pp.164-187. http://www.ccel.org/

The Second Apology of Justin, in ANF-01.PDF, pp.189-271. http://www.ccel.org/

The Discourse to the Greeks, in ANF-01.PDF, pp.272-2. http://www.ccel.org/

The Hortatory Adress to the Greeks, in ANF-01.PDF, pp.274-290. http://www.ccel.org/

Kojiki. (1882) *The Kojiki.* B.H. Chamberlain, trans., Reprint in Hare (2004).

Koran. (1989) *The Meaning of the Holy Qur'án.* Abdullah Yúsuf 'Alí (trans.) amana publication. Beltsville, Maryland.

Landa, Diego. [1566] (1978) *Yucatán Before and After the Conquest.* Dover, New York. (1st. 1937. Original title: *Relación del as cosas de Yucatán*)

(1941) *Landa's Relación del as cosas de Yucatán.* Alfred M. Tozer (trans. and ed.) Peabody Museum of American Archaeology and Ethnology, Vol.XVIII, Harvard University, Cambridge, Mass.

Lao-tzu (老子) [580-500 BC] (1891) *The Texts of Taoism. (Tao Te Cging* (道徳経)) Translated by James Legge, 2 vols., Sácred Books of the East, Volume 39-40.

(1913) *The Canon of Reason and Virtue.* Translated by D.T. Suzuki & Paul Carus, Open Court, La Salle, Illinois.

(1996) *Tao Te Ching.* Translated by J.H.Mcdonald. http://www.wam.umd.edu/~stwright/rel/tao/TaoTeChing.html

(1997) *Roshi.* (老子) A Japanese translation with the original Chinese text of the *Tao Te Ching.* Tamaki Ogawa (trans.), Chuokoran-Shinsha, INC., Tokyo. (Evisec edition of 1973)

Las Casas, Bartolomé (1545) *Peticón y requerimiento de los obispop de Guatemala, Chiapa y Nicaragua al presidente y oidores de la Audientia de los Confines. 19 de octubre de 1545.* in Assadourian 1991:440-447.

(1981) *Brevísima relación de la destruccioón de la Indias.* Editorial Fortamara, S.A., Barcelona.

402

(1967) *Apologética Historia Sumaria*. II tomos, Edmundo O'Gormn (ed.) Universidd Ncional Autónoma de México, México.

(1986) *Historia de Las Indias*. III tomos, Biblioteca Ayacucho,Caracas.

(1992b) [1552?] *In Defense of the Indians*. Northern Illinois University Press, DeKalb.(*Apologia*)

(1995) *Indeio wa Ninghen ka*. (『インディオは人間か』) Hidefuji Someda (trans.) Iwanamishoten, Tokyo.(An abbreviated Japanese translation of Las Casas 1967).

León Valdés, Carlos Rolando & Francisco López Perén. (trans.) (1985) *Popol Vuh: libro universal de la renovación del tiempo*. José de Pineda Ibarra, Ministro de Educación, Guatemala.

Lopez Medel, Tomas. [1556] *Carta a S.M. el Rey, Guatemala 20 de abril de 1556*. AGI, Aud. Santa fé, leg.188, fol.84-85v. Published in Lopez Medel (1990:114-118)

(1990) *Colonización de America*. Corpus Hispanorum De Pace, Vol.XXVIII, Consejo Superior de Investigaciones Cientificas, Madrid [1549-1572].

Luxton, Richard N. (trans.) (1995) *The Book of Chumayel: The Counsel Book of the Yucatec Maya 1539-1638*. Aegean Park Press, Laguna Hills, California.

Markham, Clements R. ed. (1873) *Narratives of the Rites and Laws of the Yncas*. Translated from the original Spanish manuscripts, and edited, with notes and an introduction, by Clements R. Markham. Elibron Classics, 2001, 269 pages Replica of edition by The Hakluyt Society, London.

María Bossú Z., Ennio. (trans. and ed.) (1990) *Un Manuscrito K'ekchí del siglo XVI*. Comisión Interuniversitaria Guatemalteca de Conmemoración de V Centenario del Descubrimiento de América, Guatemala.

Marquina, Gaspar de. [1533] *Una carta desde Cajamarca*. En Lockhart 1986:II, Appendice I, 263-4.

Martínez, José Luis. (eds.) *Documentos cortesianos*. 4 vols. Fondo de Cultura Económica, 1990-1992, México.

Matuda, Kiichi et al. (trans and ed.) (1973) *Nihon Jyunsatuki*. Heibonsha, Tokyo.

Mendieta, Fray Geronimo De. [1595] (1997) *Historia Eclesiastica Indiana: A Franciscan's View of the Spanish Conquest of Mexico*. Felix Jay (ed. and trans.) Studies in the History of Missions, Vol 14, The Edwin Mellen Press, New York, USA & Ceredigion, Wales, UK.

Molina, Christóbal de [el Almagrista o de Santiago]. (1968) [1553] *Relación de muchas cosas acaesidads en el Perú*. BAE2, *Crónicas peruanas de interés indígena* / edicion y estudio preliminar de Francisco Esteve Barba, Tomo 209, p.56-96.

Molina, Christóbal de. [de Cuzco] [1573] (1873) *The Fables and Rites of the Inca*. In Markham 1873, pp.3-66. (The original Spanish text, *Relación de las fábulas y ritos de los incas*. CLDRHP 1 Ser. Tomo I, pp.1-103)

Molina, Juan Gutíerrez de. [1570] *Información de servicios (huamanga, 1570)*. In Millones 1990:59-165.

Mooney, James. (trans). (1897-98) *"Myths of the Cherokee"*, Nineteenth Annual Report of the Bureau of American Ethnology, Part I., pp.240-427.

Motolinia, Fray Toribio de. [entre 1482~1491?-1569], *Historia de los indios de la Nueva España*. Información y Revista, Madrid, 1985.

[1555] *Carta de Toribio de Motolinia al Emperador Carlos V, Enero 2 de 1555*. in Motolinia 1985:299-326.

Murúa, Martín de. (1987) [1590-1611] *Historia general del Perú*. Ballesteros Gaibrois, Manuel (ed.) Información y Revista, Madrid.

Nihongi (1896) *The Nihongi*. W.G. Aston (trans.). In republished in Hare 2003.

Nisino, Sho. (1933) '*Mino Mission Houmurubesi* (The Mino Mission to be destroyed).', *The Minotaisho Sinbun*, 28 July. Reprinted in Wada 1972:359-360. (西濃生「美濃ミシオン葬るべし」美濃大正新聞).

Ocampo, Baltazar de, [1610] *An Account of the Province of Vilcapampa and a Narrative of the Execution of the Inca Tupac Amaru (1610)*, in Markham (1909) *History of the Incas by Pedro Sarmiento de Gamboa and The Excution of the Inca Tupac Amaru by Captain Baltasar de Ocampo*. Translated from the original Spanish manuscripts, and edited, with notes and an introduction, by Clements R. Markham, The Hakluyt Society, London. pp. 203-247.

Origenis. [246~9?] *Commentarium in Epistolam S.Pauli ad Romans*. The original Greek text is lost. I have used a Japanese translation from the surviving Latin translation. (*Roma no Shintoeno Tegami*. (『ローマの信徒への手紙』) Takashi Odaka (trans.) Soubunsha, Tokyo1990)

Otzoy C., Simón. (trans.) (1999) *Memorial de Sololá: Edición Facsimilar del manuscrito original*. Comisión Interuniversitaria de Conmemoración del Quinto Centenario del Descubrimiento de América, Guatemala.

Ozaki, Hiromichi. (小崎弘道 1856-1938) [1886] (1975) *Seikyo Shinron*. (『政教新論』) I have used a reprint found in Takeda 1975:3-41.

[1892] (1975) *Shinko no Riyu*. (『信仰の理由』) I have used a reprint found in Takeda 1975:41-80.

Pachacuti-yamqui Salcamayhua, Juan de Santa Cruz. [ca.1600] *An Account of the Antiquities of Peru*, In Markham (1873)

Pereña, Luciano. (ed.) (1988) *Carta Magna de Los Indios: Fuentes Constitucionales 1534-1609*. Madrid: Consejo Superior de Investigaciones Cientificas.

Plato (ΠΛΑΤΩΝΟΣ) [389BC?]. *Paidon* (*ΦΑΙΔΩΝ, Plato's Phaedo*), A Japanese translation by Yasuo Iwata. Iwanami Shoten, Tokyo 1998. (For citation, I have used Plato (1871)).

(1871) *Phaedo*. translated by Benjamin Jowett. C. Scribner's Sons, New York. Reprint in Hare 2003.

[360BC?] *Sophist.* translated by Benjamin Jowett. C. Scribner's Sons, New York. [1871] Reprint in Hare 2003.

Popol Vuh. See Edmonson (1971), Seler (1975), Tedlock (1996), Recinos (1950), Chávez (1979), (1994), Christenson (2003, 2004).

Poma, Huamán. (1978) *Letter to A King: A Peruvian Chief's Account of Life under the Incas and under Spanish Rule.* E.P. Dutton, New York.

Porphyry (of Tyre ca.232-ca.305AD) (1994) *Porphyry's Against the Christians: The Literary Remains.* R. Joseph Hoffmann. Trans&ed. Prometheus Books, Amherst, New York.

Proceso inquisitorial del cacique de Tetzcoco Don Carlos Ometochtzin (Chichimecatecotl) (1980) Biblioteca Enciclopedica del Estado de México, México. (1st 1910 México)

Querbeuf, Yves, Mathurin Marie Tŗeaudeŗ de. (1780-83) *Lettres édifiantes et curieuses, ecrites des missions etrangeres.* Nouvelle ed. Chez J.G. Merigot, Paris. (1st. C. Le Gobien [et al.] 1702-1776).

Quiñones Kebler, Eloise. (ed.) (1995) *Codex Telleriano-Remensis: Ritual, Divination, and History in a Pictorial Aztec Manuscriript.* University of Texas Press, Austin.

Recinos, Adrian (ed. and trans.) (1950) *The Popol Vuh: The Sacred Book of the Ancient Quiché Maya.* University of Oklahoma Press, Norman. (1st in Spanish Mexico, 1947)

(1984) *Cronicas Indigenas de Guatemala.* Academia de Geografía e Historia de Guatemala, Guatemala. (1st Universidad de San Carlos, Guatemala 1957).

Ricci, Matteo. (1982-3) *Della entrata della compagnia di Gesùe chritianità nella China.* I have used a Japanese translation published in *Chugoku Kirisutokyo Fukyoshi.* Tomo I, and Tomo II, pp.5-258. Iwanamishoten, Tokyo. (This is unique direct translation from the original Italian text. 『中国キリスト教布教史』 大航海 時代叢書第Ⅱ期8, 9 マッテーオ・リッチ セメード、岩波書店)

(1985)[1603] *True Meaning of the Lord of Heaven.* (With the original Chinese text) Institute of Jesuit Sources, St. Louis.

Rodríguez de Figueroa, Diego. [1565] *Relación del camino e viage ... hizo desde la ciudad del Cuzco a la tierra de Guerra de Manco Inga.* An English translation by Markham in Yamase (2003:9-37) [Originally in Cieza de León 1913:170-199].

Roys, Ralph L.(trans.) (1967) *The Book of Chilam Balam of Chumayel.* University of Oklahoma Press, Norman. (1st. Washington D.C., 1933)

Sancho, Pedro. (1912) *An account of the Conquest of Peru.* Translated and annotated by Philip Ainsworth Means. Milford House, Boston, Mass.

Sarmiento de Gamboa, Pedro. (1909) [1572] *The Second Part of the General History called "Indica"....* In Markham (1909), pp.1-201.

Schultze-Jena, L. (trans.) (1972) *Popol Vuh: Das Helige Buch der Quiche Indianer von Guatemala.* W. Kolhammer, Berlin. (1st Stuttgart 1944).

Seler, Eduard (trans.) (1975) *Popol Vuh: Das Heilige Buch der Quiché Guatemalas mit Schallplatte*. Gebr. Mann Verlag, Berlin.

Semedo, Alvarado. [1562] *Imperio de la China, i Cultura evangelica en el por los Religiosos de la Compaña de Jesús*. I have used a Japanese Translation in Ricci 1983:261-518.

Sepúlveda, Juan Guinés de. (1550) *Apologia Ioannis Genessi Sepulveda por libro de iustis belli causis*. The Author have used a Japanese translation by Someda *Seifukusennsou ha ze ka hi ka*. Iwaanamisyotenn, Tokyo 1992, pp.3-50.

(1984) [1544-45]*Demócrates Segundo o de las justas causas de la guerra contra los indios*. Angel Losada (ed. and trans.) 2nd ed., Instituto Francisco Vitoria, Consejo Superior de Investigaciones Científicas, Madrid. (1st. 1951 Madrid)

Shütte, Josef Franz S. J. (1951) *Valiganos Missionsgrundätze fûr Japan*. Tomo.I, Roma. (An English Translation was pubilished by Institute of Jesuit Sources, St. Louis)

(1958) *Valiganos Missionsgrundätze fûr Japan*. Tomo.II, Roma. (An English Translation was pubilished by Institute of Jesuit Sources, St. Louis)

Smailus, Ortwin. (1989) *Vocabulario en lengua Castellana y Guatemalteca que se llama Cakchiquel chi*. 3 vols. Wayasbah-Verlag, Hamburg.

Takeda, Suugen. (1999) *Teihon Takeuch Bunken*. Yawata Shobo, Tokyo.(武田崇元 編 『定本竹内文献』 八幡書房)

Takeda, Kiyoko. (ed.) (1975) *Meiji Shukyo Bungaku Senshu*. Vol.2, Tikuma Shobo, Tokyo. (武田清子 ・ 編 『明治宗教文学集』)

Tápia, Andrés de. (1939) *Relación de Andrés de Tápia*. en Agustín Yánez (ed.), *En Crónicas de la Conquista*. Universidad Nacional Autónoma de México, México, pp.25-78.

Tedlock, Dennis (trans.) (1996) *Popol Vuh*. (Revised Ed.) Simon & Schuster, New York. (1st. 1985).

Tokko Keisatu.(特高警察＝The Japanese Imperial Secret Police) (1941) *Showa 16nen chu ni okeru shakaiundo no jyokyo*. I have used a reprint of portion relared to the Christian edited by Wada 1972:127-282.

(1942) *Showa 17nen chu ni okeru shakaiundo no jyokyo*. I have used a reprint of portion relared to the Christian edited by Wada 1972:127-282.

(1943) *Showa18nen no Kirisutokyo Undo*. I have used a reprint of portion relared to the Christian edited by Wada 1973:9-183.

(1944) *Showa19nen no Kirisutokyo Undo*. I have used a reprint of portion relared to the Christian edited by Wada 1973:193-282.

Udâna. (1902) *The Udâna*. Translated from the *Pali* by Dawsonne Melanchthon Strong, LUZAC & Co, London

Valigano, Alejandro. [1583] *Sumario de las cosas de Japón*. I have used a Japanese translation by Tadashi Sakumain in Matuda et als. (1973) pp.3-155.

[1592] *Adciones del sumario de Japón*. I have used a Japanese translation by Tadashi Sakumain in Matuda et als. (1973) pp.159-227.

Vissière, Isabelle et Jean-Louis (eds.) (2001) *Lettres Édifiantes et Curieuses des Jésuites de Chine 1702-1776*. Éditiones Desjonquères, Paris.

Vitoria, Francisco de (1485?-1546) (1989) *Relectio de Indis*. L. Preña (ed.), C. Baciero (trans.) Coprus Hispanorum de Pace, Consejo Superior de Investigaciones Científicas, Madrid.

(1991) *Political Writings*. Anthony Pagden (ed. and trans.), Cambridge University Press, Cambridge.

Yamane, Kiku. (1937) *Hikari Wa Toho Yori*. Nihon to Sekaisha, Tokyo. (『光は東方より』日本と世界社) An electronic reproduction on CD for Windows available from Yawata Shoten, Tokyo.

(1964) *Nihon ni Himeraretearu Sekai no Rekisi*. Heiwasekaisha, Tokyo. (『日本に秘められてある世界の正史』平和世界社)

(1994) *Kirisuto wa Nihon de Shindeiru*. Tama Shuppan, Tokyo. (『キリストは日本で死んでいる』たま出版) (originally published in 1958 from Heiwasekaisha, Tokyo)

Yupanqui Inca, Titu Cuci (1987) [1570] *Ynstrucion del Ynga Don Diego de Castro Titu Cissi Yupangui para el muy Ilustre señor el licencidad Lope Garcia de Castro...* Japanese translation by Hidefuji Someda, *Inka no Hanran*. Tokyo: Iwanamishoten.『インカの反乱』

(1988) *En el encuentro de dos mundos, los incas de Vilcabamba: instrucción del inga Don Diego de Castro Tito Cussi Yupangui, 1570*. Prólogo de Francisco Valcárcel B. Martín Rubio, María del Carmen (ed.).Madrid: Ediciones Atlas.

(Secondary Sources)

Acuña, Rene (1975) "*Problema del Popol Vuh*", Mester, (5), pp.123-32.

(1983) "*El Popol Vuh, Vico y la Theología Indorum*", in Carmack and Morales Santos, pp.1-16.

(1998) *Temas del Popol Vuh*. Universidad Nacional Autónoma de México, México

Allen, Catherine. J. (1988) *The Hold Life Has: Coca and Cultural Identity in an Andean Community*. Smithsonian Institution Press, Washington, D.C.

Alvarez, Victoriano. (1999) "*La espritualidad Maya y la Libertad de Culto*", Centro de Estudios Mayas -Timach- 1999: 47-56.

Bassie, Karen. (n.d.) "*Maya Creator God*", http://www.mesoweb.com.

Baudot, Geroge and Tzvetan Todorov. (1994) *Azuteka Teikoku Metubouki*. Kikuchi et al (Trans.), Tokyo: Hosei University Press (*Récits Aztèques de la Conquête*. Éditions du Seuil, Paris 1983).『アステカ帝国滅亡記』

Baynes, Norman H. (1972) *Constantine the Great and the Christian Church.*. Oxford University Press, Oxford.

Berezkin, Yuri E. (2002) *"Some Results of Comprative Study of American and Siberian Mythologies: Applications for the Peopling of the New World"*, ACTA AMERICANA (Sweden), Vol. 10, No 1, p.5-28.

Boremanse, Dider. (1993) *'The Faith of the Real People: The Lacandon of the Chiapas Rain Forest'*, in Gossen 1993:324-351.

Boxer, C.R. (1951) *The Christian Century in Japan, 1549-1650*. University of California Press, Berkley & Cambridge University Press, Cambridge. (I have used a reprint of 1993. Carcanet Press Limited, Manchester, UK)

(2004) *South China in the Sixteenth Century*. Orchid Press, Bankok. Thailand. (1st 1953)

Bricker, Victoria R. (1981) *The Indian Christ, the Indian Kings*. University of Texas Press, Austin.

(2002) *"The Maya uinal and the Garden of Eden"*, Latin American Indian Literature, 18:1, p. 1-20.

Brook, Francis J. (1995) *"Montecuzoma Xocoyotl, Hernán Cortés, and Bernal Díaz del Castillo: The Construction of an Arrest"*, Hispanic American Historical Review 75(2) pp.149-183.

Bunzel, Ruth. (1952) *Chichicastenango: a Guatemalan Village*. University of Washington Press, Seattle.

Burkhart, Louise M. (1999) *"The Cult of the Virgin of Guadalupe in Mexico"*, in Gossen 1993: 198-227.

Carpenter, Edward. (1920) *Pagan & Christian Creeds: Their Origin and Meaning*. Harcourt, Brace and Company; New York. (Reprint in Hare 2004)

Carrasco, David. (1982) *Quetzalcoatl and the Irony of Empire*. The University of Chicago Press, Chicago.

Carus, Paul. (1900) *The History of the Devil and the idea of Evil from the Earliest Times to the Present Day*. Open Court, Chicago.

Cary, O. (1909) *A History of Christianity in Japan, Protestant Mission*. New York.

Castro-Klarén, Sara et al. (1990) *El retorno de las huacas: estudios y documentos sobre el Taki Onqoy, siglo XVI*. Recopilación de Luis Millones. Instituto de Estudios Peruanos; Sociedad Peruana de Psicoanálisis, Lima.

Centro de Estudios Mayas -Timach- (ed.). (1999) *Memoriarias del congreso internacional sobre el Pop Wuj*. Centro de Estudios Mayas –Timach-. Qutzaltenango, Guatemala.

Cervantes, Fernando. (1994) *The Devil in the New World: The Impact of Diabolism in New World*. Yale University Press, New Haven.

Chamberlain, Robert S. (1948) *The Conquest and Colonization of Yucatan, 1517-1550*. Carnegie Institution of Washington, Publication 582, Washington, D.C. (Reprint UMI, Ann Arbor 1991).

408

Chapman, Anne. (1992) *Masters of Animals: Oral Traditions of the Tolupan Indians, Honduras.* Gordon and Breach Science Publishers, Philadelphia. (1st in French. *Les enfants de la mort: univers mythique des indens tolupan (jicaque) du Honduras.* México 1978)

Chiappari C.L. Chiappari, Christopher Louis. (1999) *Rethink Religious Practice in Highland Guatemala.* Ph.D. Thesis at the University of Minnesota, UMI, Ann Arbour.

Chuchiak, John Franklin. (2000) *The Indian Inquistition and the Extirpation of idolatry.* Ph.D. Thesis at Tulan University, New Orleans, UMI., Ann Arbour.

Clendinnen, Inga. (1987) *Ambivalent Conquests: Maya and Spaniard in Yucatan, 1517-1570.* Cambridge University Press, Cambridge.

Coe, Michael. (1993) *The Maya.* 5th ed. Thamas and Hudson, London.

Colombres, Adolso. (1994) '*Nota Preliminar*', in Chávez 1994:7-13.

Cronin, Vincent.(1957) *The Wise Man From the West.* Doubleday Anchor, New York.

Damrosch, David.(1993) "*The Aethetic of Conquest: Aztec Poetry Before and After Cortés*", in Greenblatt 1993:139-158.

Deloria, Vine, Jr. (1994) *God is Red: a Native View of Religion.* 2nd. Ed., Fulcrum Publishing, Golden, Colorado. (1st.1973)

Douverger, Christian. (1993) *La conversión de los indios de Nueva Espana.* Fondo de Cultura Económica, México.

Dunne, George H. (1962) *Generation of Giants: The Story of the Jesuits in China in the Last Decades of the Ming Dynasty.* University of Notre Dame Press, Notre Dame.

Dussel, Enrique D. (1981) *A history of the Church in Latin America: colonialism to liberation, 1492-1979.* Translated and revised by Alan Neely., Eerdsman Grand Rapids, Michigan. (Originally published as *Historia de la Iglesia en América Latina.* 2. ed. Barcelona, Editorial Nova Terra, 1972)

Ebizawa, Arimichi. (1968) *Ishinhenkakuki to Kirisutokyo.* Shinseisha, Tokyo. （海老沢有道『維新変革期とキリスト教』新生社）

Edmonson, Munro S. (1993) "*The Maya Faith*", in Gossen 1993:65-85.

Edmonson, Munro S. and Victoria R. Bricker. (1985) "*Yucatan Maya Literature*", in Supplement to the Handbook of Middle American Indians, Victoria R. Bricker (General ed.), vol.3, University of Texas Press, Austin. pp.44-63.

Elliott, John H. "*The mental world of Hernán Cortés*" (Transactions of the Royal Historical Society [London], 5th series, 17, 1967, p. 41-58).

Eastman, Charles Alexander. (1911) *The Soul of the Indian.* Reprinted in Hare 2004.

Farriss, Nancy. (1984) *Maya Society under Colonial Rule.* Princeton University Press, (I have used a reprint with corrections in 1992), New Jersey.

Figgis, John Neville. (1921) *The Political Aspect of S. Augustine's 'City of God'*. Longmans, Green & Company, London. (reprint in Hare 2004)

Fox, Robin Lane. (1986) *Pagans and Christians*. Harper & Row, Publishers, San Francisco.

Freidel, David, Linda Schele, Joy Parker. (1993) *Maya Cosmos*. William Morrow and Company, Inc., New York.

Frost, Elsa Cecilia. (1993) *"Indians and Theologians: Sixteenth-Century Spanish Theologians and Their Concept of the Indiginous Soul"*, in Gossen 1993:119-139.

García, Laura Ibarra. (2001) *"Los sacrificios humanos. Una explicación desde la teoría histórico-Genética"*, Estudios Cultura de Nahuatl Vol.32., pp.341-358.

García Icazbalceta, Joaquín. (1947) *Don Fray Juan Zumárraga, primer obispo y arzobispo de México*. 4. Tomos. Editorial Porrúa, México.

Gernet, Jacques. (1996) *Chugoku to Kirisutokyo: Saisyo no Taiketu*. Hosei University Press, Tokio. (*Chine et Christianisme: La première confrontation*. Édition Gallimard, Paris 1991) (An English translation of the early edition of this study was published as *China and the Christian Impact: A Conflict of Cultures*. Cambridge University Press, Cambridge 1987.)

Gillespie, Susan D. (1989) *The Aztec King's*. University of Arizona Press, Tucson and London.

Girard, Raphael. (1979) *Esotericism of the Popol Vuh*. Translated from the Spanish with a Foreword by Blair A. Moffett Theosophical University Press, Pasadena, California. (1st. in Spanish in 1948)

Gonoi, Takashi. (1990) *Nihon Kirisuto Kyoshi*. Kikkawa Ko-Bunkan, Tokyo. (五 野井隆史『日本キリスト教史』)

Gosner, Kevin. (1992) *Soldiers of the Virgin: The Moral Economy of a Colonial Maya Rebellion*. The University of Arizona Press, Tucson.

Gossen, Gary H. (ed.) (1993) *South and Meso-American Native Spirituality: From the Cult of the Feathered Serpent to the Theology of Liberation*. The Crossroad Publishing Company, New York.

(1999) *Telling Maya Tales: Tzotzil Identities in Modern México*. Routledge, New York & London.

Greenblatt, Stephen. (ed.) (1993) *New World Encounter*. University of California Press, Berkley, Los Angels & London.

Guillén, Edmundo. (1978) "*Documentos inéditos para la historia de los incas de Vilcabamba: La capitulación del gobierno español con Titu Kusi Yupanki*", Historia y Cultura, Lima, vol.10. pp.47-93.

Gutiérrez Estévez, Manuel. (1993) *"The Christian Era of the Yucatec Maya"*, in Gossen 1993:251-278.

Gutiérrez, Gustavo. (1993) *Las Casas: in search of the poor of Jesus Christ*. Translated by Robert R. Barr. Orbis Books, Maryknoll, N.Y.

Hall, Manly P. (1928) *The Secret Teachings of All Ages: An Encyclopedic Outline of Masonic, Hermetic, Qabbalistic anf Rosicrucian Symbolical Philosophy Being an Interpretation of the Secret Teachings concealed within the Rituals, Allegories, and Mysteries of all Ages.* H.S. CROCKER COMPANY, INCORPORATED, San Francisco.

Hanke, Lewis. (1941) *The development of regulations for conquistadores.* In *Contribuciones para el Estudio de la Historia de América. Homenaje al Dr. Emilio Ravignani.* Ed. Peuser, ltda. Buenos Aires., p. 71-87).

(1965) *The Spanish Struggle for Justice in the Conquest of America.* Little, Brown and Company, Toronto, Canada. (1st 1949).

Harada, Minoru. (1989) *Genso no Cho Kodaishi.* Hihiousha, Tokyo. (原田実『幻想の超古代史―「竹内文献」と神代史論の源流』)

Hemming, John. (1993) *The conquest of the Incas.* (Updated Edition) Pan Macmillan Ltd., London. (1st Harcourt Brace Jovanovich, N.Y., 1970).

Hsia, Adrian. (2004) "*EURO-SINICA: The Past and the Future*", Taiwan Journal of East Asian Studies, Volume 1 Number 1, pp.17-56.

Holland, William. (1963) *Medicina maya en los Altos de Chiapas.* Instituto Nacional Indigenista, México.

Hutton, Ronald. (1991) *The Pagan Religions of the Ancient British Isles: Their Nature and Legacy.* Blackwell Publishers Ltd., London.

Jones, Grant D. (1989) *Maya Resistance to Spanish Rule.* University of New Mexico Press, Albuquerque.

(1998) *The Conquest of the Last Maya Kingdom.* Stanford University Press, Stanford.

Karino, Ryokichi. (1936) "*Amatukyo Komonjyo no Hihan*", Shiso, Vo.6. (狩野亨吉「天津教古文書の批判」「思想」昭和11年6月号.)

Kisimoto, Hideo. (ed.) (1954) *Meijibunkasi. Vol.6, Shukyohen,* Youyousha, Tokyo. (岸本英夫・編『明治文化史6宗教編』洋々社: An English translation of this title was published as *Japanese Religion in the Meiji Era.* Trans. and adapted by John F. Howes. Obunsha, Tokyo 1956)

Klor de Alva, J. Jorge. (1993) "*Aztec Sprituality and Nahuanized Christianity*", in Gossen 1993:173-7.

Kobayashi, Munehiro. (1995) *Wareraga Senzono Osieni Sitagaite: 1530Nendai Tezcoco Jyuminni Taisuru Itansinmonkirokuno Bunseki.* Kobe City University of Forgien Language, Kobe, Japan. (小林『我らが祖先の教えに従いて』)

Koepping, Klaus-Peter. (1994) "*Manipulated Identities: Syncretism and Uniqueness of Tradition in Modern Japanese Discourse*", in Stewart and Shaw 1994:161-177.

Koyasu, Nobukuni. (2001) *Hirata Atutane no Sekai.* Pelikansha, Tokyo. (子安宣邦『平田篤胤の世界』)

LaFarge, Oliver. (1949) *Santa Eulalia: the Religion of a Cuchúmatan Indian.* The University of Chicago Press, Chicago.

León Chic, Eduardo. (1999) *El Corazon De La Sabiduría Del Pueblo Maya=Uk'u'xal Ranima' Ri Qano'jib'al.* Fundación Centro de Documentación e Investigación Maya, Guatemala.

León-Portilla, Miguel. (1974) "*Quetzalcóatl-Cortés en la conquista de México*", Historia Mexicana, 24:1,p. 13-35.

(1988) *Time and Reality in the Thought of the Maya.* Second ed., University of Oklahoma Press, Norman & London. (1ˢᵗ. in Spanish. México 1968)

(1990) *Endangered Cultures.* Julie Goodson-Lawes (trans.), Southern Methodist University Press, Dallas, Texas.

(1993) "*Those Made Worthy by Divine Sacrifice: the Faith of Ancient Mexico*", in Gossen 1993:41-64.

Li, Dan J. (1969) *China in Transition, 1517-1911.* Van Nostrand Reinhold Company, New York.

Liljefors Persson, Bodil. (2000) *The Legacy of the Jaguar Prophet: An Exploration of Yucatec Maya Religion and Historiography.* Lund Studies in History of Religions, Vol.10, Almqvist & Wiksell International, Södertälje, Sweden.

Lockhart, James. (1986) *Los de Cajamarca. Un estudio social y biográfico de los primeros conquistadores de Perú.* 2tomos. Editorial Milla Batres, Lima. (The Original English Title: *The Men of Cajamarca: A Social and Biographical Study of the First Conquerors of Peru.* University of Texas Press, Austin 1972)

López Mejia, Alma. (1999) "*El movimientos Maya y las relaciones interculturales, el poder local con relación al Pop Wuj*", in Centro de Estudios Mayas -Timach- 1999: 135-6.

Luxton, Richard. (1981) *The Mystery of the Maya Hieroglyphs.*

MacCormack, Sabine. (1993) "*Demons, Imagination, and the Inca*", in Greenblatt (1993) pp.101-126.

MaGrath, Alister E. (2001) *Kirisutokyo Shingaku Nyumon* (キリスト教神学入門) A Japanese Translation of *Christian Theology: An Introduction.* (Third ed. 2001 (1ˢᵗ.1993)), Masami Kamiyo (trans.), Kyobunsha, Tokyo.

Marrou, Henri-Irénée. (1980) *Kirisutokyoshi* (キリスト教史). Sophia University Ed., Kodansha, Tokyo. (A Japanese translation of the second part of *Nouvelle Historire de l'Église*, I, Éditions du Seuil, Paris, 1963)

Marzal, Manuel M. (1993) "*Andean Religion at the Time of the Conquest*", in Gossen 1993:86-115.

(1993a) "*Transplanted Spanish Catholicism*", in Gossen 1993:140-172.

Masaki, Akira. (1996) "*Kami no Zushogaku* (神の図像学)", in Yamaori 1996:19-203.

Maurer Avalos, Eugenio. (1993) '*The Tzaltal Maya-Christian Synthesis*', in Gossen 1993:228-250.

412

Meyer, Birgit. (1994) *"Beyond syncretism: Translation and diabolization in the appropriation of Protestantism in Africa"*, in Stewart and Shaw 1994:45-68.

Michelet, Jules. *Satanism and Witchcraft: a Study in Medieval Superstition.*

Milbrath, Susan. (1999) *Star Gods of the Maya: Astronomy in Art, Folklore, and Calendars.* University of Texas Press, Austin.

Miller, Mary and Karl Taube. (1993) *An Illustrated Dictionary of the Gods and Symbols of Ancient Mexico and the Maya.* Thomas and Hudson, London.

Millones, Luis. (ed.) (1990) *El retorno de las huacas: Estudios y documentos sobre el Taki Onqoy Siglo XVI.* Instituto de Estudios Peruanos, Lima.

Minamiki, George S. J. (1985) *The Chinese Rites Controversy from Its Beginning to Modern Times.* Loyola University Press, Chicago.

Mino Mission. (ed.). (1949) *Mino Mission Hakugai Shi*（美濃ミシオン迫害史）, reprinted in Wada 1972:344-377. (Originally submitted to the Library of Japanese Diet as a report on the situation of the presecuation of the Christian in Ogaki City)

(1992) *Jinja Sanpai Kyohi Jiken Kiroku.*（神社参拝拒否事件記録（復刻版）四日市市) Yotukaichi, Gifu. Private Printing.

Mondloch, James L. (1978) *Basic Quiche Grammar.* State University of New York at Albany, Albany

Mullins, Mark R. (1998) *Christianity Made in Japan: A Study of Indigenous Movements.* University of Hawai'i Press, Honolulu.

Mumford, Jeremy. (1998) *"The Taki Onqoy and the Andean nation: sources and interpretations"*, Latin American Research Review, 33:1, pp.150-165.

Nassau, Robert Hamill. (1904) *Fetichism in West Africa.* Charles Scribners Son, New York. Reprint in Hare (2004).

Neill, S., (1964) *A History of Christian Missions.* Penguin Books, Harmondsworth.

Nohara, Kanyu. (1930) *Kinja Mondai Keika Hokoku.* Unknown Place. Reprinted in Mino Mission 1992:21-87. (野原勘由『神社問題經過報告』)

O'Bryan, Aileen. (1956) *The Dîné: Origin Myths of the Navaho Indians.* Bulletin 163 of the Bureau of American Ethnology of the Smithsonian Institution, Washington DC. Republished in Hare (2004)

Ostrogorsky, George. (1957) *History of the Byzantine State.* Translated by Joan Hussey, Rutgers University Press, New Jersey. (The Original German ed. 1940, 1952, the 1st English translation: London, 1956).

Pagden, Anthony. (1986) *The fall of natural man.* Cambridge University Press, Cambridge. (1st 1982).

(1993) *European Encounters with the New World.* Yale University Press, New Haven.

Pagels, Elaine H. (1995) *The Origin of Satan: the New TestamentOrigins.* Random House, New York.

413

Pease G.Y., Franklin.& Yoshio Masuda (1988)『図説インカ帝国』小学館, Tokyo.

Quiroa, Nestor Ivan. (2002) *The "Popol Vuh" and the Dominican Friar Francisco Ximénez: The Maya-Quiché Narrative as a Product of Religious Extirpation in Colonial Highland Guatemala.* Ph.D. thesis at University of Illinois at Urbana-Champaign. UMI, Ann Arbor.

Redfierld, Robert. (1941) *The Folk Culture of Yucatan.* The University of Chicago Press, Chicago.

Redfierld, Robert and Alfonso Villa Rojas. (1962) *Chan Kon: A Maya Village.* The University of Chicago Press, Chicago and London. (Abridged Edition of 1st 1934).

Regalado de Hurtado, Liliana. (1997) *El inca Titu Cusi Yupanqu y su tiempo: los incas de Vilcabamba; y los primeros cuarenta años del dominio español.* Pontificia Univ. Católica del Perú, Fondo Editorial, Lima.

Restall, Matthew. (1997) *The Maya World: Yucatec Culture and Society, 1550-1850.* Stanford University Press, Stanford.

(1998) *Maya Conquistador.* Beacon Press, New York.

Ricard, Robert. (1966) *The Spiritual Conquest of Mexico.* Lesley Byrd Simpson (trans.), University of California Press, Berkley, California.

Rivera Dorado, Miguel. (2000) *¿Influencia del cristianismo en el Popol Vuh?,* Revista Española de Antropología Americana, 30, p. 137-162.

Robson, Rev. James. (1929) *Christ in Ialâm.* John Marry, London.

Rosso, Antonio Sisto. (1948) *Apostolic legations to China of the Eighteenth Century.* P.D. and Ione Perkins, South Pasadena.

Rostworowski de Diez Canseco, María. (2003) *Inka Teikoku no Keisei to Houkai.* Yoshio Masuda (trans.), Toyo Shorin, Tokyo, (Japanese Edition of *Historia de Tawantinsuyu.* Lima: 1988, 1999).

Sáenz de Santamaria, Carmelo. (1964) *El licenciado Don Francisco Marroquín: Primer Obispo de Guatemala (1499-1563).* Ediciones Cultura Hispánica, Madrid.

Saitou, Akira. (1993) *Tamasii no Seifuku: Andesu ni Okeru Kaishu no Seijigaku.* Heibonsha, Tokyo. (斎藤晃『魂の征服：アンデスにおける改宗の政治学』平凡社)

Sanematu, Katuyoshi. (2000) *Maya Bunmei: Seinaru Jikanno Sho.* Gendaishorin, Tokyo (『マヤ文明・聖なる時間の書』現代書林).

(2003) *Maya Bunmei: Aratanaru Shinjitu.* Kodansha, Tokyo (『マヤ文明・新たなる真実』).

Schultze-Jena, Leonhard. (1954) *La vida y las creencias de los indígenas quichés de Guatemala.* Antonio Goubaud Carrera y Hebber D. Sapper (trans.) Editorial del Ministerio de Educación Pública, Guatemala. (Originally published in German 1933)

414

Shaw, Rosalind & Charles Stewart (1994) *"Introduction: problematizing syncretism,* in Stewart·et als. 1994:1-26.

Similox Salazar, Vitalino. (1999) *"Las iglesias fundamentalistas de Guatemala y la espiritualidad Maya, con énfais en el Popol Vuh,"* Centro de Estudios Mayas -Timach- 1999: 81-93.

Someda, Hidefuji. (染田秀藤) (1995) *Kaisetu.* In Las Casas 1995:325-343.

Spence, Lewis. (1908) *The Popol Vuh: The Mythic & Heroic Sages of the Kiches of Central America.* David Nutt, at the Sign of the Phoenix, London.

(1913) *The Myths of Mexico and Peru.* Reprinted in Hare (2004).

Stanzione, Vincent. (2000) *Ritual of Sacrifice: Walking the face of the Earth on the Sacred Path of the Sun.* University of New Mexico, Albuqurque.

Stern, Steve J. (1982) *Peru's Indian peoples and the challenge of Spanish Conquest: Huamanga to 1640.* University of Wisconsin Press, Madison.

Stewart, Charles and Rosalind Shaw. (1994) *Syncretism/Anti-Syncretism: The Politics of Religious Synthesis.* Routledge, New York.

Sugii, Rokuro. (1984) *Meijiki Kirisuto Kyo no Kenkyu.* Douhousha, Kyoto, Japan. (杉井六郎『明治期のキリスト教の研究』同朋社　京都)

Sullivan, Paul. (1989) *Unfinished Conversations: Mayas and Foreigners Between Two Wars.* Alfred A. Knopf, New York.

Sumiya, Mikio. (1975) *"Kindai Nihon no Keisei to Kirisutokyo",* in Takeda 1975:414-423. (隅谷三樹男「「近代」日本の成立とキリスト教」『近代日本の形成とキリスト教』昭和25年第5章に初出)

Tahara, Tuguo. (1963) *Hirata Atutane.* Kikkawakobunkan, Tokyo. (田原嗣郎『平田篤胤』)

Taube, Karl. (1993) *Aztec and Maya Myth.* British Museum Press, London.

Tedlock, Barbara. (1991) *Time and the Highland Maya.* (Second Ed.) University of New Mexico Press, Albuquerque (1st 1982).

Thompson, Donaldo E. (1954) *Maya Paganism and Christianity: A History of the Fusion of Two Religions.* Middle American Research Institute, The Tulane University of Louisiana, New Orleans.

Thompson, J.Eric S. (1970) *Maya History & Religion.* University of Oklahoma Press, Norman.

Thompson, Stith. (1929) *Tales of the North American Indians.* Indiana University Press, Bloomington. (Reprint in Hare 2003).

Thomas, Hugh. (1995) *Conquest.* Simon & Schuster, New York. (originally published in London 1993)

Todorov, Tzvetan. (1999) *The Conquest of America.* University of Oklahoma Press, Norman. (1st. in French 1982).

Van Oss, Adriaan C. (1986) *Catholic Colonialism: A Parish History of Guatemala 1524-1821.* Cambridge University Press, Cambridge.

Valencia Solanilla, César. (1996) *"Dualidad y transgresión en el Popol Vuh"*, Revistad e Ciencias Humanas, No.7, p.15-23, Universidad Tecnológica de Pireira, Columbia.

(2002) *"El Pop Wuj de Adrián Inés Chávez: Autenticidad, poesía y simbolismo de la cosmogonia maya – quiché"*, Revista Ciencias Humanas, No.30,

Varón Gabai, Rafel. (1990) *"El Taki Onqoy: las raíces andianas de un fenómeno colonial"*, in Millones 1990:331-406.

Villa Rojas, Alfonso. (1988) *"The Concept of Space and Time among the Contemporary Maya"*, in León-Portilla 1988:113-159.

Vogeley, Nancy. (1997) *"China and the American Indies: A Sixteenth-Century "History""*, Colonial Latin American Review, Vol.6, No.2. 1997.

Vogt, Evon Z. (1969) *Zinacantán: A Maya Community in the Highlands of Chiapas.* Harvard University Press, Cambridge, Mass.

Wada, Yoichi. (1972) *Senjika no Kirisutokyo undo.* Vol.2, Shinkyosyuppansha, Tokyo.

(1973) *Senjika no Kirisutokyo undo.* Vol.3, Shinkyosyuppansha, Tokyo.

Wagley, Charles. (1949) *The Social and Religion Life of a Guatemalan Village.* American Anthropological Association, Washington D.C.

Yamase, Shinji. (2001) *History and Legend: An Exploration of Native Guatemalan Texts*, Ph.D. Thesis, University of Essex, Colchester, England, UK.

(2002a) *Maya Bunmei.* Taiyo Shobo. Nigata, Japan: (『マヤ文明』)

(2002b) *History and Legend of the Colonial Maya of Guatemala.* The Edwin Mellen Press. New York, USA & Ceredigion, Wales, UK.

(2002c) *"Review of Richard N. Luxton 'The Book of Chumayel: the Counsel Book of the Yucatec Maya 1539-1638' (1995)"*, ACTA AMERICANA (The Journal of the Swedish Americanist Society, SAMS), Vol.10, No.1, p.125.

(2003a) *Mekisiko Seifuku: Azuteca Teikoku to Seifukusha Hernán Cortés – Shinjitu to Kyokou.* Virtual Cluster & Booking, Tokyo. (『メキシコ征服：アステカ帝国と征服者エルナン・コルテス－真実と虚構－』)

(2003b) *Document on the Conquest of the Inca.* Clements R. Markham at al. (Original trans.), Taiyo Shobo, Nigata, Japan.

(2004) *Inca Teikoku Hokai: Peru Kodaibunmei no Hametu no Rekisi.* Meta Brain, Tokyo. (『インカ帝国崩壊・ペルー古代文明の破滅の歴史』)

(2005) *Azuteca Teikoku to Seifukusha Hernán Cortés – Shinjitu to Kyokou.* Meta Brain, Tokyo. (『アステカ帝国と征服者エルナン・コルテス－真実と虚構－』 Updated and Revised Version of Yamase 2003a)

(2005b) *"Review of Adrián I. Chávez (1994) Pop Wuj: Libro del Tiempo"*, ACTA AMERICANA, Vol.13, No.1.

Yamaori, Tetuo. (ed.) (1996) *Nihon no Kami* (日本の神). Vol.3, Heibonsha, Tokyo.

Yanase, Naoya. (ed.) (1933) *Mino Mission ni Okeru Jinja Sanpai Mondai no Shinso*. Ichiryusha, Nagoya, Aichi, Japan. (published not for sale. 柳瀬直彌・編『美濃ミッションに於ける神社参拝問題の真相』一粒社 名古屋市), Reprinted in Mino Mission 1992:103-229.

Yao, Xinzhong. (1997) *Confucianism and Christianity. a Comparative Study of Jen and Agape*. Sussex Academic Press, Brighton. (Revised ed. of 1996)

Yazawa, Toshihiko. (1971) *Iezusukai Chugoku Shokanshu 2: Yoseihen*. Toyo Bunko 190, Heibonsha, Tokyo. 『イエズス会中国書簡集2』

(1972a) *Iezusukai Chugoku Shokanshu 3: Kanryuhen*. Toyo Bunko 210, Heibonsha, Tokyo.

(1972b) *Chugoku to Kirisuto kyo: Tenrei Mondai*. Kondou Shuppansha, Tokyo. 『中国とキリスト教：典礼問題』

Yoshida, Mituru. (1977) *Teitoku Ito Seiichi no Shogai*. Bungeibunshu, Tokyo. (吉田満『提督伊藤整一の生涯』文藝春秋)

(1994) *Senkan Yamato no Saigo*. Kodansha, Tokyo. (『戦艦大和の最期』)

Young, John D. (1983) *Confucianism and Christianity: the First Encounter*. Hong Kong University Press, Hong Kong.

(Electronic References)

Barton, John, and John Muddiman (Editors). (2005) *The Oxford Bible Commentary*. CD edition. Oxford University Press, Oxford & Selectsoft Publication, South San Francisco.

Biblioteca Virtual Miguel de Cervantes. Universidad de Alicante http://www.cervantesvirtual.com/index.shtml

Britannica (1999) *Encyclopaedia Britannica CD: 1999 Standard Edition for Macintosh and Windows*. Encyclopaedia Britannica, Inc., Chicago.

(2005) *Encyclopedia Britannica 2005 Standard Edition (2 CD for Mac and Win)* Encyclopaedia Britannica, Inc., Chicago.

Christian Classics Ethereal Library: http://www.ccel.org/

HLAS Online. http://lcweb2.loc.gov/hlas/

Hare, John B. (ed.). (2004) *The Internet Sacred Text Archive CD-ROM version 3.0*. The Internet Sacred Text Archive, Santa Cruz.

Metzger, Bruce M. and Roland E. Murphy (eds.) (1995) *The New Oxford Annotated Bible with Apocrypha: Electronic Edition* (Version 1.0a for MS Windows). Oxford University Press, Oxford.

Index

424